BRILLIANT BEACONS

Anderfon Del.   Tiebout Sculp.

VIEW *of the* LIGHT HOUSE *at* SANDY HOOK.

BRILLIANT BEACONS

. . . .

A

History

of the

American

Lighthouse

. . . .

ERIC JAY DOLIN

LIVERIGHT PUBLISHING
CORPORATION
A Division of W. W. NORTON & COMPANY
Independent Publishers Since 1923
NEW YORK   LONDON

FIRST EDITION

For information about permission to reproduce
selections from this book, write to
Permissions, Liveright Publishing Corporation,
a division of W. W. Norton & Company, Inc.,
500 Fifth Avenue, New York, NY 10110

For information about special discounts for bulk
purchases, please contact W. W. Norton Special Sales
at specialsales@wwnorton.com or 800-233-4830

Manufacturing by Quad Graphics Fairfield
Book design by Barbara Bachman
Production manager: Anna Oler

LIBRARY OF CONGRESS
CATALOGING-IN-PUBLICATION DATA

Names: Dolin, Eric Jay, author.
Title: Brilliant beacons : a history of the American lighthouse / Eric Jay Dolin.
Description: New York : Liveright Publishing Corporation, a division of
W. W. Norton & Company, [2016] | Includes bibliographical references and index.
Identifiers: LCCN 2015044089 | ISBN 9780871406682 (hardcover)
Subjects: LCSH: Lighthouses—United States—History. | United States. Bureau
of Light-Houses—History. | United States. Lighthouse Service—History.
Classification: LCC VK1023 .D65 2016 | DDC 387.1/550973—dc23 LC record available at
http://lccn.loc.gov/2015044089

Liveright Publishing Corporation,
500 Fifth Avenue, New York, N.Y. 10110
www.wwnorton.com

W. W. Norton & Company Ltd., Castle House,
75/76 Wells Street, London W1T 3QT

1 2 3 4 5 6 7 8 9 0

To Ruth and George Rooks

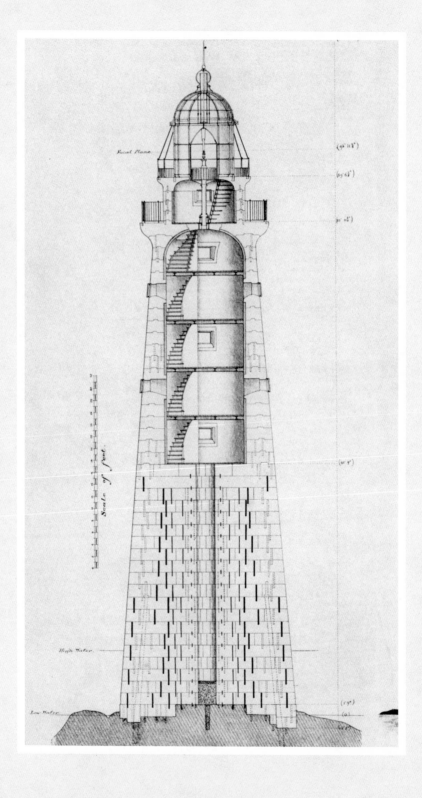

CONTENTS

. . . .

INTRODUCTION

· · · · · · · · · · · · · ·

Engraving done in 1840 of Maine's Mount Desert Rock Lighthouse,
after a painting by Thomas Doughty.

THE SEA IS A DANGEROUS PLACE, AND THE GREATEST DANGERS loom closest to shore. Although storms imperil mariners wherever they are, they can confidently maneuver their ships on the open ocean without the fear of encountering unseen hazards or running aground. But as ships graze the coast, the risks multiply. That is where jagged reefs, hidden sandbars, towering headlands, and rocky beaches threaten disaster. In the morning hours of February 24, 1817, William Osgood and his small crew—aware of such maritime portents—were intently, perhaps somewhat desperately, peering ahead for any sign of light.

Osgood was captain of the *Union*, a fine three-masted ship out of Salem, Massachusetts, sailing back from Sumatra with a cargo of nearly five hundred thousand pounds of pepper and more than one hundred thousand pounds of tin. A little after midnight Osgood spotted a familiar and most welcome sight. The beams coming from the twin towers of Thacher Island Lighthouse, off Rockport, Massachusetts, told him he was on course, thus nearing the end of his voyage. Osgood ordered his men to steer the ship southwest, keeping an eye out for the lighthouse on Baker's Island, which was not far from Salem's wharves. About two hours later they saw the lighthouse gleaming faintly in the distance and headed in that direction, but then a snowstorm obscured their view. When the lighthouse finally reappeared, however, alarm rather than relief seized the men.

When the *Union* left Salem one year earlier, in 1816, the lighthouse on Baker's Island had two towers, and cast two beams, like the twin lights on Thacher Island. Yet, during the *Union*'s journey, the Baker's Island Lighthouse was modified to exhibit only one light. Osgood and his men knew nothing of this alteration. Therefore, when they saw only a single light, confusion set in—followed by panic. Some of the men thought they must have missed Baker's Island and were instead looking at the single beam of the Boston Lighthouse, which was about fifteen miles south of Salem. Others believed, despite there being only one light, that it must be Baker's Island. But since the ship was very close to the island, there was little time to react. The steersman turned the helm in one direction, thinking it was the Boston Lighthouse in the offing, while Osgood, still certain it was Baker's Island, ordered a different course. But it was too late. Not long after Osgood barked his order, the *Union* wrecked on the northwest corner of Baker's Island. Mercifully all the men on board survived, and salvage operations later recovered much of the tin and about half of the pepper. The ship, however, was a different story: Insured for $45,000, it was a complete loss.

———

THE *UNION* DEBACLE POINTEDLY illustrates the fundamental purpose of lighthouses, which is to guide mariners safely to their destination. Had the Baker's Island Lighthouse shone two beams that frigid February morning, the *Union* would not have foundered on the rocks because the men would have known their location and reacted appropriately. The *Union* disaster notwithstanding, for three hundred years America's lighthouses have kept countless ships from wrecking, saved untold lives, and contributed mightily to the growth and prosperity of the nation.

The history of America's lighthouses is wondrously wide ranging. It is about the farsighted colonies that built the first lighthouses on the east coast to welcome commerce to their shores, embracing the founding of the nation and its dramatic expansion across the continent. When the inaugural federal Congress convened in 1789, one of the first issues it took up was whether the federal government or the states would be in charge of lighthouses; and in one of its earliest acts, Congress made lighthouses a federal concern. From that point forward, as the country grew, so too did the number of lighthouses, creating a necklace of beacons and literally lighting the way for the settlement of new territories and states.

Brilliant Beacons is also a history of government ineptitude and international competition. For a long time America's lighthouses were vastly inferior to those in Great Britain and France, even though many stubborn and misguided American officials refused to concede that fact. Only by emulating its cross-ocean rivals was America able to elevate its lighthouse system from one mired in mediocrity to one that was among the best in the world.

It is likewise a history of lighting innovation. Lighthouse illuminants changed dramatically over time, running the gamut from whale, lard, and vegetable oil to kerosene, acetylene, and finally electricity. Similarly, crude lamps gave way to more sophisticated ones, and reflectors that did a poor job of projecting the light were replaced by the crown jewels of lighthouse illumination—Fresnel lenses, which not only increased the intensity of the light, but also became one of the most important and strikingly beautiful inventions of the nineteenth century. Most of these elegant lenses have since been supplanted by modern optics, which are far less arresting to the eye, yet still effective in casting refulgent beams toward the horizon.

Lighthouses have undergone substantial structural changes. While early towers were made of wood or rubble stone, in later years cut stone, bricks, iron, steel, reinforced concrete, and even aluminum became the materials of choice. Although all lighthouses required skill to build, a few posed such significant challenges that they are truly marvels of engineering, serving as testaments to human ingenuity.

America's military history is one in which lighthouses have played a crucial role. They served as lookout towers in many conflicts, but during the American Revolution and the Civil War they also became key strategic targets, resulting in more than 160 of them being damaged or completely destroyed.

Like wars, natural disasters—especially hurricanes—have taken a terrible toll on lighthouses. The Great Hurricane of 1938 stands out, both for the extent of devastation it wreaked, and for the gripping and tragic stories of survival and death that it left in its wake.

At its core, however, the dramatic history of America's lighthouses is about people, and an intriguingly diverse cast of compelling characters brings that history to vivid life. These include Founding Fathers, skillful engineers, imperiled mariners, and intrepid soldiers, as well as saboteurs, penny-pinching bureaucrats, ruthless egg collectors, and inspiring leaders. Undoubtedly the most important actors are the male and female keepers, who—often with the invaluable assistance of their families—faithfully kept the lights shining and the fog signals blaring.

No one who has studied the history of these keepers could claim that their lives were a proverbial picnic, for they contended with loneliness, monotony, and a myriad of dangers. Not surprisingly a few died in the line of duty. Many keepers rescued people in distress on the water, some performing so heroically that America's highest award for lifesaving was bestowed on them. Above all, keepers provided a vital public service that was at once noble and altruistic. As the early-twentieth-century historian

William S. Pelletreau stated, "Among all the hosts who are called to the service of the government, . . . perhaps none is charged with duties of such moment and of such universal usefulness as is the lighthouse keeper. The soldier and the statesman protect the national honor and the person and property of the citizen, and their acts are performed in the gaze of the world. But the quiet man who trims and lights the shore and harbor lights, and watches them through the long night, . . . stands his vigil for all humanity, asking no questions as to the nationality or purpose of him whom he directs to safety."

The 1900s saw the role of keepers diminish over time. As lighthouses were decommissioned or became automated, the number of keepers dwindled, and today only Boston Lighthouse still has one. But as keepers faded from view and lighthouses began suffering from neglect, nonprofit organizations, government agencies, and private individuals stepped forward to become the new stewards of an increasing number of lighthouses, ensuring that they will be cared for and preserved for the benefit of future generations.

Lighthouses are among the most beloved and romanticized structures in the American landscape. It is not difficult to find evidence of their hold on the public's imagination. Lighthouses are emblazoned on postage stamps and license plates, while legions of artists portray them on their canvases. Many cities and towns incorporate lighthouses into their official seals, and even more businesses and organizations use lighthouses in their logos and advertising. Scores of books, movies, and television shows employ lighthouses as subjects, plot elements, or as dramatic settings. And millions of people visit lighthouses every year.

The inherent beauty of lighthouses—starkly etched against the sky—is undeniably a big part of what makes them so alluring. But America's intrinsic fascination with lighthouses runs deeper than that. Over three centuries, these brilliant beacons have indelibly woven themselves into the American fabric, and it is this rich history more than anything else that draws us in.

BRILLIANT BEACONS

CHAPTER 1

COLONIAL LIGHTS

*Engraving from 1729 depicting the Boston Lighthouse and an
armed British sloop, after a drawing by William Burgis.*

THE BOSTONIAN SAMUEL CLOUGH PUBLISHED THE SECOND EDITION
of his popular *New England Almanack* in 1701. It was a slender volume
with offerings ranging from weather predictions and local history tid-
bits to depictions of the moon's phases and trite couplets, including this
one devoted to the month of January: "Now a new year is coming in, /
with good warm clothes preserve thy skin." It contained all the typical
material of an almanac of the day, but there was one unusual item tucked

in as well, in which Clough asked his readers whether a lighthouse on Point Allerton at the edge of Boston Harbor "may not be of great benefit to mariners coming on these coasts?" It was an excellent question, and a novel one, for at the time there was not a single lighthouse in the colonies.

That a lighthouse might benefit the sailors of colonial Boston there was no doubt. Lighthouses had been fixtures in both the imagination and the actual landscape for nearly two thousand years, providing mariners with a measure of safety as they plied the world's oceans. Most historians believe that the first known lighthouse in antiquity was the magnificent Pharos, which guarded the entrance to the Greek city of Alexandria, located at the western edge of the sprawling Nile delta, where the river drains into the Mediterranean Sea. It was built sometime between 297 and 283 BC on the island of Pharos, after which it was named. From a massive square base, the Pharos rose in successively smaller tiers of white marble or limestone to an open cupola at the very top, upon which stood a statue of Zeus, the king of the gods and the ruler of mankind. The Pharos soared at least 300, and possibly 450, feet into the sky, making it one of the world's tallest structures at the time, rivaling the Great Pyramids of Egypt.

Sostratus, who seems to have been either the Pharos's architect or a major benefactor of its construction, dedicated it "to the safety of those who sail the seas." The fires continuously burning within its cupola alerted ships to the presence of treacherous reefs lying just offshore, and led them safely into the busy port. What fueled the Pharos is a mystery, but possible candidates are wood, charcoal, or animal dung. It was said that the Pharos coruscated "like a star" at night, and that during the day, the fire's billowing smoke and the colossal structure itself signaled that Alexandria was near. The ancient Greek novelist Achilles Tatius, author of the love story *The Adventures of Leucippe and Clitophon*, likened the Pharos to "a mountain, almost reaching the clouds," its flame serving as "a second sun to be a guide for ships." How long the Pharos survived is the subject of speculation, with some asserting that it shone for a thousand years and then remained dark until an earthquake toppled it in 1365. A remarkable achievement of design and engineering, the Pharos is consid-

An unknown artist's mid-eighteenth-century depiction of what the Pharos might have looked like, copper engraving circa 1759–60.

ered one of the Seven Wonders of the Ancient World.* Its fame spread so far and wide that variations of *Pharos* became the word for "lighthouse" in many languages—for example, *faro* in Spanish and *phare* in French. By the same token, the scientific study of lighthouses is known as pharology.

In the millennia since the Pharos first lit the Mediterranean's azure waters, the Romans, Spaniards, French, Italians, and Turks, among others, built lighthouses along their coasts. When Clough was peddling his 1701 almanac it is estimated that there were nearly seventy lighthouses worldwide. England boasted fourteen, many of which were well known to American colonists who traveled to and from the mother country, the most famous being the lighthouse built upon the dreaded Eddystone Rocks.

---

*Many have argued that the Greek statue the Colossus of Rhodes, another of the Seven Wonders of the Ancient World, which was erected around the same time as the Pharos, also served as a lighthouse. Although this is an intriguing claim, there is scant evidence to support it.

———

LOCATED FOURTEEN MILES SOUTHWEST of the port city of Plymouth, the Eddystone Rocks is a reef of gneiss and granite that is almost entirely submerged at high tide, when only a few feet of it break the surface. It is an oceanic hazard that had long terrorized mariners. When Christopher Jones, the master of the *Mayflower*, left Plymouth in 1620 with a motley assortment of Pilgrims and "strangers" on board, he gave the rocks a wide berth, portraying them as "ragged stones around which the sea constantly eddies, [and] a great danger . . . for if any vessel makes to far to the south . . . she will be swept to her doom on these evil rocks."

Toward the end of the seventeenth century, complaints about the great number of ships lost to the Eddystone Rocks reached a crescendo, compelling Trinity House, the English organization in charge of lighthouses, to authorize the construction of a lighthouse on one of these "evil rocks" so as to warn mariners away. Henry Winstanley spearheaded the project. Neither an engineer nor an architect, he had made his name as an entertainer and entrepreneur, his greatest claim to fame being Winstanley's Waterworks near London's Hyde Park, which featured fantastic fountains and water-drenched tableaus of classical gods. Winstanley invested his profits in shipping, and it was after two of his ships foundered on the Eddystone Rocks that he offered to finance and build the lighthouse on this desolate wave-swept location. That he had no particular qualifications to take on this tremendously difficult task bothered the exceedingly self-assured businessman not in the least.

After two years of backbreaking work, the Eddystone Lighthouse commenced operation in November 1698. In subsequent years Winstanley continued to modify his creation, resulting in a granite, wood, and iron structure 120 feet tall, which, not surprisingly given Winstanley's theatrical bent, exhibited a number of rather whimsical design elements, including an elaborate weathervane as well as six iron brackets outside the lantern room that held aloft ornamental candlesticks. A lamp and sixty candles burning within the lantern room provided the illumination.

Winstanley was extremely proud of his lighthouse, and when people

*Henry Winstanley's
Eddystone Lighthouse.*

questioned its ability to withstand the worst that the weather could offer, he confidently responded that it was his most fervent wish to be in his lighthouse during "the greatest storm that ever was" so he could prove the naysayers wrong. He should have wished for something else. When the tempest that would go down in English history as the "Great Storm" barreled into the coast on November 26, 1703, Winstanley and his work crew were at the lighthouse making repairs. All of them perished, along with the lighthouse, which was completely washed away except for a few twisted iron supports embedded in the rock.*

---

*To be fair to Winstanley, the "Great Storm" was so horrendous and lasted so long that virtually every boat on the coast was damaged or wrecked, as well as a huge number of structures on land, with the resulting loss of thousands of lives.

The Eddystone Lighthouse had proved its worth for five years, during which time the rocks had not claimed a single ship. And if anyone needed more proof, just two days after the lighthouse was destroyed, a ship full of tobacco coming from Virginia crashed on the rocks, killing all but two on board. Until the last moments before impact, the ship's master had been desperately looking for the lighthouse that was not there. Six years later a second Eddystone Lighthouse was built on the same foundation as the first, to the great relief of merchants and mariners alike.

WHILE THERE WAS NO question as to the efficacy of lighthouses, Clough's question was not whether lighthouses were valuable in general, but whether building a lighthouse at Point Allerton in particular was a good idea. Located in the town of Hull at the tip of the Nantasket Peninsula jutting into Boston Harbor, Point Allerton had in effect been a beacon of sorts for decades. In 1673 local residents built a crude stone structure upon which they burned "fier-bales [sic] of pitch and oakum" in an iron grate. This, however, was not a lighthouse, but rather a bonfire used to alert nearby towns to the approach of enemy ships. An actual lighthouse, by contrast, would be of much greater utility, safeguarding commerce because of its strategic position near the largest city and preeminent port in the American colonies.

Trade in everything from fish and leather to rum and African slaves kept Boston's wharves humming with activity, in the process creating a vibrant merchant class. As the eighteenth century progressed, thousands of vessels sailed into the harbor annually. But navigating the harbor remained difficult, for its numerous islands, shoals, and rocky outcroppings challenged even the most skillful of mariners.

Entering the harbor was particularly tricky, and shipwrecks were common. Most ships favored the southern entrance, which posed the fewest hazards, and since it was right next to Point Allerton, a lighthouse there could help guide ships safely into the harbor, and it could do so around the clock. When the sun was up, the lighthouse tower itself would be a landmark, or so-called daymark, to head for, while at night the shining beacon would light the way.

By enabling ships to enter the harbor at night, a lighthouse would solve an age-old problem. Powered only by wind, and at the mercy of the weather, sailing ships were not able to time their voyages to arrive at their destination during daylight, when visibility was greatest. Ships arriving at night would often sail around offshore waiting for the sun to rise rather than head into port in the dark. This delay only increased the chance of an accident or of encountering a storm—risks that a lighthouse could eliminate.

The pitiable quality of maritime charts at the time provided yet another argument in favor of a lighthouse. Commenting on one of the most popular charts of New England in use during the early- to mid-1700s, a contemporary labeled it "one continued error," and warned that it would likely have a "pernicious" impact on "trade and navigation." Anyone who owned a copy of the offending chart was counseled to destroy it immediately. This made lighthouses all the more valuable, since instead of relying on faulty charts to determine their location, mariners could look to the lighthouse instead.

The desire for a lighthouse took on a symbolic significance as well, for one at Point Allerton would be a sign that Boston was fast becoming a world-class city as well as a welcoming port that encouraged maritime trade. And in the ruthless competition for commerce that dominated early-eighteenth-century colonial life, a lighthouse could give a port a competitive edge.

ALTHOUGH NO DOUBT many people read Clough's provocative query, and were well aware of the potential benefits of a lighthouse, no immediate action was taken. But the seed had been planted, and in subsequent years as Boston spiraled in size, the need for a lighthouse became more compelling. Finally, in January 1713, a group of Boston merchants petitioned the Massachusetts legislature, proposing that a lighthouse be built "at some headland at the entrance" of Boston Harbor. Finding the idea attractive, the legislature appointed a committee to explore it further, and persuaded by the merits of the project, the committee surveyed the outermost reaches of the harbor to determine the best location. The committee's recommendation was to erect the lighthouse on Little Brewster, the smallest of a group of islands named after Elder William Brewster, a passenger on the *Mayflower* and Plymouth's first preacher.

Only an acre in size at high tide, Little Brewster is located about one mile north of Point Allerton, on the other side of the main shipping channel. Therefore the logic that made Point Allerton a good location for a lighthouse worked equally well for Little Brewster. This convinced the legislature, and on July 23, 1715, it passed an act to build a lighthouse on the island, noting that "the want of a lighthouse at the entrance" to the harbor "has been a great discouragement to navigation, by the loss of lives and estates of several of his majesty's subjects." Construction began

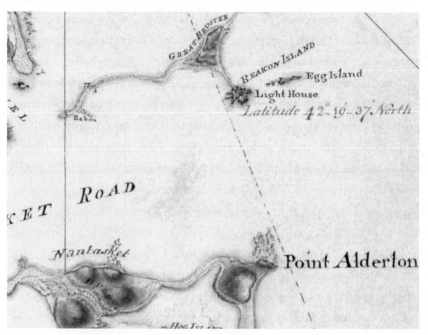

Detail of 1775 Bay and Harbor of Boston, by Thomas Wheeler. The main shipping channel at the time ran between Point Allerton (here "Alderton") to the south, and Little Brewster Island to the north, which is called "Beakon Island" on this map.

soon thereafter, and on September 14, 1716, Boston Lighthouse was lit, becoming America's first lighthouse, thus launching a new era in the colony's maritime history.

Judging by contemporary drawings and historical accounts, the lighthouse tower was sixty feet tall, conical in form, and made of rough-cut granite. On top of the stone tower sat a fifteen-foot-tall octagonal wood-and-glass enclosed lantern room, which was accessed by a spiral wooden staircase that curled up the lighthouse's core. Either candles or crude lamps that burned whale or fish oil produced the light itself.

GEORGE WORTHYLAKE, THE FIRST KEEPER of the Boston Lighthouse, assumed his job immediately. Forty-three years old, he was very familiar with the harbor, having lived for a number of years within a couple of miles of Little Brewster Island, first on George's Island, then on Lovell's Island where he kept a farm. As keeper he was responsible for "kindling the lights from sun-setting to sun-rising, and placing them so as they may be most seen by vessels coming in or going out." In addition to receiving a yearly salary of fifty pounds, Worthylake was allowed to live with his family and slaves—slaves being not uncommon then in Boston—rent-free in the modest keeper's house on the island. And to supplement his income, he was permitted to serve as a harbor pilot and continue herding sheep on the condition that doing so didn't interfere with his lighthouse duties.

During Worthylake's first winter at the lighthouse, a terrific storm pummeled the outer harbor with huge waves and driving winds. He was so busy tending the light that he had no time to tend the sheep he had placed on Great Brewster Island, which was connected to Little Brewster by a sandbar visible only at low tide. When the sheep wandered onto the bar in the midst of the gale, fifty-nine of them were swept into the churning seas and drowned. Although painful, this loss was nothing compared to the tragedy that befell him on Monday, November 3, 1718.

Worthylake, his wife, Ann, and one of his daughters, Ruth, had spent the previous day in Boston at church and visiting friends. They stayed overnight in the city, while Shadwell, one of their slaves, tended to the lighthouse. On Monday morning Worthylake collected his pay and then escorted his family and servant, George Cutler, to the wharf, where they boarded the lighthouse boat and began sailing back to Little Brewster. About a mile and a half from their destination, they were invited onto a sloop moored off Lovell's Island by a friend of theirs named John Edge. They "tarried on board about an hour," eating and drinking, "tho not to excess," after which Edge accepted an invitation to accompany the Worthylakes to the lighthouse.

Between ten and eleven o'clock, as winds freshened and whitecaps began dancing on the harbor's surface, the lighthouse boat carefully crossed the channel separating Lovell and Little Brewster Islands. Shortly after noon Worthylake's other daughter, Ann, and her friend Mary Thompson, who were on Little Brewster with one other Worthylake child, spied the lighthouse boat tying up to the mooring just offshore. Ann told Shadwell to take the canoe to ferry everyone in. No sooner had they all gotten into the canoe than it overturned, pitching them into the chilly water. They struggled for a while before drowning, and over the next few hours all the bodies except Cutler's washed up on Little Brewster. Two days passed before the weather moderated enough to enable Ann and Mary to reach Lovell's Island to get help carrying the bodies into Boston for burial.

Triple headstone for George Worthylake, his wife, Ann, and one of his daughters, Ruth, at the Copp's Hill Burying Ground in Boston.

Mid-eighteenth-century engraving
of Cotton Mather, after painting by
Peter Pelham, 1728.

This heartbreaking event caught the attention of Cotton Mather, the pompous Puritan minister of the Old North Church in Boston, arguably the most influential and famed clergyman in the colonies. A prodigious writer who rarely missed an opportunity to turn a remarkable tragedy into a vehicle for declaring God's sovereignty, Mather used the deaths as a jumping-off point for a sermon entitled "Providence Asserted and Adored," delivered on November 9. In his introduction Mather asked his parishioners to imagine the "inexpressible horror and anguish" that must have grabbed hold of Ann and her sibling as they "beheld the deadly distress of their parents and sister, and others thus perishing in the waters; unable to give the least help unto them. . . . Imagine if thou canst, the agony!" which was only compounded when one considered that "the dead bodies . . . were the only company which these poor children had upon the desolate island; for two whole days and nights together." Having set the stage, Mather then launched into his sermon, whose gist was that even in tragedy one witnesses the hand of God, and that the ultimate power of Divine Providence must not only be proclaimed by the faithful, but also worshipped.

Whereas Mather saw these untimely deaths as a means to preach the word of God, James Franklin saw them as an opportunity to make money. After learning the printing trade in London, James returned to Boston in

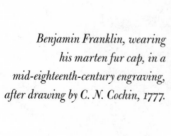

*Benjamin Franklin, wearing
his marten fur cap, in a
mid-eighteenth-century engraving,
after drawing by C. N. Cochin, 1777.*

1717 with a press and movable metal type in tow, establishing himself as
one the city's five printers. While in England he had seen local printers
capitalize on unusual or shocking incidents by quickly producing pam-
phlets of poetry immortalizing the events and then selling them to the
public, which never seemed to tire of the sensational. No sooner had the
Worthylakes and their unfortunate fellow passengers been interred than
James asked his younger brother Benjamin to write a poem commemorating the drownings.

Twelve-year-old Benjamin, one of seventeen children in an indigent
family, had only recently been apprenticed to James, but he was already
showing his great facility with words, a skill that would later help make
him one of the most influential of America's Founding Fathers, as well
as the most quotable. He quickly produced "The Lighthouse Tragedy,"
and James sent him to the streets to hawk the piece. Although Benjamin later called the poem "wretched stuff, in the Grub Street ballad
style," it "sold wonderfully, the event being recent, having made a great
noise." Such sales, Benjamin noted, "flattered my vanity," but his father
ridiculed his effort, telling him, "verse makers were generally beggars."
Thus, Benjamin concluded, "I escaped being a poet, most probably a
very bad one." Despite the popularity of "The Lighthouse Tragedy" at
the time, no copy has ever been found.

Nearly forty years later Franklin narrowly avoided becoming the subject of his own tragedy, and he had a lighthouse to thank for his salvation. In June 1757, at the age of fifty-one, Franklin sailed from New York to Falmouth, England. As the ship neared the southwestern English coast around midnight in the middle of July, the captain made a serious miscalculation. He thought he was well to the south of the dangerous Isles of Scilly, a rocky archipelago forty-five miles off the southwestern tip of Cornwall, England, when in fact he was heading right for them. The lookout, who had either fallen asleep or was otherwise distracted, didn't see the St. Agnes Lighthouse looming out of the darkness, but Franklin did, later recalling that it appeared to him "as large as a cart wheel." The captain saw it at the same instant and "ordered the ship to wear round," just in time to keep it from plowing into the rocks. "This deliverance," Franklin observed, "impressed me strongly with the utility of lighthouses." In a letter to his wife, Deborah, Franklin told her that upon arriving in Falmouth, he and his son, William, went directly to a local church and, "with hearts full of gratitude, returned sincere thanks to God for the mercies we had received: were I a Roman Catholic, perhaps I should on this occasion vow to build a chapel to some saint; but as I am not, if I were to vow at all, it should be to build a *lighthouse*."*

WITH WORTHYLAKE GONE, Boston merchants immediately recommended the veteran mariner Capt. John Hayes for the position. While the legislature debated, it also sent Robert Saunders, John Chamberlin, and a man named Bradduck to tend the lighthouse temporarily. Calamity soon followed, however. On November 14, just a few days before the court officially appointed Hayes keeper, Saunders saw a ship in the distance. When the ship raised a flag, Saunders assumed it was requesting a pilot to guide it into the harbor. Notwithstanding the inclement weather, Saunders and

---

*It is often said that Franklin wrote, "Lighthouses are more useful than churches," but he did not. This pithy saying appears to be a paraphrase of the accurate quote reproduced in the text above, which was likely concocted many years after Franklin's death.

his two assistants set out to offer their services. The ship's captain, however, didn't need a pilot. He only wanted to learn what news there was. This infuriated Saunders, who said that had he known, he never would have ventured out under such stormy conditions. While the trio headed back to the lighthouse, a wind gust upset the boat. Saunders and Bradduck drowned, but Chamberlin managed to swim to the island, resting twice along the way on rocky crags lying just beneath the surface.

Despite a curse that seemed to be associated with the lighthouse, Hayes took the job. Soon thereafter, he lobbied for an important addition to the island. Realizing that a beam of light was virtually useless in thick fog, Hayes asked the court to give him a "great gun" that he could fire periodically to warn ships away from Little Brewster and its adjacent shoals during times of reduced visibility. In response the court sent him a sizable cannon in late 1719, which became the first official fog signal in the colonies.

Hazards continued to plague the Boston Lighthouse. In 1720 and again in 1753, fires gutted the lighthouse when the whale oil lamps accidentally tipped over, underscoring the risk of having an open flame and wood in close proximity. Another combustion threat came from the sky. Since the lighthouse was the tallest structure for miles around, it is no surprise that it was occasionally hit by lightning, which could not only start

The cannon used as a fog signal at Boston Lighthouse.

a fire but also potentially crack the lighthouse's masonry shell. For the first few decades of the lighthouse's existence nothing could be done to protect against such strikes. Bostonians could only cast worried glances at the sky as storm clouds approached, hoping and praying that lightning would spare their houses, churches, and now their lighthouse. But in 1749 Benjamin Franklin, keenly aware of the danger of such natural disasters, figured out how to tame God's thunder when he invented the lightning rod. The concept was deceptively simple: By placing a metal rod atop a building and attaching it to a wire running into the ground, the enormous electrical current contained in a bolt of lightning could be safely conducted into the earth. One might have assumed that in order to safeguard their lighthouse the people of Massachusetts would have quickly adopted this means of protection. Unfortunately religion stood in the way.

Clergymen had long viewed lightning as a manifestation of God's will, used to punish the sinful. According to this way of thinking, lightning rods were frustrating God's design, and therefore they were an abomination: Installing them was a blasphemous act. Nonetheless, despite clerical opposition, many lightning rods were erected in Boston in the years following Franklin's invention, but those who "thought it vanity and irreligion for the arm of flesh to presume to avert the stroke of heaven" were successful in keeping the lighthouse rod-free. Until, that is, the lighthouse sustained significant lightning damage over the course of a few successive summers. At that point practicality trumped any lingering religious considerations, and a lightning rod was installed on the lighthouse, most likely sometime before the mid-1770s.

The Boston Lighthouse was a harbinger of things to come. The rationale that propelled Bostonians to build a lighthouse led other locales to do the same. The populations and economies of the American colonies were expanding at a near-exponential rate, and ports were one of the primary engines of that growth. Virtually all the biggest cities were ports, serving as entrepôts for colonial trade and becoming centers of finance and capital accumulation. An increasing number of ships transporting goods within the colonies and throughout transatlantic markets helped the colonies' economy grow faster than any single country's, and gave colonists one of the highest standards of living in the world. With so much of the colonies' prosperity riding on the shoulders of maritime commerce, it is no wonder that the demand for lighthouses rose over time. Yet despite this there was no accompanying boom in their construction. Each place that built one did so at its own pace, and only after complaints by local merchants became too insistent to ignore. The first to follow in Boston's footsteps was Nantucket.

NANTUCKET, OR *NATOCKETE* AS the local Wampanoag called it, translates from their Indian language as "the faraway land at sea," and it lives up to its name. "Take out your map and look at it," Herman Melville exclaimed in his classic *Moby-Dick*. "See what a real corner of the world it occupies; how it stands there, away off shore, more lonely than the Eddystone lighthouse." A crescent-shaped island just thirteen miles long and seven miles wide at its farthest reaches, Nantucket lies roughly thirty miles from Woods Hole on Cape Cod, and fifteen miles from the larger island of Martha's Vineyard.

Living on sandy soil that made for poor farming, but surrounded by an ocean teeming with whales, Nantucketers decided early on that their commercial future was on the sea. By the mid-1740s, Nantucketers had built up an impressive whaling fleet of nearly sixty ships. Roaming the Atlantic in pursuit of their quarry, Nantucket's whalemen began and ended their voyages in the island's only harbor, whose entrance was a mere three-quarters of a mile wide. Given how small and flat Nantucket was, finding the entrance in the dark was difficult in the best of circumstances. To help make that task easier not only for the island's whalemen but also other mariners, the town of Sherburne (modern-day Nantucket) voted two hundred pounds in 1746 to build a lighthouse on Brant Point, one of the sand spits bracketing the harbor's entrance.

Little is known about this structure, other than when it was erected; it was said to have been rather short, made of wood, maintained by Nantucket's shipowners, and lit by—what else?— whale oil. In 1757 it burned to the ground, likely as a result of an overturned lamp. The town

replaced the lighthouse the following year with another wooden structure, this one lasting until March 9, 1774, when "the most violent gust of
wind that perhaps was ever known" on Nantucket tore through the town,
destroying the lighthouse along with several other buildings. Once again
the Nantucketers, whose whaling fleet had grown to 150 vessels, quickly
built another beacon on the same spot.

THREE YEARS AFTER NANTUCKET built its first lighthouse, Rhode
Island followed suit. It might even have beaten Nantucket had local merchants gotten their way. In 1730 fifteen of them petitioned the colonial
legislature to build a lighthouse along the coast. Rhode Island's maritime
commerce was booming, led by both Newport and Providence's substantial involvement in the so-called Triangular Trade, which transported rum
to Africa, where it was used to purchase slaves, who were taken to the West
Indies and exchanged for molasses that was shipped back to Rhode Island
distilleries and transformed into more rum. To bolster their petition the
merchants pointed out that not only other nations but also the neighboring
colony of Massachusetts had already erected lighthouses "for the preservation of navigation . . . where it has proved of a very great advantage," a
statement that underscores how widespread and successful trading—both
in commercial goods and human beings—had become.

This compelling argument notwithstanding, it was eight years before
the legislature appointed a committee to build a lighthouse at Beavertail Point. This windswept promontory at the tip of Jamestown cleaves
the east and west passages into Narragansett Bay, and was an excellent
spot for a lighthouse to guide ships heading to nearby Newport, or to
Providence as well as other ports on the bay. Before construction of the
Beavertail Lighthouse could commence, however, the War of the Aus-
trian Succession erupted in Europe—later spilling over into the colonies,
where it was called King George's War—embroiling Great Britain and
virtually all the major European countries in nearly a decade of hostilities
and placing plans for Rhode Island's first lighthouse on hold.

After the war ended in 1748, the legislature, spurred to action by recent shipwrecks, resuscitated the project and tapped Peter Harrison, America's first professional architect, to design the lighthouse. Made of wood and reaching sixty-nine feet, the lighthouse was completed in 1749, and illuminated with whale oil lamps. As if on cue, a fire destroyed it in 1753, whereupon Harrison's services were enlisted again, but this time he wisely designed the lighthouse to be built of stone.

The Beavertail Lighthouse provides the earliest known example of the misfortunes that can occur when a lighthouse goes dark. The land on which the lighthouse stood was owned by one Josiah Arnold, who declined to sell it to the colony but agreed to hire someone to tend the lighthouse as long as the colony covered the keeper's salary. This arrangement worked well for quite a while, but in 1764 the colony stopped the payments for reasons that are unclear. For two years Arnold demanded his money to no avail, at the same time continuing to support the keeper out of his own pocket. On November 4, 1766, Arnold decided he had had enough. He told the keeper, Joseph Austin, to stop tending the lighthouse, and vowed not to relight it until he was paid.

Concerned citizens flooded the governor's office in Newport with complaints. Fearful that an accident might ensue, the governor dispatched one John Hoockey to deliver a letter to Arnold, telling him to resurrect the lights immediately, and assuring him that the issue of his back pay would be promptly brought before the legislature, and likely resolved in his favor. If, however, Arnold refused to restart the lighthouse, Hoockey was supposed to do it himself.

The colonial drama escalated day by day. Arnold did refuse, and on the night of Thursday, November 6, Hoockey lit the whale oil lamps. The next day he told the governor that he thought Austin would be willing to tend the light unless Arnold continued to forbid him from doing so. The governor then gave Hoockey another letter, this one for Austin, asking him to tend the lights until the following Monday, when he would be paid for his services.

Hoockey gave the letter to Austin, who was amenable to the plan, but Austin's wife urged him to talk to Arnold first. According to Hoockey, Arnold, upon reading the letter, flew into a rage and tossed the letter in the fire. He not only forbade Austin from tending the light but also told him to kill anyone who tried to do so. Whipped into a frenzy because he had not been paid in years, Arnold threatened to sue Hoockey for trespassing on account of his lighting the lamps the night before. After Arnold calmed down, he gave Hoockey permission to tend the lighthouse, but Hoockey was so intimidated by Arnold's irrational threats that he left early that evening. The lighthouse was dark again.

Later that night, while sailing his sloop back to Newport, Captain Spencer saw a light that he thought was the Beavertail Lighthouse. It was in fact the light of a private residence, and by following it Spencer ran his vessel onto the sands of Sachuest Beach. Fortunately no lives were lost and the sloop was later refloated, but that did not stop the recriminations. One irate letter writer to the *Newport Mercury* asked how Arnold could justify "sporting with, and endangering the lives and properties of mankind." Arnold shot back, arguing that it wasn't right for him to have to sacrifice his "private fortune" to benefit the public good. He had never threatened Hoockey, he averred, and insisted he had treated him with "hospitality" and told him he could tend the light on the evening of the accident. Any "blame" should thus accrue to Hoockey, not him. While this feud was played out, the governor hastily dispatched someone else to the lighthouse to keep it lit.

Still fuming over his treatment, Arnold submitted a twelve-page petition to the legislature in February 1767, defending his behavior and demanding his back pay. By repeatedly ignoring his requests for compensation, Arnold claimed, the legislature had treated him with "contempt" and unfairly "condemned" him for his actions "without a hearing" by his peers. He added that the legislature had even "threatened" to take his land without his consent. "How consistent with justice and how far reconcilable to English liberties these proceedings may appear," Arnold concluded, "I shall leave to every judicious man in the colony to determine." The legislature finally decided that it had in fact treated Arnold unfairly, and that summer awarded him all the money he was due, with interest. With that the squall ended almost as abruptly as it had begun, and Arnold went back to running the lighthouse for the colony.

———

New London was next. Situated at the mouth of the Thames River along the coast of Long Island Sound, New London was Connecticut's most vital port, blessed with a deep and inviting harbor. Its mariners actively traded with the West Indies, Newfoundland, and the other colonies, in products ranging from horses and beef to pipe staves and slaves. In 1760 area merchants and shipmasters petitioned the colonial legislature for permission to build a lighthouse and fund its construction with a lottery, a very common device used throughout the colonies to pay for public works, including roads and churches. Permission granted, the lottery raised five hundred pounds, and the lighthouse was completed in 1761. Located on the harbor's western edge, the sixty-four-foot tower had a base twenty-four feet in diameter and stone walls four feet thick.

While New London was building its lighthouse, New Yorkers forged ahead with plans of their own. The idea of employing navigational aids to help ships sailing to New York City had been discussed as far back as 1680, when New York's royal governor, Edmund Andros, proposed placing unlit beacons on Sandy Hook, a low-lying sandy peninsula in northeastern New Jersey, about twenty miles from the city's wharves. It was a prime location, since ships heading to the city usually followed a channel that curved around the tip of the Hook. Although Andros's proposal died, the basic idea behind it did not, and it was resurrected nearly eighty years later in a slightly different form.

One of the lottery tickets issued to raise money for the New London Harbor Lighthouse.

A few newspaper articles published in the late 1750s lamented recent shipwrecks in the vicinity of New York, arguing that a lighthouse strategically placed on Sandy Hook might have avoided such catastrophes. "It is surprising that" such a lighthouse "has not been built long before this day," one of the authors commented. Surprising indeed, since New York, on the verge of eclipsing Boston as the second largest city in the colonies, was home port for nearly five hundred vessels, and a destination for hundreds more.

Ships heading for New York had traditionally used the highlands of Navesink next to Sandy Hook as a landmark to guide them into the harbor. Rising nearly three hundred feet, these highlands—the tallest point on the coast below Maine—could be seen by ships far out to sea during the day, but were of less navigational value to mariners at night.

Finally, in 1761, forty-three of New York's leading merchants, roused to action by a long list of shipwrecks, urged acting governor Cadwallader Colden, a noted botanist, physician, and historian, to build a lighthouse on Sandy Hook. He, in turn, told the legislature that the lighthouse is "an object so worthy of your consideration, and a provision for it, so essential to the welfare of our commercial interests." In short, he could not recommend it highly enough. The legislature concurred, passing a lighthouse bill in May.

A lottery to raise three thousand pounds to buy land on Sandy Hook and construct the lighthouse proved a resounding success. Ten thousand tickets, at two pounds each, were snapped up and 1,684 winners selected, two of whom walked away with the top prize of one thousand pounds, a small fortune considering that at the time a schoolmaster might earn only around sixty pounds per year. With the money in hand, negotiations for the land began. Robert and Esek Hartshorne, the owners of Sandy Hook, demanded £1,000 in exchange for four acres at the tip of the peninsula, a steep price that the New Yorkers thought excessive for such a small and unprofitable piece of real estate. The Hartshornes stood firm, and the New Yorkers handed over the money.

But soon after construction began, the coffers ran dry. Having spent so much for the land, the New Yorkers didn't have enough money to finish the lighthouse. So they launched another lottery in April 1763, on the same terms as the first. It was just as successful, and in slightly more than a year, on June 11, 1764, the Sandy Hook Lighthouse shone for the first time. Built by the New York mason Isaac Conro, the octagonal, rubble stone lighthouse soared to 103 feet, including the copper-topped iron lantern room that displayed whale oil lamps. Conro's work was "judged to be masterly" by contemporaries, and it certainly was, for it still stands today. And since all the colonial lighthouses that preceded it have been rebuilt at least once, Sandy Hook holds the distinction of being the oldest continuously operating lighthouse in the nation.

PHILADELPHIA HAD AN EVEN greater need for a lighthouse than did New York. Located along the west bank of the Delaware River roughly 110 miles from the mouth of Delaware Bay, Philadelphia was by 1760 the largest city in the colonies, and its foremost port. Situated roughly in the middle of the thirteen colonies, Philadelphia played a dominant role in the coastal trade, serving as a north–south distribution point for goods. It also supported a healthy overseas commerce in such products as flour, wine, and iron. And given Pennsylvania's Quaker roots, its history of religious tolerance, and its wealth of arable land, immigrants in search of a better life flocked to the colony, making Philadelphia America's main port of entry.

But before ships arrived in Philadelphia they had to navigate the treacherous waters at the mouth of the bay, which had claimed many victims over the years. A particularly nasty spot was off Cape Henlopen, a broad expanse of sandy beaches, dunes, marshes, and pine forests located at the south side of the bay's entrance, where "the wrecks which lie plentifully scattered over the beach," noted a contemporary visitor to the area, "afford a melancholy proof of the necessity of a lighthouse to the approaching navigator."

Creating a colonial chorus of sorts, Philadelphia's merchants concurred heartily, but despite their lobbying for a lighthouse on Cape Henlopen, the colonial legislature failed to act. So in 1761 the merchants took matters into their own hands, launching a lighthouse lottery virtually identical to the one sponsored by New York earlier in the year. Unfortunately they were not as successful as their brethren to the north, raising only £2,260. Still, the merchants forged ahead, and in 1763 they persuaded the Pennsylvania legislature to take the money and build the lighthouse.

The legislature established a commission to oversee construction, and acquired two hundred acres on Cape Henlopen, which was part of Pennsylvania at the time (it is now in Delaware). Funding problems continued to plague the project, but timely loans, and the laying of duties on shipping provided the money necessary to proceed. On November 14, 1765, the *Pennsylvania Journal* eagerly informed its readers "that the elegant lighthouse building on Cape Cornelius (commonly called Cape Henlopen) will be very soon lighted for the direction of shipping." And less than a month later the *Pennsylvania Gazette* issued a notice to all masters of vessels, letting them know that the lighthouse was finished; the height of the stone structure being variously reported as either sixty-nine or eighty-seven feet.

THE NORTHERN AND MID-ATLANTIC colonies paved the way in lighthouse construction, but soon a southern one followed suit, led by Charleston, South Carolina (then called Charles Towne, in honor of King Charles II of England). The roots of Charleston's lighthouse reach back to the late seventeenth century. In 1673, just three years after Charleston was founded, the colonial legislature ordered that a beacon be raised on what would later be called Morris Island, located just beyond the mouth of Charleston Harbor. Nothing more than an iron grate that burned balls of oakum—rope fibers slathered in tar—the beacon guided mariners into the harbor. In the early 1700s tallow candles (presumably in a lantern) replaced the fiery balls of oakum, but before long it became clear that a simple beacon fueled by candles would not suffice.

By midcentury Charleston had emerged as the fourth largest city in the colonies, and arguably the wealthiest on a per capita basis, if one did not count slaves (who were not considered people). A brisk trade in indigo, naval stores, deerskins, rice, and other goods propelled Charleston's economy. With roughly eight hundred vessels sailing into Charleston Harbor each year, the South Carolina legislature, prompted by area merchants, decided that the time had come to build a permanent lighthouse on Morris Island, and it passed a law to that effect in 1750.

Despite the colony's slave-fueled prosperity, however, the legislature had difficulty finding funds, and by 1755 it had allocated only part of what would be needed. Moreover, the lighthouse supporters did not realize that there would be competition for the funds, and were surprised to learn that the elders of Charleston's Saint Michael's Church had also come to the legislature with outstretched hands. Needing money to finish the final third of the church's steeple, the elders argued that the funds set aside for the lighthouse should be given to them, their rationale being that since the steeple—which would rise to 186 feet upon completion—was so tall, and could be seen far out to sea, that it could serve as the city's beacon, thus saving the colony the expense of building a lighthouse. Succumbing to the persuasive powers of the cloth, the legislature promptly diverted the funds to the church.

Frustrated but undeterred, merchants continued complaining about the lack of a lighthouse. Their voices ultimately reached the ears of King George III, who ordered that the project proceed. The cornerstone of the brick Morris Island Lighthouse was laid on May 30, 1767, and in little more than a year the 115-foot structure, topped with a gilded ball, began welcoming mariners to Charleston.

A YEAR AFTER CHARLESTON built a lighthouse, Massachusetts added another to its jagged coast, the one at Gurnet Point. Christened by the Pilgrims after similarly named headlands in England, where gurnet fish—or gurnards, as they are called today—ran thick, Gurnet Point sat at the tip of a seven-mile-long peninsula at the entrance to Plymouth Bay. According to the legislators, the lighthouse would save lives "by directing the distressed, in stormy and tempestuous weather," into the protective embrace of Plymouth Harbor, the only safe anchorage between Boston and Cape Cod.

The Plymouth (Gurnet) Lighthouse began operation in late summer

1768, a little more than a month after Boston and New York merchants agreed to boycott most British goods in an attempt to force Parliament to repeal the hated Townshend Acts, which placed customs duties on tea, glass, paper, lead, and paint imported into the colonies. In a significant departure from earlier colonial lighthouses, rather than one lantern room, there were two, which poked out of the roof at either end of a wooden house thirty feet long and fifteen feet wide. This twin-lights design was chosen to differentiate it from the Boston Lighthouse so that mariners would not confuse the two. Even though the lantern rooms were not much more than twenty feet off the ground, since the lighthouse sat on a bluff they were actually some ninety feet above sea level.

A LITTLE MORE THAN seventy miles north of Gurnet Point, on the bank of the Piscataqua River not far from its exit to the sea, sits Portsmouth, New Hampshire. Its very name signifies its early connection to maritime commerce, and during the eighteenth century Portsmouth became a significant center of colonial trade, specializing in shipbuilding and the export of timber and masts, including those made from the tallest, straightest, and thickest white pines, which surveyors marked with the "King's Broad Arrow" in a largely unsuccessful attempt to reserve them solely for the Crown's use.

In light of Portsmouth's commercial importance, the king authorized the building of a lighthouse in 1742 near the mouth of the Piscataqua, and provided funding of one thousand pounds. But, for reasons that are unclear, nothing happened for decades. Finally, in 1765, one hundred of the area's most prominent merchants demanded to know why the lighthouse project had died, and what had happened to the money. "If such a building," they argued, "was then [in 1742] estimated of such importance to the safety of navigation & benefit of trade, it is much more so now by the increase in both." A committee was appointed to look into the matter, but if it produced a report, it has never been found. As for the money, it had apparently been spent in other ways.

Three years later, on December 12, 1768, New Hampshirites were reminded once again of the need for a lighthouse. That night a schooner from Guadeloupe laden with molasses wrecked within a mile of the entrance of Portsmouth Harbor. A few days later the *New-Hampshire Gazette* opined, with a tinge of sarcasm, "It is to be hoped within 50 years more we shall have a lighthouse at the entrance of this harbor, which it is more than probable would have saved this vessel, and a number of others heretofore."

One might have thought that New Hampshire governor John Wentworth, whose family had deep roots in maritime trade, would heartily support the building of a lighthouse, but when it came time for him to address the matter, he offered only a feeble proposal. In 1771 he recommended, as if applying a Band-Aid to a gushing wound, that the colony place a lantern atop the flagpole at Fort William and Mary, near the mouth of the Piscataqua, and that it be tended by the fort's commanding officer. Although this light was a minor affair that would cost a measly thirty pounds, Wentworth argued passionately for its erection. "Many valuable lives are annually lost," he told the legislature, "and much property destroyed for the want of such a friendly edifice." These shipwrecks, and the "tears" and "pitiable complaints" of the widows and orphans left in their wake, he declared, might have been prevented by the lantern he envisioned. He ended his plea by warning that if the legislature didn't approve his proposal, "every future expiring cry of a drowning mariner upon our coast will bitterly accuse the unfeeling recusant."

The legislature approved Wentworth's plan on April 12, but then the project went in an entirely different direction. Less than a week later the *New-Hampshire Gazette* trumpeted the news that a full-fledged lighthouse was being built just outside the walls of the fort. The records are mute on what caused this dramatic shift, but according to the historian Jane Molloy Porter, "the most likely explanation" is that when England reimbursed the New Hampshire for costs it incurred fighting the French and Indian War—which engulfed the colonies between 1754 to 1763—the influx of money caused Wentworth and the legislature to scrap their original plan and invest more substantially in the region's future.

The new lighthouse finally rose on the New Hampshire horizon in early July. It was made of wood, with an iron-and-glass-enclosed lantern

Detail from a 1799 print, View of Piscataqua Lighthouse from Kitterie Point, *showing the Portsmouth Harbor Lighthouse (artist unknown).*

room containing lamps burning fish oil. Its height remains unknown since it was replaced in 1804, and no plans of the original survived. Contemporary drawings of the lighthouse, however, show an attractive, tall conical structure with small windows along its side. Its value to mariners was quickly proved, as Wentworth reported to the legislature in December 1771 that it had already "been the acknowledged means of preserving two vessels and their men."

JUST AS THE FOUNDATION for the Portsmouth Harbor Lighthouse was being laid, Massachusetts decided to light up yet another part of its coast. The area chosen for the third beacon was Cape Ann, a rocky headland about thirty miles north of Boston, which had been the site of numerous shipwrecks, none more tragic than the seventeenth-century crash of the *Watch and Wait.*

On the morning of August 11, 1635, Anthony Thacher and his cousin, the minister Joseph Avery, went to the wharf in Ipswich, Massachusetts, where the *Watch and Wait* was preparing to depart. Ministers were not easy to find in the devout Massachusetts Bay Colony, and the people of Marblehead, a small fishing village north of Boston, had persuaded Avery to be their pastor, despite his lingering concerns about leading a congregation comprising mainly fishermen, whom he thought were often "loose and remiss in their behavior." The grateful Marbleheaders had sent the pinnace, or small boat, *Watch and Wait* to pick him up, along with his cousin, who had also decided to move to Marblehead. While the master and his three crewmen readied the vessel for the trip, the passengers boarded. In addition to Avery and Thacher, they included both of their large families, two servants, and another gentleman. All told there were twenty-three people on the boat.

For the first three days, with various lengthy stops along the way, the trip went well, but on August 14 "the Lord suddenly turned" the group's "cheerfulness into mourning and lamentations." About ten in the evening the wind rose to a gale force, splitting the sails. The sailors refused to replace them on account of the dark, and instead anchored for the night. By dawn the gale had turned into a hurricane. The *Watch and Wait* began dragging its anchor; then the cable snapped, casting the vessel adrift in the raging seas. Thacher, Avery, and their families prayed and comforted one another as best they could, while expecting to be consigned to the depths at any moment.

The *Watch and Wait* was then thrown onto a large rock, where it was wedged in place and pummeled by the waves. As the cabin flooded and the vessel started breaking apart, the ocean began to claim its victims, almost one by one. The master and the crewmen were the first to be swept overboard. Rather than despair, Thacher held on to his faith. While peering out of the cabin into the roiling seas, he saw treetops in the distance. This discovery raised his hopes, and he told his cousin, "It hath pleased God to cast us here . . . the shore not far from us" (one wonders, though, if Thacher questioned why God had not simply set the vessel *on* the shore). But Avery pleaded with him to stay so that they and their families could "die together" and be delivered to heaven.

No sooner had Thacher agreed to accept this fate than a thunderous wave surged into the cabin, washing him, his daughter, Avery, and Avery's eldest son out onto the rock. Clambering higher up, the four of them called to those still in the cabin to join them. The others apparently frozen with fear, only Thacher's wife responded. She began crawling through a hatch to the quarterdeck when another wave smashed into the vessel, obliterating what was left of it, sending her and all the other occupants into the water. The force of the same wave also swept everyone from the rock save Thacher, who managed tenaciously to cling to the rock face. Then, just as he was reaching out to grab a plank from the vessel, another wave dislodged him, and he too was pitched into the sea.

In the end only Thacher and his wife survived what would become one of the most dramatic and fabled shipwrecks in Massachusetts Bay Colony history. Bruised, battered, and nearly naked, they washed up on a small, uninhabited island about a mile from the mainland of Cape Ann. They covered themselves with clothing from the wreck, and survived on food that had also floated ashore. Five days passed before a boat came within hailing distance and rescued them.

The disaster quickly became the talk of New England, and many shared the deep sorrow felt by the Thachers. In September 1635 the legislature awarded Thacher "forty marks," or about twenty-six pounds, to help compensate him for "his great losses," and a year later it gave him the island "upon which he was preserved from shipwreck, as his proper inheritance." Thacher named the island "Thacher's Woe," but it is known today as Thacher Island, which is part of the town of Rockport.

Thacher never lived on his eponymous island. After being rescued, he and his wife resided in Marblehead for several years and then headed to Cape Cod, where Thacher became one of the founders of Yarmouth. Thacher Island stayed in the family for a few generations before it was sold. The rock struck by the *Watch and Wait* was part of a ninety-foot-long reef that lies about a half-mile off the northeastern edge of Thacher Island. In subsequent years the reef caused many wrecks, one of which involved the ship *London*, which gave the reef its new name, the Londoner.

When the Massachusetts legislature gathered in April 1771, the Lon-

The two towers of the Thacher Island Lighthouse. These towers were built in 1861, replacing the original towers from 1771.

doner was very much on their minds. At the beginning of the month three prominent Marblehead merchants petitioned the legislature to build one or more lighthouses on Cape Ann to warn vessels away from the Londoner and another dangerous ledge in the area. The legislature appointed a committee, headed by the Boston merchant and shipowner John Hancock, to draft a lighthouse bill, which passed on April 26, 1771, and proposed building a lighthouse either on Thacher Island or on the mainland of Cape Ann.

Another committee, tasked with deciding where to put the lighthouse, selected Thacher Island, which was promptly purchased for five hundred pounds. Rather than a single lighthouse tower, however, the legislature decided to build two to distinguish them from Boston Harbor's lighthouse. The forty-five-foot-tall stone towers, placed nearly nine hundred feet apart, were first lit on December 21, 1771. Whereas all previous colonial lighthouses were intended to guide ships safely into and out of port, Cape Ann's twin lights were the first to warn of a specific danger—the dreaded Londoner. The residents of Cape Ann, enamored of and thankful for the twin lights, soon began calling them "Ann's Eyes."

THACHER ISLAND LIGHTHOUSE would be the tenth and the last lighthouse erected in the colonies under British rule—a rule that, in large part through the emergence of a forceful and independent-minded merchant class, was rapidly coming to an end. Even as the twin towers were being built, the bond between the colonies and the mother country was already weakening. The Sugar Act, the Stamp Act, and the Townshend Acts had taken their toll, greatly angering American colonists and giving them an electrifying rallying cry—"No Taxation Without Representation." The Boston Massacre, on March 5, 1770, inflamed passions even more. And in the years following the lighting of the twin towers, the growing fracture became an open breach, as the Boston Tea Party, the punitive Intolerable Acts, the skirmishes at Lexington and Concord, and finally the Battle of Bunker Hill sundered most of the remaining ties between Britain and its American colonies, launching the Revolutionary War

Before the war, lighthouses played a significant role in the economic growth of the colonies, enhancing maritime commerce by making it safer. It can even be argued that the expansion of lighthouses correlated significantly with the dynamic and independent thrust of the colonies themselves. But once the war commenced, the role of lighthouses changed dramatically. Instead of welcoming ships from afar and warning them of hidden dangers, lighthouses became military targets.

CHAPTER 2

CASUALTIES OF WAR

. . . .

Engraving of Washington taking command of the Continental army at Cambridge,
July 3, 1775, after a painting by M. A. Wageman.

THE CONTINENTAL CONGRESS DECLARED JULY 20, 1775, AS A
day of "public humiliation, fasting, and prayer." Reflecting the strong
religious beliefs of many of its founding legislators, the newly minted
Congress asked Americans to pray to God to forgive them for their "iniq-
uities" and to "inspire" King George III with the "wisdom" necessary
to put a "speedy end . . . to the civil discord between Great Britain and
the American Colonies." It was hoped that such prayers would prevent
a "further effusion of blood." But Maj. Joseph Vose of the Continental
Army had no interest in atonement or in asking God to influence the

king's actions. Instead Vose and his men had their sights set on attacking the Boston Lighthouse.

Ever since the battles at Lexington and Concord on April 19, 1775, and even more so after the Battle of Bunker Hill nearly two months later, Boston had been under siege. While the British army and navy controlled the city and the harbor, an increasing number of American soldiers surrounded Boston itself, effectively isolating the British. Although most Americans were still hopeful that reconciliation could be achieved, many—particularly those in and around Boston—believed that an all-out war for independence was inevitable. When waging a war, the main goal, of course, is to inflict injury, lethal if possible, on the enemy, and that is where the lighthouse played a contributing role.

On July 2, less than three months after the outbreak of hostilities, the Massachusetts Provincial Congress recommended that the colony's three lighthouses—on Little Brewster Island, Thacher Island, and at Gurnet Point—be put out of commission, leaving it to the towns where the lighthouses were located to take the necessary action. The logic was inescapably clear: Lighthouses do not distinguish between friend and foe, and as long as the colony's lighthouses remained operational they would help safely guide British vessels along the treacherous Massachusetts coast and into Boston Harbor, where they could strengthen and resupply the beleaguered British forces. Disabling the lighthouses, it was hoped, would make it that much more difficult for the British to sustain the siege.

As for the lighthouse at Gurnet Point, Congress was a little late: The resolute residents of Plymouth had already extinguished it on April 23. Thacher Island Lighthouse was the next to go. The day after Congress made its recommendation, Capt. Sam Rogers, a doctor from Gloucester, Massachusetts, led a hardy band of local militia to Thacher Island, where they smashed the lighthouse lamps and the glass in the lantern room, also collecting all the whale oil. The lighthouse, however, was hardly their only target. The patriotic citizens of Cape Ann suspected Capt. James Kirkwood, the lighthouse keeper, of being a Tory, and that was reason enough to get rid of him. After finishing with the lighthouse, Rogers and his men grabbed Kirkwood and his family and deposited them unceremoniously on the mainland, where, according to a British military report, they were left "to shift for themselves." Their suspicions were correct, for soon thereafter the Kirkwoods fled to Canada, becoming part of the exodus of sixty thousand Tories who left America during the war to settle somewhere else in the British Empire, refugees whom the historian Maya Jasanoff has labeled "Liberty's Exiles."

Although the lighthouses at Gurnet Point and on Thacher Island had significant strategic value, the safety of the Boston Lighthouse remained of paramount importance to the Redcoats. Therefore disabling it became a Revolutionary grail. With that goal in mind, Brig. Gen, William Heath ordered Major Vose to lead a raid on Little Brewster Island. A farmer formerly of Milton, Massachusetts, Vose and sixty soldiers set out from Hingham, Massachusetts, in the early morning hours of July 20. After muffling the oars by covering the oarlocks in cloth, they quietly rowed seven whaleboats to the tip of the Nantasket Peninsula in Hull, and then dragged the boats across a slender ribbon of sand to a beach opposite the lighthouse. Into the water they went again. When they finally reached Little Brewster, Vose and his men burned the lighthouse's wooden portions and seized three casks of whale oil, as well as the furniture in the keeper's house, fifty pounds of gunpowder, a couple of boats, and a cannon.

At the time of the attack British marines and loyalists were tending the lighthouse, yet bizarrely there is no record of an initial confrontation. Even if there was no fight on the island, however, one soon broke out. At eight that morning a watch on the HMS *Lively*, anchored only a mile away, spotted the line of whaleboats approaching the lighthouse. Realizing that something was terribly wrong, he alerted his commanding officer, who quickly signaled other nearby ships for assistance.

Before the British could respond, Vose's men had done their damage, and were piling back into their whaleboats to race for the shore. A few minutes later eight British vessels were in furious pursuit, bearing down on the Americans and unleashing a series of broadsides in their direction. The rain of metal notwithstanding, Vose's raiders made it back to Nantasket with only two men sustaining minor leg wounds. Once on land, the Americans arrayed themselves in battle formation, in effect daring the British soldiers to come ashore. But they didn't take the bait and instead moved their vessels out of range of the Americans' muskets. An eyewitness to this entire affair said that he "saw the flames of the lighthouse ascending up to heaven like grateful incense, and the [British] ships wasting their powder."

THE DARING ATTACK ON the Boston Lighthouse heartened the patriots. As Abigail Adams wrote to her husband, John, who was in Philadelphia with the Continental Congress, "these little skirmishes seem trifling, but they serve to inure our men, and harden them to danger." And better yet, Adams added that she had heard that the British—whom she labeled, with characteristic eloquence, as "vermin and locusts"—were "very wroth at the destruction of the lighthouse."

The attack had even greater significance as part of a broader pattern of patriot defiance. In the months leading up to the attack, Americans had on multiple occasions successfully used whaleboats to raid various harbor islands to burn hay and take off crops and livestock so as to keep these valuable resources from falling into British hands. American whaleboat warriors had even harassed British ships. The attack on the lighthouse acted like a tocsin, revealing once again that although the world's mightiest navy controlled the harbor, the Americans could still fight back. This boldness led James Warren, the president of the Massachusetts Provincial Congress, to boast, "It is said they [the British] are more afraid of our whale Boats than we are of their Men of War."

While the patriots were emboldened by the attack on the lighthouse, Vice Adm. Samuel Graves was enraged. As the commander of British naval forces in North America, he was in charge of protecting British interests and defending against American attacks. Yet repeatedly the Americans had gotten the better of his fleet, the attack on the lighthouse being only the most recent example. In response to this latest indignity, Graves, who was on board the HMS *Preston* anchored in Boston Harbor, immediately issued a circular "To all Seafaring People," warning them that the lighthouses on Thacher Island and at the entrance to Boston

Harbor had been "burnt and destroyed by the rebels," and urging them to "be careful that they are not deceived by false lights, which the rebels threaten to hang out, in order to decoy vessels into destruction."

At the same time Graves sent loyalist carpenters to repair the Boston Lighthouse, and for their protection he provided a guard of thirty-two marines and one lieutenant, along with a heavily armed longboat. "With this party," Graves wrote, "the engineers were of [the] opinion the light house might well be defended, until succors arrived, against 1,000 men." Work progressed quickly, and by July 29 the British-controlled light-house was once again illuminating the besieged harbor.

That light was of no small concern to George Washington, who had assumed command of the American forces at the beginning of July. Although Washington had learned of Vose's raid only after the fact, he now went on the offensive, ordering a second attack on the lighthouse. The man chosen to lead the attack was Maj. Benjamin Tupper, another member of Brigadier General Heath's regiment.

A FORMER TANNER, schoolteacher, and veteran, like Washington, of the French and Indian War, Tupper assembled three hundred soldiers and thirty-three whaleboats along the shore of Dorchester, Massachusetts, late in the evening of July 30. According to tradition, he told the men, "If there is any one of you who is afraid, and does not want to go with us, let him step two paces to the front." He then—we can only hope slightly facetiously— whispered to one of his officers that if any man stepped forward, he was to "shoot him on the spot." Nobody moved. And soon the miniarmada began rowing to Little Brewster Island, reaching its destination at about two the following morning. As they approached, one of the marines guarding the lighthouse yelled, "The whaleboats are coming!" whereupon his superior, Lieutenant Colthurst, ordered his men to grab their arms and assemble. This proved to be a difficult maneuver, since quite a few of the marines were, as one of them later recalled, "in the liquor and totally unfit for service."

Disregarding a direct order, a few of the intoxicated marines fired their muskets at the Americans, causing them to halt their approach and raise their oars. While the Americans appeared to be considering their next move, Midshipman Christopher Hele urged Colthurst to continue firing at the Americans in the hope that it might cause them to retreat. No sooner had Hele spoken than the Americans let out a seemingly feral, warlike cheer, and split their forces into small groups of whaleboats, each making for different parts of the island. Colthurst decided that the only choice the British had, being so vastly outnumbered, was to withdraw to their schooner and longboat, and then try to reach the HMS *Lively*, which was not far off.

As the Americans swarmed onto the island, the longboat managed to escape, but the schooner grounded very close to the shore, and was soon set upon by the Americans. In the melee that followed, Tupper's men killed six, including Colthurst, who was shot through the head, wounding five more in the process. Upward of thirty prisoners were taken, mainly marines, but also a number of workers and assorted Tories who were visiting the island—thus definitively refuting the British boast that the lighthouse would be able to hold off an onslaught of one thousand men until reinforcements showed up.

While some of Tupper's men were busy engaging the enemy, others, acting to complete the guerrilla offensive, torched the lighthouse and the rest of the buildings on the island. Their mission complete, the Americans now faced a new foe—the tides. The same low water that foiled the schooner's escape now hampered their departure. By the time they set off, the British were already chasing them at close quarters, firing furiously. But Tupper had wisely planned ahead. Before the raid began, he had ordered Maj. John Crane to position his fieldpiece on Nantasket beach to cover the Americans' retreat. And now, as Crane blasted away, sinking one British boat, Tupper and his men made it safely to shore, having suffered only one fatality, a Rhode Islander named Griffin who was shot through the temple.

The prisoners were ultimately sent to a Revolutionary jail in Springfield, but before they left, a moving scene played out in Germantown (West Roxbury), where Griffin was interred on August 1. The British marines who had been wounded during Tupper's raid actually attended the funeral to pay their respects. After the service Abigail Adams told

*Early-twentieth-century
photo of Benjamin Blyth's
pastel portrait of
Abigail Adams, circa 1766.*

the marines "it was very unhappy that they should be obliged to fight their best Friends." They said "they were sorry," and hoped that God would put a speedy end to "the unhappy contest." The marines also said they "had been deceived, for they were told if they were taken alive," the Americans would kill them. Such sentiments reflected the often ambiguous division that separated the former colonists and their foes.

The same day as the funeral, Washington issued a congratulatory letter, lauding the attack on the lighthouse. Washington thanked Tupper and his men for "their gallant and soldier like behavior, . . . and for the Number of Prisoners they took there." This action, Washington claimed, would undoubtedly make the Continental Army "as famous for their mercy as for their valor."

Washington's pride was shared by many Americans, among them Elisha Rich, a Baptist minister from Chelmsford, Massachusetts, who memorialized Tupper's assault in verse. Having earlier written a ballad on the Battle of Bunker Hill, Rich now offered a new broadside called "Poetical Remarks Upon the Fight at the Boston Light-House," which included the following patriotic stanzas:

> *The Boston Light-House that did help our foe,*
> *By God's assistance thou did'st overthrow,*

By means which in danger they must be,
Should other Ships of War come against thee.

But when thy foe this Building would repair
That they may pass the channel without fear,
They met with force repulse to their surprise,
Their works were all destroy'd before their eyes.

AMERICANS behold with joyful eyes,
The lofty Light-House now in ruin lies,
It gives not light to Bloody Tyrannts here,
And tho' they fight this should not move thy fear.

The British reaction to Tupper's raid was scorn—directed not so much at the Americans but at Vice Admiral Graves, who had once again been clobbered by the forces whom the British general John Burgoyne had derisively dismissed as a "rabble in arms." From the King, members of parliament, and military colleagues, criticism rained down on the now hapless Graves, not only for the two humiliations at the lighthouse, but also for his failures and general inanition on so many other fronts.

The general feeling toward Graves was perhaps best expressed in a private letter from Burgoyne to Lord George Germain, the colonial secretary in Prime Minister Lord North's government, written on August 20, 1775. Burgoyne, at the time stationed in Boston, started off with a query. "It may perhaps be asked in England," he wrote, "'What is the Admiral doing?'" Burgoyne responded, "I wish I were able to answer that question satisfactorily; but I can only say what he is *not* doing. . . . He is *not* defending his own flocks and herds, for the enemy have repeatedly and in the most insulting manner plundered his own appropriated islands. He is *not* defending the other islands in the harbor, for the enemy landed in force, burned the lighthouse[,] . . . and killed and took a party of marines under the guns of two or three men of war." In any event, Graves's failings ultimately became too much for the British government, and he was recalled by the end of the year.

In the meantime the British desperately wanted the lighthouse relit, but that took quite a while. Work crews labored on and off for months, protected by marines on the island, and an armed transport or warship anchored nearby. To further increase safety, the workers were often shuttled to the island during the day, and then taken on board one of the ships at night. Four months later, on November 23, 1775, the lighthouse that British general William Howe said was "so necessary for the safety of vessels bound to the port" was finally guiding ships once more. British troops by year's end guarded the lighthouse around the clock to keep the Americans from staging another attack. Nonetheless the lighthouse's trials by fire were not over.

The Siege of Boston, in which the British had essentially strung a strategic noose around the city, finally ended in 1776 when royal troops, and the bulk of the Royal Navy, placed in an indefensible position by the sudden appearance of patriot cannons on Dorchester Heights, retreated and sailed to Halifax, Nova Scotia, on March 17—forever after celebrated by Bostonians as Evacuation Day. A few warships, however, remained in the vicinity of the lighthouse to warn other ships coming from Britain that the army had departed. The continued British presence infuriated the Americans, and on June 14, Continental Army troops, under the command of Col. Asa Whitcomb, fired cannons and mortars at enemy ships from batteries on Long Island, while other troops fired on them from Nantasket. This barrage forced the remnants of the British fleet to put to sea, but before they left, British marines landed on Little Brewster Island. Recognizing the lighthouse's strategic value to the insurgents, the British torched it and left a keg of gunpowder at its base. Then they returned to their ships along with the lighthouse guards. Less than an hour later, at eleven in the morning, the keg's fuse hit its mark. The Boston Lighthouse blew up, turning it into "a heap of rubbish" in the words of one eyewitness.

BY THE TIME THE British withdrew from Boston in March, the number of Americans who still thought reconciliation a possibility had diminished significantly, owing to a number of dramatic events that had transformed the rift between America and Britain into an irreparable breach. In January 1776, Thomas Paine's elegantly argued *Common Sense* appeared, further energizing American patriots by eviscerating the rationale in favor of continued British rule. The manifesto urged independence and declared that "the birthday of a new world is at hand." And in February, American fury was aroused yet again when the insurrectionary people learned that Parliament had passed the punitive Prohibitory Act, which attempted to strangle American commerce by halting all British trade with the colonies. The bill treated American ships as if they were now enemies of the Crown, thereby making them subject to seizure by the British navy. Thus, by March 1776 the question was not whether the undeclared war with Britain would continue, but where the next battle would be waged.

EVEN BEFORE EVACUATION DAY, all eyes had pivoted to New York City. As early as January 1776, Washington believed that the British were planning to invade this thriving metropolis. Given his premonition, he ordered Maj. Gen, Charles Lee to strengthen the city's porous defenses. Although New York City contained numerous loyalists, who would heartily welcome a British invasion, New York's Provincial Congress was of the same mind as Washington. It sought to prevent a British takeover, and one of its strategic steps involved the lighthouse at Sandy Hook.

Like their brethren to the north in Massachusetts, New Yorkers did not want their lighthouse to aid the enemy. Thus, on March 4, 1776, New York's Provincial Congress ordered that the lighthouse be dismantled, appointing a committee to make sure that was accomplished. The committee, in turn, selected William Malcolm, a prominent New York merchant, ardent patriot, and major in the local militia to carry out this "important enterprise." Malcolm's instructions were clear: to remove the glass from the lantern room and collect all the whale oil in casks. If Malcolm could not remove the glass, he was supposed to smash it, and if he could not find casks, or if the enemy appeared, he was to pump the oil onto the ground. "In short," the committee told him, "you will use your discretion to render the lighthouse entirely useless."

Since secrecy was paramount, the committee sent Malcolm to New Jersey alone, for fear that if he departed from New York with any appreciable force, loyalists in the city would alert the British warships patrolling the area. But the committee knew Malcolm could not complete the mission on his own, so they gave him a letter of introduction to the patriotic Committee of Inspection and Observation in Middletown, New Jersey, where Sandy Hook was located. The letter beseeched the New Jerseyans to offer assistance, and they obliged, providing a small detachment of militia led by Col. George Taylor to accompany Malcolm to the lighthouse on March 8.

The party encountered no resistance, but they had to smash the glass since they lacked the tools to take the panes out of their metal frame. In addition to three and a half casks of whale oil, they took eight lamps and two block and tackles from the lighthouse. The mission's success, however, proved only transitory.

Facing no opposition, the British in a move of geographic significance took possession of the tip of Sandy Hook in the middle of April, placing marines on land and warships just offshore. This achieved three strategic goals: First, it gave the British access to drinking water, something that was in desperately short supply since their source on Staten Island was cut off as a result of American attacks. Second, it allowed the British to monitor and control the main shipping channel into New York, which ran by Sandy Hook. And, finally, it meant that the British also controlled the lighthouse, which was expected to play a critical role in the upcoming attack on New York City, its shining beacon serving to guide the British fleet safely on its approach. But for the lighthouse to be a guide it first had to be fixed, a challenging task that was not completed until about the middle of June. While repairs were ongoing, Capt. Hyde Parker of the HMS *Phoenix* strengthened defenses by increasing the number of marines guarding the lighthouse.

THE CAPTURE OF SANDY HOOK and the resuscitation of the lighthouse understandably worried Washington, who had been in New York City since April 13 preparing the Continental Army for the impending British invasion. For the same reasons that the British wanted to hold on to Sandy Hook, Washington wanted to oust them, and disable if not destroy the lighthouse. To achieve those goals, he turned, once again, to Benjamin Tupper. Since distinguishing himself in the assault on the Boston Lighthouse, Tupper had been promoted to lieutenant colonel and put in charge of a fleet of whaleboats, schooners, and sloops, whose job it was to patrol the waters from Long Island to northern New Jersey, report on the movements of British ships, and keep those ships from communicating with American loyalists. Now Washington ordered Tupper to attack Sandy Hook.

Tupper's force of about three hundred men set out in whaleboats and other assorted craft from Perth Amboy, New Jersey, at 11:00 a.m. on June 19. By sunset they landed at Middletown, where Tupper failed to obtain any assistance from New Jerseyans, "tho," he later recalled, it was "earnestly requested." Tupper thought this refusal "a little strange," and indeed it was a marked difference from just a few months earlier, when Taylor and his men had willingly led Major Malcolm to the lighthouse. But New Jersey was a colony of sharply divided loyalties, and many residents did not stand with the patriots. By the time Tupper arrived, the number of loyalists had risen, and it would soon include among its ranks the erstwhile patriot George Taylor, Malcolm's escort. Seen in this light, Tupper's failure to enlist the help of the New Jerseyans was not so strange after all.

Without reinforcements, Tupper and his men then set off again, arriving at about two the following morning at Spermaceti Cove, a sheltered embayment near the base of Sandy Hook that derived its exotic name in 1668 after a sperm whale washed ashore there. Tupper waited until late that evening to begin the nearly four-mile march to the lighthouse over the dunes and through the dense cedar forest, moving very slowly so as to keep quiet and not alarm the enemy. The men were in "high spirits," the soldier Solomon Nash later recalled, and they made it to within about 450 feet of their target at about four on June 21, undetected by the British. While his men formed ranks on the slope of a small hill, and primed their fieldpieces, Tupper and one of his officers strode to the lighthouse and demanded to speak with the commanding officer, his plan being to persuade the British to surrender. Tupper had barely made this request before the sentry began shooting, only narrowly missing the Americans, who quickly retreated back to their party.

Tupper ordered the "artillery to play," launching twenty-one cannonballs at the lighthouse, but its walls were so thick and strong that the rounds made "no impression." At the same time Tupper's men exchanged fire with the marines guarding the lighthouse, while two British warships lying offshore unloaded their guns on the Americans. Frustrated by his failure to damage the lighthouse, Tupper ordered his men to move closer to the ships in the hope of drawing the British onto the shore to fight, but he found that he "could not provoke them." Despite the fact that this battle lasted roughly two and a half hours, and much of it was fought during the dawn's early light, only two of Tupper's men were hit, and their wounds were minor. And it appears that there were no British casualties.

After this anticlimactic encounter, the Americans returned to their camp on the other side of the cedar forest, where Tupper wrote Washington a letter in which he claimed that the heavy force waiting to meet him was proof that the British had been warned of his coming. Tupper

*Engraving of General
George Washington,
circa 1777.*

also pledged to renew the attack that evening, but instead he returned to Perth Amboy to regroup. It was just as well, since when Washington finally received the letter, only one day later, on June 22, he immediately wrote back ordering Tupper to "desist from the enterprise, as it seemed dangerous and no[t] to promise success."

Penning those words must have pained Washington, who had been anticipating a victory. Only the day before, eighty-three men, including three officers, had paraded on his orders before Assistant Quartermaster General Hugh Hughes at army headquarters in New York City. They had provisions, arms, and ammunition to last seven days, and their mission was to reinforce Tupper's troops on Sandy Hook. When Washington learned of Tupper's failure, however, the mission was canceled.

WHILE TUPPER'S MEN and the British were firing away at one another, a formidable British fleet, a veritable armada, was at sea, heading from Halifax to New York, with orders to rendezvous at Sandy Hook. It arrived on June 29. The *New-York Journal* reported that perhaps as many as 130 British ships had anchored inside the Hook, and that they had been "sent out by the tyrants of Great Britain" who had destroyed "the English constitution here, on the pious design of enslaving the British colonies and plundering their property at pleasure, or murdering them at once, and taking possession of all." Less than a week later the undeclared war became a real one when the Continental Congress adopted the Declaration of Independence on July 4. John Adams, who had long advocated breaking free of Britain, joyously proclaimed, "We are in the very midst of a revolution, the most complete, unexpected, and remarkable of any in the history of nations."

To consolidate their hold on Sandy Hook, the British added to their defenses around the lighthouse and stationed additional warships nearby. In subsequent years the Americans repeatedly attacked the British forces at Sandy Hook without success. During this time the Hook became a magnet for loyalists, as well as runaway slaves who were lured by the promise of freedom in exchange for enlisting in the British army. The

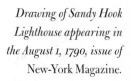

Drawing of Sandy Hook Lighthouse appearing in the August 1, 1790, issue of New-York Magazine.

temporary settlement that grew up in the penumbra of the lighthouse was called Refugee Town, and the lighthouse acquired the moniker Refugee Tower. From this crude outpost, the motley band of refugees launched numerous raids into northern New Jersey, terrorizing the local populace and leaving a trail of murdered patriots and burned homes. It wasn't until Lord Cornwallis surrendered to Washington at Yorktown on October 19, 1781, that the British occupation of the Sandy Hook Lighthouse came to an end, the Refugee Town finally disbanding.

NOT ALL LIGHTHOUSES FEATURED so dramatically during the War of Independence. Many were used as lookouts to alert the countryside to the arrival and movement of British ships. Other lighthouses were burned. Cape Henlopen's was, but it is not at all clear who torched it, or when. The most repeated account blames the British. According to this version, the

HMS *Roebuck*, sometime in April 1777, was near Cape Henlopen when the hungry men on board cast a covetous gaze at the cattle grazing around the base of the lighthouse. A party of sailors went ashore to obtain a few cows. The only problem was that the bovines belonged to the lighthouse keeper, a Mr. Hedgecock, and when the British asked him if he could spare a few, the scrappy keeper reportedly said, "I'll give you no cows, but if you don't get out I'll give you some bullets!"

This ultimatum sent the sailors scurrying back to the *Roebuck* to get instructions from their commanding officer, who ordered them to return, this time in greater numbers to get the job done. Hedgecock, who saw the longboats heading for the beach, grabbed his valuables and rushed into the woods, herding his cattle before him. When the sailors arrived only to see that their dinner had disappeared, they turned their wrath on the lighthouse, smashing the lantern room and burning the stairs.

It's a wonderful story, but most likely apocryphal. For one thing the *Roebuck*'s log has no record of the event, and such an action would almost certainly have merited at least a mention. It is also hard to believe that hardened British marines, who despised the American rebels, would have been so intimidated by a saucy lighthouse keeper. Instead it is far more likely that they would have given him the butt end of their muskets, or even shot him, before in workmanlike fashion taking what they wanted.

View of the Cape Henlopen Lighthouse, seen from the sea, 1780.

If cows and a cheeky keeper were not involved, then how did it happen? Some argue that Hedgecock accidentally burned the lighthouse and blamed it on the British. Others claim that the *Roebuck*—at a later date—or some other unidentified British warship was responsible. Whatever actually transpired, the lighthouse, after the fire, remained dark for the duration of the war.

While the culprit at Cape Henlopen remains a mystery, there is no doubt about who burned the Beavertail Lighthouse two years later. On October 24, 1779, after occupying Newport for nearly three years, British forces departed, but just before leaving they set fire to the lighthouse's wooden stairs and landings. The extreme heat shocked the masonry so badly that nearly twenty-five years later the badly damaged lighthouse still leaked during storms despite heroic efforts to make the walls tight again.

THE TREATY OF PARIS, which was signed on September 3, 1783, officially ended the Revolutionary War and rescued America's lighthouses from being used as pawns. But how the newly formed United States would organize itself and make its way in the world was yet to be determined. There was, however, no doubt that lighthouses would have a critically important role to play. They had contributed to the colonies' economic vitality, and they would now do the same for the new nation.

CHAPTER 3

LIGHTS OF A
NEW NATION

. . . .

Detail of watercolor of the Montauk Point Lighthouse,
painted in 1796 by Isaac McComb.

THE UNITED STATES CONSTITUTION, RATIFIED ON JUNE 21, 1788,
created the basic structure, or skeleton, of America's government. The
following year, the first federal Congress met in New York City to start
putting flesh on the bones by crafting laws for the infant nation. The dele-
gates to this inaugural congress were well aware of the enormity of the task
before them. "We are in a wilderness without a single footstep to guide
us," wrote James Madison to his fellow Virginian Thomas Jefferson.

"Our successors will have an easier task." During that memorable spring and summer of 1789, as Congress began charting America's course, one of the first issues to emerge was whether the individual states or the federal government would be in charge of the country's lighthouses.

In the years immediately after the end of the Revolution, the states had been in charge. Just as the colonies had once done, the states built and maintained the lighthouses within their borders. It was the states, therefore, which repaired or rebuilt the lighthouses that had been damaged or destroyed during the war. In 1783, for example, Massachusetts built a new seventy-five-foot-tall Boston Lighthouse to replace the one the British had detonated.* And it was Massachusetts that took the lead in building new lighthouses, one at Great Point on Nantucket in 1784, and another at the mouth of the Merrimack River in Newburyport in 1788.

When Congress began its deliberations in April 1789, the future of lighthouse management remained an open question. The debate hinged primarily upon funding, or more specifically on where the money for lighthouses would come from. Up to the late 1780s the colonies, and later on the states, had funded lighthouses through a combination of lotteries, direct appropriations, and, most important, by imposing tonnage duties (taxes) on ships arriving at key ports. Congress, however, quickly determined that the federal government, not the states, should levy tonnage duties. One of the main justifications was economic. In perilous financial straits, the federal government needed the money generated by such duties to run the government and repay the nation's war debts.

Having stripped the states of their main source of lighthouse funding, Congress wisely decided that the federal government should also manage the lighthouses themselves. This conclusion was based in large part on fairness and the concern that the states, bereft of tonnage duties, would not be able to support these maritime beacons. But there was more to it than that. Some congressmen believed that when the Constitution gave the federal government the power to regulate foreign and domestic commerce, it also gave it the power to regulate lighthouses, since these struc-

* In 1859, the tower's height was increased to 89 feet.

*Engraving of
Elbridge Gerry by
James Barton
Longacre, circa
1847.*

tures were so intimately tied to and necessary for the operation of the nation's commercial system.

Not all congressmen agreed with this government seizure. Antifederalists in particular, who opposed a strong centralized national government, argued that lighthouses should remain under the control of state governments. Some feared that if the government used the Constitution's commerce clause as a reason for taking over lighthouses, it might use the same clause to assume control of the mouths of rivers and other places it deemed critical to the regulation of national commerce. But they were outvoted, and the majority even included some members of the Anti-Federalist Party such as Elbridge Gerry, a representative from Massachusetts who would later go on to become vice president under President James Madison, and from whose name the term "gerrymandering" is derived.* Gerry, as it happens, grew up in Marblehead, one of America's

---

* "Gerrymandering" means redrawing the boundaries of political districts so as to favor one political party over another. When he was governor of Massachusetts in 1812, Gerry signed a bill that would redraw districts in the state to benefit the Republican party. Even though he

foremost fishing communities, part of a family that owned a fleet of ships that engaged in coastal and transatlantic trade. As a result he knew how heavily mariners relied on lighthouses. Overcoming his natural political inclinations, Gerry introduced on July 1 the first draft of the bill that would transfer to the federal government the management of existing lighthouses and other navigation aids, including buoys and unlighted beacons. After lengthy debate, and multiple revisions, that bill was sent to President George Washington on August 6, who signed it into law the following day, making August 7, 1789, the official birthday of America's lighthouse establishment.* Commonly referred to as the Lighthouse Act, it was only the ninth law passed by Congress. It also became America's first public works program. Soon thereafter the Treasury Department was tasked with overseeing the nation's lighthouses.

The transfer of lighthouses was not instantaneous, however. The law included a quid pro quo. Before the federal government assumed management responsibilities, the states had to cede their lighthouses and the lands surrounding them to the United States. Originally the states were given a year to comply, but the deadline was thrice extended to give states that were dragging their feet more time. Appropriately enough, independent and feisty Rhode Island, ever wary of federal control, and the last state to ratify the Constitution, was also the last state to relinquish its lighthouse, finally doing so in May 1793. But Rhode Island was not the only state distrustful of the federal government. When Massachusetts ceded its lighthouses in June 1790, it did so with a warning: If the federal government failed to properly maintain any of Massachusetts' lighthouses, then the state reserved the right to take back the neglected structures.

---

signed the bill reluctantly, by doing so he linked his name forevermore with this disturbing form of political manipulation.

*To commemorate the bicentennial of the passage of the Lighthouse Act in 1989, President Ronald Reagan signed a bill designating August 7 (of that year only) as National Lighthouse Day. Twenty-four years later, the U.S. Senate passed a resolution making August 7, 2013, National Lighthouse Day. Efforts are currently under way to establish National Lighthouse Day as a permanent holiday.

——

WHEN THE LIGHTHOUSE ACT passed in 1789, a mere twelve light-houses dotted the east coast. Three more were added in quick succession. The first was at Portland Head, a wonderfully scenic rocky promontory at the edge of Casco Bay in Maine. Agitation for the lighthouse had begun in 1784, when merchants from nearby Falmouth petitioned the Massachu-setts government to erect a beacon at this location (Maine was still part of Massachusetts at the time). Falmouth, which two years later was renamed Portland, boasted one of the nation's busiest harbors, and since the main shipping channel into the harbor ran alongside Portland Head, the mer-chants felt that a lighthouse there would be of inestimable value to com-merce. The petition languished until early 1787, when a sloop crashed on the rocks off Portland Head, resulting in two deaths and precipitating a plaintive plea from a local paper: "Does not this unhappy accident evince the necessity of having a lighthouse at the entrance to our harbor? It is supposed that the loss of this vessel was occasioned by the want of one."

In the wake of the disaster the merchants renewed their petition, prompting Massachusetts to provide $750 for the project. This amount, however, was far from enough, so shortly after the federal government assumed responsibility for all lighthouses, it provided another $1,500 to finish the job. Only two years later the Portland Head Lighthouse, built of rubble stone and seventy-two feet tall to the base of the lantern room, started shining, becoming Maine's first lighthouse on January 10, 1791.

Some sixty years later, in 1850, Henry Wadsworth Longfellow wrote a poem called "The Lighthouse," and the Portland Head Lighthouse is widely believed to have been his inspiration.* A Portland native, Long-fellow lived there until he went off to Bowdoin College, but he visited his hometown often, making many trips to the nearby lighthouse and befriending a few of the keepers. Two of the poem's most memorable and evocative stanzas are its first and last:

---

* Although by this time the lighthouse had been modified, having been reduced in height by about twenty-five feet.

The rocky ledge runs far into the sea,
And on its outer point, some miles away,
The Lighthouse lifts its massive masonry,
A pillar of fire by night, of cloud by day.
. . . .
"Sail on!" it says, "sail on, ye stately ships!
And with your floating bridge the ocean span;
Be mine to guard this light from all eclipse,
Be yours to bring man nearer unto man!"

The need for lighthouses was recognized from the very north to the very south of the fledgling nation. Ten months after Portland Head Lighthouse was completed, Georgia's Tybee Lighthouse became the fourteenth beacon to illuminate America's coast. Like its Maine counterpart, the Tybee Lighthouse's history antedated 1789. In 1736, four years after Georgia's founding as the thirteenth colony, an unlit beacon was erected on Tybee Island at the mouth of the Savannah River to guide mariners to the newly settled town of Savannah, which lay about fifteen miles upriver from the ocean. Described by a contemporary as "a tower of wood of prodigious height," the poorly constructed beacon quickly deteriorated and was leveled by a storm in 1741, then replaced the following year with another wooden beacon, ninety-four feet tall. This one was sturdier, but it too fell into disrepair, and in 1768 the colonial government authorized the construction of a brick lighthouse nearby. The new ninety-foot structure was finished only two years before the Revolution, in early 1773, and warmly welcomed by colonial officials, who held an inaugural celebration on Tybee Island, replete with speeches, victuals, and a healthy plentitude of spirits. But it was a lighthouse in name only. No keeper was assigned to tend it, and although it was topped with a lantern room, the lighthouse remained dark, serving only as a daymark until it was finally lit on November 10, 1791.

The Portland Head and Tybee Island lighthouses were partially or entirely completed before the states of Massachusetts and Georgia ceded them to the United States. As a result the Cape Henry Lighthouse, located at the mouth of Chesapeake Bay, holds the distinction of being the first lighthouse paid for and built entirely by the federal government.

THE IDEA OF BUILDING a lighthouse at Cape Henry preceded the Revolution by more than half a century. Alexander Spotswood, the lieutenant governor of Virginia, first broached the possibility in 1720, when he encouraged both his colony and Maryland to participate jointly in the construction. A year later, in a letter to the English Board of Trade, Spotswood noted that a lighthouse on the Cape would be of such "obvious" benefit to the trade of both colonies that he "often wondered why so useful a work has not been undertaken long ere now."

Not everyone agreed with Spotswood's assessment. While Virginia's legislature passed a bill agreeing to cover its share of the costs, Maryland's balked. In subsequent decades the clamor to build a lighthouse grew ever louder, but it wasn't until 1773 that Virginia and Maryland commenced the project. For two years a team of men, including many slaves, labored to transport the sandstone from the quarry along the banks of the Rappahannock River to Cape Henry, a distance of 135 miles. This work, employing a combination of oxen and sleds to haul the rocks overland, and flatboats to ship them to their destination, was both grueling and expensive, and in 1775 the money ran out. But before any supplemental appropriations could be made, the war intervened, and all work on the lighthouse stopped.

After the war the project was abandoned for financial reasons until the federal government finally stepped in. The Lighthouse Act of 1789 included a provision requiring a lighthouse to be erected at the entrance to Chesapeake Bay, a clear recognition on Congress's part of the importance of the region's burgeoning maritime commerce. This provision caught the attention of Virginia's governor, Beverley Randolph, who offered President Washington a deal. If the federal government agreed to build a lighthouse on Cape Henry within seven years, Randolph would not only cede two acres on the Cape to the United States, but he would add a lagniappe—the thousands of tons of sandstone that had already been transported to the site. Washington consented, and work on the lighthouse began in 1791.

As it turned out, the sandstone Randolph threw in to sweeten the deal was of little use. After sitting on the Cape for more than fifteen years, the heavy sandstone blocks had settled and were covered with twenty to fifty feet of sand. Although some of the blocks were salvaged, most were left buried, since the cost of retrieving them was too great. Additional sandstone had to be brought in, and the Cape Henry Lighthouse, more than ninety feet tall, was finished in October 1792.

OVER THE NEXT TWO DECADES, through the beginning of the War of 1812, the United States built thirty-four more lighthouses. This dramatic expansion reflected the explosive growth of America's maritime commerce, as American merchants, freed from the yoke of Britain's restrictive Navigation Acts, went on a shipbuilding binge, sending their fleets the world over in pursuit of profits. Between 1789 and 1807 alone, the tonnage of American ships engaged in foreign trade increased nearly sevenfold; a growth rate that the late-nineteenth-century economist Henry Carter Adams claimed was "without parallel in the history of the commercial world." This newly minted flotilla of American ships benefited immensely from these new lighthouses, as did the growing fleet of foreign vessels sailing to American ports.

Most of America's new beacons were constructed in New England, a fact that reflected the region's continued dominance in maritime commerce, as well as the power of its politicians and civic leaders, who used their influence to lobby Congress to build lighthouses along the coast. One of these was built in Truro, Massachusetts, a town located near the tip of the gently curving outer arm of Cape Cod, sandwiched in between Provincetown and Wellfleet. The boisterous Atlantic and the many shoals lurking beneath the surface of the waters just offshore had swallowed up dozens of ships over the years, the most famous being the sixty-four-gun British warship *Somerset*.

While prowling the waters off Cape Cod looking for French ships to capture, the *Somerset* ran into heavy weather on November 1, 1778. The next day it plowed into the Peaked Hill Sand Bars less than a thousand feet from Truro's shores, finally losing a fierce battle with gale-force winds. Its rudder sheared off and its hull pierced, the *Somerset* was pounded by immense waves, one of which lifted it off the bars and thrust it precipitously closer to the beach, where a growing crowd of Cape Codders gathered to witness the calamity and salvage whatever they could from the stricken ship. Ultimately all of the *Somerset*'s officers and crew made it to the beach save for twenty-one who drowned when their boat overturned. The 480 survivors were taken prisoner by the Americans and marched or transported by boat to Boston, where they were jailed, then released through prisoner exchanges.

The great number of shipwrecks in this area spurred the Boston Marine Society, the Salem Marine Society, and the Massachusetts Humane Society to join forces to petition Congress in 1796 to build a lighthouse on the Clay Pounds, or Highlands of Truro, a majestic bluff that rose more than one hundred feet above sea level and stretched for a mile along the coast. According to the Wellfleet minister Levi Whitman, a more perfect spot could not have been found. "That mountain of clay in Truro," he wrote in 1794, "seems to have been . . . [placed there] by the God of nature, on purpose for the foundation of a light-house." Congress supported the petition and provided the necessary funding. By November 15, 1797, the Highland Lighthouse, whose siting Reverend Whitman had believed was divine, began operating. The forty-five-foot-tall wooden tower was located about a mile from where the *Somerset* had crashed, and about five hundred feet from the bluff's edge, as if providing a memorial of sorts to all those who had perished along this unforgiving stretch of coast.

Another New England lighthouse was built on Boon Island, roughly seven miles from York, Maine. This small, barren outcropping of jagged rock, whose highest point is only fourteen feet above sea level, had been a hellish hazard to mariners since the early seventeenth century. And in 1710, it was the location of one of the most infamous shipwrecks in early American history, with gruesome details that—were they not so painfully true—might have been part of a fictional tale.

———

THE *NOTTINGHAM GALLEY* OF London with a crew of fourteen, John Deane commanding, left the Irish port of Killybegs for Boston in late September 1710 carrying a cargo of cordage, cheese, and butter. The journey across the Atlantic was plagued by bad weather, but when the merchant ship reached the American coast, conditions deteriorated markedly. On December 11, in the midst of a howling nor'easter, Deane spotted breakers in the distance, but before his men could change course the ship crashed into Boon Island.

Battered but alive, the men hauled themselves onto the island, but to their great dismay discovered that of all the food on board, only three small rounds of cheese and some old beef bones could be retrieved, the rest having sunk or floated away. In the frigid December weather, they managed to put up an improvised tent, gather mussels and seaweed to supplement their meager fare, and build a small boat from the galley's debris. A few days before Christmas, Deane and one of his crew launched the boat in a bid to get ashore and find help, but a wave caught the vessel and smashed it to pieces on the rocks. The two men hauled themselves out of the surf and rejoined the others, whose expectation of imminent salvation was dashed in less than an instant. "The horrors of such a situation," Deane later recalled, were "impossible to describe; the pinching cold and hunger; extremity of weakness and pain; . . . and the prospect of a certain, painful, and lingering death, without even the most remote views of deliverance!" It was, he said, "the height of misery."

Fatigued and famished, the few who remained able to work cobbled together a rickety raft. Two crewmen set off for the mainland, but along the way the raft was upset, pitching them into the icy water. A few days later the raft and the lifeless body of one of the men were found washed up on shore. The body of the other man was never recovered. Amazingly enough, the discovery of the raft and the body failed to elicit an immediate search of the area, and the protracted nightmare continued for those remaining on Boon Island.

At the end of December the ship's carpenter, whom Deane described

Aerial view of Boon Island Lighthouse in 1950. This tower, completed in 1855, is the third one built at this location. At 133 feet, it is the tallest lighthouse tower in New England.

as a "fat man, and naturally of a dull, heavy, phlegmatic disposition," died. Facing imminent starvation, and "after mature consideration of the lawfulness or sinfulness on the one hand, and absolute necessity on the other," the men—as if anticipating the Donner Party tragedy more than a century later—began eating the carpenter's raw flesh, accompanied by seaweed in place of bread. Initially repulsed by their own behavior, they hesitated, but unremitting hunger transformed them into cannibalistic creatures, forcing the captain to ration the carpenter's remains lest he be entirely consumed in just a few sittings.

The misery continued, the crazed survivors hardly aware that the New Year, 1711, had begun. Finally, a few weeks into January, the earlier appearance of the raft and the body prompted a search by the local townspeople, and the twelve surviving castaways were rescued. The story of *Nottingham Galley*—like a portent of Herman Melville's early fiction—became a public sensation after Deane and a couple of the crewmen published accounts that differed dramatically, with Deane's painting himself as the hero, and his crewmen making him out to be a tyrannical scoundrel who had planned all along either to give the ship to French privateers or run it ashore in order to collect insurance money.

Nearly a century later, by the end of the 1700s, Boon Island's navigational history precipitated the Massachusetts government to build an unlighted wooden beacon on the island to alert mariners. It was destroyed during a storm in 1804, and replaced with an unlighted stone tower, a structure that had its own bit of associated drama when three of the men who built it drowned coming off the island after their boat capsized. The federal government then stepped forward in 1811, erecting a twenty-five-foot-tall stone lighthouse with an iron lantern room on top.

FARTHER DOWN THE COAST, beyond New England's shores, other lighthouses sprang up, among them the one at Montauk Point, a sharply chiseled headland located at the extreme eastern tip of Long Island. Ascending roughly seventy feet from the craggy rocks and ceaseless waves below, Montauk Point is like the prow of a tremendous ship facing the full fury of the Atlantic. The British appreciated this spot's strategic value, and kept a bonfire burning there as a beacon during the American Revolution to assist the Royal Navy in maintaining its blockade of Long Island Sound. New Yorkers were equally convinced of Montauk Point's navigational importance. Numerous shipwrecks had occurred in this area, and a lighthouse on the point would help guide ships heading to New York from Europe, as well as those sailing into Long Island Sound or to nearby ports in Rhode Island and Massachusetts.

Made of finely hammered freestone from Chatham, Connecticut, the lighthouse's eighty-foot tower, which was finally lit in 1797, was topped by a ten-foot-high lantern room displaying whale oil lamps. It was an immense structure, tapering from a base twenty-eight feet in diameter, with walls seven feet thick, to the summit, where the corresponding dimensions were sixteen and a half feet and three feet. When the Congregationalist minister Timothy Dwight, the eighth president of Yale, visited the lighthouse in 1804 he averred, "Perhaps no building of this useful kind was ever erected on this side of the Atlantic in a spot where it was more necessary for the preservation of man."

Dwight's well-deserved praise notwithstanding, other lighthouses were just as important as Montauk's. High on that list was the Cape Hatteras Lighthouse in North Carolina. Located about midway along a two-hundred-mile chain of barrier islands that form the Outer Banks, Cape Hatteras is a slender elbow of sand that juts far out into the Atlantic. For hundreds of years the waters off the Cape had been the bane of mariners.

Ships approaching the Cape from the north would sail near the coast, getting an assist from the gently southward-flowing Labrador Current, and avoiding the much more powerful current of that mighty "river in the ocean," the Gulf Stream, which races northward farther offshore at speeds up to four knots. But when the ships reached the Cape, where the Gulf Stream comes very close to land, they faced a daunting task. To round the Cape and avoid having to battle against the full force of the stream, thereby losing precious time on their journey, ships hugged the shore. If, however, they got too close they could come to grief on the Diamond Shoals, those rock-strewn sandbars that extend about twelve miles from the Cape and lie, as if in wait, not far below the surface. Thus, to continue south, ships in that area attempted to thread the needle between the shoals on one side and the stream on the other. This navigational feat was made even more difficult because the confluence of the cold Labrador Current and the warm Gulf Stream created frequent fogs that reduced visibility; moreover, when the opposing currents slid past or sometimes smashed into each other, tremendous turbulence resulted, pitching ships about and causing the vast underwater dunes to shift, creating an ever-changing tableau of hazards for mariners to contend with.

These dangers were not limited to ships sailing south; they could also ensnare those heading north if they came too close to Diamond Shoals instead of staying farther offshore in the Gulf Stream's helpful embrace. And no matter in which direction ships sailed, they faced the added risk of running into the gales and hurricanes that frequently struck this tempestuous stretch of coast. Little wonder, then, that the ocean floor off the

Cape was littered with shipwrecks, leading mariners to dub this treacherous area the Graveyard of the Atlantic.

In the late 1700s there had been talk of putting a lighthouse at the tip of Diamond Shoals, where it would be of the most use to ships attempting to navigate past the Cape, but the technology of the day was not capable of such an engineering feat. So the federal government pursued the next best option, and in February 1794, Secretary of the Treasury Alexander Hamilton sent a report to the Senate recommending that a lighthouse of the "first rate" be built on Cape Hatteras. Although the project was soon approved, the challenges of land acquisition, the perennial woes of funding, and the difficulty of finding a competent contractor caused a lengthy delay. Construction didn't start until 1799; the ninety-foot stone lighthouse being completed only in 1802, and lit the following year.

RESPONSIBILITY FOR LIGHTHOUSES in these early years fell within the Treasury Department, shifting between the Treasury secretary and the commissioner of revenue. All the major decisions regarding management, such as approving lighthouse locations and construction contracts, even appointing keepers, were made at the federal level with the direct involvement of the president. Evidence of this high-level attention can be gleaned from the many lighthouse-related letters signed by the likes of Presidents George Washington and Thomas Jefferson, as well as Secretary Hamilton. The fact that lighthouse matters rose to such heights of consideration reflected both the small size of the federal government and the great importance of lighthouses to the nation's future.

Not only did the various presidents and other senior officials sign off on lighthouse decisions, but they also occasionally weighed in with more detailed advice, such as when George Washington expressed concern about the sobriety of one of the applicants for the post of lighthouse keeper at the Cape Henry. "If the person recommended by Colo. Parker is intemperate in drinking," Washington wrote to Hamilton, "it is immaterial whether you can recollect his name or not; for, with me, this would be an insuperable objection, let his pretentions and promises of reformation be what they may." Years later Jefferson wrote that the keeper at the same lighthouse should be fired for poor performance, stating his philosophy that "the keepers of light houses should be dismissed for small degrees of remissness, because of the calamities which even these produce; and that the opinion of Col. Newton in the case is of sufficient authority for the removal of the present keeper." Federal officials, however, could not manage everything; hence the oversight of day-to-day operations, as well as the construction and maintenance of lighthouses, was delegated to customs collectors in key ports.

The volume of lighthouse correspondence was prodigious, and of all the topics broached, none was brought up more often than keepers' wages. Although salaries ranged widely, most were between $200 and $350 per year, and they varied based on a number of factors, including the location of the lighthouse and the amount of work required to maintain the light. Keepers lodged numerous complaints, their most common objection being the flagrantly low salaries and the paucity of raises. Supporting a family and supplying all their needs was simply impossible on such meager amounts, they said, and the shortfall was especially significant for keepers living on islands, where conditions were particularly harsh, and obtaining supplies was made much more expensive by the necessity of transporting them from the mainland.

The government defended the salaries, noting that while they were not generous, being in the range of what an average laborer of the day might have received, there were reasons why they were relatively low. Officials pointed out that in addition to their salaries, keepers also received free lodging, and, if the circumstances of their location were favorable, they could garden, fish, or take on freelance jobs, such as piloting, to fulfill their needs and supplement their paltry income. Yet, despite the meager pay, the government had little difficulty filling keepers' positions, and stiff competition was common for the posts.

Nevertheless the government was not immune to the keepers' concerns, and on a number of occasions, wages were increased. In 1805, for example, Ebenezer Skiff, the keeper of the Gay Head Lighthouse on Martha's Vineyard, whose wondrously solid and nautical name was so appropriate for his position, wrote to Albert Gallatin, the secretary of the Treasury, requesting a raise. Skiff argued that the lighthouse's location near the eroding cliffs of Gay Head created a unique situation. The rich red, brown, and yellow clay veins that gave the cliffs the brilliant palette of colors from which the area derived its name also made his job more difficult. Winds whipping off the ocean and up the sides of the cliffs carried aloft the fine clay particles, and deposited them on the outside of the lantern room's glass panes, leaving behind a thick, opaque film that occluded the lighthouse's beams. As a result Skiff had to clean the panes from the outside regularly, which was, he said, "tedious service in cold weather, and additional to what is necessary in any other part of the Massachusetts." Furthermore, the spring near the lighthouse provided only a trickle, forcing him to cart water from another spring a mile away to satisfy his family's needs. Since these "impediments" had not been known or taken into account when setting his salary, Skiff asked that they be considered now. They were, and soon thereafter President Jefferson, in a munificent gesture, raised Skiff's annual salary by $50 to $250.

How American lighthouses were illuminated evolved over time. The earliest ones used tallow candles or crude lamps with braided cotton wicks that burned oil from whales, seals, or fish. By the beginning of the nineteenth century sperm whale oil became the illuminant of choice, and it was usually burned in so-called spider lamps, slightly more sophisticated devices that employed larger oil reservoirs and a greater number of wicks to throw off more light. Oftentimes multiple spider lamps were hung in a lighthouse, each in turn with multiple "blazes," or individual wicks, held in place by their own receptacles.

The whale oil used in lighthouses didn't come from the sperm whale's blubber but rather from the spermaceti organ located in the whale's bulbous head. This organ contained up to twenty-three barrels of a thick waxy substance called spermaceti, from which two types of oil—winter pressed and summer pressed—were made. In the fall the spermaceti would be boiled in kettles to eliminate water and impurities; the thick liq-

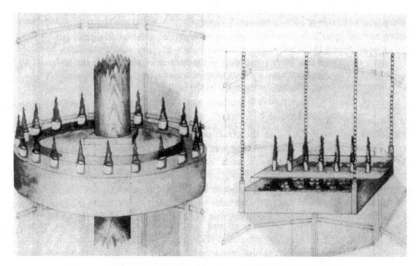

Two types of spider lamps used in lighthouses.

uid remaining was drained into casks, which were placed in storehouses for the winter, where the cold temperatures transformed the liquid into a semisolid granular mass. When the temperature rose enough during the winter to soften this mass, the casks were opened and the contents transferred into woolen sacks that were tied off and squeezed in a large wooden screw press capable of exerting hundreds of tons of pressure. The extremely high-quality oil that drained out of the sacks was called winter pressed, and it was the most expensive and cleanest burning of all whale oils. Because it stayed liquid at low temperatures, lighthouses used it mainly during the winter months, but even then, if the mercury dropped too far, keepers had to heat the oil on stoves before adding it to the lamps. The material that remained in the sacks was reheated and drained into casks to be stored until the warm weather returned in early summer, when the contents of the casks were shoveled into cotton bags and again set upon the press. The substance that issued this time, called summer-pressed oil, was of lesser quality, but it still fetched a good price. And since it congealed at lower temperatures it was used in lighthouses during the warmer months.

Though spider lamps were an improvement over earlier lamp designs, they still left a lot to be desired. Due to incomplete combustion, they generated large amounts of smoke that coated the lantern rooms' glass panes, which the keepers constantly had to clean. The smoke and acrid fumes sometimes proved so overwhelming that keepers were forced to flee the lantern room to avoid incapacitation. And worst of all, the spider lamps' light was not very strong. This was a critical issue to mariners because the light's strength helps to determine how far it can be seen at night.

The distance at which a lighthouse's beam is visible depends on two factors, the height of the light above sea level, and its intensity. Theoretically, the higher the light, the farther away its beam is visible before it disappears over the horizon due to the curvature of the earth. Thus a light that is fifty feet high could be seen at a maximum distance of fourteen and a half miles by a person standing on the deck of a ship fifteen feet above sea level; whereas a light that is one hundred feet high could be seen a little more than eighteen miles away. The distance at which the light can be seen based only on its height is referred to as its geographic range.

The maximum geographic range for a light is theoretical because it can be achieved only if the light is intense enough to reach the person on the ship. The less intense the light, the shorter the distance it can travel before it fades from view. The distance that a lighthouse's light can travel, based solely on the intensity of the light, is referred to as its luminous range.

Of course one other factor has to be taken into account in determining how far a lighthouse's beam can be seen—the weather. Unfavorable weather conditions, such as fog, rain, or snow, limit the distance light can travel. For example, a very intense light that is one hundred feet high might be visible roughly eighteen miles away on a clear night, but perhaps less than half that distance if it is raining.

Under certain circumstances, however, a lighthouse's light can be seen even beyond the horizon. The beams from very powerful lights can be refracted by water vapor or clouds, in effect allowing them to bounce over the horizon. Thus, even before a mariner can see the light, he might see its glow—or what is termed the loom of the light—a faint radiant indication that a lighthouse is not too far off.

Exactly how far the beams of America's early lighthouses traveled is not known, but since spider lamps were relatively weak, it obviously cannot have been very far. If their lights could be made stronger, however, then the effectiveness of lighthouses could be improved. In fact European scientists and engineers had already taken an important step in that direction.

EUROPEANS HAD LONG USED COAL, wood, candles, as well as oil lamps to light their lighthouses, but in the 1780s a major leap in lighthouse illumination took place. It began with the work of the Swiss-born physicist Aimé Argand. In 1782, while living in France, he developed a new type of oil lamp. Instead of a single, solid wick it used a hollow circular wick placed between two thin concentric brass tubes. This arrangement increased the amount of oxygen reaching the lighted wick by forcing air to flow up through the inside of the inner tube, as well as over the outside of the outer tube—more oxygen made for more efficient combustion, less smoke, and a brighter light. The wick could be raised and lowered by turning a knob, and oil was fed by gravity to the wick through a pipe connected to a reservoir.

But when Argand lit his prototype, the flame was relatively small; it flickered a lot and still produced considerable smoke. While he was trying to figure out how to remedy these problems, a serendipitous accident provided an answer. One day, Aimé's younger brother grabbed, as he later recalled, "a broken-off neck of a flask lying upon the mantelpiece, [and] happened to reach it over to the table, and to place it over the circular flame of the lamp: immediately it rose with brilliancy. My brother started from his seat with ecstasy, rushed upon me in a transport of joy, and embraced me with rapture." The neck of the flask acted as a chimney, causing the airflow over the wick to increase dramatically, achieving more complete combustion. Applying this insight, Aimé added a glass chimney to his design, which not only virtually eliminated the smoke and created a brighter light, but also shielded the flame from the wind and reduced flickering. Thus was born the Argand lamp, and subsequent modifications, including the use of a constricted chimney, which forced the air closer to the flame, only improved the lamp's effectiveness.

It would become a sensation in Europe, and later in America. Thomas Jefferson was an early admirer, and in 1784, while serving as minister to France, he wrote a friend about the invention, asserting that "it gives a light equal as is thought, to that of six or eight candles." Postcolonial homes and businesses were soon brighter and cleaner than ever.

But the Argand lamp's potential usefulness to lighthouses was not realized until it was combined with a parabolic reflector. When a light is placed at the focal point of such a reflector, a certain amount of the light's rays bounces off the reflector and is concentrated into a beam that shines in the direction in which the reflector is facing. How much of the light is reflected depends on a number of factors. A considerable amount of the light escapes beyond the edges of the reflector or is absorbed by the reflector's surface—the more reflective the surface, the less light is absorbed. In theory a flawless reflector will absorb about 50 percent of the light that hits it, reflecting the rest. But in practice even a high-quality parabolic reflector will reflect a little less than 50 percent, whereas a

Part of an Argand lamp,
showing its glass chimney,
concentric brass tubes, and
circular hollow wick.

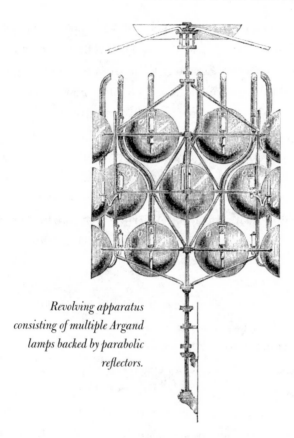

Revolving apparatus consisting of multiple Argand lamps backed by parabolic reflectors.

mediocre reflector might reflect half that amount. Either way, a parabolic reflector creates a beam of light hundreds of times stronger than the light source on its own.

Soon after the Argand lamp was introduced, Europeans began pairing the lamps with parabolic reflectors, creating lighthouse lights that were far more effective than those that had come before. The reflectors were typically made of metal clad in a thick layer of silver that was polished to a mirrorlike finish to increase its reflectivity. In a few instances a thick plano-convex glass lens—flat on one side, convex on the other—was placed in front of the lamp in an attempt to magnify the light beam and make it stronger, but this addition was soon discarded when it was discovered that rather than magnify the light, it made it worse. To maximize the amount of light emanating from lighthouses, multiple reflectors were grouped together and attached to a stationary iron framework or one that could be rotated using a clockwork-type mechanism to produce a flashing pattern of lights as the banks of reflectors came in and out of view. The pattern, or characteristic flash of the revolving lights, could be made unique to each lighthouse, enabling mariners to pinpoint their location along the coast. This system of reflection-based illumination is called catoptric (from the Greek word *katoptron*, for "mirror").

By the early 1800s a growing but still relatively small number of European lighthouses, especially in England, Scotland, and France, employed parabolic reflectors. While Europe was slowly moving ahead with its lighthouse illumination, America stuck with its ineffectual spider lamps—that is, until one Winslow Lewis arrived on the scene.

Born in the Cape Cod town of Wellfleet in 1770, Lewis traced his roots back to the 1630s, when his ancestors emigrated from England to Plymouth, Massachusetts. His father—also named Winslow Lewis—was a mariner, serving as the master and part owner of a small number of vessels. The younger Lewis followed in his father's footsteps, and from 1796 to 1808 captained a ship engaged in the lucrative packet trade between Boston and Liverpool, importing among other things coal, salt, and iron. Described as a "tall, fine-looking man, of winning address," Lewis was successful in his chosen profession, as evidenced by his having been elected to membership in the prestigious Boston Marine Society in 1797.

Lewis's prosperity, however, was upended by the Embargo of 1807, an attempt by President Thomas Jefferson to punish the British, as well as the French, for harassing American shipping while the Napoleonic Wars raged through Europe. The embargo, which went into effect that December, prohibited American ships from sailing to foreign ports, and foreign vessels from obtaining cargo at American ports. Jefferson thought that cutting off trade would cripple Britain and France's economies, forcing them to respect America's neutrality. Although the embargo failed miserably to achieve either of those goals, it did put many American mariners out of work, including Lewis.

Cut off from his livelihood, and with a family of four to support,

Winslow Lewis.

Lewis turned entrepreneur. Like other American mariners, he thought American lighthouses with their feeble spider lamps were rather dim, so he set his sights on developing a better form of illumination. After two years of experimentation, he completed what he called a "magnifying and reflecting lantern," which was an Argand-style lamp with a 9-inch metallic reflector behind it, and a similarly sized plano-convex glass lens in front. When installed in lighthouses, multiple lamp assemblies would be affixed in tiers to a stationary or revolving metal framework to increase the light output.

If this all sounds familiar, that's because it was. The basic components of Lewis's lantern had been employed in Europe for more than twenty years. Nevertheless, Lewis claimed that it was his invention. While some accused him of basing his design on reflector and lamp assemblies he had seen in England, Lewis professed complete ignorance of European advancements. Though there is no clear proof as to the true origins of Lewis's "invention," it strains credulity to think that Lewis, a man who admittedly had no optical experience whatsoever, had come up with this design on his own. It is virtually certain that he copied something he had seen. But whether he did or not, one thing is absolutely true—Lewis's lighting apparatus was not very good.

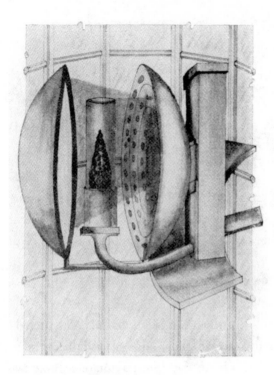

Winslow Lewis's "magnifying and reflecting lantern," with the Argand lamp in the center, the reflector to the right, and the glass lens to the left. Behind the reflector is a reservoir for oil.

The Argand-style lamp he used was of poor quality, and his reflectors, which he claimed were parabolic in form, were decidedly not. As one chronicler of lighthouse history observed, the "reflectors came about as near to a true paraboloid as did a barber's basin." In actuality they tended to be more spherical in shape—a critical difference: A parabolic reflector generates a strong beam that shines straight ahead where it is needed; a spherical reflector does not. Instead the light rays bouncing off a sphere will converge on the focal point of the light source, meaning that most of them will go up or down, with only a small amount being sent out toward the horizon where they are of most use to mariners. Early on, Europeans had experimented with spherical reflectors, but upon discovering their ineffectiveness, almost universally discarded them in favor of parabolic ones.

Another problem was that Lewis's reflectors weren't very reflective. Made of copper covered with a very thin layer of silver, the reflectors "had much the grain and luster of tin-ware, and would reflect no distinct image." And the glass lenses Lewis placed in front of his lamps—yet another design element cast off by the discerning Europeans—further limited the reflectors' usefulness. Four inches thick, made of green glass full of imperfections, and poorly positioned as well, the lenses probably blocked as much light as they let through. Still, even with all their design flaws, Lewis's lamps did throw off more light, especially when grouped together, than the spider lamps he sought to displace.

Brimming with confidence that his "invention" would revolutionize lighthouse illumination in the United States, Lewis proceeded to Washington to patent his "magnifying and reflecting lantern," hoping to inoculate himself against competition. One might have thought that the necessity of proving that his device was actually new and worthy of protection would have presented a formidable obstacle to Lewis's plans. But in the early nineteenth century the process of obtaining a patent was less than thorough, to say the least. The patent office, then part of the State Department, was run by a single administrator—a glorified clerk, really—and the issuance of patents was pro forma. All an applicant needed to do was pay the then-not-insignificant thirty-dollar filing fee, provide a description and model of the invention, and swear to the best of his knowledge that the invention had not been known or used in the United States or any other country. The overburdened and underfunded administrator would then check existing U.S. patents on file in the office, and if none were similar, issue the patent. Lewis provided all the necessary materials, and swore that his lantern was entirely new—meaning that if he had in fact pilfered the design, his oath constituted a clear case of perjury. The patent administrator found everything in order, and granted Lewis patent number 1305 on June 8, 1810.

Had the patent process been more scrupulous, it is doubtful that Lewis's application would have succeeded. Knowledgeable Americans were not ignorant of the evolution of lighthouse illumination taking place in Europe, and a little digging on the part of a curious patent examiner would likely have raised some questions as to the originality of Lewis's idea. As far back as 1790, an article in the *New-York Magazine* on the Sandy Hook Lighthouse noted that the federal government had recently assumed management responsibilities for all American lighthouses, and it ended with the following plea: "It is to be hoped that the modern European improvement of increasing the effect of the light . . . by means of lenses and reflectors, will be adopted by Congress."

Unless there were buyers, Lewis's patent would be meaningless, and he began generating interest in his device even before the patent was issued. After a successful exhibition of his lamps in the cupola of the Massachusetts State House sometime early in 1810, Lewis obtained permission from Henry Dearborn, the customs collector of the port of Boston, to place his lamps in the Boston Lighthouse for a more realistic test of their efficacy. That May a committee of three men, including two ships' captains appointed by the Boston Marine Society, accompanied Lewis to the Boston Lighthouse and watched him set up his apparatus, which consisted of six lamps in two tiers. The men then sailed out of the harbor into Massachusetts Bay to a point roughly equidistant from the Boston Lighthouse and Salem's lighthouse on Baker's Island to the north, which employed spider lamps. Over the course of the evening, and then into the early morning hours, the men compared the light coming from the two lighthouses, and not surprisingly concluded that Lewis's were far superior, the difference in brightness being "as great as would appear between a well trimmed Argand lamp and a common candle." Better than that, Lewis's lamps used much less oil than spider lamps—50 percent less, according to Lewis—thereby providing a brighter light for less money. The committee was so pleased with the result that it recommended that the government adopt Lewis's method of lighting immediately.

After reading the committee's glowing report, Dearborn was equally excited. Oil was the single greatest operational expense at lighthouses, and here was a means of cutting costs and improving the lights, the perfect combination for federal officials intent on increasing efficiency and trimming expenditures. But Dearborn thought that another, more comprehensive test was necessary to better evaluate Lewis's lighting scheme. To that end Dearborn got permission from Secretary of the Treasury Gallatin to fit up one of the twin lights at Thacher Island with Lewis's lamps so that it could be compared, side by side, with the other tower's light.

The results were equally impressive. Writing to Gallatin on December 20, 1810, two months into the lighting experiment, Dearborn noted that he was "fully convinced that Mr. Lewis's system is far preferable to the present mode practiced in the United States, both in regard to the brilliancy of the light and the saving of oil." According to Dearborn and other observers, the tower lit with Lewis's lamps appeared, next to the other one, "as a large brilliant star compared to a small star." As a result Dearborn strongly recommended that all of the country's lighthouses should be fitted with Lewis's lamps, a financially beneficial move that he said would provide the country with "much better lights," while cutting oil use in half.

Additional tests of Lewis's lamps at the lighthouses at Boston Harbor and Thacher Island continued to impress observers the following year, and the glowing reports ultimately convinced Gallatin that the government needed to change the way its lighthouses were lit. Congress concurred, and on March 2, 1812, it passed legislation instructing Gallatin to purchase Lewis's patent and hire him to install his lamps in all of America's existing lighthouses, of which there were forty-nine at the time. Later that month Gallatin and Lewis reached a deal, whose terms required Lewis to refit all the lighthouses within two years, and maintain them in good repair for seven. The government agreed to pay Lewis $24,000 for the patent and for installing the lights, at the same time covering the costs of manufacturing the lamps and transporting them to the lighthouses. Lewis would also be paid $500 per year for maintaining the lights, the government providing him with the necessary supplies.

There was, however, a catch. The government had entered into the agreemeent on the understanding that Lewis's lamps would not only be brighter than the ones they replaced, but also that they would use only half the oil. If Lewis's lamps failed to deliver on either account, he would be forced to return all the money the government had paid him.

Lewis signed the contract, and then persuaded the government to buy him a boat to visit the lighthouses, asserting that it would be cheaper than chartering a vessel. At roughly ninety tons, the schooner *Federal Jack* was outfitted with a blacksmith's shop, areas for carpenters and coppersmiths to work, accommodations for thirteen, as well as two small boats for shuttling men and supplies between the schooner and the lighthouses.

Lewis got to work right away. By December 1812 he and his four mechanics had refitted forty lighthouses, with Lewis apparently being responsible for determining the number of lamps (as many as fifteen), their configuration, the size of the reflectors, and whether the lamps would be stationary or revolving. But before Lewis could finish his contract, the War of 1812, which had been declared in June, caught up with him.

Lewis and his men knew that they were running a great risk ranging along the Eastern Seaboard while British ships were swarming the coast, but they kept at their task, hoping to avoid the enemy. Their luck ran out on March 1, 1813, when the British frigate *Aeolus* captured them not far from Charleston's lighthouse. After taking the Americans prisoner and stripping the *Federal Jack* of all its contents, including lighting apparatuses intended for multiple lighthouses in the southern states, the British commander set it ablaze. Four days later Lewis and his men were paroled and sent to Providence, while the *Federal Jack*'s captain was shipped to Bermuda, where he stayed until being swapped in a prisoner exchange in June.

LEWIS REMAINED OUT OF COMMISSION for the rest of the war, along with much of the lighthouse establishment. As was the case during the Revolutionary War, Americans didn't want to give the British any advantages, and that meant darkening the lighthouses. The number quenched during the War of 1812 is unknown, but many if not all of them were dark at one time or another. For some Britons, at least, this was no imposition at all. As one British officer recalled long after the war, "The enemy, contrary to his own interest, (a rare occurrence with citizens of the United States), had extinguished the light on Cape Henry: This gratuitous act saved us the trouble of 'dowsing the glim.'"

The War of 1812, in contrast to the Revolutionary War, produced only a few relatively minor lighthouse incidents of note. Busy blockading the coast, the British sometimes plundered the locals to replenish their provisions, and on February 14, 1813, a band of sailors landed at the

Cape Henry Lighthouse with that goal in mind. According to a Delaware paper, reporting in the jingoistic style of the period, the sailors "attacked the pantry and smoke house of the keeper, captured his hams, mince pies and sausages, leaving not a link behind!—after when they effected their retreat in the greatest good order and regularity to their ships, with flying colors, without the loss of a ham! So much for British heroism and discipline—HUZZA! 'England expects every man to do his duty!'"

Another instance of damage was more lasting. In July 1813 the British commodore Thomas Hardy, whose squadron was stationed off Block Island to harass American ships and blockade the coast, sent a message to Giles Holt, the keeper of Little Gull Lighthouse, located at the eastern end of Long Island's North Fork. Hardy ordered Holt to extinguish the light to keep it from aiding American vessels wanting to run the blockade. As a conscientious and patriotic federal employee, Holt refused, responding that only orders from the U.S. government could make him take such an action. About a month later British marines overruled Holt's objection by force; they landed on Little Gull Island, grabbed the lighthouse's lamps and reflectors, and threw them into the ocean, effectively blotting out the light for the rest of the war.

The war's most memorable story occurred at Scituate Lighthouse in Massachusetts. In June 1814 two British ships sent raiding parties into Scituate Harbor, burning a few American vessels and capturing others. As the ships departed, Simeon Bates, the lighthouse keeper and a member of the local militia, fired a few cannon shots in their direction from the brass artillery piece next to the lighthouse at the tip of Cedar Point. Come September, one of the British warships returned, but neither Bates nor any of his fellow militiamen, who used Cedar Point as a lookout, was around to mount a defense or alert the town. The only people at the lighthouse were Bates's wife, and two of his daughters, twenty-one-year-old Rebecca, and seventeen-year-old Abigail. When Rebecca spied the ship lowering its boats in the distance, she exclaimed to Abigail, "The old *La Hogue* is oft' here again!" Fearing that another attack on the town was imminent, Rebecca grabbed the fife and drum the militia kept at the lighthouse, and with her sister in tow, ran behind a ridge of cedars. As the

The "Lighthouse Army of Two," Rebecca and Abigail Bates, in Harper's New Monthly Magazine, *June 1878.*

boats came by the point, the two sisters began playing *Yankee Doodle* to scare the British into thinking that the militia was on the way. The ruse worked. The boats turned around, and the *La Hogue* soon left.

Pointing out among other things that the *La Hogue* was not in fact near Scituate at the time, some claim that this story, based solely on the recollection of the two sisters, is a bit of confabulated folklore. But Rebecca might have simply misidentified the ship, and she and her sister swore the story was true, even signing affidavits to that effect. Many locals, siding with the two intrepid sisters, believed it too. True or not, the tale of the plucky female "Lighthouse Army of Two" has become a staple of lighthouse lore.

WHEN WORD OF THE Treaty of Ghent, the peace accord signed in neutral Belgium, on Christmas Eve 1814, officially ending the war, reached America in early 1815, Lewis got back to work. By the fall he had already installed lamps in the remaining lighthouses. The government was so impressed with his performance that on January 1, 1816, it gave him another job, signing him to a seven-year contract to deliver sperm oil to the lighthouses, keep the lamps in good repair, and provide any needed supplies. The government agreed to provide Lewis with the oil, and pay him twelve hundred dollars per year to deliver it. He was paid an additional five hundred for the other responsibilities.

While the salary was impressive, it was the oil that proved to be the real bonanza. Lewis's lamps were supposed to use only half the oil that spider lamps required, so the government provided that amount. After making his deliveries, Lewis was free to keep any leftover oil, and fortunately for him there was an abundance, because in practice his lamps used far less oil than he had originally predicted; in fact they used only 30 percent of the oil that spider lamps did. In 1816 alone this resulted in a surplus of more than nine thousand gallons, which, given the high price of the sperm oil, enabled Lewis to realize a profit of roughly twelve thousand dollars, or about half of President James Madison's salary at the time. His earnings from surplus oil, added to the large sum he got from selling his patented lamps to the government, made Lewis a very wealthy man.

When Lewis began installing his lamps, American lighthouses had been the responsibility of Albert Gallatin, the secretary of the Treasury. In 1813, however, with the war absorbing an increasing amount of his attention, Gallatin decided to hand off that responsibility to the commissioner of the revenue. When that position was abolished at the end of 1817, lighthouses reverted back to the secretary, the baton handovers so frequent in one decade alone as to be almost dizzying. Then, in 1820, the responsibility shifted yet again, this time to Stephen Pleasonton, the Treasury Department's fifth auditor.* Thus began what would become the most controversial and the "darkest period" in the history of America's lighthouses.

---

* At the time, there were multiple auditors within the department, each one designated by his numerical ranking—e.g, first auditor, second auditor, and so on.

CHAPTER 4

ECONOMY ABOVE ALL

. . . .

*Stephen Pleasonton,
the fifth auditor and
superintendent of
lighthouses.*

STEPHEN PLEASONTON OWED HIS JOB AS AMERICA'S FIFTH
auditor in large part to being in the right place at the right time during
the waning days of the War of 1812. On August 24, 1814, as British troops
were bearing down on Washington, Secretary of State James Monroe,
who had been monitoring the British advance, sent a rider back to the
State Department with urgent instructions. Believing that a British takeover of the capital was a virtual certainty, Monroe ordered his staff to do
whatever it could to keep critical state papers from falling into enemy
hands. Pleasonton, a senior State Department clerk at the time, immedi-

ately purchased bolts of linen, and with the assistance of coworkers fashioned the fabric into carrying bags, in which they carefully placed many of the jewels of American history, including precious documents such as the Declaration of Independence, the secret journals of Congress, and George Washington's correspondence. Witnessing this frantic activity, Secretary of War John Armstrong told Pleasonton there was no need for such alarm since he thought a British attack unlikely. Pleasonton replied that Monroe held a different view, and in any case it was better to be prudent and save the documents, rather than risk them being purloined or even destroyed by an enemy force.

Pleasonton loaded the bags into carts and took them across the Potomac River to Virginia, hiding them in a gristmill not far from Washington. Fearing that this was still too close to the threatened capital, Pleasonton took the documents to Leesburg, thirty-five miles away, and locked them in an empty house. Exhausted by this ordeal, Pleasonton retired to a local hotel, and the next morning learned that the capitol had been engulfed in flames the previous night. Fortunately for the nation, the documents Pleasonton secreted away, much like the paintings Dolley Madison had ordered removed from the White House, survived the war.

A few days after James Monroe was inaugurated president in early March 1817, he rewarded Pleasonton, his faithful clerk, by appointing

British engraving of the capture of Washington on August 24, 1814,
showing the capitol ablaze, circa 1815.

him fifth auditor. This position as yet had nothing to do with lighthouses. Pleasonton's responsibilities included managing all the financial affairs of the State Department, the Post Office, and those relating to Indian trade. He was, in effect, a government accountant, tracking expenses, paying bills, and balancing ledgers. It wasn't until 1820 that the secretary of the Treasury expanded Pleasonton's portfolio by giving him oversight of lighthouses, a position that earned him the unofficial title "superintendent of lighthouses."

Forty-four years old at the time, Pleasonton was a hardworking, methodical government bureaucrat. The only known portrait of him is not very flattering. Jaws clenched, his lips turned sharply downward at the corners, he appears to be a very serious if not mirthless man. But one image cannot truly capture someone's personality, and according to at least one of his friends, Pleasonton "was a very kind hearted gentleman with much dry humor," who exhibited considerable "bonhomie."

Pleasonton had no particular skills that would recommend him for his new task, which required him not only to manage the nation's lighthouses, but also other navigational aids, including unlighted beacons, buoys, and, in later years, lightships, which were ships that shone lights from their masts and were moored in locations where it was impracticable to locate lighthouses. Pleasonton knew virtually nothing about lighthouses; neither did he have any experience with maritime issues or any engineering or scientific background. His strengths were those an auditor would be expected to have. He focused on the money, and his primary professional goal was to protect the government purse and cut costs wherever possible.

In 1820 there were 55 lighthouses nationwide, a number that spiraled to 325 by the time Pleasonton's extraordinary thirty-two-year tenure ended in 1852. Pleasonton's method of lighthouse management remained relatively unchanged throughout this period. After Congress decided where lighthouses were needed, usually based on petitions from state and local officials, and appropriated requisite funds, Pleasonton's office issued the design plans for the buildings and then sent them to the customs collectors where the lighthouses were to be located. The collectors put the plans out for bid, and then Pleasonton, per government rules, chose the lowest bidder for the job. The collectors typically oversaw the selection and purchase of the building site, and in making the selection usually relied on the advice of local mariners and officials. When the contractor finished the project, a mechanic was required to certify that the work was done properly before final payments were made and the lighthouse accepted by the government. While the secretary of the Treasury officially appointed keepers, customs collectors were responsible for nominating, hiring, paying, and firing them. Collectors also were supposed to visit the lighthouses annually, report back to Pleasonton on their condition, and arrange for any necessary repairs. Contractors were hired to supply oil to the lighthouses and install the lighting apparatus, which invariably were Lewis's patent lamps.

In line with his cost-cutting philosophy, Pleasonton rigidly controlled lighthouse finances, with every significant expenditure having to gain his approval. He was especially proud of consistently spending less than Congress appropriated, and returning a surplus to the federal Treasury. At one point he claimed that his sterling record of coming in under budget was "unexampled, so for as I know, in the annals of government."

While he focused obsessively on costs, he was far less engaged in the technical aspects of lighthouse operations, which did not fall naturally within the realm of his expertise. As a result he relied heavily on advice from both collectors and contractors in assessing the effectiveness of the lighthouses.

Pleasonton relied most of all on Winslow Lewis, viewing him as the lighthouse expert, and often turning to him for guidance on lighthouse design and operations. After all, when Pleasonton arrived on the scene, Lewis *was* the accepted expert. The government had purchased his patent, making his lamps the nation's official standard of best lighting practice, and Lewis was intimately familiar with every lighthouse in the country, having visited and illuminated all of them. Furthermore, Lewis knew a great deal about broader maritime issues, and was well connected within the shipping community, having just completed a two-year term as president of the Boston Marine Society.

The two of them, Pleasonton and Lewis, developed a strong professional and personal relationship, built in part on their shared parsimoniousness and eagerness to keep costs to a minimum. Lewis not only continued to be the main supplier of oil until the late 1820s, when the contract went to New Bedford whaling merchants, but he also became deeply involved in lighthouse construction, ultimately building, according to his own estimate, eighty lighthouses, an impressive record achieved as a result of his ability so frequently to submit the lowest bid. Lewis's influence on lighthouse construction went far beyond just building them, for he provided Pleasonton with designs for lighthouses, which Pleasonton often used as the basis for the building plans issued by his office.

With the same ruthless cost-cutting approach he used to win building contracts, Lewis also won the vast majority of the contracts to illuminate the lighthouses, providing them, of course, with his patented lamps. Commenting on Lewis's penchant for underbidding the competition, Pleasonton noted that Lewis "would work for nothing . . . sooner than give up a branch of business in which he has been engaged for more than thirty years." Although there have been murmurs over time that the relationship between Pleasonton and Lewis might not have been entirely aboveboard, as the lighthouse historian Francis Ross Holland, Jr., has pointed out, there isn't any " 'hard' evidence that there were any shady dealings between" the two, and given Pleasonton's pristine reputation for rectitude it seems unlikely that the national overseer of lighthouses would have accepted kickbacks.

As many as ten clerks worked for Pleasonton, but not all of them focused on lighthouse issues. Their assistance was essential, especially since Pleasonton's responsibilities as fifth auditor later expanded to include the Patent Office and settling a wide range of accounts concerning foreign commerce. This added workload stretched Pleasonton thin, further reducing the amount of time he could devote to lighthouse affairs.

The management scheme that Pleasonton devised served his needs, but as would become painfully clear in the coming years, it didn't serve the best interests of the nation or the mariners who plied its shores.

UP THROUGH THE MID-1830S, roughly 150 new lighthouses were built, an expansion that reflected the dizzying industrial growth of the adolescent nation. Most of these beacons were located along the coasts of the New England and the mid-Atlantic states, but lighthouses were also added in places farther afield. The opening up of what would become America's heartland, and the increasing flow of goods such as grain and timber over the Great Lakes, made lighthouses a necessity for safer travel. What early traders and shippers quickly apprehended was that these magnificent inland seas, covering roughly 95,000 square miles, were every bit as dangerous to shipping as the oceans of the world, capable of generating enormous waves and punishing conditions that could, and often did, sink ships. Even before Pleasonton's responsibilities expanded, the first lighthouses on the Great Lakes were built in 1818 on Lake Erie, at Buffalo and Presque Isle (now part of Erie, Pennsylvania), and lit the following year. Others followed, including the Rochester Harbor Lighthouse on Lake Ontario (1822), the Cleveland Lighthouse on Lake Erie (1829), the Thunder Bay Island Lighthouse on Lake Huron (1832), and the St. Joseph Lighthouse on Lake Michigan (1832), forming a ribbon of sorts that illuminated the Great Lakes.

When the Erie Canal opened in 1825, connecting the Hudson River at Albany to Lake Erie at Buffalo, it not only increased the amount of shipping on the Great Lakes, as traffic between New York City and the heartland soared, but it also created a need for lighthouses along the Hudson to help ships navigate to and from the canal. The first one, built in 1826 at Stony Point, just below West Point, warned ships away from the rocks of Stony Point Peninsula.

Lighthouse expansion was hardly an exclusively Yankee affair, for this period also saw the addition of lighthouses along the Alabama, Mississippi, and Louisiana coasts. Arguably the most important extension of the lighthouse establishment was on the Florida coast, in particular along the Florida Keys. A 185-mile-long coral archipelago that curves in a graceful arc from Virginia Key off Miami to the Dry Tortugas, the Florida Keys had long been one of the most perilous places for ships. Beginning in the 1500s, Spanish vessels transporting the riches of the so-called New World back to the Old, had skirted the Keys on their way from the Gulf of Mexico to the Atlantic, trying to avoid crashing into the jagged reefs and sandbars lying just offshore. After the United States acquired the Louisiana Territory in 1803, American mariners were forced to run the same gauntlet as the watery passage by the Keys became a busy commercial highway, connecting the burgeoning port of New Orleans with the rest of the United States as well as Europe. An untold number of ships failed to negotiate the Keys, and the resulting wrecks became the foundation for an extremely lucrative industry, in which individuals called wreckers salvaged the disabled vessels for profit.

In 1819, under the terms of the Adams-Onís Treaty, Spain dramatically ceded Florida to the United States, and two years later the treaty was ratified. Soon after, the idea of lighting the Keys in an effort to reduce the number of wrecks gained currency. In early 1822 the navy ordered Lt. Matthew C. Perry, who would later gain fame for "opening up" Japan in the 1850s, to officially take possession of Key West and explore its potential as a naval base. While performing this duty, Perry wrote a letter to Smith Thompson, the secretary of the navy, encouraging him to tell the Secretary of the Treasury that there was a "great want of lighthouses on the Florida Keys," adding that building some there would render Florida's shores "more safe and convenient." At the same time merchants, shipowners and captains, and insurance companies were also busy lobbying in favor of lighting the Keys. Congress responded on May 7, 1822, issuing the first of many appropriations, and over the next six years lighthouses were built at Cape Florida (1825), the Garden Key in the Dry Tortugas (1826), Key West (1826), and Sand Key (1827).

Other than the Indians who were forcibly and tragically expelled from their land, perhaps the only people who weren't happy about the lighthouses in the Florida Keys were the wreckers. The business of salvaging ships was not peculiar to Florida. Since time immemorial, wreckers have worked shores the world over, and there were wreckers all along America's eastern seaboard seeking to profit from other people's misfortune. Wreckers were often called, in high American slang, "mooncussers" because they supposedly prayed for dark and cloudy nights, and were thought to curse the brightly shining moon since it helped mariners find their way. By the same logic, wreckers were also assumed to be, and were often accused of being, against the building of lighthouses. There doesn't appear to be any evidence of this in the Keys, but farther to the north, in New England in particular, there are many such anecdotal stories. In the early 1850s, while touring Cape Cod, Ralph Waldo Emerson, for example, was told by the keeper of the Nauset Lighthouse in Eastham that local wreckers, eager to keep their business brisk, strongly opposed the building of the lighthouse. To overcome such resistance, local proponents of the lighthouse had to venture to Boston to obtain the recommendation of the city's marine society.

Wreckers were also accused of a far worse activity—using false lights on dark nights to lure ships into danger in order to generate more business. In some accounts wreckers would tie lights to horses or cows and walk them along the beach, simulating a ship's light, potentially drawing ships unfamiliar with the area to follow the light and come to grief on a reef or shoal. At other times it was claimed that lights placed atop poles were intended to confuse mariners into thinking they were the beam from a lighthouse, with similar baleful results. Such tales were often bandied about all along America's Eastern Seaboard, from the Keys on up, but there is great debate over whether wreckers ever acted so abominably. And, understandably, given the nature of such nefarious activity, and the desire of perpetrators to hide their deeds, there is no known reliable evidence that false lights were actually used in the United States. Nevertheless there must be some truth to the tales, because in 1825 Congress passed a law that made it a crime to "hold out or show a false light, or lights" with the intent of causing a wreck, and anyone found guilty of this felony could be fined up to five thousand dollars and imprisoned up to ten years.

CAPE FLORIDA LIGHTHOUSE on Key Biscayne was not only the first lighthouse in the Keys, it was also the site of one of the most dramatic stories in the history of America's lighthouses, which took place on July 23, 1836. Florida at the time was contested land. The Second Seminole War had begun in 1835, with the Indians fighting American efforts to relocate the tribe beyond the Mississippi. In early January 1836 a band of Seminoles took control of the lighthouse, which had recently been abandoned due to the outbreak of hostilities. Given the lighthouse's importance to shipping, Floridian merchant William Cooley agreed to lead a group of men to retake it.

Cooley and his armed retinue took up residence near the lighthouse at the end of January, and the Indians soon departed. A little while later the lighthouse keeper, John Dubose, returned to take over his duties, and until the early summer things were quiet, but there remained a residual fear that the Indians might come back. In July, Dubose went to Key West for supplies, leaving the lighthouse in the care of the assistant keeper, John W. B. Thompson, and a black man named Aaron Carter, who likely was Thompson's slave.

At about four in the afternoon on July 23, as the sun in the bright blue sky was arcing toward the horizon, bringing to a close another scorching Florida day, Thompson was heading to the keeper's house when out of the corner of his eye he spied a large group of Indians—as many as fifty—about twenty yards away. Sprinting for the lighthouse, he yelled for Carter to follow. The Indians discharged their rifles, and a few of the balls ripped through Thompson's clothes and hat, while most of the rest blew small holes in the lighthouse's door. As soon as Thompson and Carter were within the tower, Thompson locked the door, only moments before the Indians reached it.

Thompson had prepared for trouble, placing three loaded muskets in the lighthouse. He grabbed the guns and ran up the stairs to the second window, at the same time telling Carter to watch the door and let him know if the Indians attempted to break through. Thompson shot his guns in quick succession at the Indians gathered around the keeper's house, and then he reloaded, ran to another window, and fired again. Finally Thompson ascended to the lantern room, firing, he said, whenever he "could get an Indian for a mark." While Thompson was shooting, the Indians smashed the windows of the keeper's house, and returned fire.

Thompson kept the Indians away from the lighthouse until dark.

Then, however, his pursuers fired a furious volley and rushed forward, setting the lighthouse door and an adjacent boarded window ablaze. The flames breached the tower and rapidly raced up the wooden stairs. When they reached the landing where Thompson kept his bedding and clothes, the inferno exploded, fed by the 225 gallons of whale oil spewing from the tin storage tanks that had been pierced by the Indians' bullets. Thompson grabbed a keg of gunpowder, his muskets, and ammunition, and raced to the lantern room. Then he went below to cut away the stairs. While Thompson was furiously sawing, Carter climbed from the bottom of the tower to join him. The scorching flames and acrid smoke drove Thompson back before he could saw all the way through the wood, whereupon he and Carter rushed to the lantern room.

Thompson covered the lantern room's entryway, but the flames finally burst through, forcing him and Carter to retreat to the two-foot-wide iron platform outside. There they lay flat on their backs, the fire roaring on one side and agitated attackers down below on the other, firing up at them. With the "lamps and glasses bursting and flying in all directions," his clothes on fire and his "flesh roasting," Thompson attempted to put an end to his "horrible suffering" by throwing the keg of gunpowder into the fire, hoping to blow the tower to smithereens.

Attack on Cape Florida Lighthouse, 1836, *as imagined by artist Ken Hughs in 1975.*

The tower shook violently, and although it failed to fall, the stairs and the upper landings collapsed. This temporarily tamped down the fire, but then it rebounded as intensely as before. Carter, his body riddled by seven balls, was already dead. Thompson, too, had been shot, with three balls in each foot. Believing that he had no chance of surviving, he went to the outside of the iron railing, and after commending his "soul to God" was about to launch himself into the air, when something he could not describe caused him to stop and lie down again. He was lucky he had the chance, because while he was exposed at the railing, bullets from the Indians whizzed around him like "hail-stones."

That night the Indians plundered and torched the keeper's house. At about ten the next morning, one group of Indians loaded Thompson's sloop with their booty and left, while the rest went to the other end of the island. "I was now almost as bad off as before," Thompson later recalled, "a burning fever on me, my feet shot to pieces, no clothes to cover me, nothing to eat or drink, a hot sun overhead, a dead man by my side, no friend near or any to expect, and placed between seventy and eighty feet from the earth, and no chance of getting down, my situation was truly horrible."

In the afternoon Thompson spied two ships in the distance. Marshaling his fast-waning strength, he used some of Carter's bloody clothes to signal them, and soon the United States schooner *Motto*, accompanied by the sloop-of-war *Concord*, arrived. Having heard the explosion the night before, the men on board were coming to investigate, and on the way they recovered Thompson's sloop, which had been stripped by the Indians.

A group of marines strode ashore, and quickly discovered that getting Thompson down was not going to be easy. To no avail, they tried using a makeshift kite to fly a line to the top of the tower. With night imminently approaching, the marines went back to their ship, promising Thompson they would return in the morning. When they did, they attached twine to a ramrod, shooting it from a musket to the top of the tower. Thompson grabbed the twine and fastened it to an iron stanchion. He then used the twine to pull up a two-inch-thick rope, which he also tied to the stanchion. Two marines then climbed up the rope and jerry-rigged a sling to bring Thompson back to earth. After a short stay in Key West, during which all but one of the balls in his feet were extracted, Thompson retired to Charleston. "Although a cripple," he later wrote, "I can eat my allowance, and walk about without the use of a cane." As for the Cape Florida Lighthouse, it was not repaired until 1846, due to delays caused by the continuing hostilities between the U.S. military and the Seminoles.

AT ABOUT THE TIME that the Cape Florida Lighthouse was being attacked, America boasted a string of more than two hundred lighthouses. Pleasonton, though a skinflint in so many ways, was very pleased with that growth. He was especially proud of the quality of the light that Lewis's lamps produced. Many of America's mariners, however, were less enthused. For years they had been complaining that the lighthouses in Great Britain and France were far superior to the ones in America—and they were right.

CHAPTER 5

EUROPEANS TAKE
THE LEAD

. . . .

French inventor
Augustin-Jean Fresnel.

WHILE AMERICANS UP THROUGH THE MID-1830S REMAINED wedded to Lewis's mediocre lamps, the British and French continued developing and advancing their forms of illumination, with dazzling results. Unlike Lewis's poorly constructed reflectors, the ones widely used in Britain in the early decades of the century were manufactured by hand with exacting precision. Highly trained craftsmen took copper sheets heavily clad in silver and, using molds, meticulously hammered

the sheets into the parabolic form. Gauges were used to check the perfection of the shape, and needed modifications were applied; then lighting
tests were conducted to ensure optimal reflection. Another improvement
involved the positioning of the Argand lamp. Lewis's design, besides
straying from the parabolic form, had the lamp too far in front of the
reflector and not positioned to ensure the best reflection. The orienta-
tion of the lamp was made worse when it had to be tipped forward to
allow for the cleaning of the reflector, or to improve the flow of oil to
the burner. In contrast, the British reflectors had a hole cut in the lower
portion, through which the lamp was inserted, thereby placing the flame
at the proper focal point. When the reflector needed cleaning, the lamp,
which sat on an adjustable arm, could be lowered, and once the cleaning
was done, raised back to the same exact and correct position. As a result
of these differences, the British lamps were much better than Lewis's,
producing a significantly stronger focused beam of light.

Meanwhile, improvements in lighting in France were even more
dramatic, and were due to the brilliance of Augustin-Jean Fresnel (pronounced *freh-NEL*). Born in the French province of Normandy on the

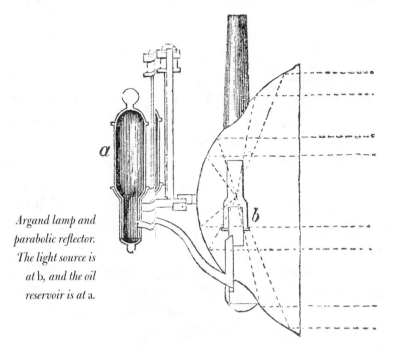

*Argand lamp and
parabolic reflector.
The light source is
at* b, *and the oil
reservoir is at* a.

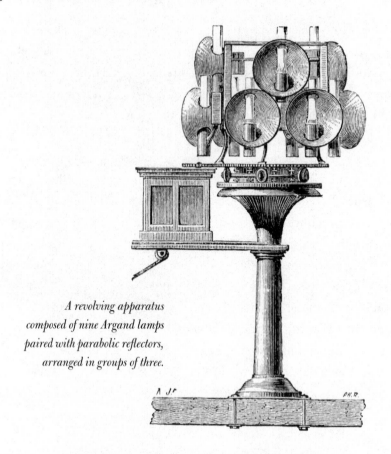

*A revolving apparatus
composed of nine Argand lamps
paired with parabolic reflectors,
arranged in groups of three.*

eve of the French Revolution in 1788, Fresnel was a sickly child, exhibiting a frailty of body that would always plague him. A slow and unenthusiastic learner in his early life, Fresnel was only just beginning to read at eight years old. While his parents and other adults worried about his lack of educational progress, Fresnel's childhood friends were convinced that he was a "genius," pointing to his many triumphs in building mechanical devices—among them, popguns and bows that were so effective in their design that they were no longer just toys, but dangerous weapons, which adults banned lest they lead to serious injury to Fresnel or one of his playmates.

After his less than auspicious initiation into formal education, Fresnel focused his sharply honed and inventive mind and soon blossomed, attending the finest science and engineering schools in France and impressing his teachers with novel solutions to complex mathematical and technical problems. He graduated in 1809, at the age of twenty-one, from France's National School of Bridges and Highways, the oldest civil engineering school in the world, and began working for the government, overseeing the building of roads and bridges.

Though important and honorable, this job was hardly challenging to a man of Fresnel's cast of mind. The leveling of roads, the quarrying of stone, and the laying of roadbeds, along with the occasional building of a small bridge over an irrigation ditch, were tasks that Fresnel found dull and enervating. He especially disliked being the superintendent. "I find nothing more tiresome than having to manage other men," he complained in a letter to his parents, "and I admit that I have no idea what I'm doing."

In his spare time Fresnel pursued his interest in science, and began experimenting with optics. After receiving encouragement from the dashing and charismatic French physicist François Arago, who, although only two years older than Fresnel, was already seen as a gifted scientist with a deep understanding of the behavior of light, Fresnel continued his explorations, focusing most intently on diffraction. His work led him to support and further develop the wave theory of light, which posited that light was composed of waves—similar to the ripples one sees after dropping a rock in water—that could either cancel out or amplify one another depending on how they interact. The wave theory was considered somewhat radical at the time, especially since it disputed the more widely accepted particle theory of light established by Isaac Newton more than 125 years earlier, which argued that light was made up of discrete particles called corpuscles. When the French Academy of Sciences announced a competition in 1817, with diffraction as the topic to be investigated, Fresnel entered a paper based on the wave theory, and was awarded the grand prize in 1819. The acclaim and renown this afforded enabled Arago to have Fresnel detailed from his current assignment (working on canals) to join him at the Commission de Phares (Lighthouse Commission), created by Napoleon in 1811 to make France's navigational lighting system the envy of the world, and a symbol of France's modernity and great engineering skill. Arago was trying to improve the parabolic reflectors then used in France, and he thought Fresnel could help with that endeavor.

Over the next few years Fresnel applied his extensive knowledge of optics to take up Arago's challenge. Fresnel's idea was not to improve the reflector but, in a bold revolutionary stroke, to get rid of it entirely and instead place a lens in front of the flame. As the science historian Theresa Levitt points out, "A lens, by refraction, or the bending of light, could do the same thing that mirrors [reflectors] did by reflection; that is, it could take . . . the light emanating from the source and direct it into a beam." And it could do so more effectively. Even the best reflector reflected only about half of the light that hit it, but a lens of the right thickness could let through more than 90 percent of the light.

The problem was making the lens a manageable size. If the lens were placed close to the light, so as to catch most of the light's rays, it would have be thin at the edges and very thick in the middle to refract the rays into a parallel beam. But such a thick lens would absorb, rather than transmit much of the light. This in fact was the main problem with the thick lenses that Europeans had used in conjunction with early parabolic reflectors, as well as with the lenses Lewis used with his patented lamps (his lenses were made worse by being colored, which caused them to absorb even more of the available light). And given the limitations of glassmaking at the time, the thicker the lens, the more likely it would be marred by imperfections, such as bubbles or differences in glass density, only further diminishing the lens's ability to transmit rays cleanly without deviation. Alternatively, if Fresnel placed the lens farther away from the light source, the lens could be thinner, but for it to capture and refract most of the light's rays effectively, it would have to be huge in diameter, making it too large and heavy for the intended use.

What Fresnel wanted to do was produce a relatively large lens that was not too heavy, and he did so by creating what he called "lenses by steps," which eliminated much of the bulk of the lens while still retaining its refractive properties. Fresnel's solution to this problem utilized a central bull's-eye lens surrounded by concentric rings of triangular prisms. When a flame was placed behind the Fresnel lens at the proper focal

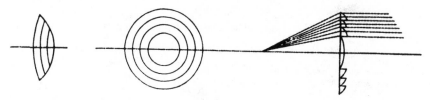

Augustin-Jean Fresnel's drawing illustrating his concept of "lenses by steps." On the left is a thick convex lens, and on the right is the thinner Fresnel lens, with much of the bulk of the original lens cut away, leaving the central bull's-eye, and the surrounding prisms, which refract the light rays as shown.

length, the light emanating from the flame would be refracted as it passed through the bull's-eye lens and the prisms into parallel rays, creating the desired beam shining out toward the horizon. An illuminating system based on refraction like this is called dioptric (from the Greek *dioptrikos*, a surveying instrument). Fresnel was not the first person to come up with this idea of "lenses by steps," but he was the first to perfect it and apply it to lighthouse illumination.

Because the Fresnel lens used so much more of the available light, its beam was much stronger and could travel much farther than the beams coming from even the very best reflectors. To make the beams even stronger, Fresnel and Arago developed modified Argand lamps, which had up to four concentric wicks and, as a result, threw off a much brighter light than traditional lamps with a single wick.

The first major test for the Fresnel lens came in 1823, when one was placed in the magnificent Cordouan, France's most famous and oldest continually operating lighthouse, located at the mouth of the Gironde Estuary in southwestern France, not far from the port city of Bordeaux. Completed in 1611, the 223-foot-tall Cordouan was more like a palace than a lighthouse, earning the well-deserved nickname, "Versailles of the Sea." Among its many unusual features was a richly decorated "King's Chamber"—although no king ever stayed there—with two fireplaces, a reception hall, side offices, and marble throughout. There was also an ornate gilded chapel boasting Corinthian columns, four stained-glass windows, and exquisite sculptures. The keepers had their own

The Cordouan Lighthouse.

The Fresnel lens placed in France's Cordouan Lighthouse in 1823. The lens is currently on display at the Musée des Phares et Balises in Ouessant, France.

decidedly less sumptuous quarters, and used a servants' entrance and a separate staircase adjoining the main tower to climb to the lantern room and tend the light.

The lens that Fresnel installed at Cordouan used eight square lens panels, with each panel having a bull's-eye lens in the center and prisms encircling it. The panels were arrayed in a belt on a metal frame around a lamp in the center. With this configuration alone, much of the light thrown off by the lamp would escape above and below the lens belt. To capture some of that light, Fresnel placed above the lens belt, at an angle, smaller lens panels that directed the light traveling up from the lamp onto a series of inclined mirrors that, in turn, reflected the beams toward the horizon. Below the lens belt Fresnel used inclined mirrors for the same purpose.

A clockwork-type mechanism rotated the Cordouan lens. As each panel came into the line of sight of a distant mariner, it sent out a bright flash of light, which would be followed by an interval of increasing dimness, then relative darkness, then another flash of light when the next panel came into view. At the same time the mirrors above the panels

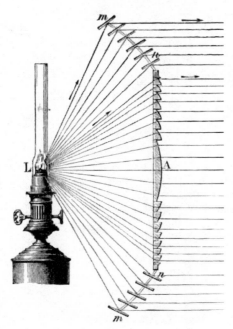

Diagram showing light being transformed into a beam as it passes through a Fresnel lens, comprised of the central bull's-eye panel surrounded by concentric rings of triangular prisms. Above and below the lens are inclined mirrors, which also direct the light in the desired direction.

threw off an intermittent beam, while the more numerous mirrors below sent out a constant fixed stream of light.

The test was a great success. French mariners pronounced the Cordouan light excellent, far better than any they had ever seen. Fresnel calculated that his lens produced a light equivalent to thirty-eight of the best British reflectors, while using only about half the oil. France soon committed itself to placing Fresnel lenses all along its coast at intervals, so that when the beam from one lighthouse faded from view, another one would take its place, meaning that mariners would never be out of sight of a helpful guiding light.

Fresnel's goal was to perfect the lens by getting rid of the mirrors above and below and replacing them with prisms, which would allow more of the lamp's light to be effectively directed toward the horizon. He could not do this with the prisms he was using in his current lens panels because the laws of optics allowed those prisms to bend light only up to forty-five degrees. Therefore, if those prisms were placed higher or lower than the lens panel, they wouldn't refract the light enough for it to be sent out in a parallel beam straight ahead, since that would require bending the light at a greater than forty-five-degree angle.

Again Fresnel devised an elegant solution. If light travels through a

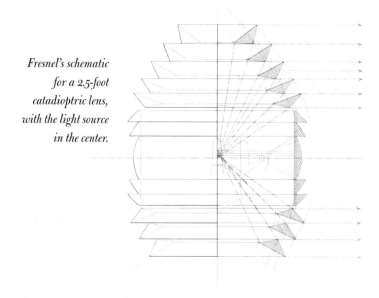

*Fresnel's schematic
for a 2.5-foot
catadioptric lens,
with the light source
in the center.*

prism of a certain shape, it will refract off the first surface, then reflect off the second, internal surface, and be refracted again upon exiting the third surface. This "pinball" effect meant that the light could be bent at more forty-five degrees. Fresnel envisioned placing these internally reflecting prisms above and below the bull's-eye lens panels in such a way that they could capture the lamp's light and direct it to be parallel to the beam generated by the panels—in effect creating one large, unified, and very bright shaft of light. Because internally reflecting prisms rely on both reflection (catoptric) and refraction (dioptric), they are called catadioptric.

In the mid-1820s when Fresnel—who had since been appointed secretary of the Commission des Phares—first conceived the idea of using internally reflecting prisms, no glass manufacturers were capable of making them large enough to be used with full-size Fresnel lenses. (Fresnel was, however, able to produce a small-scale model that worked.) But before glass technology could catch up with Fresnel's vision he died, on July 14, 1827, at the age of thirty-nine, after a long battle with tuberculosis, a vicious infectious disease that typically attacked the lungs, causing its victims to cough up blood, and was at the time the leading killer throughout most of Europe. "I could have wished to live longer," Fresnel confided to his mother and brother on his deathbed, "because I perceive that there are in the inexhaustible range of science, a great number of questions of public utility, of which, perhaps, I might have had the happiness of finding the solution."

Despite his early death, Fresnel's legacy in the field of lighthouse illumination was secure, and continued to grow after his demise. By the mid-1830s there were an increasing number of French lighthouses with Fresnel lenses, and other countries, among them the Netherlands and Great Britain, were also slowly making the switch to this newer, improved form of illumination. And as the innovation took hold, the Fresnel lenses would come in four orders, or sizes, based on the distance between the lamp and the inner surface of the lens. The first order was the most powerful and had the largest lens, with an interior diameter of nearly six feet; it was used for major seacoast lights. At the other extreme, the fourth order was for harbor lights, and it was only about a foot in diameter.

———

LÉONOR FRESNEL TOOK HIS brother's place as secretary of the Commission des Phares, and continued to pursue Augustin's dream of perfecting the lens by replacing the mirrors with prisms. But in 1836, when Pleasonton remained so smugly content with the quality of America's lights, that dream was years away from being realized. Most of the Fresnel lenses then in use, with the exception of the smallest, were similar to the one at Cordouan, employing mirrors above and below the central lens panels. Even so, they created a light that far surpassed anything shining on American waters.

CHAPTER 6

THE "RULE OF IGNORANT AND INCOMPETENT MEN"

. . . .

Sea view of the Cape Poge Lighthouse, on Chappaquiddick Island, Martha's Vineyard, Massachusetts, painted by Charles Hubbard, circa 1840–49.

AMERICAN MARINERS PLYING EUROPEAN WATERS WEREN'T the only ones who noticed the superiority of British and French lighthouses. So, too, did Edmund and George W. Blunt, brothers who in 1826 took over from their father the publication of the *American Coast Pilot*, a periodical that provided mariners with sailing directions and charts, as well as detailed descriptions of the nation's lighthouses. The Blunts, in the tradition of their father, Edmund March Blunt, developed close ties to mariners, and had long listened to their complaints about the inferior quality of America's lighthouses, to which they soon added their own. And it was not only the quality of the lights that concerned them, but also the poor management of the American lighthouse establishment as a whole.

After visiting France in the early 1830s, touring lens factories, and meeting with Léonor Fresnel, Edmund returned a fierce advocate of employing Fresnel lenses in America, a cause shared equally by his brother. They wrote to Secretary of the Treasury William John Duane, a member of President Andrew Jackson's cabinet, in 1833, pointing out the "the great deficiency in our present light-house system," and urging him to buy Fresnel lenses for use in major seacoast lighthouses. Neither Duane nor Pleasonton responded, but that didn't stop the Blunts from continuing their fight for reform, and in 1837 they sent another letter to the latest secretary of the Treasury, Levi Woodbury, with a long list of grievances. This missive and Pleasonton's response became fodder for public consumption when the Senate published both.

The Blunts painted a bleak picture of the lighthouse establishment. Based on the opinions of scores of shipmasters who frequently traveled to Europe, the Blunts argued that American lighthouses, when compared with those of Great Britain and France, were "greatly inferior in brilliance, in the distance they may be seen, and in good management." For many years, they contended, America had lagged far behind other nations in taking advantage of improvements in lighthouse illumination. Lewis's much-touted lamps were dismissed as "nothing but the Argand lamp, with miserable arrangements." The thick green glass lenses that were still used on a number of Lewis's lamps were ridiculed for worsening an already poor light, leading the Blunts to imply with considerable irony that Congress should consider launching an inquiry into the "cost to the public of this ingenious patent, to obscure lights." By contrast the English lamps, they said, were far superior to Lewis's, and France's Fresnel lenses much better than the English ones. Not only that, but the lights of Great Britain and France were less expensive to operate and maintain than their American counterparts.

The Blunts claimed that since lighthouse construction was left to contractors with no engineering background, it inevitably resulted in shoddily built structures. Yet, they added, "the system which produces such structures is called the best in the world; and the deceived superintendent congratulates himself on its good management." With their pointed comments about Pleasonton, the litany of charges continued: Sperm oil was not tested for quality, and was often not very good; keepers were frequently absent from duty; and customs collectors were too busy with their other responsibilities to perform an adequate number of inspections. On the importance of inspections, the Blunts were adamant: Until frequent inspections and examination of every aspect of the lighthouse system, from construction to lighting to keepers, is "enforced, our light houses will remain a reproach to this great country, feebly and inefficiently managed, and at the mercy of contractors."

The Blunts had long been frustrated by the lighthouse establishment's decisions to modify the characteristics of a lighthouse, for example, from flashing to stationary, or, even worse, to alter a lighthouse or build a new one without providing adequate notice, which could lead to serious accidents when mariners were unaware of the changes. (It was just such a disaster that took place in 1817, when the *Union* wrecked off Salem on account of the Baker's Island Lighthouse being changed from a twin to a single light.) The Blunts underscored the importance of advance notice by pointing to the case of the *Galaxy*, which was away on a voyage when the Barnegat Lighthouse, located at the northern tip of Long Beach Island, New Jersey, was built. When the ship returned, the captain, knowing nothing of this new light, thought it another, and steered for it only to founder on the rocks, resulting in a loss of fifty thousand dollars.

The lighthouse establishment had, the Blunts concluded, "increased beyond the ability of any single individual at Washington" to manage. Pleasonton, a myopic and narrow-minded bureaucrat at best, was far too reliant on the reports of self-serving contractors, which were invariably favorable. While the Blunts complimented Pleasonton on his intelligence and his "skill, and promptitude" in carrying out his duties, they noted somewhat caustically that those duties revolved entirely around financial matters, "and, there can be no doubt, this least important part of the whole system has been exceedingly well managed."

Pleasonton bristled at the Blunts' charges, claiming that they were all "either frivolous, unimportant, or entirely unfounded." He asserted, reflecting his biases, that America's lights were as good as any in Europe and better than most, and appended testimonials from customs collectors and ship's captains vouching for their quality. Pleasonton offered figures showing that British lights were more expensive, and he disputed the claim of shoddy construction. As for Fresnel lenses, Pleasonton said he had some years earlier explored the possibility of purchasing a few, but found them too costly to justify, especially since he thought American lights "were satisfactory," and his "chief object was economy." Finally Pleasonton made an effort to defend Winslow Lewis, "to whose experience and knowledge in all that relates to light houses, I have been greatly indebted for the present and past good condition of the whole establishment."

Since Lewis was so deeply implicated in the Blunts' letter, Pleasonton asked him to respond as well. Calling the letter "an unjustifiable and gross attack," Lewis, the skilled salesman whose impact on America's lighthouses was as profound as it was troubling, began by impugning the Blunts as people who didn't know much about the subject at hand, and were thus not in a good position to criticize. If the American lights were so bad, Lewis said, then surely complaints would have been heard from one of the many thousands of ship's captains who entered the port of Boston, yet Lewis had not heard a single one. He too said he had explored the potential of the Fresnel lens, but found it "too complicated" and "too expensive, and too liable to injury, to be introduced into our lighthouses." To show the Blunts just how good America's lighthouses were, Lewis appended a chart that listed what he claimed were the impressive distances that the lights could be seen in clear weather.

The Blunts responded unmercifully, writing again to Secretary Woodbury and using the information provided by Pleasonton and Lewis to show just how clueless they actually were. The first line of attack focused on Lewis's chart: The distances he indicated were physically impossible. Given the height of the lighthouses, their beams, no matter how strong, could not be seen as far away as he claimed because of the curvature of the earth. For example, Lewis said that the Boston Lighthouse was visible thirty miles to sea, but for that to be true the observer would have to be at a height of 289 feet, a complete impossibility. The shipping captains whom Pleasonton and Lewis had corraled to support their claims were, the Blunts pointed out, almost all masters of coasting vessels or long retired, and therefore in no position to testify as to the relative merits of European and American lights. As for the quality of construction, the fact that in the previous year alone, more than one-quarter of the costs of maintaining the lighthouses was spent on repairs was clear evidence of shoddy work. The Blunts reiterated their belief that British and French lights were cheaper to maintain than the American, and supported it with figures, but that was not the most important issue—the quality of the light and its ability to aid mariners was. To drive this point home, the Blunts brought up the *America*, which had been wrecked off the Dry Tortugas on account of a bad light; a loss that totaled $350,000. Focusing solely on the bottom line, as Pleasonton was wont to do, the Blunts argued was a shortsighted approach that was bad for mariners and their ships, especially since one loss like the *America* cost more than what the lighthouse establishment spent in a year maintaining all of its lighthouses and lightships.

The Blunts were most troubled by Pleasonton's overall attitude. They thought, perhaps naively, that once they showed him the problems with the current system in such a persuasive manner, he would endeavor to implement needed reforms. But instead of such a reasonable response, the Blunts said they found Pleasonton "making common cause with a contractor, and claiming, in the face of all evidence, that this establishment needs no improvement."

THE BLUNTS WEREN'T ALONE in raising questions about the lighthouse establishment. After the election of 1836, a new Congress, concerned that too many lighthouses were being built without adequate justification, placed a hold on all lighthouse appropriations until the Board of Navy Commissioners could determine whether the proposed lighthouses were actually needed for navigational safety. The board concluded that thirty-one lighthouses, at a proposed cost of $168,000, were unnecessary; as a result Congress cut them from the budget. At the same time, however, Congress inexplicably made no changes to the lighthouse selection process.

The next year Senator John Davis of Massachusetts, chairman of the Committee on Commerce and a close friend of the Blunts, launched his own investigation, and in May 1838 his committee concluded that the English and French lighthouse establishments were notably far superior to America's, and that the Fresnel lens clearly produced the best light available. But the committee realized that there still might be doubters, so it was necessary to conduct a test. At the committee's instigation, therefore, Congress required Woodbury to import two Fresnel lenses, one of the first order (fixed), and the other the second (revolving), so that they could be compared with existing reflectors to see which was better.

That was not the committee's only recommendation. Concerned about the large number of lighthouses that had been deemed unnecessary, as well as the purported inferiority of the lighthouse establishment, the committee urged Congress to determine where the problems lay, and recommend fixes. To that end Congress authorized President Jackson to divide up the coast and Great Lakes into districts, have naval officers inspect the lighthouses, and report their findings.

The eight naval officers chosen by the president did their work quickly, submitting their reports in the fall of 1838. While many lighthouses were found to be in relatively good condition, about 40 percent had significant problems such as weak foundations, leaking lanterns, poor ventilation, and too many lamps, often with bent or dull reflectors. In some places there were also too many lighthouses, often with similar characteristics, which only confused mariners and wasted money.

Of all the officers, Lt. George Mifflin Bache, one of Benjamin Franklin's great-grandsons, was the most candid when it came to criticizing the lighthouse establishment. Reflecting on a host of ills, among them too great a reliance on customs collectors for making site selections and unskilled contractors for doing the work, he said, "It cannot be denied that, under this system, many buildings have been badly constructed." Bache lamented that in other countries "the aid of science has been called in to render more perfect the different methods of illumination," while in America, those who should be most interested in such advances had remained woefully ignorant. To remedy some of the problems, he recommended that the lighthouse establishment employ knowledgeable inspectors, engineers, and opticians to ensure quality buildings and lighting.

Despite the problems identified by the investigation, Congress took no action, and those hoping to spark reform placed their hopes on the arrival of the Fresnel lenses from France. Surely that would turn the tide.

THE REFORMERS WOULD HAVE to wait. Matthew Perry, now a captain in the navy, had been tasked with acquiring two Fresnel lenses while in Europe on other business, and he signed a contract with the French lens manufacturer in August 1838. But it would be nearly two and half years before the lenses made it to the United States, and were set up for view. Manufacturing and weather delays, including a storm in the Atlantic— which damaged the delivery ship, waylaying it in Bermuda for repairs— conspired to slow the process.

In the meantime, however, anticipation grew for the arrival of the Fresnel lenses and their storied light-bending properties. "If well authenticated evidence may be relied on," Davis wrote in May 1840, "the brilliancy of the beam of light formed by these lenses, has never been surpassed in lighthouses." Should they live up to their much-vaunted reputation, Davis said, "We shall soon lay aside our reflectors for lenses."

A few months later Perry reported to Congress, previewing what was to come. Although he said he greatly preferred the Fresnel lenses to the English parabolic reflectors, "the brilliancy of both . . . is so remarkable, compared with the dimness of the American lights, that no one can avoid noticing the difference." And to drive the point home, and subtly further the cause of reform, he added, "The imperfection of . . . [the American reflector's] form and the inferiority of its construction, as to material and workmanship, are so apparent, that it has always been a matter of surprise among nautical men why the evil has been so long permitted to exist, while in most other respects we have taken the lead in practical improvements."

Pleasonton, however, remained true to his almost Dickensian lapidary nature. Whether out of sincere conviction or political inertia, he was not excited at all, as rigidly committed to his opposition to the Fresnel lens as he was to his seemingly unshakable faith in Lewis's lamps. In fact Pleasonton's anger at those who were trumpeting the cause of reform led him initially to refuse to pay for lenses, even though Congress had already appropriated the money. He soon relented, his foot-dragging having put off the arrival of the lenses by only a few months. Reflecting on this, Perry wrote to a friend, "Mr. Pleasonton has purposely thrown these difficulties in the way. He always strenuously opposed any innovation upon the existing lighthouse system of our country[,] shamefully defective as it is." At a later date Perry pinpointed the source of Pleasonton's intransigence. "The truth is the old egotist has pronounced his America[n] lighthouse system the best in the world, and was excessively annoyed at the exposure of its utter worthlessness."

After much to and fro, the two lenses were finally installed in March 1841 in the twin towers of the Navesink Lighthouse, located in the New Jersey Highlands. The lenses lived up to their billing, greatly impressing all who saw them, including Naval Commander Thomas R. Gedney, who was asked by Congress to compare the lights at Navesink with the ones at Sandy Hook and Cape Henlopen. "The lenticular lights at the Navesink," he concluded, "so far surpass in brilliancy the lights at Cape Henlopen and Sandy Hook, as scarcely to admit a comparison."

Even Pleasonton was impressed with the lenses, noting the "beauty and excellence of the *light* they afford. They appear to be the perfection of apparatus for lighthouse purposes." But as soon as he uttered this praise, he tamped down expectations of any dramatic shift to lenses in the United States, and devised a new strategy for forestalling their implementation on American soil. Rather than attack the lens itself for being unnecessary—their superiority now evident—Pleasonton attacked the lighthouse keepers themselves. The lamp and the clockwork associated with the Fresnel lens, he claimed, were so complicated that not one keeper out of the 240 then employed in America had the technical skill to operate them effectively. Although this was clearly untrue—as evidenced by the fact that Fresnel lenses had been operated quite well for years in France by men culled from the ranks of ordinary day laborers—Pleasonton never wavered in his belief. He also still balked at the high cost of purchasing and installing the lenses, which in this case reached $18,975.36.

Not surprisingly, Winslow Lewis leveled the very same criticisms. After noting that the lenses "are a brilliant affair & produce a strong light," Lewis added that that they were "too complicated & liable to get out of order," because of which they would require "constant attendance" by multiple keepers. Claiming that his reflectors worked exceptionally well, and were visible as far as could be wished, he recommended against unnecessarily spending money on French lenses.

Nonetheless Pleasonton had to admit that he was interested in importing one more Fresnel lens for further evaluation. Again, however, Congress took no action. There would not be another Navesink experiment. America, for the foreseeable future, would stick with the antiquated lights it had.

THE NEXT ASSAULT ON the ossified and obdurate American lighthouse establishment came from an unusual direction. It was spearheaded by Isaiah William Penn Lewis, or IWP, as he liked to be called, who, as it just so happened, was Winslow Lewis's nephew. After an early career at sea he became a civil engineer and, with his uncle's assistance, was introduced to lighthouse work. From the late 1830s to 1840, Pleasonton hired IWP for a number of projects, ranging from supervising lighthouse construction to shoring up building foundations undercut by the relentless sea, as well as installing new lanterns, lamps, and reflectors.

IWP's exposure to America's lighthouses caused him to hold them in contempt. At every turn, it seems, he saw incompetence. Poor construction practices and optically deficient reflectors were a particular concern, and he shared many of his complaints with Pleasonton, arguing that engineers or architects should be hired to oversee site selection and construction, and that American reflectors, like those in England, needed to be manufactured to more exacting standards. Such criticism did not sit well with Pleasonton or Winslow Lewis, and soon Pleasonton wanted nothing more to do with IWP, whose lighthouse work dried up.

Frustrated by his failed efforts at reform from within, and bitter about his experience working for the lighthouse establishment, IWP directed his complaints to a seemingly obstinate Congress. Early in 1842 he sent a blistering letter to Massachusetts congressman Robert Charles Winthrop. "Instead of order, economy and utility, in the administration of our lighthouse system," he wrote, "we have confusion, extravagance, and impotence. . . . We have two hundred and thirty-six witnesses in the shape of as many lighthouses, that all order, economy, and utility in the construction, illumination, and administration, are set at utter defiance by rule of ignorant and incompetent men, who are still pursuing the same career unnoticed and uncared for." IWP urged Winthrop to investigate the lighthouse establishment, and transfer its responsibilities to the Corps of Topographical Engineers, which had been formally established in 1838 and oversaw civil engineering projects for the federal government. Not until engineers took the place of "incompetent" contractors, he argued, could the many problems he identified be remedied. To garner support for his cause IWP traveled to Washington to lobby other congressmen and encourage action.

After IWP's scathing letter was shared with Pleasonton and Winslow Lewis, who were predictably furious, Lewis contacted his political allies in the House and, echoing IWP, urged them to conduct another thorough investigation—but Lewis's goal for the investigation was quite different, in that he hoped it would discredit IWP's damning accusations.

Prodded into action by both Lewises, the House Commerce Committee launched an inquiry. In communications from Pleasonton and Lewis the committee received a spirited defense of the current system, one that boasted of the economy of America's lighthouses as compared with those in Great Britain and France, and argued that Lewis's reflectors were parabolic in shape, and that American lighthouses were well designed and built. Both men added that they saw no reason to employ engineers for lighthouse work, with Pleasonton observing that they were not only very expensive but there were plenty of nonengineers who had the requisite "practical knowledge of lighthouses," and could be employed for a "moderate sum." In contrast, the testimony provided to the committee by IWP and Edmund Blunt presented an entirely different image, of a dysfunctional lighthouse establishment that needed a complete overhaul.

Unfortunately for IWP, the committee's ranks included many Pleasonton and Lewis supporters. And in coming to its conclusions, the committee relied most heavily on information provided by those two, as well as by the customs collectors who had a vested interest in touting the system they were part of. The committee also still placed great weight on the comments of the shipmasters whom Pleasonton and Lewis had trotted out years earlier—the same ones whom the Blunts had said were in no position to testify on the relative merits of European and American lights because they were mostly masters of coasting vessels or long retired. Most shockingly, the committee looked at the investigation done by naval officers in 1838—the one that found serious problems at 40 percent of the lighthouses examined—and claimed it was *not* evidence of poor management. And to discredit IWP's claims even further, the committee said that his "great zeal for change" was not fueled by a desire to serve the public good but rather by his selfish wish to have the Corps of Topographical Engineers take over so that he could be gainfully employed again. Such a person, the committee observed, "should be listened to with distrust, and taken with much allowance."

Given all this, it is not surprising that the committee found that many of the complaints leveled at the lighthouse establishment were without merit, and that the resulting report was largely an affirmation of the status quo. It allowed that some improvements could be instituted, including more inspections, and said that once those relatively minor changes were made, America's lighthouse establishment would be the equal of any in the world. As for Pleasonton, the committee averred that his twenty-two-year incumbency had given him valuable experience and "a practical knowledge of his business, which should not, for slight causes, be lost to the public," and that transferring his "duties to other and inexperienced hands" would likely cause problems and increase costs. "Every innovation is not an improvement," the report concluded, and (using a mid-nineteenth-century version of "If it ain't broke, don't fix it") "when an old and well-tried system works tolerably well, change and experiments should be avoided."

IWP was more than chagrined at this outcome, but he would soon have another chance to expose the lighthouse establishment's failures. On May 25, 1842, the very same day that the Commerce Committee issued its report, Walter Forward, the latest secretary of the Treasury appointed by President John Tyler, gave IWP an assignment. Concerned that in recent years nearly half the annual maintenance expenses for the country's lighthouses went to repairs, Forward instructed IWP to examine lighthouses in Maine, New Hampshire, and Massachusetts and identify what defects in construction were causing this troubling trend.

Predictably IWP's report, delivered in January 1843, was a searing indictment of the lighthouse establishment. He visited seventy lighthouses in four months, interviewed scores of keepers, finding almost nothing worthy of praise and nearly everything deserving of condemnation. To the criticisms already leveled, IWP added leaky roofs, misaligned reflectors, lamps shining uselessly on land, bad mortar, cracked walls, smoky lanterns, poor ventilation, too many lighthouses bunched close together (thereby confusing the mariner), unattended lights going out at night, and a host of other problems, most of which were blamed on unnamed contractors, but it was abundantly clear that his uncle, of all people, was the main target of his attack. Especially troublesome to IWP, apparently a heroic figure not swayed by considerations of nepotism, was the close relationship between his uncle and Pleasonton. When a contractor provides the specifications for lighthouses to the superintendent, and then that contractor so often becomes the successful bidder for the contract, it should come as no surprise, IWP contended, that it "prevents any honorable man of reputation and professional skill from becoming a bidder, knowing, as he must, that such a practice effectually destroys all competition." IWP also found instances of fraud, such as one case in which the walls of a lighthouse, which were supposed to be solid, were instead dangerously filled with sand and rubbish. About the only positive thing he had to say was that in recent years virtually all the thick green lenses, which diminished the light, had been removed from the reflectors.

Just as predictably Pleasonton and Lewis reacted to IWP's report with a fusillade of protests and criticism of their own. Pleasonton pronounced the report as being full of "calumnies," and he forwarded comments from nearly one thousand masters of ships and other vessels, all of whom he said attested to the quality of American lights (if Pleasonton had read the responses more closely, he would have seen that many of the respondents complained about America's lights, and thought them greatly inferior to ones in Europe—one respondent even claimed that America's lights were "the worst I ever saw in any part of the world"). Ever a master political strategist and fighter, Pleasonton also forwarded favorable testimony from the Boston Marine Society—whose members included many of Winslow Lewis's friends and supporters—, as well as from a large group of shipowners in Portland, who, not surprisingly, primarily owned coasting vessels, not ones that crossed the Atlantic. And in a letter to Secretary Forward, Pleasonton repeated what had become his mantra—"I do not hesitate to say, that no similar establishment in the world now presents better lights [than the United States], or is conducted with any thing like the economy." To support his position Pleasonton claimed that British lighthouses cost, on average, nearly three times more than American lighthouses to maintain.

Lewis was not to be intimidated or placated. He published a sixty-page rebuttal to his nephew's report, defending his own work and belittling IWP, claiming that while he had "a talent for drawing," he had "little practical knowledge of engineering" or optics, and whatever knowledge he had was gotten from books, not from actual work in the field (Lewis conveniently ignored his own lack of engineering or optical experience). Lewis gathered testimonials supporting his work and the quality of the lights, and got a few keepers to state that the nega-

Schematic for the tower of the Monhegan Lighthouse, circa 1849. This lighthouse, on Monhegan Island, Maine, was completed in 1850, replacing the original lighthouse built in 1824.

tive comments attributed to them by IWP did not accurately represent what they said.

The internecine battle between the Lewises made for dramatic reading, but it didn't sway legislators.* While Secretary Forward came down firmly on IWP's side, and recommended that no more appropriations for lighthouses be made until a competent engineer was appointed to oversee the lighthouse system, Congress ignored the report and the recommendation. The report, however, did have an impact. According to the *Journal of Commerce*, it "was a severe blow to the defenders of the old

---

* Unfortunately it appears that neither Lewis nor IWP left behind any letters that reflect on their personal feelings toward each other, and how their very public and vicious battle over the nation's lighthouses affected their relationship (or the dynamics of the broader Lewis family). But it may be safely assumed that they loathed each other.

system . . . [and] it compelled the General Superintendent of Lighthouses to bestir himself and get things a little more to rights." In what might amount to a largely symbolic move, given his campaign to maintain the status quo, Pleasonton did in fact refit a number of lighthouses with new, better-designed lanterns and larger, improved reflectors. He had actually been pursuing such upgrades for a couple of years, showing that he was taking to heart at least some of the many complaints that had been made against the lighthouse establishment. The changes to the system, however, were marginal, and the technology of America's lighthouses at the time remained a sorry affair at best.

UNDAUNTED, THE REFORMERS CONTINUED to press their case. In 1845, just months after the inauguration of President James Polk, his secretary of the Treasury, Robert J. Walker, initiated a study of European lighthouse organizations with an eye to comparing their operations with those in the United States. Navy lieutenants Thornton A. Jenkins and Richard Bache (another of Benjamin Franklin's great-grandsons) were sent to evaluate lighthouse management and technological advances in France, England, Ireland, and Scotland. Their wide-ranging report, submitted in June 1846, lauded lighthouse management in Europe while ridiculing the American system. Its main point was that in Europe, especially in France and Great Britain, the very best scientific, engineering, and administrative talent was brought to bear in building and managing lighthouses. As a result sites were chosen wisely, construction was excellent, inspections were frequent and thorough, oil quality was high, keepers were well trained, and the lighting apparatus were the best of their kind (truly parabolic reflectors and Fresnel lenses). With respect to lighting, Jenkins and Bache urged that America should immediately adopt the Fresnel lens: "The interests of commerce and the cause of humanity forbid that the lights on our coasts should be in any respect inferior to those on the coasts of the other great commercial nations of the world," they said, but unfortunately America's were. And most of all, the two lieutenants argued that highly qualified engineers were needed for the lighthouse establishment to run properly. Based on this report, Walker urged Congress to appoint a board composed of Pleasonton, the head of the Coast Survey, two naval officers, two engineer officers, and a secretary, and instruct it to develop a detailed plan for improving the lighthouse establishment. Again, however, no action was taken.

THE CRITICISM RAINING DOWN on the lighthouse establishment raises the question of why the status quo persisted. One reason is that for most of the period in question, Democrats dominated the national government, and they generally opposed expenditures on public works and internal improvements, such as lighthouses and canals, because they didn't want to benefit one branch of commerce or industry over another. As a result, many of them supported Pleasonton's cost-cutting approach, which kept expenditures down. Inertia also played a role. Change of any kind in government, even in a country as young as America then was, is often difficult, and Pleasonton, as skilled a political brinkman as any nineteenth-century technocrat, had an impressive ability to marshal testimony and data supporting his perspective on the situation. Even though his opponents effectively disputed his views, those seeking to avoid change could point to the information Pleasonton provided to claim that the lighthouse establishment was adequate. The vehemence of some of the attacks on Pleasonton and Lewis also had an influence on the course of events. IWP's report, in particular, was so intense—and so seemingly personal, especially since it was leveled against a relative—that it allowed those who opposed change to discredit the messenger along with the message. Finally, there is little doubt that Pleasonton's extraordinary political connections helped him defend the lighthouse establishment. He was on good terms (to say the least) with a number of presidents and congressmen, who often relied on him for advice pertaining to his various duties as fifth auditor. And even though a contemporary, Rear Adm. Charles Wilkes, who led the United States South Seas Exploring Expedition (1838–42), claimed that Pleasonton "was not a bright man," he noted that the fifth auditor was nevertheless "intimate with most of the leading men of his day. . . . [And] with his accomplished and handsome wife they had much influence in the intricacies of the Govt., and from her beauty and sprightliness, had great power over the distinguished men by whom the Government was administered and were always well posted of what was going on." The numerous soirees the Pleasontons hosted at their DC home further enhanced their influence.

FACING POLITICAL INERTIA, congressional intransigence, and a particularly well-connected and dogged opponent in Pleasonton, IWP, more than ever convinced that he was in the right, would not give up the fight, and it appeared that Pleasonton had finally met his match. After his blistering report in 1843 failed to result in change, IWP spent nearly two years in France, befriending Léonor Fresnel and learning as much as he could about France's daringly innovative lenses. Upon returning to the United States in 1845, he entered the fray once again, this time petitioning the men whose business would benefit from the superior technology. To that end IWP mounted demonstrations before curious merchants' organizations in New York, Boston, and Washington, urging them to write to the secretary of the Treasury and encourage him to support the adoption of the Fresnel lens as the American standard. He also lobbied Congress to have the U.S. Army Corps of Topographical Engineers, which had already constructed a few lighthouses, build more.

Even though Congress was preoccupied with the Mexican-American War, which had begun in May 1846, and would conclude in early 1848 with the signing of the Treaty of Guadalupe Hidalgo, the legislators responded to IWP's earnest calls for change in 1847, giving the corps control over four lighthouses that posed engineering challenges. One of these was the Brandywine Shoal Lighthouse in Delaware Bay. Army engineers Hartman Bache, yet another of Benjamin Franklin's great-grandsons, and George Gordon Meade, who would later gain fame as the Civil War general who bested Robert E. Lee at Gettysburg, were put in charge, and they employed the relatively new screw-pile technology imported from Great Britain. Invented in 1838 by an Irish engineer, Alexander Mitchell, this system used multiple iron pilings tipped with spiral flanges up to three feet across that were corkscrewed into the ocean floor to hold

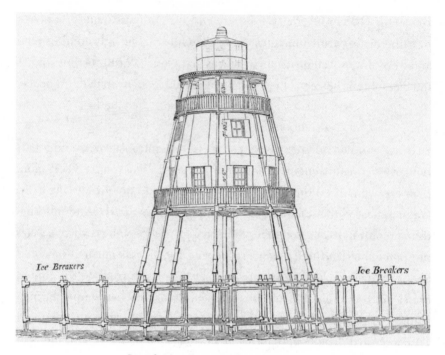

Brandywine Shoal Lighthouse, circa 1850s.

the lighthouse structure fast. Screw piles were particularly useful in areas of soft of mud, sand, or clay, which required the extra stability or gripping power the flanges provided. The nine iron pilings of the Brandywine Shoal Lighthouse rose well above the high-water line and held up a platform upon which sat the small cottage-style keeper's quarters, with the lantern room on top. The forty-six-foot-tall Brandywine Shoal Lighthouse, the first screw-pile lighthouse in the nation, was lit on October 28, 1850, its beam coming from a third-order Fresnel lens.

The lens at Brandywine was actually the fourth Fresnel lens in America, because earlier in 1850, a second-order lens had been installed in the newly built Sankaty Head Lighthouse on the southeastern edge of Nantucket. In his 1843 report IWP had called the waters off Sankaty Head, which covered the dangerous Nantucket shoals, a "fatal spot upon the coast of Massachusetts, where many a brave heart and many a gallant ship lie buried in one common grave." Sankaty Head Lighthouse was not built by the Corps of Engineers, however, but rather by naval engineer

Benjamin F. Isherwood, and Pleasonton was forced to equip it with a Fresnel lens by virtue of a congressional mandate. The lighthouse earned the instant admiration of mariners, who took to calling it the "rocket light" and "blazing star." Fishermen claimed to be able to bait their hooks by its gleam, and many said it was the best light they had ever seen. So much of a tourist attraction did the Fresnel lens become that in 1856, the entryway to the lantern room had to be widened so that women sporting hoopskirts could climb up to see it.

Another of the projects undertaken by the Corps of Engineers was the Carysfort Reef Lighthouse, located in four and a half feet of water off the island of Key Largo, at the tip of Florida. Scores of ships had wrecked on the reef between the mid-1830s and the early 1850s, providing a persuasive argument for a lighthouse on this spot. The engineers hoped to build the lighthouse on iron piles screwed deep into hard coral, but test borings at the site determined that beneath the thin coral crust lay soft sand, which was not stable enough to bear the lighthouse's weight. So corps engineers came up with a novel solution. They slid large cast-iron disks over the iron pile legs, and when the legs were screwed into the sand, the disks (called foot plates) sat firmly on top of the coral crust, adding extra surface area, and therefore creating a larger load-bearing surface and enhanced stability.

Meade supervised the final stages of construction, and the 112-foot Carysfort Reef Lighthouse sprang into operation on March 10, 1852. The keeper's quarters were located on a platform well above the water, and the lantern room was located higher still, at the top of the structure. To get to the lantern room the keeper ascended a narrow, enclosed cylindrical staircase that rose from the top of the quarters. Eight iron legs formed the outer structure of the lighthouse, and because of its skeletal design this type of screw-pile lighthouse is commonly referred to as a skeleton tower. As a result of their open structure, skeleton towers offered little resistance to wind and waves, and therefore were especially useful in offshore areas buffeted by severe weather.

An astonishing turn of events, however, deprived the Carysfort Reef Lighthouse of the first-order Fresnel lens IWP had purchased for it. The

Carysfort Reef Lighthouse, circa 1962.

French lens arrived in plenty of time at the Customs House in New York City, but for some unknown reason, the corps was not informed that it was there. For nine months the valuable lens, packed in thirteen unusually large crates, languished in a warehouse waiting for someone to claim it and pay the excise taxes due. As was standard practice, the unclaimed boxes were put up for auction, and since nobody had bothered to open any of them, they were simply labeled "machinery." Believing that such a large quantity of machinery must have appreciable value, Customs House employee Stephen Lutz, along with a few of his friends, submitted a winning bid of five hundred dollars. They carted the boxes to a vacant lot some blocks away and, with great anticipation, began prying them open. While the contents amazed them, they had not a clue what they were. Only after consulting with others did they discover what they had purchased. Soon after that, the New York agents for the French manufacturer, Henry Lepaute, found out what had happened, and became enraged, leading American authorities to dispossess Lutz and his friends of the lens and return it to the government. But it was too late for the Carysfort Reef Lighthouse, which in the meantime had been fitted with eighteen lamps and twenty-one-inch reflectors based on Winslow Lewis's patented design.

THE INCREASED INVOLVEMENT OF engineers, and the addition of two more Fresnel lenses were encouraging signs for the future, but they were just that—signs, and not any indication of the fundamental change that so many had been calling for. However, the increasing disconnect between the lighthouse establishment and trends in the country was cause for some optimism that further changes might soon take place.

Fresh from new territorial gains as a result of its victory over Mexico in 1848, the United States at midcentury was an emerging world power, its strength fueled by rapid industrialization, and bustling with confidence that progress, especially technological progress, was not only possible but also inevitable, if not unstoppable. Nevertheless, progress was clearly wanting when it came to the nation's lighthouses. As a contemporary article in the *American Review* noted:

> Our whole [lighthouse] system lacks *method*; and nothing can ever supply this radical defect, until science and experience are systematically introduced into its supervision. The establishment is not adapted either to the wants of our commerce, or to the advanced state of science and of art. And yet, in all other branches of industry and social economy, we are prompt to seize upon all improvements. We use the very best steam engines, the best machinery in manufactures, and even the Magnetic Telegraph. . . . In these departments we should

rightly deem it niggardly and narrow to reject the new because the old was cheaper. There, certainly, is no reason why similar improvements should be rejected or neglected, in so important a branch of the public service as our Light-House Establishment—a branch on the efficiency and perfection of which depend, not only the wealth with which our ships are freighted, but the lives of the thousands who follow the sea.

In 1851 Congress decided it was time to take another shot at reform, in the hope that the result would give America the lighthouse system it deserved.

IN MARCH 1851 CONGRESS ordered Secretary of the Treasury Thomas Corwin to convene a board to conduct an extensive study of the condition of the lighthouse establishment, and prepare a plan to improve its operations. The so-called Lighthouse Board was composed of two navy officers, two army engineers, a civil engineer of high scientific attainments, and a junior officer of the navy to act as secretary. Corwin, a close friend of the Blunts, staffed the board with an impressive array of high-level talent. Alexander Dallas Bache, the chosen civil engineer, was head of the United States Coast Survey and among the nation's foremost physicists, who had performed groundbreaking work on the fundamentals of electromagnetism, leading to the development of the telegraph. One more of the seemingly endless number of Benjamin Franklin's great-grandsons to become involved with lighthouses, Bache also had a strong engineering background, having graduated first in his class from West Point at age nineteen. The two navy slots went to Cdr. Samuel Francis Du Pont, a member of the famed gunpowder manufacturing family of Delaware, and Commodore William B. Shubrick. The army engineers were Brevet Gen. Joseph G. Totten, the chief engineer of the army, and the topographical engineer Lt. Col. James Kearney. Navy lieutenant Thornton A. Jenkins was tapped as secretary. Every member of the board was united in their respect for science and engineering, and were supporters of the Fresnel lens—Jenkins was the coauthor of the 1846 report that denigrated America's lighthouses and urged the immediate adoption of lens technology. There was absolutely no doubt that these men would come down hard on the lighthouse establishment, and they did.

Over four months the board visited nearly forty lighthouses, soliciting information from a wide range of individuals, including military and civilian ship captains and European lighthouse officials. The board's 760-page tome covered virtually every aspect of lighthouse management, and much of the information and findings repeated what had already been said in earlier reports, but this time the sheer weight of the evidence, marshaled in one place, made the report authoritative and compelling.

Everywhere the board looked it found serious problems and deficiencies. Virtually all lighthouses were poorly constructed, the report said, and some of the best lighthouses in the country, it was stated, had actually been built in the colonial era, specifically Sandy Hook, Cape Henry, and Cape Henlopen. Although Winslow Lewis was not mentioned by name in the report, he and other contractors were called out for their lack of engineering knowledge, which resulted in lighthouses that were "anything *but creditable to the reputation of those who had the charge of erecting them.*" Such shoddiness led the board to observe, "Our lighthouse establishment seems to be the sole exception to our practice of building for the future as well as for the present. In it there seems to be ever a lurking apprehension that our naval and commercial existence is but *temporary.*"

Most reflectors were found to be spherical, not parabolic, and virtually all the lamps examined were poorly adjusted. Keepers were often not competent to tend the lights and had been given little or no instruction. Pleasonton had sent around a circular of instructions to keepers, but it was so brief (a single page) that it was not particularly useful, and more often than not it was nowhere to be found at the lighthouses. Inspections were virtually nonexistent. The identifying characteristics of lighthouses often confused rather than aided the mariner, and there were too many lighthouses in areas of high population, and not enough on deserted stretches of the coast that posed significant dangers.

Mariners canvassed for their opinions piled on the criticism. Lt.

David D. Porter's comments were typical. "Our light-houses as at present arranged are so wretched," he said, "that any seafaring man must desire a change." Cape Hatteras Lighthouse, which he called "the most important on our coast," was, he said, "without a doubt, the *worst* light in the world. . . . The first nine trips I made I never saw Hatteras light at all, though frequently passing in sight of the breakers." Lt. H. J. Hartstene opined, "The lights on Hatteras, Lookout, Canaveral, and Cape Florida, if not improved, had better be dispensed with, as the navigator is apt to run ashore looking for them."

The board complained that the lighthouse establishment had remained stagnant while the rest of the world passed it by. More than a dozen maritime nations, most especially Great Britain and France, were already widely employing Fresnel lenses, making their coasts safer. Yet the only improvements Americans had made in more than three decades were putting Fresnel lenses at Navesink, Sankaty, and Brandywine, and as a result the nation's lighthouses were "not as efficient as the interests of commerce, navigation, and humanity demand." The board also pointed out that since the first Fresnel lens had been imported for Navesink, lens technology had dramatically improved with the addition of catadioptric prisms above and below the central panels, which served to direct even more of the light in a concentrated beam seaward. Commenting on the largest lenses then available, Alan Stevenson—part of the extremely talented Stevenson dynasty that had built Scotland's most magnificent lighthouses—said, "Nothing can be more beautiful than an entire apparatus for a fixed light of the first order . . . I know no work of art more beautiful or creditable to the boldness, ardour, intelligence, and zeal of the artist."

As for the supposed excessive cost of Fresnel lens, the board obliterated that argument. Relying on its careful observations of the Fresnel lenses at Navesink and Brandywine Shoal, in comparison with nearby lighthouses using the best reflectors, the board concluded that the light from the lenses was roughly four times more powerful and effective than that coming from the arrays of reflectors, while at the same time the reflectors were roughly four times more expensive to operate and maintain than the lenses, based on the cost of oil alone. Additionally, other savings would ensue from employing lenses in place of reflectors. While a lens required only one lamp, each reflector needed a lamp, and since American lighthouses often had as many as eighteen or more reflectors in an array, that meant that switching to a lens would save on supplies, including wicks and glass chimneys. It would also save on the major cost of keeping all those lamps in good repair. As a result the board calculated that if all the country's lighthouses were fitted with Fresnel lenses, at a cost of roughly five hundred thousand dollars, the annual savings in oil, supplies, repairs, and transportation costs would be large enough so that in five or six years the cost of switching to lenses would have been covered, and from thereon out, the government would benefit from the continued savings coming from the use of less expensive lenses. And whereas reflectors had to be replaced every ten to fifteen years, lenses could serve for perpetuity. The board declared that the superior brilliance of the Fresnel lens alone "furnished an unanswerable argument in favor of the lens system," and factoring in the lens's great economy only made the argument stronger.

The board moreover reported that to expect the lighthouse establishment, as constituted, to "compare, in point of excellence and economy," with systems in France and Great Britain "would be to expect order out of anarchy and confusion, and perfection out of such various and imperfect elements." Whereas Scotland's lighthouses, for example, were under the supervision of distinguished engineers of the Stevenson clan, and France had long included its top scientists and engineers in lighthouse matters through the Commission des Phares and other professional organizations, the United States had for the most part stuck with amateurs, and suffered the consequences.

What was needed, the board reported in a seemingly direct refutation of everything Pleasonton had done, was a radical overhaul of the system that put the best scientists and engineers in charge. The current lighthouse establishment should be replaced with a board that had the same range of individuals as the current Lighthouse Board, while adding another civilian with high scientific skills, and an officer of the army engineers as a second secretary. Since the board would be housed in the Department of Treasury, the secretary of the Treasury would serve as its president ex officio. The new nine-member board, with the exception of the two secretaries, would be unpaid, meet four times a year, and be responsible for bringing the highest degree of professionalism to America's lighthouses. Among other things, lighthouse plans would be drawn up by skilled engineers and approved by the board, engineers would oversee building construction, inspections would be frequent and performed by competent individuals, and the Fresnel lens would be adopted throughout the system.

THE LIGHTHOUSE BOARD DELIVERED this stinging report on January 30, 1852. Despite the call for immediate action, and the overwhelming nature of the case presented, Congress took its time debating what to do. In the meantime, predictably, Pleasonton, fearing that the end of his career was near, defended himself. In a letter to Corwin he expressed incredulity that after all the years of attacks that he had successfully repelled, yet another was made, and he disparaged this latest assault by saying that it had little new to offer. Pleasonton once again discredited his past attackers and rehashed all the arguments he had made for decades as to why the system he ran was good enough. He threw in more time-worn testimonials from mariners attesting to the quality of the lights, and in general made it clear that the world he—a figure almost worthy of a Shakespearean tragedy—saw bore almost no resemblance to the one the Lighthouse Board had revealed. In a letter to President Millard Fillmore he claimed, "The great object of this attack was to introduce the French lenses into our light houses, which do not suit this country and for that reason I opposed and still oppose the employment of them." As for Lewis, he was spared the board's drubbing of the system he helped create, having mercifully died in 1850.

Come summer, debate over the creation of the board was still plodding along. Some congressmen did not like the idea of a board, preferring to vest control in a single individual. Others, remarkably, felt that further study was needed. In a particularly startling volte-face, Senator Davis of Massachusetts, the same man who had urged the United States to import its first Fresnel lens back in 1838, was now having second thoughts, fearing that the lenses were too expensive, and that if they were adopted nationwide, America would be far too dependent on the French for its lights, which might be problematic in the event of conflict between the two countries. Davis also maintained that it was suspicious that the board's report found not a single thing to praise about a system that had been in place for more than thirty years. As a result he believed that the report was "an unfair, unjust, and exaggerated statement of facts."

In the end it took an outside force to help implement the report. As George Blunt described it, "In 1852, the bill for creating the Light-house Board was pending in Congress, but being opposed by parties interested in keeping up our bad system, its passage was doubtful." At the same time the steamer *Baltic* was heading from Washington, DC, to New York, with a contingent of congressmen on board. Just miles from Sandy Hook the ship was detained by heavy fog, unable to proceed because the offshore buoys—aids to navigation under Pleasonton's control—were inadequate to guide the ship's captain into port. This delay, and especially the reason for it, angered the congressmen, and when they finally returned to the capital they threw their weight behind the stalled and seemingly endangered bill, and it passed on August 31, 1852.

AFTER THIRTY-TWO YEARS PLEASONTON was abruptly out of a job, and a repressive and anachronistic lighthouse era was now drawing to a close. "We are very glad to learn that Mr. Pleasonton has lost his office," crowed the *Vineyard Gazette*. "It is astonishing that our government has kept a regular antediluvian old Granny like Pleasonton in office for almost half a century." Many shared the same opinion. But before placing all the blame for the lighthouse establishment's pitiful state on Pleasonton, and, to a lesser extent, his accomplice, Winslow Lewis, it is essential to recall Congress's role. After all, it held the purse strings and controlled the legislative agenda, and could have forced any number of changes on Pleasonton

Joseph Henry,
circa 1860–75.

if it had wanted. Presidents, too, could have stepped in. That politicians did not take action for so long, even in the face of such overwhelming evidence that all was not well with America's lighthouses, is an indictment of the system within which Pleasonton operated. Whatever the causes, the inherent tragedy is that America's lighthouses were allowed to remain in such a parlous condition for so long. As the lighthouse historian Francis Ross Holland, Jr., noted, "One wonders how many ships that wrecked during Pleasonton's thirty-two-year administration would have been saved had more effective lights been available."

Affronted by his ouster, Pleasonton refused to put down the cudgel. In February 1853 he wrote to his friend James Buchanan, whom he knew from the latter's days in the Senate, and asked if he might put in a good word with the president-elect, Franklin Pierce, in the hope of landing a job with his administration. "I feel under great obligation to you," wrote Pleasonton, "for your obliging offer to interpose on my behalf: for to be turned out of office now, when I am too old to engage in any other business, with my slender means to live on . . . would destroy me." As a means of bolstering his case for government employment, Pleasonton added, striking a familiar note, that he had saved "at least ten million dollars in conducting the Light-House Establishment." It didn't matter. Pierce had no position for him, and Pleasonton died in 1855 at the age of seventy-eight, bitter until the end about the denouement of his career.

THE LIGHTHOUSE BOARD CONVENED for the first time in October 1852. Membership on the new board was the same as on the old, with three additions, the most significant being Joseph Henry, who was appointed as the second civilian scientist. Henry, a former Princeton professor and the founding director and secretary of the Smithsonian Institution, was one of America's foremost scientists, who, like his close friend, A. D. Bache, had also performed groundbreaking work on electromagnetism that contributed to the development of the telegraph. The two other additions to the board were Capt. E. L. F. Hardcastle, as the engineering secretary, and Treasury Secretary Corwin, who became its president ex officio. The job facing the board was immense, and they got to work immediately.

CHAPTER 7

BRIGHTER LIGHTS

. . . .

*Cape Disappointment Lighthouse, near the mouth of the Columbia River,
circa 1857. The drawing was rendered by T. E. Sandgren, based on
a sketch by Maj. Hartman Bache.*

Pleasonton's reign—as well as his tight rein—had left
America's lighthouses in a deplorable state, and it was up to the Lighthouse Board to fix existing problems and take the lighthouse establishment in a new and more efficient direction. This was a daunting task to
say the least, but the board proved equal to it. Not only were board members competent and thoroughly knowledgeable about lighthouse matters,
and dedicated to the cause of improving navigational aids, but they also
shared a commitment to civic duty that imbued their work with a sense
of purpose. As Henry wrote to his friend Asa Gray, America's foremost

botanist, "I would not of my own accord have engaged in the business of the Light-House Board but as I was especially requested by the President [Millard Fillmore] to assist in reorganizing this important part of the executive duty of the government I could not well decline."

The board's first task was to set up a management system to guide their actions. They divided the Atlantic, Gulf, Pacific, and Great Lake coasts into districts, each one being assigned a navy inspector who visited the lighthouses every three months, and was responsible for lighthouse maintenance and the supervision of keepers. The districts also had an assigned army engineer, who oversaw construction of and repairs to the buildings and the lighting apparatus. Reports from the inspectors and engineers were sent to the board so that it could monitor progress and promptly address problems.

Once Congress authorized the construction of a lighthouse, with extensive advice and input from the board on technical and fiscal issues, the board's engineering secretary drew up the plans, specifications, and contracts for lighthouse construction, which the board reviewed and approved. The board also awarded all construction contracts and made sure that no contract was let unless the contractors possessed the skills necessary to do the job. To tackle specific issues and conduct experiments, the board divided its members into executive committees, including ones for lighting and engineering. To ensure that all lighthouses had the supplies and equipment they needed, the board established a central depot on Staten Island (not yet part of New York City) and employed tenders to bring the materials where they were needed. In later years, depots were located in each district.*

Realizing that the economy and success of lighthouses were only as good as the people who tended them, the board issued an extremely detailed list of instructions for keepers, which covered everything from how to clean the lantern room and the lighting apparatus to the proper times for lighting and extinguishing the lights. The board also began

---

*Today some of the buildings of original Staten Island depot serve as the home for the National Lighthouse Museum.

training keepers and, in another break from the past, began making literacy a job requirement, so they could better attend to their duties and fill out the many reports they had to submit. Applicants for keeper positions had to be between eighteen and fifty years old, and also had to be physically capable of performing a myriad of manual and mechanical tasks, including whitewashing the lighthouse and associated buildings and repairing machinery. Unannounced visits by lighthouse inspectors helped ensure that keepers maintained high standards, and those found wanting could be reprimanded or penalized. Severe infractions, such as letting the light go out during the night, resulted in immediate dismissal.

A critical deficiency of the old system was the lack of a useful light list that contained detailed information about all the navigational aids, such as their locations and characteristics, mariners could rely on in sailing the coast. The board's extensive annual light list remedied this situation. The board also tried to eliminate potentially deadly surprises by sending out notices that informed mariners well in advance of any changes in lighthouses or if new ones had been built, so that accidents like those of the *Union* and the *Galaxy*, which occurred near the Baker's Island Lighthouse in Massachusetts and the Barnegat Lighthouse in New Jersey, respectively, could be avoided.

DURING THE BALANCE OF the 1850s, as the sharp divisions between the Northern and Southern states widened, and the tenor of political discourse grew increasingly strident and less conciliatory, the board implemented a wide range of improvements to the nation's lighthouses and imposed a uniform set of standards and practices. Inferior lighthouses were either repaired or replaced, and new ones were built using engineer-approved designs and the best available materials, such as finished stone, brick, and iron. Lighthouses that were no longer necessary to aid navigation were discontinued. Taking a leaf from the French lighthouse book, the board pursued the goal of placing lighthouses along the coast in such a way that mariners were never out of sight of one. This meant locating more lighthouses in less populous areas, which had been somewhat ignored during

Pleasonton's tenure, largely because those sites had smaller political constituencies to lobby on their behalf. So as to keep mariners from being confused as to where they were and which lighthouse was in view, the board adopted a clear classification scheme, which differentiated lighthouses based on the light's characteristics, such as whether it was fixed or flashing.

Declaring that "a light placed on a prominent cape or point should be not less than 150 feet above the mean sea-level, to enable the mariner to be warned of his danger in time to shape his course," the board set out to make such lighthouses taller. This is what happened to the nearly 100-foot-tall Cape Hatteras Lighthouse, which had long been an object of complaint, when it was elevated to 150 feet in 1854, much to the relief of mariners attempting to make it past the deadly Diamond Shoals. The Fire Island Lighthouse, located on a barrier island just south of mainland Long Island, was another one that received a much-needed lift.

Originally built in 1826, standing eighty-nine feet tall, the Fire Island Lighthouse was implicated in the crash of the bark *Elizabeth* in the summer of 1850, which took the lives of the leading Transcendentalist, tireless advocate of women's rights, and insightful journalist and literary critic Margaret Fuller, along with her Italian husband and their two-year-old son, as well as five other passengers and crewmembers—only seventeen people survived. The *Elizabeth* had departed Livorno, Italy in mid-May, heading for New York City. Its cargo, valued at two hundred thousand dollars, included oil paintings, silks, almonds, and a marble statue of the recently deceased John C. Calhoun, a full-throated defender of slavery and former vice president, secretary of state, and senator from South Carolina. Seven days after the trip commenced, and just before the *Elizabeth* was to sail out of the Mediterranean, the captain died of smallpox and was buried at sea. The relatively inexperienced first mate, Henry Bangs, took over, and early in the morning of July 19, in the midst of a furious gale, he sighted the American coast. Tragically he mistook the Fire Island Lighthouse for one on the New Jersey shore, which led him to miscalculate the ship's position. As a result, at around four o'clock the *Elizabeth* plowed into a sandbar a little more than three miles from the lighthouse, and a mere three hundred yards offshore.

Margaret Fuller.

The ship quickly swamped and began to break apart under the merciless pounding of the waves. According to contemporary accounts, the locals who had gathered on shore, showing a callous disregard for the sufferings of their fellow humans and a keen interest in their own well-being, focused on salvaging valuable objects from the ship rather than retrieving the lifeboat near the lighthouse in order to mount a rescue attempt. Seeing that nobody was coming to their aid, many on board the *Elizabeth* launched themselves into the boiling surf in an effort to reach the beach. But Fuller, who could not swim, and her family remained on the ship as it slowly disintegrated around them. Finally, more than ten hours after the *Elizabeth* had grounded, just as they were preparing to make a desperate attempt to follow the others, they were swept into the water and under the still mountainous waves.

Fuller's death was a story of international significance. Horace Greeley, the legendary editor of the influential *New-York Tribune*, for whom Fuller had worked, wrote the paper's obituary of its star journalist, concluding, "America has produced no woman who in mental endowments and acquirements has surpassed Margaret Fuller." The great amount of publicity surrounding the wreck of the *Elizabeth*, due to its celebrated passenger, plus the fact that the Fire Island Lighthouse was critical to transatlantic steamer traffic, led Congress to replace the lighthouse with a new one, nearly 170 feet tall, that was built in 1858 and still stands today. And by the end of the 1850s, nine brick lighthouses, all at least 150 feet tall, proudly stood guard at prominent points along the Eastern Sea-board, ranging from Fire Island down to the Dry Tortugas Lighthouse in Florida.

WHILE THE TALLER LIGHTHOUSES in key locations were being con-structed, the single most important change to the lighthouse system as a whole was the adoption of the Fresnel lens. After years of being in the rel-ative dark, America's lighthouses were steadily reborn with the brightest lights of all. Keeping two French lens manufacturers working at full tilt, the board slowly but surely began fitting America's lighthouses with new lenses, a process that often required the lighthouses' lantern rooms to be rebuilt to handle the larger apparatus.

American pride in adopting these lenses was on display at the Exhi-bition of the Industry of All Nations in New York City in 1853, which was intended to showcase the world's industrial achievements—of course with a particular emphasis on the progress of the host nation. The exhi-bition's organizers were eager to have a Fresnel lens on hand, and the board was happy to comply, wanting to share with the country the dra-matic changes underway at the nation's lighthouses, and to build public support for the exciting, and very expensive, new direction it was taking. The timing proved excellent. The French first-order lens slated for the Cape Hatteras Lighthouse was languishing in the New York Customs House. It couldn't be installed because the new, taller lighthouse was still under construction. So the $6,500 lens was redirected to the exhibi-tion and placed in the Crystal Palace, an imposing and visually stunning iron-and-glass structure in midtown Manhattan—in what is today Bryant Park—patterned after the Crystal Palace that had been the centerpiece of the Great Exhibition in London two years earlier.

The board tasked George Gordon Meade with setting up and exhibit-ing the lens, on account of his experience building the Brandywine Shoal and the Sand Key Lighthouses, both of which had first-order lenses. The spectacular Cape Hatteras lens had twenty-four flash panels and 1008 prisms, and it delighted visitors who had the treat of viewing it lit up at

night, illuminating the darkness with its brilliant beams. A great booster
of the Fresnel lens, Meade too became almost rhapsodic over the dramatic display: "This marvelous contrivance darts forth its dazzling flash,
and revolving as it flashes, only intermits its light still more to startle the
beholder." Exhibition organizers proclaimed that by exposing the lens to
the public in this way, it would "in a few months [be] as familiar to the
whole of our mechanical world as . . . a common compass."

America's adoption of this state-of-the-art lens came at a propitious
time, just when Augustin Fresnel's dream was finally being realized. As a
result of the work of both French and Scottish engineers, even the largest
Fresnel lenses were using an array of internally reflecting (catadioptric)
and refracting (dioptric) prisms to create glistening glass towers held in

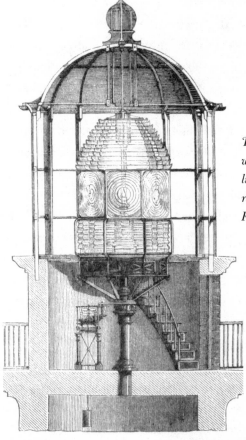

*The lantern room and
watch room (below) of a
lighthouse with a
revolving first-order
Fresnel lens.*

*The third-order Fresnel lens
destined for Cape St. Elias
Lighthouse, in Alaska,
circa 1915.*

place by gleaming brass frames, that could capture and effectively redirect toward the horizon more than 80 percent of the available light. To many these marvels of optical brilliance resembled a sparkling glass beehive. They were quite simply one of the most useful and exquisite products of the Industrial Revolution, worthy of being considered not only technological masterpieces but also splendid works of art.*

Fresnel lenses now came in six sizes or orders, which was based on the distance between the flame and the lens. They ranged from first-order lenses, which were twelve feet tall and six feet in diameter, down to sixth-order ones that were less than two feet tall, and just shy of a foot in diameter (in later years a 3.5-order lens was added to the lineup). The

---

*Today Fresnel lenses are used not only in lighthouses but also in many other applications. For example, many automobile head- and taillights, overhead projectors, and spotlights employ lenses based on Fresnel's design to focus light into powerful beams.

first-order lenses were the most powerful, and were used for primary lights, the ones that mariners would see upon first upon approaching the coast. Smaller lenses served different roles. For example, lighthouses warning of such dangers as a reef might require only a third- or fourth-order lens, while a lighthouse at a smaller harbor's entrance, not needing to shine a beam so far over the waves, might use a sixth-order lens.

Beyond this there were many configurations of lenses. For example, fixed, or stationary, lenses shone a continual beam up to 360 degrees over the entire horizon. Such lenses would have a central band of convex glass that went all the way around the lens, with dioptric and catadioptric prisms laddered above and below. Revolving, or rotating, lenses consisted of multiple panels with a central bull's-eye panel surrounded by prisms. Each time a panel passed in front of the light it would emit a bright flash. This flashing effect could also be achieved with a fixed lens when a moving screen, or shutter, was employed, which would occult the light at certain intervals. Additionally there were also fixed lenses varied with a flash, which revolved. With these the bull's-eye panels and prisms above sent out an intermittent flash, while the circular prisms below sent out a continuous beam. That way the mariner would always see a light, along with a characteristic flash identifying the specific lighthouse.

While most lights were white, others were red or green, as well as some combination of these hues. Colored lights were employed for a variety of reasons. If there were many lighthouses close to one another along a particular stretch of coast, interspersing ones displaying a colored light would differentiate them from the neighboring white lights, thereby helping mariners fix their position. A red light could also be employed to warn of a specific danger, such as rocks lurking beneath the surface. In such cases the light would be split into sectors of different colors. Thus, when approaching a lighthouse, if the captain saw a red light, he would know to be especially cautious until he saw the light turn green or white, which was an indication that the danger had passed. The colored effect could be achieved in a number of ways. The lens itself could be colored,

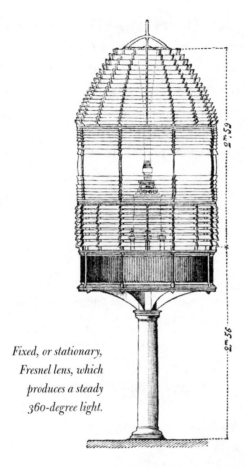

Fixed, or stationary,
Fresnel lens, which
produces a steady
360-degree light.

the lantern's glass panes could be colored, or colored glass panels could be placed either around the lamp or on the outside of the lens. The one drawback of using colored glass was that it absorbed a significant percentage of the light, thereby weakening the beam.

Fixed lenses were perched on pedestals, and revolving lenses were mounted on a chariot, or carriage, which "was a series of large bronze or steel wheels that rolled on a circular table below the lens" and sat on the pedestal. A revolving lens was rotated by a clockwork mechanism powered by a slowly falling weight on a cable. The cable was wrapped around a drum, and as the weight descended it turned the drum, which was attached to a drive shaft and gears that rotated the lens as it rolled on the chariot wheels. The speed at which the lens rotated depended on how fast the weight descended. The rate at which the lens flashed was determined by a combination of the speed of rotation and the number of flash panels: The faster the rotation and the greater the number of flash panels, the more flashes during a set period of time. To keep the lens rotating, the keeper would have to crank the drum periodically to pull up the cable and weight so that it continued to fall. The weight itself would either descend through the center of the lighthouse, within a column inside the spiral stairs, or it could be hidden within an enclosed shaft that ran down the lighthouse's wall.

ONE OF THE BOARD'S greatest challenges—perhaps even more so than having to modernize the Augean stables left by Pleasonton—was keeping up with America's growth. With Texas and California gaining statehood in 1845 and 1850, respectively, and the Oregon Territory being added to

Keeper Edwin J. Moore winding the clockwork mechanism for rotating the second-order Fresnel lens at the Grosse Point Lighthouse, in Evanston, Illinois, circa 1900. Note the chariot wheels near the top of the pedestal.

Matagorda Island Lighthouse, in Texas, circa 1945.

the nation in 1846, the length of the country's coastline had expanded dramatically. Even before the board came into existence, efforts were under way to light these new areas.

Texas officials began lobbying Washington for lighthouses soon after Texas became a state. Although legislators quickly came through with appropriations for lighthouses at the mouth of Galveston and Matagorda Bays, delays in gaining access to the land put off construction, and these first two lighthouses in Texas were not lit until 1852. The Bolivar Lighthouse (Galveston) and the Matagorda Island Lighthouse were identical cast-iron towers, lined with brick for added strength, corrosion protection, and insulation. Fitted with fourteen of Lewis's patented lamps and reflectors that shone seventy-nine feet above sea level, both lighthouses served busy ports of entry that were conduits for a vibrant trade with England, France, and the rest of the United States in a range of goods, including lumber, cattle, molasses, and cotton—the most lucrative export of all. Toward the end of the 1850s, after determining that neither lighthouse was tall enough to provide a sufficient warning to mariners, the board raised both of them another twenty-four feet and, to improve them even further, gave them third-order revolving Fresnel lenses. By the end of the 1850s more than a dozen lighthouses and lightships were spread along the Texas coast.

———

THE WEST COAST POSED another challenge. Extending from the bottom of California to the northern tip of the Oregon Territory, this thirteen-hundred-mile-long coastline is a jagged stretch of rocky, towering headlands with numerous offshore reefs and ledges. It is swept by mighty currents, regularly enveloped in thick fogs, blasted by fearsome gales, and buffeted by mammoth waves that have thousands of miles of open ocean to build. All these factors conspired to wreck many Spanish, Russian, English, and American ships between the sixteenth and mid-nineteenth centuries. And throughout all that time there was not a single lighthouse on the west coast to help mariners avoid disaster and find a welcoming port.

When the United States organized the Oregon Territory in 1848, it authorized the construction of two lighthouses—one at Cape Disappointment* near the mouth of the Columbia River, and the other at New Dungeness Spit in the Strait of Juan de Fuca (both of these falling within the boundaries of what would later be Washington State). The discovery of gold in California that same year dramatically expanded the government's plans for west coast lighthouses, as gold fever, which had already infected California, engulfed the rest of the country. Soon hundreds of ships from eastern ports ran the gauntlet around the deadly and unforgiving waters of Cape Horn on their way to California, where they deposited hordes of people all drawn to what largely remained a mirage of precious gold. The population of San Francisco, formerly a sleepy little town, swelled to more than twenty thousand by the end of 1849, and

---

*It was so named by the English explorer and fur trader Capt. John Meares, who was disappointed that on his voyage to the Pacific Northwest in 1788 he was unable to find the mouth of a great river (later called the Columbia) that was noted on Spanish charts. Since Meares was just off the Cape at the time—and thus very near the mouth of the Columbia, although he was oblivious to that fact—he christened the promontory Cape Disappointment.

continued growing at an exponential rate. With so many ships heading to the new El Dorado, Congress decided that California too would need lighthouses to help guide the way.

During the presidency of Zachary Taylor, Congress tasked the Coast Survey in 1849 with determining where lighthouses should be placed along the west coast, and the survey recommended that sixteen be built. Although Congress authorized eight of these as early as 1850, it wasn't until 1852 that the Baltimore builders Francis A. Gibbons and Francis S. Kelly were awarded the contract, the delays resulting primarily from lags in appropriations plus a congressional investigation into improprieties resulting from the contracting process.

The delays didn't sit well with west coast merchants or politicians. In 1851 a group of San Francisco merchants wrote to Stephen Pleasonton, telling him of the "great and immediate necessity" of building a lighthouse at the mouth of the harbor, "the want of [which] has caused great detention, inconvenience, as well as the total loss of many vessels bound into this port." That same year the California senator William McKendree Gwin complained to his congressional colleagues that although his state had paid millions to the Treasury in customs duties the previous year and was more than four times the geographic size of New York, with a much larger seacoast, it still was "utterly destitute of light-house establishments, necessary and indispensable to our commercial marine in approaching her coasts." A little more than a month after Gwin delivered his impassioned speech, Gibbons and Kelly got the contract, and the first eight west coast lighthouses were finally given the green light.

Seven of the lighthouses were to be built in California, including ones at Alcatraz Island (in San Francisco Bay), not yet a prison, Fort Point (at the entrance to the bay), Southeast Farallon Island (about twenty-five miles west of the Golden Gate), Point Loma in San Diego, Point Conception in Santa Barbara, Point Pinos in Monterey, and Humboldt Harbor near California's northern border. The lone lighthouse in the Oregon Territory was to be at Cape Disappointment.

All the lighthouses were slated to have the same design, that being a keeper's house with the tower rising from its center. The towers would not have to be very tall because of geography. Unlike the east coast, where many lighthouses were located close to sea level, and therefore needed to be tall so that their beams could be seen far away, the great height of much of the west coast's shoreline gave even relatively short lighthouses an impressive elevation. If anything, the problem on the west coast was making sure that lighthouses were not *too* high, for if they were their beam could be obscured by the low-hanging clouds or the fogs that often blanketed the region. And, in fact, a number of west coast lighthouses had to be relocated to lower elevations for that very reason.

Gibbons and Kelly dispatched the bark *Oriole* from Baltimore on August 12, 1852, with twenty-eight men and all the construction materials that would be needed to build the lighthouses, save for the bricks and stone, which were to be obtained locally. After rounding Cape Horn, the *Oriole* sailed into San Francisco at the end of January 1853. Another construction party had already arrived via the Panama route and was working on the foundations of the lighthouses at Alcatraz and Fort Point. Soon the lighthouses at Point Pinos and the Farallons were also underway. But at this last location Gibbons and Kelly's men ran into a problem caused by eggs.

FARALLÓN IS SPANISH FOR "rocky islet in the ocean," but an even better name for these islands is the "the Devil's Teeth," which is what nineteenth-century mariners called them on account of their fearsome appearance and the threat they posed to ships. The Farallons' tall, jagged granite peaks and ridges had long been a magnet for wildlife, and in the early 1800s the islands were raided by Russians and Americans who killed thousands of fur seals and sea otters, the pelts being sold for great profits in China. The Russians also harvested eggs from a bird called the common murre, whose breeding colonies blanketed the islands. Soon after the gold rush began, common murre eggs became a coveted commodity in California.

Since there weren't many chickens in California in the mid-1800s, Californians hankering for omelets, cakes, or any other food that relied

*A common murre
pair looking down on
their egg, on the
Farallon Islands.*

on eggs as an ingredient would have to do without these gustatory plea-
sures unless they could find a replacement. Enter the common murre.
With its distinctive black-and-white coloration, the common murre looks
a bit like a penguin, especially as it waddles about on land, and is about
the size of a small duck. The common murre's flesh is not very palatable,
but its eggs are as big as a goose's and were more than adequate as a substitute for chicken eggs. While some claimed that common murre eggs
had a slightly fishy taste, one nineteenth-century commentator said they
were "rich, delicate, and altogether desirable,—dropped,* fried, boiled,
or cooked in any of the hundred ways known to Frenchmen."

By the time that Gibbons and Kelly's men arrived at Southeast Farallon Island in April 1853, the Pacific Egg Company was engaged in a
lucrative business collecting as many as a million common murre eggs
and selling them in San Francisco for a dollar or more a dozen, generating annual sales as high as two hundred thousand dollars. The egging

---

*This word, still in use in parts of New England, means "poached."

season lasted from early May to the middle of July, and that is when the eggers, as the collectors were called, descended on the islands. They donned large cotton flour sacks with holes cut in the bottom for their head and arms, as well as a v-shaped slit in the front, into which the eggs were deposited. Tightly tied around their waist, the sack, or "egg shirt," became a capacious carrying pouch able to hold two hundred or more eggs. Instead of leather, the soles of their shoes were made of braided rope studded with nails, which offered better purchase on the steep, sharp, and often slippery slopes. Thus attired, large crews of eggers would search the island for nests to plunder. And all the while swarms of ravenous, noisy seagulls with sharp beaks and talons shadowed the eggers, swooping in at every opening to try to snatch the eggs before the men could. At the end of the day the eggs were deposited in baskets, cleaned with salt water, and placed in a storage shed, from which they were taken a few times a week and shipped to San Francisco's markets. It was dangerous business, and more than a few eggers lost their footing and fell to their death.

The Pacific Egg Company, not unnaturally, viewed the island as its domain and didn't want the government building a lighthouse whose beams might threaten their lucrative enterprise by scaring away the birds. The eggers, therefore, refused to let the lighthouse builders come ashore. When the local customs collector learned of this standoff, he dispatched a Coast Survey ship with a complement of heavily armed soldiers who quickly persuaded the eggers to back down.

Soon after the builders landed, however, they realized they had another problem. The best location for the lighthouse was at the peak of the island, 348 feet above sea level, but it was not big enough to serve as a foundation for the keeper's quarters and the lighthouse tower. Instead they built the tower on the peak, and the quarters on a flat plain closer to the water. Constructing the tower, in particular, was a grueling ordeal. Its walls were made from granite quarried on the island, and were then finished off with a facing of bricks. To ascend to the peak, the men had to scale slopes that were a dizzying forty-five to sixty-five degrees. In an effort to make that task a little easier, the men chiseled more than four

An egger on South Farallon Island, his shirt filled with common murre eggs, circa late 1800s.

hundred steps out of the rock, creating a path that snaked its way to the summit. Even with this assist, the men were forced to use their hands as well as their feet, or risk losing their hold and plummeting in some spots as much as two hundred feet to an almost certain death. The bricks were transported four of five at a time on the men's backs, and to get them the final distance to the top a windlass had to be employed. These difficulties notwithstanding, the quarters and the forty-one-foot tower were completed by August 1853.

The *Oriole* next headed north to build the lighthouse at Cape Disappointment, but on September 19 it wrecked on the bar of the Columbia River—an ironic twist given the men's mission to establish a lighthouse intended to save ships from destruction. Although all the men on board were rescued, the ship and its contents were a total loss. In the coming months the men obtained additional ships and supplies, and, splitting up, continued work not only the lighthouse at Cape Disappointment, but also the ones at Humboldt Bay, Point Conception, and Point Loma.

The first eight lighthouses were completed by August 1854, but only one of them had been lit by that time—Alcatraz, whose third-order Fresnel lens came to life on June 1, 1854. Part of the reason the other lighthouses remained dark was delays in getting Fresnel lenses from France, whose lens makers were being overwhelmed by the great volume of orders, not only from the United States but also other countries as well as France itself. Another reason was that some of the lantern rooms were too small.

The original contract called for each of the lighthouses to be fitted with Lewis's patented lamps and reflectors, and the designs for the lantern rooms reflected those dimensions. Even though the secretary of the Treasury amended the contract before the *Oriole* left, telling Gibbons and Kelly that the government would provide Fresnel lenses for all the lighthouses, the specifications for the lighthouses themselves were not altered, which posed a problem since many of the lenses were taller and wider than Lewis's apparatus. This disconnect resulted in some of the towers being modified, and three of them—at South Farallon, Point Conception, and Cape Disappointment—had to be completely torn down and rebuilt. Not surprisingly, rebuilding Farallon Lighthouse proved to be the greatest challenge of all.

The Farallon's first-order Fresnel lens arrived in San Francisco in December 1854 on board the French clipper *St. Joseph*, which also brought an eagerly anticipated cargo of French wine for the locals. The enormous lens came in seventy-three crates, some as large as sixty-seven cubic feet, or about the size of a commercial refrigerator. Gibbons and Kelly's men immediately realized that the lens would not fit in the lighthouse's lantern room, so the boxes were left at the docks. It wasn't until the next summer, when the engineer Hartman Bache arrived on the scene to take over as west coast lighthouse inspector that the problem was resolved.

Bache told his superiors about the struggle involved in building the lighthouse the first time, yet he was confident that, "however great the difficulties," the lighthouse could be rebuilt. But there was one major obstacle. The lens would have to be taken to the summit in its boxes, which, given their size and "ungainly" shapes, would be a task "only second to an impossible one." The sole solution, Bache said, was to build

Farallon Island Lighthouse on Southeast Farallon Island, off the coast of California, circa 1856. The lighthouse is visible at the top of the highest peak. The drawing, by T. E. Sandgren, was based on a sketch by Maj. Hartman Bache.

a zigzag road to the top, and get a mule to help with the labor. When his bosses in Washington balked at the tremendous cost, Bache replied if the road weren't built, "the light will never be exhibited." Bache got the money, his road, and a mule, and the lighthouse was rebuilt and shining forth by the end of 1855.

After the ship *Lucas* lost its way in the fog and crashed off the Farallon Islands in 1858, Bache decided that a fog signal was an absolute necessity. His solution was novel to say the least. He found a cave at the edge of South Farallon Island that had a hole in its roof. When conditions were rough and the waves were large and frothy, they slammed into the island and surged into the cave, violently displacing the air, which, having only one avenue of escape, rushed out the hole with tremendous velocity. Taking advantage of this naturally explosive vent, Bache inserted a train whistle into the hole. When the air rushed out of the cave, the whistle screamed. Any time the surf was high the ingenious fog signal worked beautifully, but there were a number of problems inherent in the design. It was often the case that the wind and waves were high when the weather was clear and visibility not an issue. Still the whistle would blow. And unfortunately, more often than not, when the fog was dense, the sea was relatively calm, and the whistle silent. Furthermore, at extreme low tide, regardless of the conditions of the ocean, the signal would stand mute because the mouth of cave remained exposed. This unique and fickle signal remained in operation until 1875, when a violent storm obliterated it. Not until five years later did South Farallon get a brand-new steam-powered siren.

BY THE END OF 1856 the first eight lighthouses were all shining with Fresnel lenses, but at that point there were already other lighthouses on the west coast, reflecting the rapid growth in Southern California as well as to the north, in Oregon. Not long after the *Oriole* left Baltimore, Congress funded eight more beacons, including three in California located at Point Bonita, Santa Barbara, Crescent City; and five in the Oregon Territory located at the mouth of the Umpqua River, Smith Island, New Dungeness Spit, Willapa Bay, and Tatoosh Island, the most northwesterly point in the contiguous United States, which today is part of Washington State. All these were built by local contractors, and lit by the end of 1858.

The building of the Tatoosh Island Lighthouse proved to be the most controversial, at least to the local Makah Indians. *Tatoosh* is the Makah word for "thunderbird," one of their native gods. According to Indian legend, when this fantastical bird opened it mouth, lightning fractured the sky, creating a thunderous noise. Since time immemorial the Native Americans had used the eighteen-acre island, located about three-quarters of a mile off of Cape Flattery, as a place to fish, whale, farm, celebrate rituals, and sometimes bury their dead. When the first survey crews arrived in the early 1850s to scout the island for a suitable location for the lighthouse, they were greeted by about 150 Indians who were understandably none too happy about the white men tramping on their land. George Davidson, the head of the survey team, fearing an Indian attack, built a breastwork, behind which stood armed sentries. This show of force maintained the peace.

Reflecting the growing animosity between the Indians who had inhabited these lands for thousands of years, and the increasing number of American settlers in the area, tensions flared again when another survey team arrived on the steamer *Active* in the summer of 1853. Earlier that year a smallpox epidemic had decimated the Makah population, killing some five hundred, about half the tribe. (The disease was most likely introduced by American fur traders, whom the Indians called "Bostons," since so many of the traders hailed from that city.) This devastating loss, plus the arrival of a new contingent of whites, put the Makah in an angry mood, eager to fight to avenge the deaths of their fellow tribe members, and to preserve the land that they felt was rightfully theirs. They were soon joined by a large party of Haida, who were well known and feared for their fierceness in battle. So as not to arouse suspicion, the Haida disguised themselves as traders. Any thoughts the Indians had of attacking, however, disappeared as soon as the heavily armed *Active* fired a salvo of menacing warning shots from its cannons.

In predictable fashion in 1855 the Makah signed the Treaty of Neah Bay with the governor of the recently created Washington Territory, relinquishing their rights to many of their ancestral lands, including Tatoosh Island, for thirty thousand dollars, and leaving them in return a small reservation. Nevertheless, when the workers arrived in 1855 to build the lighthouse, the situation continued to simmer and remained tense. The Indians wandered about the island, occasionally stealing tools, food, and other items from the workers. To protect themselves from a possible attack, the workers built a blockhouse and stocked it with muskets and gunpowder—which they fortunately never had to use.

Despite interference from the Indians, stretches of miserable weather, and delays in obtaining materials, the Tatoosh Island Lighthouse was completed in late December 1857 and staffed by four keepers. Retaining keepers, especially in the early years, proved difficult. Within six months after the lighthouse began operating, five keepers resigned. One of their complaints—along with concerns about poor living conditions and inadequate pay—was the fear of being attacked by the Indians, who often showed up on the island in large numbers and forced their way into the lighthouse, which fascinated them because of the unfamiliar tools and technologies it contained. This fear was not without grounds. In at least two instances Indians had struck a keeper, and a few times they threatened to kill one. New keepers were brought in, however, and with

Cape Flattery Lighthouse, 1962.

the U.S. military ready to take action if need be, an uneasy truce was maintained. In later years the friction between the Indians, long since subjugated, and the keepers was largely eliminated, and the name of the station was changed to Cape Flattery Lighthouse.

A SENSE OF THE great transformation that had taken place on the west coast can be gleaned from the comments of Richard Henry Dana, a prominent Boston lawyer and author of the phenomenally successful book, *Two Years Before the Mast*. Published in 1840, the book recounts Dana's voyage on the brig *Alert* in the mid-1830s, cruising the coast of California collecting and curing cowhides. In an addendum to that book, written years later, Dana recalled the first time the *Alert* sailed into "the vast solitude of San Francisco Bay," where there was little sign of human habitation, adding that "on the whole coast of California there was not a lighthouse, a beacon, or a buoy." But in 1859, when Dana returned to San Francisco, now a "great center of world-wide commerce," he noted how, "miles out at sea, on the desolate rocks of the Farallons, gleamed the powerful rays of one of the most costly and effective lighthouses in the world. As we drew in through the Golden Gate, another lighthouse met our eyes." Farther down the coast, while sailing by Point Conception at night, Dana recorded seeing "a cheery light gleaming over the waters from its tall lighthouse standing on its outermost peak."

THE INTRODUCTION OF LIGHTHOUSES and the transformation on the west coast and in Texas was only part of the much larger, and equally dramatic, change that was being wrought. The Lighthouse Board had taken a poorly functioning, poorly managed lighthouse establishment and, in relatively short order, turned it into an efficient, effective, and respected system of national illumination. In 1856 America already had more than twice as many lighthouses as Great Britain, and almost one-third as many as the rest of the nations combined. By the end of that politically fraught decade there were 425 American lighthouses, an impressive increase from the 325 lighthouses the board had inherited. Virtually every one of those

Point Conception Lighthouse, in Santa Barbara, California, circa 1856. In the foreground is the fog bell being carted to the lighthouse by horses and oxen. The drawing, by T. E. Sandgren, was based on a sketch by Maj. Hartman Bache.

lighthouses now boasted a Fresnel lens. As Levitt points out, "In a few short years, the United States had gone from having the least number of . . . [Fresnel lenses] to the most, by a staggering margin."

Léonor Fresnel, observing these changes from his native France, marveled at America's achievement. "The prodigious development of this service within so short a time under the Lighthouse Board has truly astonished me. My old experience, in fact, enables me the better to appreciate how much energy and activity were necessary to bring to this degree of perfection the lighthouse service of such a vast expanse of coast." Not only were the lights brighter, but also they were cheaper to operate, contrary to everything that Pleasonton had claimed. As the Lighthouse Board's report in 1852 had predicted, the lenses generated at least four times the illumination of the reflectors they replaced, and used only about one-fourth the oil. Therefore, with every year that passed, the lenses were helping to pay for themselves.

After years of bureaucratic obstinacy and official shortsightedness, America's lighthouses were finally up to par, yet at this very moment of great success troubling signs loomed on the horizon. The long-simmering conflict between the Northern and Southern states, primarily fueled by unresolvable differences over slavery, was reaching a veritable boil, and threatening to sunder the Union in two. And when the Civil War finally broke out, many of America's lighthouses would become targets in the nation's bloodiest war, strategic assets that would figure among its many casualties.

CHAPTER 8

"EVERYTHING BEING RECKLESSLY BROKEN"

. . . .

Rubble was all that was left of the Charleston Lighthouse after Confederate forces blew it up in December 1861. This daguerreotype was made in the summer of 1863.

No PRESIDENTIAL ELECTION IN AMERICAN HISTORY CAUSED more political reverberations than that of Abraham Lincoln, an outspoken opponent of the expansion of slavery, who was elected on November 6, 1860. The acrimony that characterized the campaign only intensified in the period immediately afterward, fanning the long-smoldering embers of secession into an outright conflagration. Nowhere was this felt more deeply or intensely than in South Carolina. When South Carolina's secession convention met six weeks later on December 17, it was a fore-gone conclusion that the state would break from the Union, and that when it did, it would move to take control of all federal property within its bor-ders. That is what greatly concerned naval commander T. T. Hunter, the lighthouse inspector in charge at Charleston. Accordingly, he wrote to the Lighthouse Board on December 18, asking what he should do when the state demanded that he turn over all the lighthouses.

The secretary of the Treasury responded on behalf of the board, curtly telling Hunter that although the department couldn't give him any specific instructions, he was still accountable under the law for all the lighthouse property in his district. This "you're on your own" response undoubtedly shocked Hunter, telling him that not only was he solely responsible for holding out against a state bitterly hostile to the federal government, but that if he capitulated in any way he would liable for the loss.

There was, however, one person at the board who knew exactly what Hunter should do—naval commander Raphael Semmes. Semmes had fought in the Mexican-American War, and just prior to being appointed secretary of the board in 1858 he served as a lighthouse inspector for the Caribbean and Gulf Coasts. He was the first to see Hunter's letter, and it prompted him to write a note to the secretary of the Treasury, Philip

Raphael Semmes,
circa 1862.

F. Thomas, arguing that the lighthouses should be handed over to the state, adding that it would be a grave mistake to have "the coast of South Carolina be lighted by the Federal Government against her will." Semmes's perspective, amenable of course to South Carolina residents, made perfect sense given his loyalties, and his secret plans for the future.

Born in 1809 in Charles County, Maryland, along the banks of the Potomac, Semmes was a slightly built man, weighing around 130 pounds and standing about five feet seven, just below the average height for the time. He had piercing gray eyes, and in addition to a small goatee, he sported a conspicuously long mustache that flared out on both sides of his face, the ends of which he waxed into fine points and kept well trimmed and continually groomed to retain their proper shape. Semmes's cool and forceful personality, as well as his keen intellect, commanded the respect of those around him.

Semmes with his family moved to Alabama in 1841, and it was in the Deep South that his allegiances lay. Lincoln's election had convinced him that there was no hope for reconciliation between the North and the South, although he didn't think that a war would have to be fought to effect the separation. When the split occurred, Semmes planned to resign from federal service and follow his conscience. A little more than a week before Hunter's letter landed on his desk, Semmes had written to Alexander H. Stephens, the future vice president of the Confederate States of America, asking him to support his admission to the "Navy of the Southern Republic" when the time came. "I am still at my post at the Lighthouse Board," Semmes told Stephens, "performing my routine duties, but listening with an aching ear, and a beating heart for the first sounds of the great disruption which is at hand." That disruption was not long in coming.

So VIRULENT WERE THE feelings toward Lincoln that on December 20 South Carolina became the first state to secede. The situation in Charleston's harbor had become quite tense by the end of the month. Maj. Robert Anderson, who was in charge of federal troops in the area, gathered them together at the yet-to-be completed Fort Sumter, a three-tiered, pentagonal fortification located at the harbor's mouth on an artificial island made of thousands of tons of granite. He chose that location believing that it would give his relatively small number of men the best chance of defending themselves against a possible attack by the South Carolina troops who were taking up positions along the shore.

Concerned that Washington might send reinforcements to Fort Sumter, South Carolina governor Francis Pickens, a wealthy landowner and former American ambassador to Russia, resolved to make their approach as difficult as possible. Thus he had all the buoys in the harbor removed, and he ordered his troops to take control of three of the lighthouses located in and around the harbor—at Castle Pinckney, Sullivan's Island, and Morris Island—and extinguish their lights. Pickens also ordered Hunter to leave the state, which he did in early January. (He was not, however, ultimately held responsible by the board for the loss of the lighthouses.)

The federal reinforcements Pickens anticipated and feared arrived not long after midnight on January 9, 1861, aboard the *Star of the West*, a civilian steamer leased by the army, which had departed New York City four days earlier. The only lighthouse in the harbor still shining was the one at Fort Sumter with its fourth-order Fresnel lens, now operated by Major Anderson's troops. That light alone, however, was not enough of a guide for the *Star of the West* to risk trying to get over the Charleston Bar, a series of submerged shoals about eight miles southeast of the city, forcing the Union men to wait until dawn to make their approach.

The *Star of the West*'s expedition was supposed to be secret, but word of its mission had leaked to the press, and the South Carolinians were ready. Pickens, worried that Morris Island might be taken over by Northern troops, and had already had the lighthouse's first-order lens taken down and buried in the sand to keep it from being used by the enemy. As soon as the *Star of the West* approached the harbor, South Carolinian troops began firing cannons, hitting the ship twice but causing little damage. The *Star of the West* was not prepared for this assault and incapable of mounting a defense, so the captain put the ship about and returned to New York.

Over the next few months, as the standoff continued between Ander-son's troops at Fort Sumter and the growing number of Southern troops massing along the harbor's edge, the Confederacy, as it would be known, came into being. By the beginning of February, six more states had seceded, including Alabama, and they had hammered out a provisional Confederate constitution that would be formally adopted a month later.

In the late afternoon of February 14, Semmes was at home with his family in Washington, DC, still biding his time, embedded within the bureaucracy of a federal government to which he felt no loyalty, when a messenger delivered a telegram that changed the trajectory of his life. The Committee on Naval Affairs of the Provisional Confederate States of America wanted Semmes to come to Montgomery as soon as possible. "Here was the sound for which I had been so anxiously listening," Sem-mes later wrote. "Secession was now indeed a reality, and the time had come for me to arouse myself to action." That evening he composed a let-ter to the committee, telling them that he would be there "immediately."

The next morning Semmes severed all his ties with the North. First, he submitted his resignation as commander in the U.S. Navy. Next he resigned from the Lighthouse Board, having only two days earlier been promoted from secretary to one of the board's two main naval positions after the death of one of the other members. His letter to the board was gracious, thanking the members for their courteous treatment of him over the years, but it was not acknowledged with so much as a receipt. Semmes attributed this slight to the fact that there were other Southern-ers on the board, including its chairman, Commodore Shubrick, a South Carolinian, who had also been wooed to join the Confederacy but had decided to stay put—a decision Semmes viewed with no small amount of disdain.

Semmes said his tearful good-byes to his Ohio-born wife and family—who would spend the next few years in Cincinnati—and headed for Montgomery, where Confederate president Jefferson Davis ordered him to travel to New York to buy arms for the South, this still being a time, before the actual outbreak of war, when Southerners and North-erners were relatively free to travel anywhere in the States and conduct business. Soon after returning to Montgomery on April 4, Semmes was appointed head of the Confederate Lighthouse Bureau, which had been created just a month earlier as a result of his own recommendation. He barely had time to settle in and appoint clerks before, as he later recalled, "Fort Sumter was fired upon, and the tocsin of war was sounded."

IN HIS INAUGURAL ADDRESS on March 4, 1861,[*] Lincoln proclaimed that he would use his "power" to "hold, occupy, and possess, the property and places belonging to the Government." One of those places, in his estimation, was Fort Sumter. This created an immediate problem, because Major Anderson and his men—having held out for months, besieged by Southern forces—were desperately low on food, and if they weren't resupplied soon they would have to surrender. On April 4 Lincoln sent unarmed transports with provisions for Sumter, along with an armed escort of ships. Not wanting to provoke the South into starting a war, Lincoln told Jefferson Davis this was strictly a humanitarian mission, and that the armed ships were only to respond if the transports were fired upon. Davis's government, however, had already decided that it couldn't allow the North to retain control of Sumter because, as the historian James McPherson has pointed out, "The Confederacy could not be considered a viable nation so long as a foreign power held a fort in one of it principal harbors." At 4:30 in the morning on April 12, Confederate batteries began shelling Fort Sumter, and thirty-four hours later, having withstood a thunderous barrage that gravely damaged much of the fort, Anderson raised the white flag and surrendered. With that, the bloodiest war in American history commenced.

Semmes knew what he had to do. He hated working behind a desk, and longed for military glory, especially now that his beloved South had struck the first salvo and he could devote his life to a cause he believed

---

[*] Not until the Twentieth Amendment was ratified in 1933 was Inauguration Day moved to January 20.

in. The "Light-House Bureau was no longer to be thought of," Semmes wrote. "It had become necessary for every man, who could wield a sword, to draw it in defense of his country, thus threatened by the swarming hordes of the North, and to leave the things of peace to the future." On April 18 he resigned his post at the newly formed bureau he created, and was given command of the CSS *Sumter,* one of the few ships in the nascent Confederate navy. Over the next few years, captaining both the *Sumter* and the CSS *Alabama,* Semmes terrorized Union merchant ships on the high seas, capturing or burning more than eighty-six vessels, in the process becoming a hero to the South and a villain to the North.

The day after Semmes resigned, Lincoln announced a blockade of most of the Southern coast from South Carolina to Texas. Eight days later he expanded the blockade to include the coasts of Virginia, which seceded on April 17, and North Carolina, which would do so on May 20. Rather than blanket the entire Southern coast, which stretched 3,500 miles, the blockade was intended to put a stranglehold on the major Southern ports, thereby keeping the South from importing the materials it needed to wage war, including arms, iron, machinery, medicine, and food, while at the same time cutting off exports of such Southern products as turpentine, tobacco, and, most important, cotton, the South's number one source of revenue.

The South responded to the blockade by extinguishing its lighthouses, just as the United States had done during the War of 1812, and the colonies had done during the Revolutionary War. It is not clear from the records who issued the order to put out the lights, but it appears that it came from either the Lighthouse Bureau, local military officials, or possibly both. No matter who gave the order, it was strategically motivated. Confederate blockade-runners were very familiar with the coast and could dart in and out of harbors and bays, running along the shore in the dark of night without having to rely on lighthouse beams to show them the way and keep them from harm. Union ships didn't share that familiarity, and the darkened coast put them at a grave disadvantage. With the lights out, Union ships would find it more difficult to navigate and would be placed in greater jeopardy of wrecking, making the extensive blockade that much harder to enforce. Despite this wartime logic, some keepers were conflicted about executing this order. The purpose of lighthouses was to aid mariners, and the keepers took that responsibility seriously. Dousing the lights went against their professional and, in some cases, moral sensibilities. Nevertheless most keepers promptly complied, and in a number of instances, military men took the lead in turning off the lights. As a result, by the end of April almost the entire Southern coast was dark.

Many in the North decried this purported dereliction of duty. The popular weekly *Frank Leslie's Illustrated Newspaper* wrote, "After the bombardment of Fort Sumter, the Confederate Government, with that murderous indifference to human life which has distinguished them from the first, extinguished all the lights they could reach." To the South, however, it wasn't a case of "murderous indifference" but rather a sensible decision to make under the exigencies of war. And it was one that proved effective. As Theresa Levitt observes, "The blackened coast made life difficult for the Union, which lost more ships in grounding accidents than in all of the war's naval battles."

Not long after the lights went out, the Confederate Lighthouse Bureau ordered that lighthouse materials, including the lamps, the rotating machinery, and especially the valuable Fresnel lenses be removed for safekeeping. This, too, was a strategic decision. By eliminating these materials the Confederacy attempted to achieve two goals: the first being to keep them out of the hands of the Yankees, thereby making it more difficult for the Union to relight darkened towers if they recaptured Southern lighthouses. The second goal was to protect the lighthouse equipment so that if the Confederacy emerged victorious—as it fervently believed it would—it could quickly reestablish the lighthouses and welcome back the crucial trade and commerce they facilitated. At many lighthouses, keepers, customs collectors, and military personnel removed the materials and shipped them inland to warehouses or stored them near the lighthouses, sometimes burying them in the dirt or even in riverbeds.

———

AS THE NORTH AND SOUTH squared off against each other, Southern lighthouses were drawn into the fight. Some were the focal point for battles, while others were ruinously set ablaze, blown up, or otherwise vandalized. On the east coast Cape Hatteras Lighthouse, North Carolina's towering sentinel, was one of the first to be caught up in the action.

During the war Cape Hatteras retained its distinction as the most dangerous stretch of coast in the country. No fewer than forty Union navy ships grounded in the area, leading some to quip that "a few more shoals might have helped the South win the war." It wasn't only the navy that suffered, however. After the Cape Hatteras Lighthouse was darkened in April 1861, the Cape became especially perilous to Northern commercial vessels as well, which began foundering on the shoals in increasing numbers. The *Linwood*, bound from Rio de Janeiro to New York with six thousand bags of coffee on board, was one such casualty. Near midnight on July 17, while off Cape Hatteras, the captain of the *Linwood* posted a man to keep a lookout for the lighthouse's beam to guide the ship past this treacherous spot. As the captain later testified, it was "in consequence of the absence of the light that the ship struck."

Merchants and the companies that insured them complained bitterly to government officials about these accidents, demanding that the Cape Hatteras Lighthouse be relit as soon as possible. Sensitive to these pleas, and wanting to reestablish the lighthouse as well, Union officials also had other reasons for wanting to control Cape Hatteras, especially Cape Hatteras Inlet, the narrow passageway between Hatteras and the Ocracoke Islands, which connected the Atlantic Ocean to Pamlico Sound. For months Confederate vessels, part of the so-called Mosquito Fleet—named for the small size of the gunboats comprising it—had been launching raids from the inlet, attacking Northern merchantmen and taking them as prizes; this too raised howls of complaint from Northern shipping interests. Additionally, the inlet was an important supply route for the Confederacy, and cutting it off would be a boon to the Union. Thus, to eliminate the threat posed by what Union secretary of the navy

Gideon Welles called "nests of pirates," to capture and reestablish the lighthouse, and to cut off the supply route, the U.S. Navy sent seven warships south in August 1861 to take Cape Hatteras.

When the fleet arrived it attacked Forts Hatteras and Clark, both of which the Confederates had only recently finished building near Hatteras Inlet to protect the channel. Neither fort was awe-inspiring, their outer walls being made of mounded dirt and sand, covered by wooden planking and marsh-grass sod. Although the men in the forts did their best to defend their positions, they were severely overmatched. The fort's relatively small cannons had a limited range, and their shells fell harmlessly in the water, far short of the Union ships. Those ships, by contrast, were armed with enormous cannons that unleashed a tremendous barrage, which, during a single three-hour stretch, pummeled Fort Hatteras with three thousand shells. On August 29, a day after the Union onslaught began, the battle was over, both forts having surrendered.

Though this was a fairly minor battle in the terrible scheme of the Civil War, since it was the Union's first real victory it nonetheless had a huge impact on the North. Reportedly, when Lincoln was awakened and informed what had happened, he dashed into the Cabinet Room and danced a jig in his nightshirt. One of the Union officers, who had been providing reports to the *New York Evening Post*, added his own thoughts on the engagement's significance. Cape Hatteras, he wrote, is "a place which is of such vast importance to us. It is the key of the State of North Carolina, and to the ports north and south of this. . . . With the possession of this port we can easily keep alight Hatteras lighthouse."

This officer, however, spoke too soon: Cape Hatteras's first-order Fresnel lens had been removed earlier that summer. Thus the hopes of the Union naval commander, S. C. Rowan, of quickly rekindling the Cape Hatteras Lighthouse were dashed. As he wrote to Welles, "I was desirous of lighting Hatteras light, but to my great regret I learn that the lens has been taken down and is now in Washington [NC] or Raleigh." Before any attempt could be made to recover the lens, Cape Hatteras Lighthouse itself was threatened.

———

AT THE END OF SEPTEMBER, Col. Rush C. Hawkins, who commanded the Union troops guarding Fort Hatteras, heard rumors that Confederate forces to the north on Roanoke Island were planning to retake Cape Hatteras. To foil such an attack, Hawkins led six hundred troops from the Twentieth Indiana Regiment north to the small town of Chicamacomico (modern-day Rodanthe) located about halfway between Hatteras Inlet and Roanoke Island. Soon thereafter the Union tug *Fanny* was dispatched to supply the men at Chicamacomico, but Confederate ships captured it. After interrogating Union troops on board the *Fanny*, the Confederate commander on Roanoke Island, Col. A. R. Wright, came to believe that the forces at Chicamacomico were planning to attack Roanoke Island. As it eventually turned out, neither the Union nor the Confederate forces had intended to attack the other, but as a result of the mistaken assumptions on both sides, a strange chase ensued.

Wright decided that the best defense was a good offense, so his plan was to land troops from the Third Georgia Regiment to the north of Chicamacomico, and to land additional troops from the North Carolina regiment below Chicamacomico, trapping the Twentieth Indiana. Once the Union troops were captured, Wright planned to march farther down the Cape, destroy the lighthouse, and then retake Forts Hatteras and Clark.

Things didn't work out the way Wright had hoped. On the morning of October 5, Hawkins saw Confederate vessels approaching from the north, as well as ones heading farther to the south. Realizing they were trying to surround him, Hawkins ordered an immediate retreat back to Cape Hatteras. As soon as the Third Georgia Regiment landed, it set off in pursuit of the fleeing Twentieth Indiana.

Since the Union troops had expected to be resupplied by the tug *Fanny*, they only brought one day's worth of supplies with them to Chicamacomico. As a result they had almost no food or water, and their retreat turned into a miserable slog over the sand under an unusually hot autumn sun. "The first ten miles were terrible," recalled one of the Indiana soldiers. "No water, the men unused to long marches, the sand heavy,

*Union soldiers of the Twentieth Indiana, encamped around the
base of the Cape Hatteras Lighthouse.*

their feet sinking into it at every step. As the regiment pushed along, man
after man would stagger from the ranks and fall upon the hot sand."

The planned landing of the North Carolinians never happened
because their transports grounded far offshore, and this allowed the
Twentieth Indiana to make it to the lighthouse at midnight, having covered twenty-eight miles in fifteen hours. "Here we found water," one of
the soldiers said, "and using the lighthouse as a fort, we encamped for
the night." At the same time the Georgian troops, also exhausted, set up
camp about six miles north of the lighthouse.

The next morning the tables were turned as the Ninth New York Regiment arrived at the lighthouse. With their force added to the Indiana's,
the Union troops took off after the Georgians, who were now forced to
retreat to Chicamacomico, whereupon the Union forces called off the
chase, and headed back to Fort Hatteras. This two-day affair, full of
energy and effort but of no real military consequence, was later dubbed
by historians the "Chicamacomico Races." The Confederates finally

made it back to Roanoke Island, and the lighthouse remained under Union control for the duration of the war.

BUT THE LIGHTHOUSE WAS still dark, much to the consternation of a group of Northern insurance company presidents, who wrote to the Lighthouse Board in early October 1861, pointing out that Hatteras was "a very important point on our coast and it is desirable the light be re-established as speedily as possible." Such pleas notwithstanding, it would be many months before the lighthouse shone again, in large part because the military situation remained unsettled, and Union officials, including the board, feared that if the lighthouse were relit, it might be attacked and destroyed by Confederate forces.

By the middle of March 1862, however, as more of the coast of North Carolina came under Union control, the board decided to relight Cape Hatteras. The lighthouse engineer W. J. Newman was dispatched to the Cape to evaluate the situation, and he found that the only machinery missing was the first-order lens and the lamps—the lens pedestal, base-plate, and revolving mechanism were all still intact. Although the board wanted to supply Newman with a first-order lens, the best it could do was scrounge up a second-order lens, which finally arrived at the Cape in early May. By the end of the month Newman's crew had the lens installed and operational, much to the delight of insurance companies, shipowners, and the Union navy. A year later the illumination improved when the second-order lens was replaced with one of the first order that had been purchased from France.

At the same time that the board decided to relight Cape Hatteras, the Union navy began searching for the missing lens. Informants told Union forces that the lens was in Washington, North Carolina, a small town located about twenty-five miles up the Pamlico River, whose mouth lies due east of Cape Hatteras. But when a naval expedition arrived in the town of Washington on March 21, the purloined lens was no longer there.

When the lens had first been removed from the lighthouse in the summer of 1861, it had indeed been transported to Washington and placed in the warehouse of John Myers, a merchant and shipbuilder. Washington was also the home of H. F. Hancock, the local lighthouse superinten- dent as well as the town druggist, who was supposed to take care of the lens. However, as Union forces advanced on Washington, the Confed- erate troops there fled, as did many of the town's residents, including Hancock.

This left Myers with a problem. If he left the lens in his warehouse, Union forces would surely find it, and as a loyal Southerner, this was an outcome he wanted to avoid at all costs. So, just hours before the Union expedition arrived, Myers had the boxes containing the lens and all its parts loaded onto the deck of the sternwheeler *Governor Morehead*, and accompanied them nearly fifty miles upriver to Tarboro.

When Rowan learned that the lens had been shipped to Tarboro, he demanded that it be given back, vowing to "hold the authorities respon- sible for the return of the lens before I promise protection to the inhab- itants" of Washington. Rowan also wrote to his superior officer that he would consider taking armed boats to Tarboro and "frighten[ing] the people out of their boots unless the lens was returned." These threats notwithstanding, Rowan didn't follow through, and the lens continued its dramatic inland odyssey.

Upon arriving in Tarboro, Myers handed the lens over to Confeder- ate army quartermaster George H. Brown, who immediately fired off a letter to the Confederate Lighthouse Bureau in Richmond urging it to send someone to take possession of the lens. Brown noted that he had been told that force would be used to get the lens back, and that Union officers had even threatened "the destruction of the town of Washington if the apparatus was not forthcoming." If the lens was not removed to a safer location, Brown feared that Tarboro might be the next target in the Union's campaign to reacquire it.

The Confederate Lighthouse Bureau sent J. B. Davidge—apparently a scoundrel more interested in drinking at the local bars than doing his duty—who soon left town, making off with the money to cover the costs of moving the lens. Fortunately for Brown he soon made the acquain- tance of a "very responsible gentleman," Dr. David T. Tayloe, a physician from Washington who had escaped the city and was on his way to join his family at Hibernia Plantation on the outskirts of Townsville, North Carolina, near the Virginia border. Tayloe agreed to take the lens with him, free of charge, as long as he was furnished with a means of transporting it. A railroad car was quickly requisitioned, and loaded with forty-four boxes and two cases containing the lens's prisms, along with sixty-four castings, fourteen fixtures, and two sheets of copper, all of which were also part of the lens apparatus.

Departing on April 14, 1862, Tayloe and his valuable cargo began an arduous five-day journey to Townsville, the trip taking far longer than expected on account of the decrepit condition of the train tracks, and the need to switch cars at one point. Soon after arriving and reuniting with his family, Tayloe wrote to the Lighthouse Bureau, proving his credentials as a trustworthy and responsible man, "I have had the apparatus removed to a good store house in the country and safely stored." And it remained hidden for the remainder of the war.

SHORTLY BEFORE UNION FORCES attacked the forts on Cape Hatteras in August 1861, another lighthouse drama played out in Florida, where "a band of lawless persons," as the Union's Lighthouse Board called them, took matters into their own hands. The problems began at the Jupiter Inlet Lighthouse, located on a small hill on the northern bank of the Loxahatchee River, as a result of a strong difference of opinion between the head keeper, Joseph Papy, and one of his assistants, Augustus Oswald Lang. Lang, an ardent Confederate, aware that lighthouses throughout the South had been extinguished as part of the war effort, repeatedly demanded that Papy pitch in and do the same. Papy refused, claiming that he would not do so until he received orders from the board. Some of his contemporaries argued that Papy's intransigence had more to do with his desire to continue receiving pay and provisions from the Union government than with any concern about protocol. Yet whatever the reason, Papy's stance infuriated the devoted partisan Lang, who quit his position on August 9, and headed forty miles north to discuss the matter with James E. Paine, another loyal

Southerner. The two of them quickly decided to preempt matters and do what Papy would not.

On August 15 Lang and Paine, along with one James Whitton, arrived at the Jupiter Inlet Lighthouse. Papy demanded to know their intentions, and upon being told, he asked under what authority they were acting. As Paine later wrote to the Confederate Secretary of the Treasury, "I informed him that we came as citizens of the Confederate States, to discharge a duty to our country . . . and that our acts would meet the approbation of our government." Papy, outnumbered and outgunned, stepped aside, and the raiding party went to work disabling the light. In keeping with the strategic goal of putting out the light, while maintaining its readiness should the South prevail, they later recalled, "we destroyed no property whatsoever, the light being a revolving one and of very costly make, we took away only enough of the machinery to make it unserviceable," and then locked the parts, as well as various tools and oil, in a shed near the lighthouse.

The group now set its sights on raiding the Cape Florida Lighthouse farther to the south, at the tip of Key Biscayne. And they had a new recruit, Papy's second assistant, Francis A. Ivey. Although Paine remained behind, Lang, Whitton, Ivey, and another man traveled on foot and by boat roughly ninety miles to the lighthouse, a grueling trip that tested their allegiance to the Confederate cause since they had very little food and were alternately pelted by torrential rains and baked by a scorching sun.

Lang and his associates had heard that the keepers at the Cape Florida Lighthouse were heavily armed, under instructions by Union officials not to surrender the facility, and had in fact "repeatedly boasted that they would defend the light to the last." These rumors were confirmed when the raiding party arrived near midnight on August 21, and discovered the two keepers holed up in the tower, barricaded behind its iron door, which they had bolted shut. Despite this fortification, a clever deception got the keepers to open the door. Lang knew the head keeper, Simeon Frow, and he also knew he was expecting supplies to be delivered from Key West. So the enterprising Lang shouted to Frow, telling him he had news from Key West. This brought both keepers down, and when they opened the door and saw four guns pointed at them, they gave up without a fight.

The raiding party decided that merely disabling the light would not do. As they later wrote in a letter to the governor of Florida, "The light being within the immediate protection of Key West and almost indispensible at this time to the enemy's fleet, as well as knowing it to be useless for us to try and hold it, we determined to damage it so that it will be of no possible use to our enemies." They smashed the lens and loaded the lighthouse boat with lamps, burners, and the keepers' guns before sailing back to the Jupiter Point Lighthouse, where they stored the materials.

These raids notwithstanding, Florida provided one of the few bright spots for the Lighthouse Board during the war. In mid-December 1860, when it was already quite clear that Florida would soon secede, forty-one-year-old Capt. James M. Brannan, who led the First Artillery stationed at Key West, sent a message to Washington asking if he should "endeavor at all hazards to prevent Fort [Zachary] Taylor [located on Key West] from being taken or allow the State authorities to have possession without any resistance on the part of his command." When Florida seceded on January 10, 1861, Brannan still had received no instructions. Three days later, unwilling to wait any longer, he made a crucial decision. In the dead of night as the city's residents were sleeping, Brannan marched his small force of forty-four men the four miles from their barracks to the still-unfinished fort. Brannan's quick action secured Key West for the Union, and with the fort as a base of operations, the Union navy was able to launch attacks, support its blockade of Southern and Gulf Coast ports, and also maintain control of most of the Florida Keys. This was not only a strategic windfall for Union forces, without which the outcome of the war might well have been different, but it also meant that the Keys' lighthouses, minus the severely damaged one at Cape Florida, could be protected. In fact the lighthouses at the Dry Tortugas, Key West, Sand Key, Sombrero Key, and Carysfort Reef were the only ones in the South that remained lit throughout the entire war, providing Union naval forces with much needed guiding lights as they traversed the treacherous waters off the south Florida coast. When Union Cdr. John R. Goldsborough visited Key West in January 1862, he noted with satisfaction that these lighthouses were "shining as the safeguards and symbols of fraternal commerce and peaceful civilization."

BEYOND CAPE HATTERAS AND FLORIDA, lighthouses at many other locations up and down the east coast found themselves caught in the crosshairs of war. In late March 1862, Samuel Francis Du Pont, the brave and highly competent commander of the South Atlantic Blockading Squadron, which patrolled the coast from South Carolina to Key West, visited some lighthouses in his area of jurisdiction and shared his findings with the Lighthouse Board (his interest in this activity, of course, was amplified by virtue of his having served on the board in the 1850s). What he found was a trail of destruction. While the tower at Cape Romain, South Carolina, remained still standing, the iron railing at the top was broken, and the lens "ruthlessly destroyed." The Bull's Bay Lighthouse, also in South Carolina, had been subjected to similar treatment, "everything being recklessly broken, down to the oil cans." Charleston's venerable lighthouse on Morris Island had been blown up the previous December because the Confederates feared that Union forces might capture the island and use the tower as a lookout in the event of an attack on the city. The *Charleston Mercury*'s report of the explosion observed that "nothing save a heap of ruins now marks the spot where" the lighthouse stood. And at Georgia's Tybee Island Lighthouse, when Confederate troops abandoned the island in November 1861 to consolidate their forces at nearby Fort Pulaski, they torched the interior of the lighthouse, leaving the lantern, according to Du Pont, "much injured" (the lighthouse's second-order Fresnel lens had already been removed and sent to Savannah).

Many other lighthouses could be added to Du Pont's list, among them the Cape Charles Lighthouse, located in Virginia near the entrance to Chesapeake Bay. Originally built on Smith Island in 1828, the lighthouse was just 55 feet tall, and in the mid-1850s the board decided that this critically important spot needed a 150-foot tower with a powerful first-order lens.

Burning of the Tybee Island Lighthouse by Confederate forces in November 1861.
Note the soldiers' barracks to the left of the tower.

The new tower had progressed to a height of 83 feet by the outbreak of the war, but in 1863, a party of Confederates, or "guerillas," as the board called them, destroyed the old tower, and "subjected" the construction materials stored on the ground to "indiscriminate pilfering and spoliation."

While virtually all the lighthouses damaged during the war were in Confederate states, there was at least one exception to this rule. In May 1864, twelve Confederates led by Capt. John M. Goldsmith landed on Blackistone Island (now St. Clement's Island), in Maryland, intent on destroying the lighthouse, which consisted of the keeper's house with a tower and lantern room rising from its center. The keeper, Jerome McWilliams, begged the attackers to spare the building: His wife was close to giving birth. If he were forced to take her to the mainland, he feared, both her life and the life of their unborn child would be jeopardized. Goldsmith, who had grown up on the Maryland mainland not far from the lighthouse and had joined the Confederacy at the start of the war, was swayed by McWilliams's earnest pleas, but true to his mission, he made sure the lighthouse itself was disabled, smashing its lens and lamp, and confiscating fifteen gallons of sperm oil. However, this proved a short-lived victory, as the light was quickly reestablished, and a Union gunboat was stationed nearby to protect it from further raids.

———

THE TIDE OF DESTRUCTION visited upon lighthouses by the war extended well beyond just the east coast; those on the Gulf of Mexico, where the blockade was also enforced, suffered just as much. In September 1861, before abandoning Ship Island off the coast of Mississippi in the face of advancing Union naval ships, Confederate forces tossed wood into the base of the island's lighthouse and set it on fire, destroying the stairs and damaging the lantern. And true to form, upon departing, the Confederates took the lighthouse's Fresnel lens with them.

Sand Island Lighthouse was another target for the Confederates. Located near the entrance of Mobile Bay, a key port for blockade-runners attemping to supply the besieged Confederacy, this magnificent two-hundred-foot-tall conical brick lighthouse was the tallest on the Gulf Coast, and had been completed only in 1858 under the direction of the army engineer Danville Leadbetter, a native of Leeds, Maine, who had graduated third in his class from West Point in 1836. Ever since Union ships began blockading Mobile Bay in 1861, Northern forces used the darkened tower as an observation post to track the movements of blockade-runners, and also to spy on Confederate forts in the area. And in December 1862, under the protection of Union gunboats, a lighthouse engineer was able to install a fourth-order lens in the lighthouse so as to provide Union forces with a guiding beam that could be relied on during the planned invasion of Mobile, Louisiana.

This relighting obviously didn't sit well with Confederate troops, and in late January 1863, Lt. John W. Glenn led a small number of men to the island to destroy the lighthouse. All they were able to do, however, was set fire to a number of buildings before being chased off by gunfire from the USS *Pembina*. Not a man to be easily deterred, Glenn promised to return and "tumble the lighthouse down in their teeth." True to his word, less than a month later he landed on the island again, buried seventy pounds of gunpowder at the base of the tower, and lit the fuse. But Glenn had miscalculated the burn rate and had run only a short distance when the explosion knocked him to the ground and showered him with huge chunks of the lighthouse's walls, including one that was several tons and fell mere inches from his body. All that remained of the lighthouse was a fifty-foot-high sliver about one to five feet wide, which Glenn claimed would be toppled by the next storm. Proud of his achievement, despite nearly being crushed to death, Glenn sent a report of his activities to the commanding Confederate officer in the region, who was none other than Brig. Gen. Danville Leadbetter. Although Leadbetter didn't record his feelings at the time, it is not hard to imagine him feeling a twinge of sadness or regret upon learning that perhaps his greatest engineering accomplishment lay in ruins, a victim of the very cause for which he was so fervently fighting.

According to the lighthouse historian David L. Cipra, "There was only one documented instance on the Gulf Coast where mass destruction of lighthouses was deliberate and coordinated." This was during 1862–63, when the Confederate general John Bankhead Magruder ordered six lighthouses along the gently curving and barrier-island-strewn Texas coast to be burned or blown up so that the Union's Southern Blockading Squadron would not be able to use them as lookouts. Magruder's orders were carried out, and most of the lighthouses were severely damaged. At the Aransas Pass Lighthouse, for example, two kegs of gunpowder blew apart much of the top of the brick tower, and some reports said that the force of the explosion sent the lighthouse's spiral staircase shooting skyward. At the Matagorda Lighthouse, a brick-lined tower with a cast-iron-plate skin, a similar explosion damaged much of the foundation, but only a few of the heavy metal plates.

Using lighthouses as lookouts was ubiquitous during the war, as lighthouses were by design placed at critical points and provided a wide panoramic view of the surrounding terrain, and in the case of the Sabine Pass Lighthouse, a heavily buttressed eighty-foot-tall brick tower located at the mouth of the Sabine River in Louisiana, this not unnaturally led to a series of skirmishes when both sides had the same idea. While blockading Sabine Pass, the Union lieutenant commander Abner Read would frequently send small parties to the lighthouse to monitor enemy movements. The Confederates often did this as well, but for some time the two sides did not cross paths. That changed on April 10, 1863, when one of Read's parties, led by Lt. Benjamin Day, was at the lighthouse on reconnaissance. While at the top of the tower, Union observers saw a small enemy sloop approaching. Day immediately ordered his men to hide in tall grass near the lighthouse. Once the sloop came within a few feet of the shore, Day's men stood up with guns trained on the four Confederates in the boat, who, caught completely off guard, promptly surrendered and were taken prisoner. One of captured men, Capt. Charles Fowler, was a great prize, given his role as commander of the confederate fleet in the area.

But the Confederates would have their revenge. On April 18, only a few weeks before Gen. Robert E. Lee would achieve his greatest victory, routing Union forces during the Battle of Chancellorsville, Virginia, Read led thirteen men to the lighthouse to make more observations of Confederate activities. Although Read was wary, given the earlier confrontation, he saw no movement on the shore and decided to land, feeling somewhat reassured since he had brought along a well-armed party. The boats were pulled up on the shore, and the men approached the lighthouse. They did not get far before a band of thirty Confederates, who had concealed themselves behind the keeper's cottage, rushed forward, guns blazing. In the brief battle that ensued, most of the Union soldiers were killed, captured, or injured. Read, who lost an eye, made it back to his ship with a couple of his men. From that point forward, Union forces, at least, never again used the Sabine Pass Lighthouse as a lookout.

There was at least one case in the Gulf in which Union and Confederate forces damaged the same lighthouse. On July 12, 1863, a little more than a week after the momentous Battle of Gettysburg, a critical victory for the North that resulted in a staggering toll of more than fifty thousand casualties, Union forces visited the St. Marks Lighthouse in Florida, a brick tower near the edge of Apalachee Bay, and burned the interior so that it could not be used as a Confederate lookout. Two years later, when Union forces landed at the lighthouse to launch an attack further inland, they discovered that retreating Confederates had set off multiple explosions that blew out one third of the circumference of the lower tower to a height of eight feet, cracked other parts of lighthouse's walls, and shattered the lantern's glass panes.

The Mobile Point Lighthouse was not damaged due to mutual sabotage, but because it got in the way during the Battle of Mobile Bay. In the summer of 1864, the Union fleet, commanded by Rear Adm. David G. Farragut, came under heavy shelling from Fort Morgan as it passed by Mobile Point. Next to the lighthouse the Confederates had built a furnace that turned cannonballs into glowing projectiles that could ignite enemy ships—illustrating the fact that despite technological advances over the centuries, in some cases the state of warfare resembled nothing so much as a medieval siege. When Farragut's fleet fired on the furnace and the guns surrounding it, the lighthouse, although not the intended target, was shelled nonetheless. Subsequent firefights further damaged the structure, blasting away the outer layers of bricks on one side of the tower, and leaving a few gaping holes. Farragut, who purportedly spurred on his men—fearful of torpedoes, the term then used for naval mines— with the infamous cry, "Damn the torpedoes, full speed ahead!" went on

Damage inflicted on the Mobile Point Lighthouse during the bombardment of Fort Morgan by the Union fleet in 1864.

to win the battle, handing the Confederacy one of its worst defeats and giving the Southern Blockading Squadron control over the Gulf east of the Mississippi River.

One of the strangest instances of the war's impact on a Gulf Coast lighthouse occurred at Bolivar Point Lighthouse at the mouth of Galveston Bay. Sometime after the Confederates put out the light and packed up the lens, the entire tower vanished, leaving behind only its concrete base. Apparently someone had decided that the lighthouse's iron plates were too valuable to the war effort to be left in place. Whether they were melted down to make arms and munitions, or used to plate ships is unknown.

BY THE END OF the war the Confederacy had darkened, damaged, or destroyed some 164 lighthouses. Neither the Union Blockading Squadrons nor the board sat idly by while this was happening. Whenever possible the squadrons tried to track down missing lenses and other valuable lighthouse supplies. This is what developed in St. Augustine, Florida, in March 1862, when the city surrendered to Samuel F. Du Pont. The previous August, the St. Augustine customs collector Paul Arnau led a group of men to the St. Augustine Lighthouse, where they removed the lens, which Arnau hid in an undisclosed location. Next he ordered a few of his men to venture south to the Cape Canaveral Lighthouse, the only one in the country that did not have a Fresnel lens but still used reflectors and lamps based on Winslow Lewis's design. The keeper, Mills O. Burnham, obligingly helped the men dismantle the reflectors, the lamps, and the clockwork for the revolving mechanism. While the lamps and clockwork were delivered to Arnau in St. Augustine, Burnham buried the rest of the materials, along with more than two hundred gallons of sperm oil, in his orange grove.

Soon after arriving in St. Augustine, Du Pont had Arnau—who had resigned as mayor rather than surrender the city to Union forces—arrested and placed aboard the steamer *Isaac Smith* to be interrogated by the ship's commander, J. W. Nicholson. When Arnau pleaded ignorance as to the whereabouts of the lighthouse materials, Nicholson threatened to imprison him on the ship, holding him hostage until they were produced. This none-too-gentle form of persuasion brought Arnau around, and he promptly sent men to recover the hidden items, at which point he was released from custody.

Another case of retrieval took place on May 12, 1862, when the Union lieutenant C. W. Flusser obtained information on the whereabouts of the fifth-order Fresnel lens taken from the Wade's Point Lighthouse, a screw-pile structure in the shallow, frequently windswept waters of Albemarle Sound near the mouth of North Carolina's Pasquotank River. That same night Flusser led seventy-six seamen and thirty-eight soldiers on a three-mile march into the countryside on the outskirts of Elizabeth City, North Carolina—which had only recently been captured by Union forces—where they found the lens and other lighthouse machinery in a barn. Flusser then forced the barn's owner and other local residents to transport the materials back to the waiting ships.

For its part, the board did its best to reestablish lighthouses as soon as areas came under Union control, so that the blockading squadrons could benefit from the resumed navigational assistance. Cape Hatteras provides one of the best examples of this, but there were many others. In its annual report for the year ending on June 30, 1862, the board proudly reported, "Immediately upon the restoration of the eastern shore of Virginia to governmental control by the military operations in that quarter, the lights at . . . Cherrystone, and Hog island were re-established, and have rendered assistance of no small importance to the immensely increased navigation of Chesapeake bay and tributaries."

After the South's largest city, New Orleans, fell in the spring of 1862, delivering a terrific blow to the Confederacy, the board sent an engineer, Capt. William A. Goodwin, there to assess the situation and begin relighting the area. Upon arriving in early August, Goodwin found the German-born Treasury special agent Maximilian F. Bonzano, who counted among his other skills being a physician and a printer, feverishly at work, recovering and repairing fifty thousand dollars' worth of lenses and other lighthouse apparatus that had been stored at the New Orleans Mint. Within a mere four months Bonzano, whom Goodwin appointed acting engineer and lighthouse superintendent for the region, had orchestrated the relighting of eleven lighthouses from New Orleans down to the Gulf.

Given that the war was still raging, and passions were running high, reestablishing lighthouses in the heart of the Confederacy could be dangerous work. Such was the case for Thomas Harrison, who was shot just two days after he became keeper at the recently relit West Rigolets Lighthouse, near the eastern end of Lousiana's Lake Pontchartrain, murdered within a few steps of the lighthouse. His killer was never found, but one theory was that it was a Confederate who was angry to see Harrison working for the enemy. Whatever the cause, Harrison became the only known lighthouse keeper to die on duty during the war.

On some occasions the board acted prematurely. With the Wade's Point Lighthouse lens back under its control, the board repaired and relit the damaged lighthouse early in 1863 on the assurance that it would be adequately protected by the military. But in May of that year "it was visited by a guerilla force from the mainland and again destroyed."

Sometimes the board's efforts were imperiled by the very troops sent to protect the restored lighthouses. Not long after Confederates destroyed the old Cape Charles Lighthouse and stole construction materials intended for the new tower, the board resumed work. To ensure there would be no more trouble from the Confederates, Union soldiers were stationed at the site. But according to the district engineer, the soldiers were anything but helpful. "They are amenable to no discipline," wrote the engineer. "Their dilapidations and injury to government property exceed all that has been done by the rebels." Notwithstanding the soldiers' unruly behavior, however, the new lighthouse began shining on May 7, 1864, and it suffered no more at the hands of either Union or Confederate forces.

WHILE THE LIGHTHOUSE BOARD was moving ahead with substantial success, the Confederate Lighthouse Bureau had virtually disappeared. Not long after the orders to darken the lights and pack up lighthouse materials had gone out, almost all the Southern lighthouse keepers were

*Rather than create new stationery, the Confederate Lighthouse Bureau
simply modified the lighthouse stationery it had on hand.*

relieved of their duties, and bureau headquarters was left with a lone
employee, the interim chief, Thomas Martin. In his final annual report,
penned in January 1864, just a few months before Lt. Gen. Ulysses S.
Grant assumed command of all Union armies, Martin wrote, "The operations of the Lighthouse Establishment during the past year have been
very limited in extent, being confined almost exclusively to the care and
preservation of the Light House property which has been taken down
and removed to places of safety." Martin was still sanguine that the South
would win, and that the bureau would spring back to life, but his hopes
were not to be realized.

THE CIVIL WAR OFFICIALLY ended on April 9, 1865, when General
Lee surrendered to Grant at Appomattox Court House in Virginia. Upon
hearing the news, the Union troops began firing their rifles and cheering,
but Grant put a halt to the celebrations, telling his men, "The war is over,
the rebels are our countrymen again, and the best sign of rejoicing after
victory will be to abstain from all demonstrations." Less than a week later,
the North's joy and relief at having won the war were replaced with overwhelming sorrow when the Confederate sympathizer John Wilkes Booth
assassinated President Lincoln, shooting him in the head while he was
attending a play at Ford's Theater in Washington, DC, adding yet another
horrific casualty to the war's grisly tally.

By the time of the surrender dozens of Southern lighthouses had
already been relit, but the job still facing the board in the South was

monumental, and they attacked it with zeal. Board engineers fanned out to assess damage and begin repairs, while board and military personnel scoured the countryside and questioned former keepers or anyone else who might have relevant information, in order to recover lighthouse materials hidden during the war.

One of the most spectacular finds took place in Raleigh, North Carolina. Soon after Gen. William Tecumseh Sherman entered the city in mid-April 1865, he had some of his men do a sweep of the Capitol Building, during which they came upon a most unusual sight. As a correspondent for the *Philadelphia Inquirer* reported, "In the rotunda, between the two chambers, is stored a vast pile of lighthouse apparatus: costly lamps and reflectors of Fresnel and Argand. . . . The glass concentric reflectors of Fresnel are viewed with novel curiosity by the Western men [soldiers from inland states], to whom lighthouse paraphernalia is something new."

Local workers were hired to pack the lighthouse apparatus in crates, and the quartermaster general of the Union army, Montgomery C. Meigs, was tasked with having the crates shipped to the board. In a letter to the board chairman, Adm. Shubrick, Meigs noted, "Some broken prisms or portion[s] of lenses have been seen in possession of boys in the street, but the greater part of the lens apparatus will, I think, reach Washington in good order." Meigs also shared with Shubrick a startling discovery: The workers had used the most readily available packing material—papers that were strewn about the Capitol. When Meigs took a closer look, he found that the papers were quite old, many reaching back before the Revolution, some signed by eminent statesmen including Thomas Jefferson and Charles Thompson, the secretary general of the Continental Congress. In other words the lighthouse materials had been packed in North Carolina's irreplaceable historical archive. After the crates arrived in Washington, the papers were salvaged, stored at the Treasury Department, and promptly forgotten. It was forty years before a shocked Treasury employee accidentally rediscovered them, and a large chunk of North Carolina's historical heritage was returned to the state.

Although hopes were raised when the stash of lenses was discovered in Raleigh that the missing first-order lens from Cape Hatteras Lighthouse would be among them, it was not. Four months later, however, in August, the storied lens, which the board wanted to recover more than any other, was found by Union soldiers on patrol in Henderson, North Carolina, not far from Townsville, where the dependable Dr. Tayloe had originally hidden it during the early days of the war. The discovery revealed a problem: Sometime after the war ended, local residents had helped themselves to pieces of the precious apparatus, hoping to get a reward for their return. The board, however, was in no mood to barter, and it got the Union forces on site to pressure the locals to return the stolen pieces. Within a few weeks they were recovered, and the lens was on its way to New York.

THE FLOOD OF DAMAGED lenses coming from the South, many with chipped or missing prisms, was overwhelming. The repair shop at the board's Staten Island depot, where most of the lenses ended up, did not have the capacity or skill to fix them all, so the board sent many of them back to the French manufacturers. At one point Shubrick urged the manufacturers to make repairs "as soon as possible in order that the apparatus may be re-established upon our Southern coast and the commerce of the world be benefited thereby." The board also ordered new lenses to replace those that were too damaged to repair or couldn't be found.

The pace of restoration overseen by the board was impressive—much faster than that of the South itself. By the end of 1866 it had rebuilt or repaired ninety-four Southern lighthouses. But still, with so much work yet to be done, and so many lenses to be fixed or replaced, many of the Southern lighthouses that were darkened or damaged during the war would not be relit until the early 1870s, while many others were deemed no longer necessary for navigational purposes. Thus they remained among the permanent casualties of a war that had taken an immeasurable toll on the nation.

CHAPTER 9

FROM BOARD
TO SERVICE

. . . .

A busy day of sailing near the Isle of Shoals Lighthouse is depicted in this engraving,
titled Off Portsmouth Harbor, N.H., *after a painting by Julian Oliver Davidson, 1878.*

T HE CIVIL WAR LEFT IN ITS WAKE RUIN AND DESTRUCTION NOT
seen since in America, and like so much of the country's infrastructure,
lighthouses bore much of this toll. Yet the war was also a time of triumph for the Lighthouse Board. Not only did it work diligently and effectively at relighting the South as soon as conditions became safe enough
to do so, but it also redoubled its efforts to maintain and operate light-

houses throughout the rest of the country, and even built a few new ones. The board's commitment to improving the nation's lighthouse system remained steadfast in the decades following the war. Befitting the times, board chairman Joseph Henry wrote in 1873, "The character of the aids which any nation furnishes the mariner in approaching and leaving its shores marks, in a conspicuous degree, its advancement in civilization." With this philosophy firmly ensconced, the board endeavored to provide mariners with the best lighthouses possible.

One of the most dramatic changes during this frenetic period of growth involved the source of illumination. The origins of this shift reach back to the early 1850s, when the board realized it faced what appeared to be an insuperable problem. The price of the sperm oil that kept the lighthouses shining was rapidly increasing, due to the law of supply and demand. As American whalemen spent more money and time than ever before, traveling further across the globe to chase an ever-dwindling number of whales, the cost of obtaining sperm oil soared, and the amount of oil brought back to America's shores plunged. At the same time demand grew, inevitably leading to rising prices. Most of the sperm oil went to lighting American homes, businesses, and city streets, and also to lubricating the gears of industry. While only a small part of the demand actually resulted from lighthouse needs, the average price the board paid for a gallon of sperm oil rose exorbitantly from 55 cents in 1840–41, to $2.25 in 1855.[*] And there was every indication that the price was only going to go higher as the cycle of diminishing supply and rising demand continued.

Even though the Fresnel lenses used less sperm oil than the reflectors they replaced, the amount of oil flowing through the arteries of America's lighthouse system was considerable. As a result, the board faced a decision. It could continue to spend an increasing percentage of its budget on sperm oil, straining its resources and sacrificing other parts of the lighthouse system, or it could find another, cheaper illuminant. It wisely chose the latter.

---

[*] This price includes the expense of delivery to the lighthouses.

The board first focused on colza oil, also called rapeseed oil, which came from a species of wild cabbage that grew widely in Europe.* The French had used colza oil as a lighthouse illuminant since the early 1800s, and the British adopted it in later years. It produced a light that was equivalent to that of sperm, but at a much lower cost. The main obstacle to using it in America was the lack of a domestic source. The board tried to remedy this in the late 1850s and early 1860s by distributing colza seeds to farmers and encouraging them to raise the crop. A few farmers pursued this new venture, but they did not produce nearly enough oil to come even close to supplanting sperm oil.

At the same time that the board was promoting colza, it was also exploring the possibility of using lard oil and kerosene. Lard oil came from rendered hogs, while kerosene, also called mineral oil, had been derived primarily from coal and was available in only limited quantities throughout most of the 1850s. However, this all changed in 1859, when "Colonel" Edwin L. Drake drilled a well seventy feet deep into the ground in the isolated hamlet of Titusville, Pennsylvania, releasing a gusher of oil. This so-called black gold suddenly provided a new and much more plentiful raw material for the production of kerosene, and as the number of oil wells exploded, cheap kerosene flooded the market.

By the early 1860s, kerosene and, to a much lesser extent, lard oil were illuminating an ever-increasing number of homes and businesses, displacing sperm oil in the process. The board, however, was reluctant to switch to kerosene, claiming that its quality at this early date of introduction was "too volatile and combustible to be safely employed for lighthouse purposes." Lard oil, in contrast, proved much more promising, since it was not only a relatively safe fuel, being less combustible than kerosene, but it also burned brighter than sperm oil and was much cheaper. Indeed, a small number of lighthouses had been experimenting with lard oil as far back as the early 1840s, with encouraging results. The primary impediment to using it was that it congealed and didn't burn well at low

---

*Colza oil is a close relative of canola oil, which was developed in Canada in the late twentieth century.

temperatures, but Joseph Henry's experiments proved that there was an easy solution—simply burn it at a higher temperature by using larger lamps that generated more heat. Still, in very cold climates keepers often had to warm the lard oil on stoves to liquefy it before adding it to the lamp. With these fixes addressed, the board quickly adopted lard oil, and by 1867 virtually all the lighthouses in the system were using it.

The iron law of supply and demand, however, asserted itself again: With lighthouses consuming so much lard oil, its price skyrocketed, leading the board to take another look at kerosene. The board was still wary of this fuel, especially in light of an accident that had taken place in 1864, when a keeper on Lake Michigan decided to replace the lighthouse's lard oil lamp with one that used kerosene. For a few nights this substitution appeared to be a great success, with the new lamp providing a penetrating light, but one morning, while the keeper attempted to douse the lamp by blowing down its chimney, the lamp suddenly exploded, spewing flaming oil about the lantern room and onto the keeper's clothes. He barely made it down the stairs and out of the tower, only moments before another much bigger explosion blew apart the lantern room and destroyed the lens.

By the 1870s, however, kerosene was getting progressively cheaper, and the distillation process had improved to the point that the quality of the kerosene was much higher and less volatile than had been the case in earlier years. Although the board still considered lard oil the better illuminant, it slowly shifted to kerosene for economic reasons, since it was roughly half the cost. At first only the smaller-order lenses made the switch, but over time, and with the use of improved lamp designs, the use of kerosene expanded to larger lenses, to the point that by 1885 the transition from lard oil to kerosene was complete.

Yet the forward momentum of technology continued to increase, and about the same time that kerosene supplanted lard oil, the board began experimenting with electricity. The main type of commercial electric light widely available at the time came from carbon arc lamps, a technology invented by the Englishman Sir Humphry Davy in the early 1800s, in which an electrical current arcing between the tips of two carbon rods

The Great Bartholdi Statue,
Liberty Enlightening the World,
holding aloft a kerosene lamp.
Currier & Ives print, circa 1885.

caused the resulting superheated carbon vapor to glow incandescently, creating an extremely bright light. Because of their intense brilliance, arc lamps were too powerful for domestic use indoors, but they quickly were adopted for use in streetlamps and in industrial settings. The board's first opportunity to evaluate this technology came with the arrival of the Statue of Liberty, which was erected on Bedloe's (now Liberty) Island in New York Harbor in the mid-1880s.

When the Frenchman Frédéric-Auguste Bartholdi designed the Statue of Liberty—or *Liberty Enlightening the World,* as it was originally known—in the 1870s, he intended this gift to America to serve not only as a historical metaphor of sorts, a towering exemplar of the friendship between the two countries who had fought side by side to achieve America's independence, but also as an actual beacon or functioning lighthouse welcoming the world to America's shores. To that end the interior of the torch that Lady Liberty held aloft was fitted with nine carbon arc lamps that were to shine through two rings of circular openings cut from the lower portion of the sculpted flame, which were fitted with glass. The lamps would then be powered by an on-site generator. When the statue was illuminated for the first time on November 1, 1886, however, it produced only a weak light, due to the small size of the openings and their configuration. The public and the press alike ridiculed this feeble performance. Joseph Pulitzer's *New York World* branded it "more like a glow worm than a beacon."

Although an engineer detailed from the board designed the torch's illumination, the board itself had no formal responsibility for the statue itself until two weeks later, November 16, when President Grover Cleveland signed an executive order officially giving it the job of operating the statue as a lighthouse. While the board was able to improve the quality of the light somewhat over time, it never considered the statue to be an effective lighthouse. The secretary of war, Elihu Root, agreed with that assessment, writing to President Theodore Roosevelt in December 1901, "The light in the statue is useless so far as navigation is concerned." Root asked Roosevelt to transfer responsibility for the statue to his department, a move that was heartily supported by the board, and by the end of the year Roosevelt approved the move, ending Lady Liberty's transitory days as a lighthouse.

The board had more success with electricity at the Navesink Lighthouse in New Jersey, which had been built in 1862 to replace the one that had stood on that spot since 1828. Both lighthouses had a north and a south tower, and the towers of the earlier lighthouse were used in 1841 to test the first Fresnel lenses brought to America. Nearly sixty years later, in 1898, the south tower of the new lighthouse became the site of an equally novel test, when the board fitted it out with a carbon arc lamp, making Navesink the first primary lighthouse in the country lit by electricity.

The lamp was enclosed in a relatively new type of Fresnel lens called a bivalve, or clamshell, lens, which had two halves, each with a bull's-eye surrounded by prisms. The lens weighed more than seven tons and made a complete revolution in ten seconds, sending a flash of light out toward the horizon every five seconds. And a great flash it was, estimated

The twin lights of the Navesink Lighthouse, built in 1862, with the south tower in the foreground.

to have a candlepower of 25,000,000. Navesink was by far the most powerful lighthouse in the country. The light could be seen twenty-two miles away before disappearing over the horizon, with some observers reporting that the loom of the light, or its reflection off the sky, was visible as far as seventy miles away. While turn-of-the-century mariners welcomed the almost sun-like beam, area residents were understandably none too happy having their houses lit up nightly like the Fourth of July. Numerous complaints induced the board to blacken the lantern room's landward-facing panels, to the great relief of the locals.

These tentative steps in using electricity foreshadowed a point when electricity would become the only illumination source in America's lighthouses, but, in the meantime, there was another major advance in the burning of kerosene—the incandescent oil vapor lamp (IOV). In this lamp the kerosene was first heated and vaporized, then the gas was mixed with air and ignited by a Bunsen burner under a mantle, producing a brilliant white light. IOV lamps were eight times brighter than traditional kerosene lamps, and better yet, they used much less fuel to generate the same amount of light. If the IOV lamp sounds familiar, that is because it is similar in design to modern camping lamps that use propane as fuel. The first IOV lamp was installed at the North Hook Beacon at Sandy Hook in 1904, and from there this new technology quickly spread to many other lighthouses.

Other changes to the illuminating apparatus involved the manner of rotating the lens. The clockwork mechanism, whether powered by falling weights or a motor, could turn the larger lenses only so fast on account of the great weight of the lens and the goodly amount of friction created as it rolled over the chariot wheels. To speed the rate of rotation, two new mechanisms were employed starting in the late 1800s. Some lighthouses replaced the chariot wheels with ball bearings, while others began using mercury flotation systems. According to the lighthouse historian Thomas

Navesink's bivalve, or clamshell, Fresnel lens, on display at Boston's Museum of Science, circa 1951.

Assistant keeper Gus Axelson, preheating the incandescent oil vapor (IOV) lamp at the Fire Island Lighthouse, December 1934.

Tag, "The mercury bath consisted of a doughnut-shaped basin in which a relatively small amount of mercury was placed. Attached to the base of the lens was a large doughnut-shaped ring that was submerged in, and supported by, the mercury, which was placed in the basin. This assembly provided a nearly frictionless base for the lens to ride upon, allowing lenses weighing several tons to be started in motion with the push of a single finger." A large first-order lens on chariot wheels could take up to eight minutes to make a single revolution, so unless the lens had numerous panels, the flash pattern would be relatively slow, which might limit the mariner's ability to fix his position. With the mercury system, the lens could have far fewer panels, and provide not only a very rapid but a far brighter flash, since humans perceive rapid flashes of light as being more intense than ones of longer duration.

Augustin Fresnel had many decades before come up with the idea of using mercury flotation systems, but it wasn't until the late nineteenth century that the French and then the British began manufacturing them. The Americans purchased foreign systems and even built a few of their own, all of which were installed between 1893 and 1920 at roughly forty American lighthouses. At the time there was no concern about the negative health impacts of mercury vapors because such linkages had yet to be discovered. Given what we know now, however, one might wonder if any American lighthouse keepers were adversely affected by mercury exposure. Although there are no documented cases of cause and effect, some have speculated that a few keepers who went insane and were removed from their positions might have gotten that way as a result of inhaling too many fumes.*

THE EVOLUTION OF LIGHTHOUSE illumination coincided with progress in lighthouse design and construction. Some of the trends that were initiated by the board in the 1850s continued after the war and throughout the end of the nineteenth century. The extremely tall towers the board built in that earlier period were joined by others in the 1870s and 1880s. All these giants were in the South, including Florida's statuesque 175-foot Ponce de Leon Lighthouse (1887), the third tallest in the United States. And when the Cape Hatteras Lighthouse, already raised to 150 feet in 1854, was found to be suffering from cracks and other structural problems, it was replaced in 1870 with a brand-new masonry tower, composed of more than one million bricks, that soared to 193 feet, giving it pride of place as the nation's tallest lighthouse.

Similarly, in the 1850s the board began painting lighthouses with individual markings that made them more visible and distinguishable during the day, and these daymarks were widely replicated in the years after the war. Designs included the now-iconic black-and-white candy-stripe, or spiral-banding, pattern on the Cape Hatteras Lighthouse, and the black-and-white checkerboard pattern on North Carolina's Cape Lookout Lighthouse. Some lighthouses were painted attractively red as

---

*Similarly, the expression "mad as a hatter" originated in eighteenth-century England, where mercury was used in the hatmaking process.

well, with the Sapelo Island Lighthouse in Georgia sporting alternating horizontal red and white stripes.

The board also expanded the use of cast-iron plates—a common building component in those years—in lighthouse construction. Cast iron was durable, noncombustible, water-resistant, and cheaper than masonry, and pieces of the lighthouse could be prefabricated into virtually any shape desired and transported to the site for easier assembly. Although typically lined with brick for additional stability and insulation, cast-iron towers were nevertheless lighter than masonry lighthouses of the same size, which made them a good choice for areas that did not provide a strong foundation for a very heavy structure. When the old Cape Henry Lighthouse began to exhibit cracks in its masonry, the board replaced it in 1881 with a 163-foot, cast-iron-plate tower, which is the tallest such tower in the United States. Interestingly enough, despite the board's fear that the old lighthouse was in imminent peril of toppling over, it still stands today, about 350 feet from its replacement.

Iron, and later steel, was also used to build skeleton-tower lighthouses on land. Skeleton towers were prefabricated and constructed on site.

West Quoddy Head Lighthouse in Lubec, Maine, is painted with red and white stripes.
It is located at the easternmost point of the United States mainland.

Cape Charles Lighthouse in Cape Charles, Virginia, circa 1895.

They could be easily raised in height by adding sections, and a few of them were even disassembled and moved from one location to another. Relatively lightweight, skeleton towers were especially useful in unstable sandy or muddy areas. The tallest skeleton tower lighthouse in the United States is the one at Cape Charles, Virginia, completed in 1895, and 191 feet high, making it the second tallest lighthouse in the nation.

The board continued building cottage-style screw-pile lighthouses at relatively shallow, somewhat protected sites, mainly along the northeastern and mid-Atlantic coasts. At more exposed sites, however, the board increasingly opted for caisson lighthouses. While screw-pile lighthouses were basically a small house on stilts—and as such fairly delicate and subject to being damaged or swept away by violent storms, strong currents, and ice floes—caisson lighthouses were far sturdier and better able to withstand the elements. With the most common type of caisson lighthouse, iron plates were bolted together on land to create a hollow cylinder enclosed on the bottom. The caisson was then towed to the desired location, and sunk into the water by pouring in stone and concrete. As

The caisson for the Ship John Shoal Lighthouse being towed to the construction site.
The lighthouse is off Downe Township, New Jersey, in Delaware Bay.

the structure sank deeper, additional iron sections were bolted to the top, and more stone and concrete were poured in until the caisson was sitting on the bottom, forming a very strong, solid foundation. The keeper's quarters and the lantern room—usually made of iron, and often cylindrical in shape—were then built on top of the caisson, above the water level. This type of caisson worked well on flat, relatively stable sand or mud bottoms. In more challenging locations, however, where the bottom was unusually soft, or it had to be leveled or obstructions removed, pneumatic caissons were employed.

Pneumatic caissons began on land as well, with a prefabricated iron cylinder, but the cylinder was enclosed higher up, rather than at the bottom, creating a work chamber below, into which a hollow iron access shaft was inserted. This entire structure was then towed to the site and sunk to the bottom. At this point compressed air—hence the term "pneumatic"—was continuously pumped into the work chamber, forcing all the water out through the bottom of the caisson. Men then entered the work chamber through the access shaft and began digging, with the sand, mud, and gravel they dislodged being pumped out and over the side of the caisson into the water. As the men dug, the caisson slowly sank deeper into the bottom, and more iron sections were bolted to the top to keep the caisson's lip above water. Once the caisson reached the desired depth, the men exited, and the shaft, chamber, and upper portions of the caisson were filled with concrete. Then the lighthouse was placed on top.

Erecting pneumatic caissons was punishing work. Not only was the digging hard, but the men also had to deal with the intense air pressure and, often, extreme heat and humidity. When the caisson had to be sunk particularly deep, the process of equalizing the pressure in the chamber frequently gave the men severe headaches and caused blood to drip from their noses and ears. In extreme cases, men who stayed down too long and then left the pressurized chamber too quickly could get caisson disease, a painful condition very similar to decompression sickness, or the bends, exhibited by divers who ascend too quickly.

On account of their distinctive shape, caisson lighthouses were often called spark-plug or coffeepot lights. Many caisson lighthouses replaced screw-pile lighthouses that had been damaged or destroyed by ice, Maryland's Sharps Island Lighthouse being a case in point.

Sharps Island—which has since eroded away—was located on the eastern side of Chesapeake Bay near the southern tip of Tilghman Island. The first lighthouse in this location, a simple wooden house with a lantern room on top, was built in 1838. It conveniently had wheels so it could be moved in case the wind and tides ate away the lighthouse's foundation— which is exactly what happened, and the lighthouse was wheeled farther inland in 1848. This relentless erosion continued its assault, and by 1864 the lighthouse was again teetering on the edge. Fearing that the light-

Craighill Channel Lower Range Front Light, circa 1873. This caisson-style lighthouse is located in Chesapeake Bay off the coast of Maryland.

house would not survive much longer, in 1866 the board replaced it with a screw-pile structure located near the island in seven and a half feet of water. It, too, however, was destined to have a relatively short life.

Late on Wednesday, February 9, 1881, Columbus Butler, the head keeper at Sharps Island, and the assistant keeper, Charles L. Tarr, were growing increasingly nervous. Over the years a number of screw-pile lighthouses in the Chesapeake had been destroyed by ice, and now the ice floes were running thick and picking up speed, pushed along by the steady winds from a southeast gale. As the ice groaned and scraped against the lighthouse's iron legs, Butler became convinced that the entire structure would soon topple. His prediction came true in the morning, when a massive ice floe careened into the lighthouse with such a ferocious punch that in less than five minutes it knocked the wooden keeper's house off its legs and into the ice-choked waters.

As the surging ice floes surrounded the lighthouse, jamming shut the doors and windows, the keepers hastily clambered into the lantern room. For sixteen and a half hours, without any food or warmth to sustain them, Butler and Tarr hung on desperately as the lighthouse took them on a terrifying ride through the bay. Pitching from side to side and bouncing violently off the ice, the lighthouse often seemed on the edge of shattering to pieces or going under, as it quickly filled with water. Butler feared that they wouldn't survive, but after drifting about five miles, the lighthouse ended up not far from where it started its harrowing journey, grounding at high tide on the edge of Tilghman Island at about one in the morning on February 11. Once they were confident that the lighthouse would not float away, the two men—famished, numb, and exhausted—slogged their arduous way to the shore, finding refuge at a nearby house. Remarkably, true to their duty as keepers and fortified by food and warmth following their icy ordeal, they then returned at low tide to retrieve the Fresnel lens, the pedestal, and other items, before reporting the loss to their superiors. For staying with their lighthouse and saving its valuable apparatus, Butler and Tarr received commendations from the board.

Concluding that another screw-pile lighthouse in the same location would likely meet a similar icy fate, the board wisely opted in 1882 to

The Sharps Island Lighthouse, with the tilt. The lighthouse is no longer an active aid to navigation.

build a caisson lighthouse instead, which became the third and final Sharps Island Lighthouse. As strong as this caisson structure was, ice battered it during a few particularly severe winters in the mid-1970s, which left the lighthouse tilted at a fifteen- to twenty-degree angle.

It wasn't only ice that threatened screwpile lighthouses. On the morning of December 27, 1909, the four-masted schooner *Malcom Baxter, Jr.,* was being towed to Norfolk by a tugboat in rough seas, high winds, and snowy conditions, when it veered off course, heading straight for the Thimble Shoal Lighthouse, located near the mouth of Chesapeake Bay. Keeper Charles S. Hudgins and his two assistants were inside at the time wrapped in blankets and sitting around the stove trying to keep warm, when the schooner's jib boom crashed into the lighthouse, nearly cleaving it in two, flinging the men off their chairs, and toppling the stove. The burning coals skittering along the wood floor set the building ablaze, forcing the men to flee in the lighthouse boat. Before the flames could engulf the *Malcolm Baxter*, the current pushed it clear of the lighthouse, which was now a fireball visible for miles around. Almost everything, including the lens and the fog bell machinery, was destroyed, and all that remained was the lighthouse's twisted iron legs. In 1914 the board built a much sturdier caisson-style lighthouse on Thimble Shoal right next to the forlorn skeletal frame of the screwpile it replaced.

In the early 1900s, as new technologies began to transform American engineering and building, the board began using a relatively novel construction material—concrete reinforced with steel or iron to add tensile strength to the towers. The first experiment with this came on the heels of the San Francisco Earthquake on April 18, 1906, still the most famous temblor in the country's history. A little after five in the morning, the tectonic plates lying on either side of the San Andreas Fault ground past each other, moving as much as twenty feet or more in just over a minute, setting off a cataclysm of monstrous proportions. Estimated to have registered close to 8.0 on the Richter scale (which would not be invented until the 1930s), the earthquake destroyed nearly thirty thousand buildings, killed about three thousand people, and left hundreds of thousands homeless.

Area lighthouses didn't escape the earthquake's wrath, and the Point

Point Arena Lighthouse, Point Arena, California.

Arena Lighthouse, located on a bold promontory about 130 miles north-west of San Francisco, and just to the west of the fault, suffered the worst. According to the keeper on watch, "A heavy blow first struck the tower from the south. . . . The tower quivered for a few seconds, went far over to the north, came back, and then swung north again, repeating this several times. Immediately after came rapid and violent vibrations, rending the tower apart, . . . while the lenses, reflectors, etc., in the lantern were shaken from their settings and fell in a shower upon the iron floor." The violence of the quake damaged the tower and keeper's quarters so severely that both had to be torn down. The replacement lighthouse, 115 feet tall and made of reinforced concrete, was first lit in 1908, and in later years many other lighthouses, especially in areas subject to earthquakes, used the same material.

GIVEN THE FEVERISH PACE of inventions during this time, the board made great gains in the area of fog-signal technology as well. By the early 1900s the days of blasting cannons, shooting guns, or manually struck bells were over, and instead keepers were employing a great variety of technologically advanced whistles, sirens, and trumpets powered by steam, hot air, or electricity. Bells with automatic strikers, regulated by falling weights, provided another means of sounding an alarm, warning mariners slowly making their way through pea-soup fog that land—and potential danger—was close at hand.

Since such signals are only needed where fog heavily envelops a region, many lighthouses didn't have them. Hardly any lighthouses south of the Chesapeake Bay had fog signals, and there were none in the Gulf of Mexico. However, in New England, along the Pacific coast, and on the Great Lakes, where fog is often present hundreds or even thousands of hours per year, fog signals were an absolute necessity. Maine's Seguin Island Lighthouse, just offshore from the mouth of the Kennebec River, in the southern part of the state, set the record for fog in 1907, when it was blanketed for 2,734 hours, or roughly one-third of the year.

Although undeniably helpful to mariners, fog signals were often a

Fog-signal machinery, circa 1873.

great annoyance to people who lived near them and had to withstand hours or perhaps days of listening to the varied and plaintive cries of these powerful noisemakers. A reporter from the *New York Herald* in 1905, in an article titled, "Siren is Breaking Up Happy Homes," employed rich literary metaphors to describe the sound of the new fog signal installed at the Great Captain Island Lighthouse, off the coast of Greenwich, Connecticut. It began, he wrote, with "a screech like an army of panthers, weird and prolonged, gradually lowering in note until after a half a minute it becomes the roar of a thousand mad bulls, with intermediate voices suggestive of a wail of a lost soul, the moan of a bottomless pit and the groan of a disabled elevator." Complaints led the board to build a house for the fog signal, and make other modifications to reduce the din.

It wasn't only the lighthouse's neighbors who could be rattled by the noise. Keepers as well had to withstand the acoustic barrage, and at much closer quarters. Although most of them adjusted to the sound, and could even sleep through it, there were times when the auditory onslaught pushed them to the edge of incoherence. At one point in 1887, the keepers at the Point Reyes Lighthouse, which is located about thirty miles northwest of San Francisco on a towering jagged headland jutting far out to sea, kept the fog signal running for 176 hours straight, with each blast of the siren lasting five seconds and recurring every seventy seconds. As if proving that it wasn't just mercury fumes that posed a risk to the sanity of a lighthouse keeper, a reporter on hand noted that the "jaded attendants looked as if they had been on a protracted spree."

IN FACT THE BOARD focused its attention not only on the lighthouses but also on the keepers who ran them. In 1876 it began distributing books to keepers at the more isolated lighthouses, the very people in most desperate in need of entertainment, who didn't have the option of walking to a nearby town to get reading material. This was not a purely altruistic act, for by providing them with books, the board believed that the keepers would "be made happier and more contented with their lot, and less desirous of absenting themselves from their post."

Thus seeking to prevent or ameliorate the psychological isolation keepers were prone to, the board started with fifty minilibraries, each containing about forty books, housed in an attractive, sturdy,

One of the many minilibraries that traveled from lighthouse to lighthouse, providing keepers with entertainment and education.

and portable wooden box. These stayed at each lighthouse six months before being swapped for another. Donated by private individuals or purchased by the board, the books included the obligatory Bible and hymnbooks, along with a great variety of fiction and nonfiction—everything from novels to poetry and books on science. Upon opening the latest personal "athenaeum," a keeper might find *Robinson Crusoe* and *The Last Days of Pompeii* alongside a new installment of the series *The Five Little Peppers and How They Grew*. These libraries proved so popular that within a few decades the number in circulation grew to more than five hundred.

In 1883 the board began requiring male keepers to wear dress uniforms (female keepers—more about them later—were exempt from this rule). The uniform was a spiffy indigo-blue, wool outfit, including a double-breasted jacket with ten buttons, trousers, and a vest. There was also a visored blue cap, to which a brass lighthouse badge was pinned. The keepers were supposed to wear the uniform while on duty but had to take off the jacket and wear an apron while cleaning the delicate lighting apparatus. Also, when working outside, they could exchange their dress uniform for a brown working suit. Relying implicitly on the theory that clothes make the man, the board believed that the uniforms would "aid in maintaining [the lighthouse system's] . . . discipline, increase its efficiency, raise its tone, and add to its *esprit de corps*."

Another keeper-related issue the board tackled was patronage. Political favoritism and graft were rampant at the time throughout all levels of government. Ever since the earliest years of the lighthouse establishment, there had been keepers who were appointed as a result of whom they knew and which party they backed, rather than their suitability for the position. This had become a much more common practice beginning in the early 1800s, when customs collectors got more directly involved in nominating keepers. After all, customs collectors, themselves political appointees, often viewed keepers' jobs as plums to be handed out to party supporters. Furthermore, the secretary of the Treasury, who approved or rejected keeper nominations, was just as likely to let politics, not merit, determine hiring decisions.

Rhode Island's Block Island Southeast Lighthouse, built in 1875.

While some keepers appointed as the result of patronage performed admirably, many were literally and figuratively out of their depth, as was the case for an "efficient party man" and a "shining light . . . on election days," who had been appointed keeper at a Maine lighthouse in 1849. According to the *Portland Advertiser*, this man hailed from the center of the state and was wholly ignorant of maritime matters. Soon after the keeper took over, mariners began complaining that the light at his lighthouse didn't burn after midnight. When informed of these complaints by an official from the lighthouse establishment, the exasperated keeper replied, "Well, I know they don't, for I put' em out myself then, for I thought all the vessels had got by by that time, and I wanted to save the oil." Whether the keeper was forced to change his "lights out by midnight" policy or was sacked is not known.

This story notwithstanding, patronage was no laughing matter. It had more serious and corrosive effects, often putting lives in the hands of the incompetent and sapping the system of its most talented employees.

As board chairman Henry lamented in 1873, "In regard to light-keep-ers, the most efficient and faithful men, who from years of practice have acquired the skill necessary to a proper discharge of their duties, have been in many cases changed by collectors of customs for new men, for no other reason than to give place to some political favorite." Consider the fate of the keeper at Massachusetts's Wing Neck Lighthouse, who was callously dismissed in 1854. According to a local paper, "Mr. Law-rence was a faithful, capable man and was appointed at the time the lighthouse was built. His crime consisted in having been appointed by the Whigs." During President Lincoln's first term of office, 75 percent of keepers were replaced with friends of the administration, notwith-standing the fact that Lincoln himself often complained bitterly about the seemingly endless lines of office-seekers demanding their due. This patronage onslaught led one Republican newspaper to propose in 1861 a "new plan for lighting the coast"—simply to let every man who has applied to be a lighthouse keeper stand on the shore with a "torch in his hand. There will be no need of government oil." It is no wonder, then, that the journalist, short-story writer, and scathing social critic Ambrose Bierce, whose bitter, sardonic taunts entertained the nation for several generations, defined a lighthouse in his infamous *Devil's Dictionary* as "A tall building on the seashore in which the government maintains a lamp and the friend of a politician." The regularity of the dismissal of keepers in the mid- to late-nineteenth century, often for political reasons, is evidenced by the cursory form letter used to tell them that it was time for them to go, which simply stated, "You are superseded as keeper of _____ light station on _____, 18___, by _____." And usually it was the keeper's replacement, ready to move in, who delivered this most unwel-come news.

The board did its best to dull the impact of patronage by, among other things, requiring prospective keepers to meet certain standards, placing keepers on probation for three months, and at the end of that period test-ing their skills and firing those who didn't pass. The board also set the process at a further remove from the machinations of politics by stripping

Impressive array of Fresnel lenses displayed at the 1898 Trans-Mississippi and International Exposition, held in Omaha, Nebraska.

customs collectors of their power to nominate keepers, transferring that task instead to lighthouse inspectors. Such measures did have a positive impact, and toward the end of the nineteenth century it became increasingly common for keepers to serve an apprenticeship and rise through the ranks, moving from assistant to head keeper over time, rather than being appointed from the outside for political reasons.

But the single greatest tool in the fight against patronage arrived in 1896, when President Grover Cleveland, a tireless foe of influence peddling and political corruption, issued an executive order that included lighthouse keepers in the classified civil service. Applicants now had to be qualified and pass written and oral examinations to get the job, and political affiliation was not allowed to influence appointments or dismissals. Furthermore, the job became permanent only after the successful completion of a six-month probationary period. As a result of both the board's efforts and the executive order, patronage appointments were largely eliminated. America's lighthouse keepers were now part of a true career civil service in which merit, not connections, drove hiring and promotion decisions. This progressive change provided them, and the mariners who depended on their dedication and skills, a greater measure of security.

THE GEOGRAPHIC REACH OF the lighthouse system expanded dramatically under the board's watch. When U.S. Secretary of State William H. Seward negotiated the purchase of Alaska from the Russians in 1867 for $7.2 million—roughly two cents per acre—nearly seven thousand miles were added to America's coastline overnight. At the time there was just one navigational light in the territory that could, charitably at best, be called a lighthouse. It was located in Sitka in the cupola of the governor's mansion, usually referred to as Baranov's Castle in honor of Aleksandr Baranov, the first governor of the Russian colony in Alaska and manager of the Russian-American Company, which had operated a lucrative fur-trading business in the area since 1799. (The company's fortunes were built on the backs of Native Alaskans, or Aleuts, who were treated brutally by the Russians and forced to kill hundreds of thousands of sea otters for their pelts.) The light in the cupola was very primitive, consisting of four copper cans filled with seal oil, each with a wick, and backed by a single large reflector. Though relatively feeble, this light had long been a welcome sight for Russian mariners heading to Alaska. Upon sighting the lighthouse at Sitka in 1839, the Russian naval officer Lavrentiy Zagoskin wrote, "There are no words to express the feelings that induce a sailor to offer fervent prayers when he sees this mark of sympathy expressed by his fellow men. Suddenly he sees that he is no longer alone in the midst of the ocean waves; he sees that people are caring for him with paternal solicitude." An American army sergeant at the garrison in Sitka operated the lighthouse until 1877, but when the army left that year, the light was extinguished.

A couple of years after the purchase of Alaska, the Coast Survey submitted a report recommending where lighthouses might best be located in the territory. While this resulted in the establishment of many unlighted buoys, a new lighthouse would not be built in Alaska until the early 1900s. The specific reason for this delay is not clear, although one possible explanation is that there were more pressing demands for lighthouses in the rest of the United States, where maritime commercial needs were greater. As some have claimed, it could also have been that lighting such a long and remote coastline was simply too expensive or difficult to contemplate at the time. Or perhaps it was because too few politicians viewed Alaska, derisively referred to for decades as "Seward's Folly" and "Walrussia," as a valuable addition to the country, worthy of development.

By the late 1800s, however, the pressure to build lighthouses in Alaska reached a tipping point. The rapid expansion of the lumbering and fishing industries brought many ships north, but what really triggered a maritime stampede was the discovery of gold in northwestern Canada's Klondike region in 1896. An estimated one hundred thousand prospectors headed to Alaska during the Klondike gold rush, most of them landing in Skagway before attempting to hike over the Coast Mountains to the goldfields; a grueling trek that forced the vast majority to turn back before reaching their destination. Among the ranks of this deluge of fortune seekers was the twenty-one-year-old Jack London, who later drew from his year-long Alaskan adventure to pen the literary classics, *The Call of the Wild* and *White Fang*.

With so many ships traveling the treacherous waters off Alaska—especially those of the territory's sinuous Inside Passage, which were strewn with rocky reefs and small icebergs—there were numerous wrecks. One of the worst was that of the steamer *Clara Nevada*, which was heading from Skagway to Juneau in February 1898. Battling hurricane-force winds as high as ninety miles per hour, the *Clara Nevada* sank off Eldred Rock about thirty miles south of Skagway, killing all on board. Exactly how many perished is a mystery since the only passenger list went down with the ship, but estimates of the death toll range from 60 to more than 130 lost. The cause of the wreck is also a mystery. While it appears that there was a fire on board, whether it started before or after the ship foundered on the ledges off Eldred Rock is unknown. Reflecting on the accident, the *New York Times* noted, "The *Nevada* affair simply emphasized the conditions that prevail in northern waters. Ships of all sorts and conditions are being pressed into the service to carry crowds to the gold fields." And the *Clara Nevada* was not the only unfortunate ship that year. Thirty-three others wrecked along Alaska's southeastern coast in 1898.

This dreadful record of disaster spurred demands that the government take additional steps to ensure the safety of ships traveling Alaska's breathtakingly scenic but too often deadly marine highway. As a result the congressional funding spigot finally opened during Theodore Roosevelt's presidency, and the board built the first two lighthouses in Alaska in 1902—the Five Finger Island Lighthouse, located south of Juneau in Frederick Sound, and the Sentinel Island Lighthouse, between Juneau and Skagway. A lighthouse on Eldred Rock, a sliver of an island located in the Lynn Canal, set against the soaring backdrop of the majestic Chilkat Range, was completed in 1906.

By the end of the decade, there were thirteen Alaskan lighthouses, most along the southeast coast and the Inside Passage. A few were much farther away, including the Scotch Cap Lighthouse (1903) and the Cape Sarichef Lighthouse (1904), which were on opposite sides of Unimak

Eldred Rock Lighthouse, circa 1915.

Island at the eastern tip of the Aleutians, a gracefully curving chain of rugged volcanic islands stretching more than one thousand miles from the Alaskan Peninsula into the Pacific Ocean. The Russians called Unimak Island the "roof of hell" on account of its smoke-belching volcanoes. The lighthouses marked Unimak Pass, the main shipping channel from the Pacific into the Bering Sea, which is only about ten miles wide at its narrowest point. This was a particularly dangerous stretch of water, subject to strong currents and thick fog, and the two lighthouses were soon dubbed the "Tombstone Twins" because of the great number of shipwrecks that occurred in the area.

TWO OTHER MAJOR ADDITIONS to the board's purview were Puerto Rico and Hawaii, both of which became American territories in 1898, during the administration of President William McKinley. Puerto Rico's annexation came about as a result of that burst of aggressive imperialism known as the Spanish-American War, in which the United States easily and soundly defeated Spanish forces in Cuba and the Philippines, and effectively ended Spanish colonial rule in the Western Hemisphere. In the subsequent Treaty of Paris, signed in December 1898, the United States wrenched from Spain not only Puerto Rico, but also the Philippines and Guam. In contrast, the American takeover of the sovereign Kingdom of Hawaii didn't require a war, but rather was initiated with a coup, in which a group comprised mainly of American sugar growers, with the tacit support of the United States government, and backed by a threatening contingent of U.S. Marines, ousted Queen Liliuokalani in 1893. The provisional government that took over lobbied hard for the United States to annex Hawaii, which it did five years later, in August 1898, at the tail end of the Spanish-American War, when the strategic value of the Hawaiian Islands rose due to their usefulness as a military base for protecting America's growing interests in Asia.

The board didn't take over the responsibility for Puerto Rico's lighthouses until 1899, one year after the end of the Spanish-American War, and when it did it found that the territory's lighthouse system was in very good shape. Its thirteen lighthouses had been well built and fitted with Fresnel lenses by the Spaniards. In addition to repairing existing lighthouses, the board established two new lighthouses—one on Mona Island (1900), and the other on Cabras Island (1908)—that ended up being the last two lighthouses built in Puerto Rico.

The board gained the responsibility for Hawaii's nineteen lighthouses in 1904, and found that they were "generally of a very crude character," poorly built, and had relatively weak, antiquated lights. The board immediately initiated repairs, upgraded many of the lights with Fresnel lenses, and built new lighthouses, one of the most important of which was located at Makapu'u Point at the southeastern tip of Oahu, the third largest island in the Hawaiian archipelago. The point is nearly 650 feet high, with jagged lava cliffs plunging precipitously down to the sea. Hawaiians had been clamoring for a lighthouse at this spot since the late 1800s, on account of the many wrecks in the vicinity, but it wasn't until 1906 that plans for the lighthouse moved ahead. Congress appropriated funds for the lighthouse at the end of June, and just

Makapu'u Point Lighthouse atop Makapu'u Point, Oahu, Hawaii.

two months later a wreck near Makapuʻu Point confirmed the wisdom of that decision.

In the early morning hours of August 20, 1906, J. W. Saunders, captain of the six-hundred-foot-long American-owned Pacific Mail steamer *Manchuria* was proceeding slowly not far from Makapuʻu Point, in heavy rain and low visibility. According to Saunders's later testimony, he mistook one small island for another, and as a result was far closer to the shore than he assumed. As soon as he heard breakers crashing, he shouted the order to reverse the engines. Billowing clouds of smoke belched from the ship's funnel, as the *Manchuria* shuddered almost to a complete stop before getting hung up on a reef. The more than two hundred startled but uninjured passengers were safely evacuated, and a few weeks later the badly damaged ship was towed to Honolulu Harbor and repaired. Although Saunders mostly blamed poor visibility for the wreck, he also cited the lack of a lighthouse on Makapuʻu Point as an important contributing factor.

The Makapuʻu Point Lighthouse, located roughly four hundred feet above the water and first lit three years after the accident in 1909, is only forty-six feet tall, but it houses a truly Brobdingnagian hyperradiant lens, the largest type of Fresnel lens ever made. Designed by members of the lighthouse-building Stevenson family and manufactured by Barbier and Company in France, the fourteen-ton lens boasts 1,188 prisms, and is twelve feet high, with an inside diameter of eight feet nine inches. The board had purchased the lens in 1877 and included it as part of the lighthouse exhibit at Chicago's World's Columbian Exposition of 1893—a world's fair commemorating the four-hundredth anniversary of Christopher Columbus's voyage of discovery (albeit, one year late), at which forty-six countries assembled and displayed many of their greatest technological and artistic achievements—among which those of the host nation ranked high. People flocked to see the huge lens, helping to make the lighthouse exhibit one of the most popular at the fair. The lens was then placed in storage until the board installed it at Makapuʻu Point. Very few hyperradiant lenses were manufactured, and the one at Makapuʻu Point is the only one ever used in the United States.

IN THE SPAN OF nearly sixty years, the board had transformed America's lighthouse establishment from one that was widely ridiculed during Pleasonton's reign into one that was among the best in the world, and by far the largest, both in terms of the number of navigational aides and the territory they covered. The more than 2,500 buoys, smaller beacons, and lightships that existed when Pleasonton was sacked in 1852 had mushroomed to nearly 11,000 by 1910. At the same time the number of lighthouses had risen from 325 to about 800, the majority of which were outfitted with the most up-to-date and effective illumination technology known to man, and operated by professional and competent keepers. The board employed around five thousand people—roughly fifteen hundred of whom were lighthouse keepers. Its far-flung network of navigational aids stretched over tens of thousands of miles of coastline and rivers, the result being that most of the

*Thirty Mile Point Lighthouse, in Barker, New York,
overlooking Lake Ontario, circa 1873.*

New London Ledge Lighthouse, New London, Connecticut, which was built in 1909.

dark spots that had long bedeviled mariners had been illuminated. This dramatic expansion mirrored and contributed to the phenomenal growth of the United States, which had transformed America into the world's largest industrial, economic, and agricultural power by the early 1900s.

Despite this great success, however, there was widespread concern that the lighthouse establishment had become too unwieldy for the board to manage effectively. Instead of an unpaid, nine-member organization with diffuse responsibility, which met only four times a year, many argued that what was needed was a centralized authority with a full-time chief executive at its helm to manage day-to-day operations and focus more tellingly on increasing efficiency and reducing operational costs. Another problem with the board was the role of navy and army personnel, who constituted seven of the nine members and also served as lighthouse inspectors (navy) and engineers (army) in the lighthouse districts. Although the branches had worked together well for many years, over time there had been increasing friction and disputes between the two groups, as each jockeyed to exercise control over administrative decisions and projects.

President William Howard Taft shared these concerns. In his 1909 Annual Message to Congress he urged the legislators to completely reorganize the lighthouse establishment. Congress did so the following year, abolishing the board, and replacing it with a civilian Bureau of Lighthouses located in the Department of Commerce and Labor (which became the Department of Commerce in 1913). A single individual, the commissioner of lighthouses, headed the bureau, more commonly known as the Lighthouse Service. Lighthouse inspectors were to be culled from civilian ranks, and although army engineers could still consult on and oversee construction and repair projects, they reported directly to the civilian inspectors.

In June 1910 Taft chose George Rockwell Putnam as the first commissioner of lighthouses. Forty-five years old, Putnam was born in Davenport, Iowa, in 1865 and grew up in a large family, in a house located on a bluff overlooking the banks of the Mississippi. Curious and adventuresome, he built a canoe to explore the mighty river, which, he said,

George R. Putnam,
the first commissioner
of lighthouses.

"rolled in an irresistible magic current through the days of" his youth. After high school he briefly worked as a surveyor, studied law for while, and then spent two years at a desk job in a Chicago railroad office before enrolling at the Rose Polytechnic Institute in Indiana.

Engineering degree in hand, Putnam—now a dapper, confident, and good-looking young man sporting a neatly clipped mustache—got a job at the Coast and Geodetic Survey, where he spent the next twenty years. This work took him to nearly every state in the Union, as well as the "bitter wastes of the Far North," and the "balmy warmth of the Far East." One of his most exciting assignments came in 1896–97, when he accompanied the intrepid explorer and naval officer Robert E. Peary to Greenland. While Putnam conducted magnetism and gravity experiments, Peary—who would later become embroiled in a heated controversy over his still-contested claim to have discovered the North Pole—focused his energies on digging up and bringing back to America the 4.5 billion-year-old Ahnighito, which at the time was the world's largest iron meteorite, tipping the scales at thirty-four tons.

After his adventures in Greenland, Putnam went on multiple voyages to Alaska; then, in 1900, he was sent to the Philippines, which had recently become an American territory as a result of the Spanish-American War. As director of the Coast and Geodetic Survey in the Philippines, Putnam oversaw the mapping of this extensive archipelago, only reluctantly returning to another survey job in Washington in 1906. It was in the Philippines that Putnam had met future president Taft, who became the territory's first civil governor in July 1901. Impressed by Putnam's administrative and technical skills, dedication, and work ethic, Taft had no qualms appointing him commissioner of lighthouses. According to Putnam, shortly after he got the job, Taft briefly met with him, and he "made no other stipulation than that he wanted the work done so well as to justify the new law."

PUTNAM'S PASSION FOR THE Lighthouse Service's work was undeniable. "The lighthouse and the lightship," he wrote, "appeal to the interest and better instinct of man because they are symbolic of never-ceasing watchfulness, of steadfast endurance in every exposure, of widespread helpfulness. The building and the keeping of the lights is a picturesque and humanitarian work of the nation." During his twenty-five-year tenure, Putnam's sought to preserve America's position as one of the best lighthouse establishments in the world, while modernizing the system and reducing expenditures.

Putnam strove to take the fullest advantage of new technologies, such as radio beacons, which could transmit radio signals in Morse code hundred of miles. With the installation of radio beacons at lighthouses, mariners with radio compasses on their ships could pick up the signals and determine their position relative to a lighthouse well before the lighthouse's beam could be seen or its fog signal heard, allowing mariners to accurately and safely plot their course. And if mariners were able to pick up signals from two radio beacons, they could use triangulation to pinpoint exactly where they were on the water. Radio beacons were particularly valuable during bad weather. As Putnam observed, "Only the radio signal penetrates the fog and rain which may blot out a light, however brilliant; it alone is unaffected by the roar of the storm which drowns the sound of the most powerful [fog] signal." Putnam began installing radio beacons at lighthouses and on lightships in 1921, and by the mid-1930s more than one hundred were in operation. Evidence of their effectiveness can be gleaned from the Great Lakes, where the number of vessels that stranded in the four years after radio beacons were installed was 50 percent less than the number that did so in the four years prior.

Putnam was also a strong advocate of electrification, which was rapidly sweeping the country, lighting cities and rural communities alike and powering the nation's ever-expanding industrial base. Thanks to the groundbreaking work of Thomas Alva Edison in his laboratory at Menlo Park, New Jersey, where he experimented with thousands of lightbulb filaments before finding ones that could burn for an extended period of time, America was becoming increasingly illuminated with the warm glow of incandescent lights. These not only often replaced the harsh glare of carbon arc lamps, but also spread the benefits of artificial light throughout society, thus spurring economic development while at the same time dramatically improving the quality of life for large numbers of Americans. The board had tentatively begun converting lighthouses to electricity around the turn of the century, and Putnam greatly accelerated that process. Relying on generators, batteries, and an expanding network of power lines, an ever-growing number of lighthouses were electrified, and by the 1930s the majority of them were lit with electric lamps using incandescent bulbs that were considerably brighter than the lights they replaced.

Electrification helped Putnam move ahead with lighthouse automation, a key part of his strategy to reduce costs. Innovative timers that turned lights on and off according to a preset schedule, along with electric devices for operating smaller fog signals, made it possible for many lighthouses to run on their own, a process that was facilitated by the use of lightbulb changers that automatically replaced burned-out bulbs with new ones.

But it was not only electrification that led to increased automation. About the same time as Putnam was appointed, acetylene gas began to be used as a lighthouse illuminant. The gas, fed to the lamp from a pressurized tank, was mixed with air and burned under a mantle, in the same manner as kerosene was burned in an IOV lamp. With the addition of an ingenious device called a sun valve, lights fueled by acetylene could be run automatically.

The Swedish engineer Nils Gustaf Dalén invented the sun valve in 1907, which won him the Nobel Prize for Physics in 1912. The valve was composed of four metal rods enclosed in a glass tube. The central rod had a dull, black, heat-absorbing surface, and was connected to a valve that controlled the flow of acetylene from the tank. The other three rods, which supported the black rod, were gilded, highly polished, and heat resistant. During daylight hours, while the outer rods stayed relatively cool, the black rod absorbed solar radiation (heat) and expanded, thereby closing the valve and extinguishing the lamp. As the daylight diminished and the black rod cooled, it contracted, opening the valve and letting the gas flow freely to the lamp, where a continually burning pilot ignited the gas. Sun valves, combined with acetylene tanks and automatic mantle changers, were particularly useful for automating remote lighthouses that couldn't easily be supplied with electricity, or where it was difficult to maintain keepers.

Automation was a great financial boon. A single keeper could in some instances run lighthouses that formerly required multiple keepers, and many automated lighthouses didn't need a keeper at all (although they would still have to be visited periodically for maintenance). During Putnam's tenure, hundreds of lighthouses were automated, resulting in annual savings of hundreds of thousands of dollars.

On the other hand, automation could have been an unmitigated disaster for the keepers whose jobs were being eliminated, had it not been for Putnam's obvious concern for their well-being. By proceeding cautiously and planning appropriately, Putnam avoided layoffs by transferring displaced keepers to other lighthouses that had vacancies. But the trend was clear: Automation was the wave of the future, and Putnam had begun a process that would ultimately do away with the keeper's profession entirely, forever relegating it to being a relic of the more romantic past.

PUTNAM'S RELUCTANCE TO FIRE the displaced reflected his deep respect for the keepers themselves. "Although the pay is small, the life sometimes lonely, and the work often hazardous," Putnam wrote, "the Lighthouse Service attracts an excellent class of faithful men,* willing to take large risks in doing their duty and in helping others in distress." With each passing year Putnam grew more impressed with keepers' devotion to their jobs, and he claimed that there were only a few instances in which his confidence was misplaced. Viewing them as the backbone of the service, he firmly believed that they should be treated fairly. This perspective led him to fight on their behalf on a number of important fronts, one of which involved pensions.

When Putnam became commissioner, many keepers were well into their seventies and had been working for many decades. While some of these older keepers no doubt wanted to continue working, most wanted to retire, but they couldn't afford to because they had no retirement system and therefore were not eligible for a pension. Putnam viewed this as shabby treatment, especially given the immense value to the nation of the keepers' work, plus the fact that almost all the lighthouse services in other countries provided pensions for their keepers.

The elderly keepers posed a serious dilemma for Putnam, as many of them were getting too old and infirm to perform their job adequately. If he fired them, they might soon be destitute, and if he kept them on, the quality of the Lighthouse Service would eventually suffer. Despite the risks, Putnam decided that he wouldn't force any keepers to retire until a pension plan was in place. For eight years Putnam used his considerable political connections to lobby Congress to create a retirement plan for keepers, and he was aided in this cause by people from around the country, particularly mariners and newspaper editors in coastal communities, all of whom knew the keepers quite well and could testify that their good

---

*Typical of his time, Putnam wrote "men" although there were already some female keepers.

work and dedication to saving lives warranted more than a handshake on the way out the door.

These efforts finally bore fruit on June 20, 1918, when President Woodrow Wilson signed legislation enabling keepers to retire after thirty years of service at age sixty-five, and to collect a generous pension (the mandatory retirement age was seventy). Soon thereafter, not unpredictably, a large number of keepers who had been hoping that this day would arrive cheerfully submitted their resignations. The pension law was both a real coup and a landmark, as it was the first retirement system enacted in the United States for federal civil service workers. At the signing ceremony Wilson remarked to Putnam, "I am heartily glad to have been of any service to the men who served the government in the lighthouses. I know how important their work is and feel that nothing but justice has been done them."

Just a year later Wilson had good reason to be very thankful for the exemplary work performed by the nation's keepers, because it may have saved his life. After attending the Paris Peace Conference and signing the Treaty of Versailles that officially ended World War I, Wilson headed back the United States in July 1919 on the ocean liner turned troop transport *George Washington*. Off the coast of Massachusetts, the 723-foot-long steamer encountered dense fog that reduced visibility to near zero. Unaware of his exact location, and oblivious to the danger that lay directly ahead, the captain had no idea that his ship was on a collision course, plowing straight toward the jagged, rocky shore of Thacher Island. In such miserable conditions the bright beams of Thacher Island's twin light were utterly useless, but the sonorous blasts from its foghorn were finally heard by the sailor on watch, who immediately informed the captain, giving him enough time to change course and avoid certain disaster.

USING THE SAME DRIVE he employed in the pension battle, Putnam helped persuade Congress to provide disability benefits to keepers who were disabled by disease or injury, as long as the impairment was not "due to vicious habits, intemperance, or willful misconduct." And the families of keepers who died in the line of duty were finally able to collect survivors' benefits. Putnam also threw down the gauntlet on an issue that had long troubled keepers—their pay.

Keepers began complaining about their pay almost as soon as the federal government took over the responsibility for lighthouses, and when Putnam arrived on the scene they were still complaining. The average annual pay for a keeper in 1840 was four hundred dollars. In 1867 it rose to six hundred, where it stayed for fifty years. In contrast, by 1900 the average federal worker was earning roughly a thousand dollars per year. These keepers' salaries being averages, there were those who got more or less, depending on the circumstances, and of course head keepers received higher pay than assistants. For example, in the 1850s, when gold fever had blistered people's minds, head keepers on the west coast were paid a thousand dollars because that was necessary in a hyperinflated market in which a domestic servant or lowly clerk might earn nearly that much. (In later years, however, west coast keepers' salaries were reduced, though they remained still higher than most places in the country.) Keepers at particularly isolated or dangerous lighthouses, or those that were more difficult to run by virtue of their size or complexity, were also paid on the upper end of the scale. And on the Great Lakes, where most lighthouses were closed during the winter months when the ice made ship traffic impossible, keepers would often be paid less than the average. Of course keepers got many other benefits besides pay, including rent-free housing and a variety of supplies provided by the government periodically throughout the year, including food at remote locations. Nevertheless, no matter where it fell on the spectrum, keepers' pay was never munificent, and when it stagnated for fifty years that only exacerbated their situation.

Putnam believed keepers should be paid more, not only to benefit those already in the service but also to ensure that salaries remained competitive enough to hire competent people. Year after year Putnam pleaded for keepers' pay to be increased, and many keepers themselves submitted petitions urging the same. At last Congress responded, and in 1918 the average annual keeper's pay climbed to $840. In subsequent years there were other raises, and by the early 1930s keepers' salaries ranged from $1,080 all the way up to $2,100. Though still not extravagant, the pay scale was certainly very welcome, especially during the Great Depression when so many people were out of work.

AT THE SAME TIME that the supportive Putnam was fighting to improve the financial status of keepers, he was also forcing them to be thrifty. According to the historian Hans Christian Adamson, the "Lighthouse Bureau was not only dollar conscious; it was actually penny-pinching. *Save, stretch,* and *substitute* had become a policy and a creed." The detailed stories of keepers being asked to be frugal were legendary. It was not uncommon for paintbrushes to be used until they were worn down to the nubs, chipped screwdrivers to be filed back into shape, or used lens-cleaning rags to be repurposed to patch clothes. One lighthouse district superintendent, upon learning that a keeper was going to throw out a can opener with a broken blade, put an immediate halt to such wastefulness. "Well," the superintendent said, "the corkscrew on it is all right. It could still be used for opening a bottle. And I don't mean a bottle of wine!" In the course of saving money, sometimes the bureau allowed the secondary buildings at lighthouses, such as the keeper's quarters, to deteriorate. Given his emphasis on thriftiness, it is not surprising that Putnam had a picture of Stephen Pleasonton hung prominently in his office. But there was a major difference between Putnam's and Pleasonton's economies: Unlike Pleasonton, Putnam had an extremely competent workforce beneath him, and he never let his cost-cutting efforts diminish the quality of the navigational aids that mariners relied on.

Most keepers didn't seem to mind Putnam's frugality, and in fact many took a measure of pride in making do with less, and in being creative when it came to solving problems. And that pride extended to their broader job as well. Putnam made keepers feel that their work was important, and he frequently expressed his faith in them, both privately and publicly. They, in turn, had great admiration for and loyalty to their commissioner, who had done so much to improve their lives, and had made them feel good about being in government service.

Putnam also imbued his workforce with a shared sense of pride, community, and professionalism by awarding efficiency stars to keepers, and launching the *Lighthouse Service Bulletin*, a monthly newsletter that provided informative and entertaining reading material. Articles covered a great range of topics, including technological advances, legislative developments, new construction projects, and retirements. Some of the coverage was more lighthearted, such as when the bulletin offered recipes or shared a humorous anecdote. In the May 1921 issue, for example, L. D. Marchant, a keeper who had worked at three lighthouses in Chesapeake Bay for more than thirty-eight years, yet had never been sick for a single day, was asked how he achieved that remarkable record. "The secret of my good health," he replied, "is that I have been where the doctors could not get to me."

Sometimes, however, the stories were tragic. In May and June 1925, the *Bulletin* told of a horrific accident at the Makapuʻu Point Lighthouse. Early in the morning on April 9 of that year, assistant keepers Alexander Toomey and John Kaohimaunu were getting ready to change the watch. In the process of putting alcohol into the lighter that was used to heat the IOV lamp, a small amount of alcohol dripped on the floor. When Toomey struck a match, the alcohol fumes ignited, causing a fiery explosion. Both keepers were severely burned, but Toomey got the worst of it, his clothes having caught fire, leaving him "charred black and crinkled." As the head keeper was about to rush the two injured men to the hospital, Toomey's wife begged to come along. Toomey, however, insisted that she remain at the lighthouse, since with all three keepers gone, she was the only one who could watch the light. According to the *Bulletin*, before being taken away Toomey gathered his wife and children around him to recite the Lord's Prayer, and then he turned to his wife and said, "Stand by the light and keep it burning." Those were the last words he and his wife ever shared, for he died the next day.

———

JUST AS EARLIER AMERICAN WARS affected lighthouse operations, so too did World War I, and not in an insignificant way. Even before the Declaration of War on April 2, 1917, the U.S. government instructed keepers at primary seacoast lighthouses to keep a "bright lookout" for German submarines and report any sightings. Soon after the declaration, President Wilson transferred twenty-one of those lighthouses and their keepers to the navy for the duration of the war. Navy signalmen were stationed alongside the keepers, and together they maintained a round-the-clock vigil, scanning the horizon for enemy submarines. To help with that task, the government provided a "Submarine Silhouette Book," which included illustrations depicting German submarine profiles at the surface, as well as photographs of submarines. Keepers at all other seacoast lighthouses, while not under naval supervision, were also instructed to be on the lookout for the enemy. Some lighthouses were darkened or dimmed to avoid having the lighthouses' beams silhouette American vessels at night, making them easier targets for German submarines. And telephone service was extended to many lighthouses to facilitate quick reporting of sightings or suspicious activity.

Lighthouse keepers also did their part to help alleviate war-related food shortages. In May 1917 President Wilson appointed future president Herbert Hoover head of the newly created United States Food Administration, whose mission was to provide food for American and Allied troops, as well as the American and Allied populations. With the rallying cry "Food Will Win the War," the Food Administration urged every American to pitch in, and lighthouse keepers were no exception. The secretary of commerce encouraged keepers to cultivate as much land as possible on lighthouse property. Even keepers at lighthouses with virtually unarable land were urged to plant crops, and to spur them on the service published reports of keepers who had succeeded despite formidable obstacles. One example was Henry L. Thomas, the keeper at Nantucket's Great Point Lighthouse, who was praised for growing "good quality" potatoes in the sand. And at the Turn Point Lighthouse on Stuart

Island off the coast of Washington, instead of cultivating the land Louis Borchers, the head keeper, farmed the sea. The waters surrounding the island were teeming with a veritable cornucopia of different fish, which Borchers loved catching and canning. In 1918 alone he preserved 311 cans of fish, including salmon, sardines, and grayfish, as well as salmon caviar. Hoover was greatly impressed by Borchers's success, and urged other keepers to follow his lead.

Lightships too were enlisted in the war effort, with a few being transferred to the navy, and all of them being required to keep a watchful eye on the horizon for the enemy. The Diamond Shoal Lightship, moored off Cape Hatteras, gave its last measure of service performing this duty. On August 6, 1918, the lightship's crew saw a German submarine attacking an American merchant vessel, whereupon the lightship's radio operator alerted other American ships in the area. But the Germans were listening in, and they trained their guns on the lightship. Before sinking it, however, the Germans allowed its twelve-member crew to escape in lifeboats. The lightship's warnings, however, had not been in vain. At least twenty-five American ships heard them, and headed inshore, out of range of the prowling German submarine.

WHEN PUTNAM RETIRED IN 1935 at age seventy, in the midst of the deepest depression the country has ever experienced, he was proud of his achievements—and he had every right to be. During his tenure the number of navigational aids had more than doubled—including the addition of many new lighthouses—while at the same time the number of people working for the service had been reduced by about 15 percent. Much of that reduction was due to automation, which enabled hundreds of lighthouses to operate without keepers, thereby launching a trend that served as a harbinger of the future, a time when keepers would no longer be needed at all. Not only had the Lighthouse Service become more efficient, it had also become more effective in carrying out its primary mission of safeguarding the nation's waters. According to *Lloyd's Register of Shipping*, between 1920 and 1935 the United States rose from being the sixth safest country in the world, measured by the percentage of ships lost in maritime accidents, to the second safest, with only the Dutch having a better record. Yet another measure of Putnam's success is the sense of pride and accomplishment he instilled in his employees for a job well done. The morale among keepers in particular had never been higher. The *New York Times* offered a fitting coda to Putnam's career in its editorial announcing his retirement: "He was one of those quiet, capable, hardworking chiefs of the permanent government service of whom the general public hears little, but to whom it owes much. When you think of men of his character and devotion, the word 'bureaucracy' loses its sting."

Harold. D. King, an engineer who had twenty-four years' experience working in the Lighthouse Service and had most recently been the deputy commissioner for lighthouses, succeeded Putnam. King had known Putnam since their days working together for the Coast and Geodetic Survey in the Philippines, and he looked forward to further modernizing the service. But he had a only short time to make his mark, for in 1939 the Lighthouse Service was transferred to the U.S. Coast Guard, inaugurating the modern era of lighthouse history. Before getting to the modern era, however, it is important to circle back to what has often been called the golden age of lighthouses—the period from the inception of the Lighthouse Board in 1852 up through the last days of the Lighthouse Service. It was during those decades that the lighthouse system experienced its greatest expansion, and America's lighthouses, both literally and metaphorically, shone brighter than ever before. It was also a time when many of the most fascinating and, at times, heartwrenching stories in the history of lighthouses took place—stories about keepers and their lives, dramatic rescues, marvels of engineering and construction, birds, and a particularly deadly hurricane.

CHAPTER 10

KEEPERS AND
THEIR LIVES

· · · · · · · · · · · · · · ·

*Engraving of the
keeper on duty at the
Farallon Island
Lighthouse, 1892.*

I N ENVISIONING A TYPICAL LIGHTHOUSE KEEPER IN THE
late-nineteenth and early-twentieth centuries, one might easily conjure
up a pastoral and romantic scene of a bewhiskered man smoking a pipe,
sitting on a porch, and soaking in the beautiful scenery and sounds
of the waves gently breaking on the shore. Of course the keeper had

to tend the light, and the fog signal if there was one, and maintain his quarters and other lighthouse property, but that wasn't particularly taxing work, and it still left plenty of time to pursue other interests, ruminate about life in general, or simply to enjoy the splendid view. Although this simplistic and pleasant image contains elements of truth, it falls short of reality and the historical record. A keeper's life was hardly one of relative leisure—and furthermore the profession itself was not limited to men.

The primary responsibility of lighthouse keepers was to maintain a good light and fog signal. In the late-nineteenth and early-twentieth centuries this was no simple task. The government issued extremely detailed instructions that told keepers what to do, how to do it, and when to do it. The 1881 instruction manual included more than one hundred pages of text and diagrams, and the manual for 1918 was twice as long. The number of keepers who performed this work depended on the circumstances. Lighthouses with smaller-order lenses and no fog signals to maintain typically had only one keeper, whereas those with larger lenses and more complicated fog signals could have as many as five—the head keeper, and assistants who were ranked in descending order based on their time in service and experience.

At lighthouses with two or more keepers, work was divided between "departments." A keeper in the first department focused on the lighting apparatus. Before sunrise the keeper ascended the stairs to the lantern room and donned a linen apron to keep the lens from being scratched by contact with coarse clothes or buttons. After extinguishing the lamp at sunrise, the keeper hung curtains or shades around the inside of the lantern room. This kept the sun's rays from damaging or discoloring the lens and degrading the litharge, the lead-based compound that held the glass prisms in place within the lens's brass frame. An even greater concern, however, was the very real and persistent fear of fire. It must be realized that light can travel through a Fresnel lens in both directions. At night, when the lamp is on, the light travels out toward the horizon, but during the day, if the sun's rays were allowed to stream into the lantern room unobstructed, they would reflect and

Keeper Unaka Jennette, cleaning the first-order Fresnel lens at the Cape Hatteras Lighthouse in 1933. This is a staged picture, which is why Jennette is not wearing an apron.

refract through the lens and concentrate much of their heating power on the oil- or kerosene-filled lamp within, leading to a potentially fiery or explosive situation.

Once the curtains were hung, the keeper, feather brush in hand, removed dust from the lens, and wiped it down with a soft linen cloth before giving it a good polish with a leather buffing skin. The lamp and the revolving clockwork mechanism were also cleaned, and the lamp was filled with oil, while a spare lamp was readied for operation in the event that the main lamp needed to be replaced during the night. One of the most important tasks was trimming the wicks with a scissors to remove the residue of burning. The trimming of the wicks, which also had to be performed during the night to keep the flame steady and bright, was something that keepers had been doing for as long as lighthouse lamps had been using wicks to burn whale, lard, and colza oil, or kerosene. And it is because of this ritual trimming of the wicks that keepers affectionately referred to themselves as "wickies."

While the first department focused on the lighting apparatus, the second department was responsible for a variety of maintenance activities, including cleaning the walls and floors of the lantern room and the watch room below, as well as the balconies encircling the lantern, and all the lantern's glass panes, inside and out. Cleaning the outside of the glass panes required steady nerves and no fear of heights, for to get to the upper panes the keeper usually had to stand on the balcony railing, or on the narrow lip of the ironwork muntins, or bars, that held the glass in place. Even though there were typically handgrips for the keeper to hold, this high-wire act was dangerous, especially if the outside of the lantern was coated with water or ice. In a few instances keepers engaged in this activity slipped and fell to their death.

One of the most labor-intensive jobs in the second department was polishing the brass fixtures on the lighting apparatus and the machinery clockwork, as well as the many brass tools and appliances. After years of listening to keepers complain about this job, lighthouse machinist Fred Morong wrote a poem in the late 1920s, entitled *Brasswork or The Lighthouse Keeper's Lament*, a few stanzas of which will suffice to drive home the message.

> *O what is the bane of the lightkeeper's life*
> *That causes him worry, struggle and strife,*
> *That makes him use cuss words, and beat his wife?*
> *It's brasswork.*
>
> *What makes him look ghastly consumptive and thin,*
> *What robs him of health of vigor and vim,*
> *And cause despair and drives him to sin?*
> *It's brasswork.*
> . . . .
> *And when I have polished until I am cold*
> *And I'm taken aloft to the Heavenly fold*
> *Will my harp and my crown be made of pure gold?*
> *No, brasswork.*

Keepers were supposed to have all the above tasks completed by ten in the morning, so that the lighthouse would be ready for lighting in the evening, promptly at sunset. The light had to be cared for during the night, as well. Where there were multiple keepers, watches were established, usually of four to six hours, when the keeper on duty would stay awake in the watch room below the lantern room, and tend the light as necessary. When there were no assistants, the keeper visited the light at least twice between 8:00 p.m. and sunrise. During storms the keeper remained in the tower throughout the night, for that was when mariners were most in need of a steady, strong light, and when the lighting apparatus was most vulnerable to being upset by the rough conditions. In the midst of a tempest, keepers often had to go outside the lantern room to clear the glass panes of salt accumulation, snow, or ice. If cleaning the glass panes during the day and in perfect conditions required nerves of steel, under stormy conditions it could be all the more frightening, as George Easterbrook discovered one nasty night in January 1860.

Just seventeen, Easterbrook was the second assistant keeper at the Cape

"Christmas Eve in a Lighthouse," which appeared in the December 30, 1876, issue of Harper's Weekly.

Disappointment Lighthouse, a fifty-three-foot-tall brick tower located at the extreme southwestern corner of Washington State on a rocky promontory at the mouth of the Columbia River. Around midnight during a violent rainstorm with whipping winds, he ventured outside to the balcony to clear glass panes of salt spray and grime. Since the door had a faulty latch, he planned to prop it open while he worked, but no sooner had he made his exit than a gust slammed the door shut, locking it from the inside. After yanking on the door to no avail, the conscientious Easterbrook spent the next half hour cleaning the glass panes, only then focusing on his predicament. He didn't relish the thought of staying on the balcony until morning, when the other keepers would come looking for him, and he was greatly concerned that if he didn't get back into the lighthouse within the next two hours, the light would go out. If that happened, he would not only risk losing his pay, and possibly his job, but, more important, he might be held responsible for any shipwrecks that occurred.

According to Easterbrook, all these thoughts rushing through his head nearly drove him "insane," but he finally came out of his fear-induced stupor, put on his thick buckskin gloves, and began climbing down the side of the tower using the one-inch-thick copper lightning rod wire as his lifeline. This slender thread was affixed to the tower only at the top, thus as he slowly lowered himself, the tremendous gusts swung him "like a pendulum of a clock," and "twirled and twisted" him about in "mid-air," at times leaving him dangling perilously close to the edge of the cliff. After what seemed like an eternity, Easterbrook's feet touched the earth, but then a new problem arose. He was on the side of the lighthouse where the flat ground at the tower's base was not very wide before it sloped precipitously toward the water. Every time he swung toward the tower and tried to let go of the wire and stand erect, the wind would send him and the heavy wire flying back into the air toward the ocean. He knew that if he lost his grip at one of those moments, he "would fall headlong down, down, bounding from rock to rock, and at last be tossed about a disfigured corpse in the shallow water at the cliff's" base. With his strength fading fast, he couldn't hold on much longer. So, summoning his last reserves, he let go of the wire with one hand and waited "for the next heavy blast" to fling him against the tower. When his body slammed into the lighthouse, he cast the wire behind him, then hugged the brick tower with his outstretched arms, and slowly edged his way around the structure's base until the ground was "wide enough to drop safely on." Thoroughly spent, Easterbrook blacked out. After coming to a little while later, he crawled to the lighthouse door, undid the bolt, then laboriously climbed up the stairs to the lantern room, where he soon revived the now-dim light. Although Easterbrook had triumphed, this close call proved too much for him. A few weeks later he resigned, and went on to become a medical doctor.

Keepers were also responsible for the fog signal, which had to be frequently cleaned, and checked to make sure it was in working order. Operating the fog signal during extended periods could be backbreaking work. For example, in 1887, when the keepers at the Point Reyes Lighthouse had to keep the fog signal running for 176 hours, they had to shovel nearly 25,000 pounds of coal into the boilers.

Looking up the spiral staircase at the Dice Head Lighthouse, in Castine, Maine.

When lighthouses began using electricity in the late 1800s and early 1900s, the keepers' routine changed, assuming the keeper's position had not been eliminated as a result of automation. No longer did they have to lug heavy cans of kerosene up to the lantern room. Since the light burned clean, there was no soot or oil residue to wipe from the lamp, the lens, or the lantern room's glass panes. Without wicks to trim, "wickies" became "switchies," who simply flicked the lights on and off. Special sensors that set off an alarm when the light went out eliminated the need for keepers to stand watch. And in some cases electrically operated fog signals meant that keepers could dispense with the job of feeding coal to a hungry boiler. Some of the routine, however, remained the same, such as cleaning the lens and the brass too.

Beyond the primary responsibility of operating the light and the fog signal, keepers had many other duties. Lighthouse boats required attention, broken glass panes had to be replaced, and lighthouse buildings had to be repaired and painted periodically. Keepers were also busy filling out paperwork, including monthly reports on the lighthouse's condition, quarterly reports on expenditures, and when necessary, reports on damage to the lighthouse, as well as shipwrecks that occurred in the vicinity. In addition, keepers maintained a daily logbook that recorded weather conditions, official visits, lighthouse-related projects, and any unusual occurrences.

Although most logbook entries were unexciting, laconic, and usually written in the matter-of-fact style of a police blotter, there were times when—revealing both the ecstasies and sorrows of life—they were anything but mundane. In 1875 James Corgan, the head keeper at the Manitou Island Lighthouse, a skeletal tower located about three miles off the tip of Michigan's Keweenaw Peninsula in Lake Superior, penned the following in the station's log. "Principal keeper started at 8:00 p.m. in the station boat with wife for Cooper Harbor (distant 14 miles), in anticipation of an increase soon after arriving. When one and one half miles east of Horseshoe Harbor, Mrs. Corgan gave birth to a rollicking boy; all things lovely, had everything comfortable aboard. Sea a dead calm." While Corgan joyfully recorded his son's entry into the world, James A.

*Stannard Rock Lighthouse, circa 1882. Located in Lake Superior,
twenty-three miles from the nearest land, Stannard Rock Lighthouse was often
referred to as "the loneliest place in America."*

McCobb, the keeper at Burnt Island Lighthouse, a squat granite tower located just off the coast of Boothbay Harbor, Maine, noted a melancholy exit in his log entry for March 22, 1877: "[My] wife died this morning about two o'clock of congestion of the lungs and cankers in the throat, stomach, and bowels. She had been in feeble health all winter but able to be about the house attending to her work until about two weeks before her death. . . . Her age was fifty three years and four months."

Personal illnesses notwithstanding, lighthouses had to be staffed 365 days a year, unless they were automated, or located on the Great Lakes where most lighthouses were closed during the winter. While keepers were allowed to go to religious services on Sundays, and leave their posts on other important public occasions or to procure supplies, active light-houses were never to be left wholly unattended. Whenever a keeper was away, either an assistant keeper had to remain at the lighthouse, or, if there were no assistants, a family member, or someone hired by the keeper, had to stay behind. At lighthouses with a lone keeper, vacations were few and far between, and if taken at all, they were contingent upon having someone cover while the keeper was off-site. Where there were multiple keepers, work rotations were established to provide much-deserved breaks. The keepers at remote Cape Sarichef and Scotch Cap lighthouses in Alaska, for example, were given one year off for every three years of duty; at other sites closer to civilization, leaves were more frequent and of much shorter duration.

SINCE LIGHTHOUSES WERE PUBLIC structures, and objects of respect and veneration in the larger community, it was expected that people would visit them, and, in turn, that keepers would act as welcoming ambassadors of the lighthouse establishment. Keepers were supposed to be courteous and polite to visitors, and show them around as long as it didn't interfere with other lighthouse duties. Tours were limited to daylight hours, and under no circumstances were the keepers to allow intoxicated people to enter the lighthouse. They were also to watch visitors closely to make sure that they didn't handle the lighthouse apparatus, or worse, carve their initials into the lens, the glass panes, or the tower itself. (Fortunately, such vandalism was a rare occurrence.)

While visiting lighthouses had been a popular pastime in the first half of the nineteenth century, it developed into an even more fashionable activity in the second half of the century, and on into the early twentieth, a time when people were being increasingly exposed to stories about, and images of, lighthouses, and came to regard them in a romantic way, as captivating symbols of America's glorious maritime heritage. The press helped fuel this surge in interest. Beginning in the mid-1800s, as the number of newspapers and magazines exploded, lighthouses became a popular topic, covered by well-known authors in major publications. Many of these pieces focused on engineering feats, daring rescues, and the unusual lives that keepers led. Not only articles but also numerous books used lighthouses as a motif, the most popular of which was the bestseller *Captain January*, published in 1890 by Laura E. H. Richards, the daughter of Dr. Samuel Gridley Howe, the famed abolitionist and founder of the Perkins School for the Blind in Watertown, Massachusetts, and Julia Ward Howe. Her mother, a committed abolitionist in her own right, is best remembered for having written the lyrics of the patriotic Civil War song "The Battle Hymn of the Republic," which became the anthem of the Union and begins, "Mine eyes have seen the glory of the coming of the Lord."

In Richards's story, Januarius Judkins, a former sea captain better known as Captain January, is the kindly keeper of the fictitious Cape Tempest Lighthouse, located on a rocky island in Maine. After a ruinous storm batters the coast, sinking a ship within sight of the lighthouse, Captain January spies some wreckage floating toward the shore. His eyes focused on a white sail wrapped around a broken spar, he notices something moving. Thinking that there might be a survivor, Captain January rushes down to the rocks, pulls the spar out of the water, and cuts the sail away only to find a dead woman clutching her baby girl, who miraculously is still alive but asleep. As soon as Captain January lifts the baby from her mother's cold, lifeless arms, the girl opens her eyes, stares up at her rescuer, and laughs. Captain January views the girl as a gift from God, christens her "Star," and vows to raise her.

Captain January's blissful life with Star is thrown into disarray when a Mrs. Morton from Boston visits the area, sees Star on the mainland, and notices a strong resemblance between the girl and her sister, who died ten years earlier when the ship she was on foundered off Cape Tempest. Mrs. Morton is convinced that Star is her sister's long-lost daughter. Once this is proved, Mrs. Morton wants to take Star to Boston, but when she sees how much Star loves Captain January, she cannot bear to break them apart. So Star stays with Captain January until he dies, and then she is taken to Boston to be with her aunt and uncle.

Captain January had an even larger cultural impact when the legendary Hollywood mogul Darryl F. Zanuck, producer of films such as *The Grapes of Wrath* and *All About Eve*, brought the story to the silver screen in 1936, with America's most famous child actor, the talented Shirley Temple, playing the part of Star. The storyline, however, was shifted to make it more dramatic and to give it a happier ending that would better appeal to American audiences suffering through the depths of the Great Depression.

In the movie version the local truant officer threatens to take Star away from Captain January, who hadn't legally adopted her, while at the same time Captain January loses his job after the lighthouse switches to electricity and becomes automated. Trying to help ameliorate the difficult situation, one of Captain January's friends tracks down Star's wealthy aunt and uncle in Boston, who gladly take her into their home. Although Captain January realizes this is in Star's best interest, he grieves the loss, until he is joyously reunited with Star when her aunt and uncle hire him to captain their yacht.

THE PUBLIC'S INTEREST IN lighthouses was also piqued by the publication of numerous histories of lighthouses, as well as more technical treatises on lighthouse design, construction, and operation. Well-known poets, too, incorporated lighthouses into their work. Among them was Celia Thaxter, who, as a young girl in the late 1830s to mid-1840s, lived at the Isle of Shoals Lighthouse on White Island, off the New Hampshire coast, where her father was keeper. Her 1872 poem "The Watch of Boon Island" includes a stanza that captures the fervent prayer of keepers everywhere.

> And, while they trimmed the lamp with busy hands,
> "Shine far and wide through the dark, sweet light" they cried;
> "Bring safely back the sailors from all lands
> To waiting love,—wife, mother, sister, bride!"

It wasn't only literature that focused on lighthouses. With the rise of photography in the late 1800s, and particularly the introduction of relatively inexpensive, easy-to-operate cameras such as the Kodak No.1, millions of Americans were transformed into instant shutterbugs, passionately snapping pictures of anything that seemed worth remembering, including lighthouses, which—standing as solitary and visually appealing bulwarks of human ingenuity against the harsh beauty of a rugged coastline—presented a ready-made photographic composition.

Then, at the beginning of the twentieth century, the use of postcards exploded, and scenic lighthouses quickly became one of the most popular images to depict. Many businesses, too, began using lighthouses to hawk their products. For example the Armour Company's Lighthouse Cleanser sported a lighthouse on its label, whose "arms" held a metal scrub bucket emblazoned with the phrase "Show Me Dirt," while the lighthouse's beam illuminated where that dirt might be hiding. Smokers too were exposed to lighthouse imagery. Some cigarette manufacturers

A postcard from 1911 showing the old (right) and new (left) Cape Henry Lighthouses, in Virginia Beach, Virginia.

Early twentieth-century advertisement for Lighthouse Cleanser.

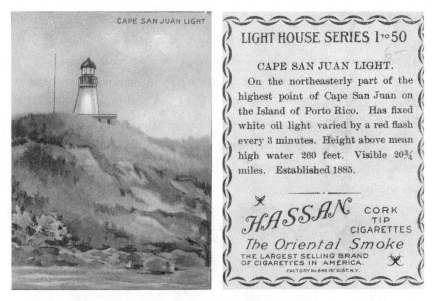

*The San Juan Lighthouse card (front and back), which was part of
the fifty-card series put out by Hassan Cigarettes in 1912.*

inserted cards into their packs that had colored drawings of lighthouses
on one side and interesting information about the lighthouses on the
other. These stiff, collectible cards were intended to entice the smoker
to purchase the cigarettes, and also to protect the cigarettes from being
crushed.

As descriptions and images of lighthouses saturated the public imagination through print, advertising, and in the movies, it was only natural that people became increasingly eager to visit them. Beyond mere
curiosity, other major draws were the resplendent locations, the fresh
air, the sun, the surf, and the picturesque buildings themselves, all of
which made lighthouses destinations that could delight the senses, uplift
the soul, and even restore the body. Remote lighthouses understandably
got few if any visitors, but sightseers often deluged more accessible lighthouses closer to population centers. And with the rise of automobiles in
the early twentieth century, a jaunt to the local lighthouse for a picnic, or
just to look around, became that much easier.

Some visitors were quite famous. The Transcendentalist writer Henry

David Thoreau rambled the length of Cape Cod four times between 1849 and 1857, and once stayed overnight at the Highland Lighthouse, where, in order "to make the most of so novel an experience," he accompanied the keeper on his rounds. Thoreau marveled at the amount of light generated by the fifteen Argand lamps, each with a twenty-one-inch reflector. "I thought it a pity that some poor student did not live there," mused Thoreau, "to profit by all that light, since he would not rob the mariner. 'Well,' [responded the keeper] . . . 'I do sometimes come up here and read the newspaper when they are noisy down below.'" Think of it, Thoreau wrote, "Fifteen argand lamps to read the newspaper by! Government oil!—light, enough, perchance, to read the Constitution by! I thought that he should read nothing less than his Bible by that light."

Robert Louis Stevenson, the Scottish author of *Treasure Island* and *Kidnapped*, and one of the few members of the famed Stevenson clan who didn't build lighthouses, visited the Point Pinos Lighthouse, perched on the tip of California's majestic Monterey Peninsula, in 1879 during his sojourn in the United States. Stevenson later wrote that at Point Pinos "You will find the light-keeper playing the piano, making models and bows and arrows, studying dawn and sunrise in amateur oil-painting, and with a dozen other elegant pursuits and interests to surprise his brave, old-country rivals."

A half century later, in September 1928, while on vacation in Wisconsin, President Calvin Coolidge and his wife visited the Devil's Island Lighthouse in Lake Superior for a pleasant lunch and tour of the facility. The head keeper, Hans F. Christensen, who served as guide, commented, "It's the first time in my four years here or my twelve years at Eagle Harbor [Lighthouse], Michigan, that anything so great has happened." And according to a journalist who reported on the momentous occasion, Christensen declared that "he was going to write to his inspector, telling him that the lighthouse had been inspected and OK'ed by the President of the United States himself."

The number of people visiting lighthouses increased almost exponentially, generating attendance figures that were often quite impressive. Between 1896 and 1916, roughly four thousand people visited the rather

Tourists visiting the Gay Head Lighthouse, on Martha's Vineyard, in 1877.

remote Cape Blanco Lighthouse in southwestern Oregon, and from July through September 1912, more than ten thousand people signed the register at the more easily reached Absecon Lighthouse in Atlantic City, New Jersey, which was not far from the major metropolises of Philadelphia and New York, thus making it the most visited lighthouse in the nation at the time. On the other hand, for example, before the highway was built near Minnesota's Split Rock Lighthouse on the northern shore of Lake Superior, tourist traffic was very light, but after the highway opened in 1924, the number of visitors boomed, with an estimated sixty thousand making the trek in 1937 alone. This flood of humanity led the service to add another keeper during the busy summer months to handle the influx. But when it was discovered that visitors had scratched the lens, the lantern room was promptly taken off the tour.

Keepers were usually happy to show off their lighthouses, but sometimes the throngs could be overwhelming, and visiting hours often had to be restricted to ensure that keepers had enough time to do their jobs. Entertaining visitors would certainly have been less of a burden if keepers were allowed to accept tips, but both the board and the service strictly prohibited such gratutities, frustrating those who felt that such compen-

*Split Rock
Lighthouse.*

sation was only fair. Still, a number of keepers flouted the rule, and those who got caught were reprimanded.

In the spirit of the long-standing American tradition of the tall tale, mischievous keepers occasionally had some fun with the visitors, pulling their leg and telling them fanciful stories about their lighthouse. According to a reporter in 1883, during a group tour of California's Pigeon Point Lighthouse, located on a rocky headland between Santa Cruz and San Francisco, the keeper "was of a very talkative disposition and took great pride in dilating upon the wonders of the establishment. As we stood inside the immediate lens which surrounds the lamp, he startled us by stating in impressive tones that, were he to draw the curtains from the glass, the heat would be so great that the glass would melt instantly, and that human flesh would follow suit; we begged him not to experiment just then, and he kindly refrained."

———

THERE WAS ONE VISITOR in particular whom keepers did not relish seeing—the lighthouse inspector. At least twice a year the inspector came by to see how well keepers were performing their job. Although inspections were unannounced, keepers were rarely caught completely off guard. As the tender with the inspector on board approached the lighthouse, it would raise the inspector's ensign and sound the ship's horn to alert the keepers to his impending arrival, giving them enough time to quickly don their uniforms and put things in their proper place. By the 1920s and 1930s, when many lighthouses had phone service, keepers established informal phone trees so that once the inspector arrived in an area his presence was broadcast as a welcome heads-up.

Inspectors made sure that all the rules and regulations were being followed, and that the lighthouse station was clean and everything was in order, including the keeper's logbook and other records. Nothing escaped the inspector's critical gaze. The lantern room and the lighting apparatus garnered a thorough review, as did the living quarters and the storage areas. Inspectors often slipped on white gloves to better detect dust and grime, and even went as far as running their fingers underneath the kitchen stove to see if it was dirty. It might seem odd that the inspectors focused almost as much attention on the keeper's house as they did on the lighting apparatus, but this merely reflected the government's belief that if one were not cleanly in one's private life, that would inevitably spill over into the professional realm.

Inspectors were respected and sometimes feared. Philmore B. Wass, who spent part of his youth in the 1920s and 1930s at the Libby Island Lighthouse in Maine, near the entrance to Machias Bay, later recalled his feelings about a district inspector named Luther. "There were times during my early years," Wass wrote, "when these two all-powerful forces—God and Luther—became confused in my mind. I thought they were one in the same, the only difference being that Luther occasionally appeared in uniform." Keepers worked hard to get a 100 percent rating from inspectors, not only because they wanted to earn an inspector's star, but also because a low rating could affect pay, merit an official reprimand, or in egregious instances of failure, result in dismissal.

One of the most endearing stories of an inspection comes from Anna Bowen Hoge, whose father, Vern Bowen, was the keeper at Passage Island Lighthouse in Lake Superior, just a few miles from the Canadian border, in the 1930s and early 1940s. When she was a young girl in the mid-1930s, Annie, as her family called her, took matters into her own hands soon after the inspector arrived. Not wanting her father to get any bad marks, she grabbed the inspector's hand as he walked by and asked him to sit beside her for a moment. As soon as he did, the precocious Annie launched into her pitch: "Mr. Inspector, I want to show you some things that are very RIGHT with our lighthouse and island. You should concentrate on the GOOD things instead of the old BAD!" Her parents, nervous about what she was going to do next, asked her to stop, but the inspector said that he wanted her to show him around. Annie led the inspector on a tour of the grounds, the oil-storage building, and the tower, where, she said, "He pretended to be impressed with the sparkling glass of the storm panes and the gleaming prisms as they cast their spectrums upon the lantern room." After this triumphant tour, Annie went back to the kitchen, while the inspector finished his inspection with her father. "The only thing I noticed while I gloated in my moment of glory," Annie recalled, "was that mother looked a bit pale. After the inspector had left, my mother and father banned me to my room forever." Though Annie was effectively grounded, fortunately things turned out acceptably. While the inspector issued a reprimand to her father, he passed the inspection, and Annie said she learned "to stay out of adult business after that!"

Keepers had to follow the rules not just during inspections but also throughout the year, or else face the consequences. Accusations of falsifying records, insubordination, drunkenness, or sleeping on the job led to an immediate investigation, and if the charges were found to be true, the keeper in question could be rebuked, demoted, or fired. The most serious transgressions, which usually resulted in immediate dismissal, were letting the lights go out or not operating the fog signal during times of low visibility.

Most keepers were conscientious about their jobs, but more than a few disobeyed the rules, and were dealt with accordingly. In 1877, for example, a reporter for the *San Francisco Chronicle* wrote about a keeper at the Point Reyes Lighthouse who was let go on account of his "love of the flowing bowl. It is said that he even regaled himself, when out of whiskey, with the alcohol furnished for cleaning lamps, and a familiar sight to the ranchman was this genial gentleman lying dead drunk by the roadside, while his horse, attached to the lighthouse wagon, grazed at will over the country." The early issues of the *Lighthouse Service Bulletin* often included a section titled, "Punishments," detailing an array of offenses, which served as a warning to any potentially wayward or lackadaisical keeper. The section in the March 1912 issue was particularly long. It told of an assistant keeper who was fired for threatening the keeper and for "fomenting trouble between the keeper and others," a keeper who was reprimanded for lying, and one who was demoted to assistant keeper "for not keeping his station in proper condition, and on account of his slovenly appearance."

When it came to a choice between personal safety and protecting the light, the government was clear as to what was expected. "It is the duty of every light-keeper to stand by his light as long as the lighthouse stands," the board proclaimed. "For him to desert it when it is in danger is as cowardly as for a soldier to leave his guns on the advance of an enemy." This philosophy was certainly displayed by the keepers at the Sharps Island Lighthouse in Chesapeake Bay, who stood by their post and even rode it into the frozen bay after the ice collapsed its supports and their entire building was carried away. While the keepers at Sharps Island remained with their lighthouse despite the treacherous conditions, two keepers at another lighthouse on the bay made a different choice that day. They abandoned their screw-pile lighthouse even though it was still standing, only to return after the danger had passed. As a result the board fired the deserters and gave their jobs to the Sharps Island keepers who no longer had a lighthouse to tend. Given the government's uncompromising martial philosophy, it is no wonder that the unofficial motto of keepers was, "The light first; myself afterwards."

ALTHOUGH THERE WAS NO requirement that keepers be married, most were, and the board and the service preferred it that way. Not only were married men believed to be more dependable, content, and sober, but also their wives (and children, if they had any) almost always pitched in to help perform many of the jobs at the lighthouse. Thus families were seen as a valuable source of free labor and support.

There were, however, lighthouses where women and families were not allowed. These so-called stag stations were the ones that were deemed too remote, too cramped, or too dangerous for families. Mainly offshore lighthouses and many of those in Alaska fell into this category. Single men were usually preferred for duty at stag stations, but when married men were appointed, their families often lived nearby on the mainland so that periodic visits were possible.

The keeper of the Cape Flattery Lighthouse, along with his wife and dog, 1943.

A somewhat amusing example of the bias in favor of married men as keepers comes from the records of the Isle Royal Lighthouse in Lake Superior, built in 1875. A bachelor named Francis Malone, who worked on the construction crew for the lighthouse, fell in love with it and its location, and a few years after the lighthouse was finished applied for the job of assistant keeper. The district inspector told him that he was looking to fill that job with a married man, whereupon Malone asked him to wait a few weeks before appointing anyone. The determined young Romeo returned a short time later, brand-new wife in tow, and got the job. It seems that Malone had already been dating a local woman, and the matrimonial requirement got him to pop the question sooner than he had planned. Malone, who was later promoted to head keeper, was so thankful to have gotten the position that he began a tradition of naming each one of his children—twelve in all—after the current district lighthouse inspector. This system worked well for a number of years, even the one in which there were two inspectors—almost incredibly, that same year the Malones had twins. But the system broke down in 1898, during

Norman Rockwell painting, The Lighthouse Keeper's Daughter, *which graced the cover of the July 28, 1923, issue of the* Literary Digest.

the Spanish-American War, when three inspectors cycled through the district. Francis apparently floated the idea of naming that year's child "Three," but Mrs. Malone promptly vetoed that, and instead they gave the name of one of the inspectors to their newborn.

One of the most important functions that family members could provide was running the lighthouse while the keeper was away, and there is no more famous instance than that of Abbie Burgess. In 1853 Abbie's father, Samuel Burgess, was appointed keeper at Maine's Matinicus Rock Lighthouse, located in outer Penobscot Bay on a rock-strewn thirty-two-acre island eighteen miles from the mainland, and twenty-five miles from Rockland, the nearest port. The highest point on the island is only fifty feet above the water. The lighthouse's two granite towers were attached to either end of the keeper's quarters, one rising eighty-five feet, and the other ninety feet above mean high water. The only other structures on the island were a chicken coop and the old keeper's house, which was made of stone and served as a storage shed.

Samuel brought his invalid wife and four youngest daughters to the island. Fourteen-year-old Abbie, the oldest of the four, became her father's unofficial assistant. Samuel often left the island for days at a time to pursue lobstering or to sail to Matinicus Island, about six miles away,

Matinicus Rock Lighthouse, circa 1890s.

to replenish supplies and retrieve medicine for his wife. While he was away, Abbie became *the* keeper of the light. "I took a great deal of pride in doing the lighthouse work," she said, "and tried to do my duty." On January 18, 1856, when Abbie was sixteen, Samuel headed out on one of his trips. Before shoving off he turned to his daughter and said, "I can depend on you, Abbie."

The following day, a savage storm barreled into Penobscot Bay. Thundering seas swept over the island and flooded the keeper's quarters. Despite the danger, Abbie decided she had to save the hens, who were, she said, "her only companions." Her mother pleaded with her not to go, but Abbie was resolute. As she later recalled:

> The thought . . . of parting with them without an effort was not to be endured, so seizing a basket, I ran out a few yards after the "rollers" had passed and the sea fell off a little, with the water knee-deep, to the coop, and rescued all but one. It was the work of a moment, and I was back in the house, with the door fastened, but I was none too quick, for at that instant my little sister, standing at the window, exclaimed, "Oh, look! look there! The worst sea is coming." That wave destroyed the old dwelling and swept the rock.

As the tide continued to rise and the seas became even rougher, Abbie led her mother and younger sisters to the north tower, praying that they would be safe there.

The worst of the storm passed in a few days, but the weather remained rough and the seas so violent that Abbie's father could not get back to the island for four weeks. Abbie stayed calm and not only took care of her mother and sisters but also kept the lights in both towers burning nightly until her father's return. "Though at times greatly exhausted with my labors," Abbie said, "not once did the lights fail. Under God, I was able to perform all my accustomed duties, as well as my father's."

A little over a year later, in the spring of 1857, Abbie was tested anew. After her father took off for Matinicus Island, another storm rolled in. The bad weather persisted for many days, once again keeping her father,

*Painting of
Abbie Burgess.*

from returning. All the while Abbie, her mother, three sisters, and older brother, Benjamin, who was visiting the island between fishing trips, watched their supplies dwindle. Fearing that they all might starve if this went on too long, Benjamin set off in a small skiff with a sail stitched together by Abbie, hoping to find their father and bring back food. Abbie watched her brother sail away but soon lost sight of him as he disappeared behind the whitecapped crests of the mountainous waves.

Three weeks passed before Abbie's father and brother reappeared. During that time the island's five inhabitants were forced to ration their food, each of them surviving on one cup of corn meal gruel and one egg per day. Throughout this ordeal, like its predecessor, the redoubtable Abbie faithfully tended the lights while taking care of her mother and sisters.

THE VAST MAJORITY OF the many thousands of lighthouse keepers were men, but there were a significant number of women as well. According to the lighthouse historians Mary Louise and J. Candace Clifford, 140 women served as principal keeper between 1776 and 1939, meaning that they were either the sole or the head keeper. The first woman to gain that position was Hannah Thomas. Her husband, John Thomas, was appointed keeper of the Plymouth or Gurnet Point Lighthouse in the early 1770s, and when he went off to fight in the American Revolution, she took over the tending of the lights until they were extinguished during the war. John died of smallpox while on a military mission in Quebec, and after the war, his widow became the principal keeper, although for how long is not clear. It appears that one of her sons, John, as well as men hired as helpers, might have taken over the chief responsibility for keeping the light at various times, but according to some accounts, she was the principal keeper when the lighthouse was transferred to the federal government in 1790, relinquishing her position that same year to John.

In one of his few forward-thinking moments, Stephen Pleasonton had the distinction of being the first U.S. government official to appoint women as principal keepers. His motivation had nothing to do with promoting gender equality in the workplace, but rather he saw it as a practical way to avoid the problems often associated with patronage. "It must be apparent to all who reflect upon the subject," Pleasonton wrote to Secretary of the Treasury Thomas Corwin in 1851, "that I have had much inconvenience and difficulty to encounter from the frequent changes incidental to our form of government, in the [politically appointed] keepers, who for a time do not understand the management of their lamps, and consequently keep bad lights and waste much oil." To deal with this issue, whenever possible Pleasonton replaced a deceased keeper with his widow, as long as she was "steady and respectable." Pleasonton viewed widows as being far more competent than inexperienced political appointees because women typically helped their husband tend the lights, and thereby learned through experience as de facto apprentices. As a result, during his tenure Pleasonton appointed thirty widows as keepers.

The practice of appointing women as principal keepers continued under the board and the service, and many of the appointees were widows who succeeded their husbands, as was the case with Elizabeth Whitney Van Riper. In August 1869 her husband, Clement Van Riper, became keeper at the Beaver Island Harbor Lighthouse, which was located on the largest island in Lake Michigan and had a cylindrical brick tower housing a fourth-order Fresnel lens that cast a fixed red light. On a squally night in the fall of 1872, while trying to aid the passengers of a ship that had sunk within sight of the lighthouse, Clement drowned, and his body was never recovered. "Life to me," his widow later wrote, "then seemed darker than the midnight storm that raged for three days upon the deep, dark waters. I was weak from sorrow, but realized that though the life that was dearest to me had gone, yet there were others out on the dark and treacherous waters who needed to catch the rays of the shining light from my lighthouse tower. Nothing could rouse me but that thought." Her deep commitment to mariners in danger led her to apply to replace her husband, and in a few weeks her appointment came through.

When Van Riper decided to marry Dan Williams in 1875, becoming Elizabeth Whitney Williams, she worried that she would lose her position. This was not an unfounded concern, since women keepers who married were often replaced by their new husbands, this being an era in which women were almost uniformly viewed as being subservient to their spouse. Other times, women keepers who married were simply dismissed. Williams, however, needn't have been apprehensive. She remained keeper at Beaver Island until 1884, when she and Mr. Williams moved to the Little Traverse Bay Lighthouse, located at the northeastern corner of Lake Michigan, where she served as keeper for twenty-nine years.

Katherine Walker was another widow turned keeper. Born in Germany, she had immigrated to the United States in the late 1860s with her young son, Jacob. Landing in New Jersey, she got a job at a boardinghouse and soon met John Walker, a widower and retired sea captain, who was the keeper at the Sandy Hook Lighthouse. John took a fancy to Kate and began teaching her English. Soon they were married and quickly added a daughter to their family. Mrs. Walker liked her new life at Sandy Hook, where she could garden and raise flowers. In 1885, however, her life was upended when John was transferred to the Robbins Reef Lighthouse, a forty-six-foot-tall iron caisson tower completely surrounded by water, located on the west side of New York Harbor about a mile north of Staten Island. The lighthouse's fourth-order Fresnel lens, which flashed every six seconds, warned ships of the submerged reef as it guided them

*Kate Walker,
circa 1909.*

into and out of the harbor. Laying eyes on her new home, Kate Walker was crestfallen: There would be no gardening here. As she later recalled, "The day we came [to Robbins Reef] . . . I said, 'I won't stay. The sight of water whichever way I look makes me lonesome and blue.' I refused to unpack my trunks and boxes at first. I unpacked them a little at a time. After a while they were all unpacked and I stayed on."

Her life was upended again in 1890, when John caught pneumonia. As he was being taken from the lighthouse to the mainland for treatment, he turned back to his wife and uttered the last words he would ever say to her, "Mind the light, Katie." He died ten days later. With two children to care for, she applied to be keeper, but the board initially rejected her, fearing that she was too diminutive for the job, standing just four feet ten and weighing barely one hundred pounds. After several men turned down the position, the board relented, and Walker was appointed. She proved to be every bit as capable as any other keeper, remaining at her post and performing admirably until retiring at the age of seventy-three in 1919, and for much of that time her son Jacob served as assistant keeper.

Walker grew to love the lighthouse. "I am happy as any queen in her castle," she said. "I am happy because I have no time to worry. For me, it is work, work, work. The lights must never fail, the glass never grow dim. Next to work, service to others is the secret of my happiness. My work helps speed safely on their voyage thousands of ships from all of the seven seas."

A tiny oasis, the lighthouse was the only place she felt truly comfortable and safe, her lone outpost of sanity just outside the madness of urban life in New York, the nation's largest city. Her occasional forays into the city for business terrified her. "I am in fear from the time I leave the ferry-boat," she told an interviewer in 1918. "The street-cars bewilder me. And I am afraid of the automobiles. A fortune wouldn't tempt me to get into one of those things."

Happily for local boaters, Walker had no fear of getting into the lighthouse boat and aiding those in distress. According to her own estimate, she rescued about fifty people, mostly fishermen, whose boats foundered on the reef in bad weather. "It has surprised me how lightly the men and women I've rescued seemed to value their lives," Walker told a newspaper reporter. "Only three or four ever knelt down and thank[ed] God for their deliverance from death. Usually they joke and laugh about it. Often they say, 'please don't tell anyone of this,' they're ashamed of having mishandled their boats." Even more disappointing to Walker was that these people showed little gratitude for her heroic actions. In fact, she said, "the only manifestly grateful creature I ever saved was a dog."

One freezing winter's day, with the wind howling and the waves pounding the lighthouse, Walker watched as a three-masted schooner plowed into the reef and turned on its beam-ends. She immediately lowered the lighthouse dory, rowed to the stricken vessel, and helped the five stranded sailors climb on board. One of the men cried, "Where's Scotty?" and through the din, a dog's whining voice was heard. A few moments later Scotty, a small shaggy brown dog, paddling furiously to get through the waves, made it to the dory, whereupon Walker hauled him out of the water. "I'll never forget the look in his big brown eyes as he raised them to mine," she later recalled.

After a lengthy battle rowing against the turbulent seas, they made it back to the lighthouse. Walker gathered Scotty in her arms, wrapping him tightly in her cloak. She then climbed the lighthouse ladder and brought him to the kitchen. As soon as she put Scotty down, he collapsed, so she gently set him on the cushion of her rocking chair, covered him with a dry shawl, and forced down his throat some of the warm coffee she had sitting on the stove. Scotty "gasped and snorted" and "quivered," again giving Walker that look she had seen in the boat. As for the men, she received not a word of thanks for risking her life to save theirs. They rested for an hour until the storm abated, then rowed to shore, leaving Scotty behind. For three days Scotty never left Walker's side, and when the captain returned to claim the dog, Scotty didn't want to leave. As the captain climbed down the lighthouse ladder with the dog in his arms, Scotty looked up at Walker and "whined" once more.

When Walker died in 1931, at the age of eighty-three, she had apparently become something of a New York City folk hero or legend in the great metropolis already suffering from the fallout of the Depression. Her obituary in the *New York Evening Post* offered eloquent praise of a life well lived, while at the same time painting an uplifting portrait of the city's own fortitude in adversity. "A great city's water front is rich in romance," the paper said. "There are queenly liners, the grim battle craft, the countless carriers of commerce that pass in endless procession. And amid all this and in sight of the city of towers and torch of liberty lived this sturdy little woman, proud of her work and content in it, keeping her lamp alight and her windows clean, so that New York Harbor might be safe for ships that pass in the night. It was a brave job and bravely done. In doing it, Kate Walker became a little lighthouse herself, for there is inspiration and good guidance in her story."

IN ADDITION TO WIDOWS succeeding their husbands, there were many instances in which the daughters of head keepers took over that position after their father died, Laura Hecox being one example. Laura was fifteen years old in 1869 when her father, Adna, became the first keeper of the brand-new Santa Cruz Lighthouse, located on a thirty-foot-high bluff at the northern edge of Monterey Bay, and comprising a one-and-a-half-story wooden keeper's house with a short square tower and an octagonal lantern room rising through the roof. Like many keepers' daughters, Laura helped her father tend the light, but her workload was a bit heavier than most because of her father's condition. Adna had been a clergyman prior to his stint as keeper, but the stress and strain of his pastoral duties had left him in ill health, and for much of the time he was keeper, Laura did a significant amount of the work. When Adna died in 1883, his son-in-law, Capt. Albert Brown, urged government officials to have Laura replace her father, since she was already quite skilled in performing lighthouse duties. Within a week the twenty-nine-year-old woman got the job, which she held for the next thirty-three years, retiring in 1916.

Hecox, whom one contemporary—in the sexist language typical of the period—described as a "pleasant little woman" was particularly fastidious, and she kept the lighthouse in immaculate condition. She greeted the many people—often more than a thousand—who visited the lighthouse each year standing at the front door with a feather duster in hand. Before letting them enter, she would brush them off, lest any dirt or dust be tracked in.

Throughout her life Hecox indulged her passion for natural history, and her job afforded her many opportunities to explore nearby beaches and tide pools, and collect a great variety of sea life. Shells intrigued her most of all, and through her own investigations she became an authority on malacology—the branch of zoology that deals with mollusks—often consulted by scientists eager to tap her expertise. After she sent specimens of a shell-less Pacific mollusk—an unusual banana slug—to a zoology professor at the University of Cincinnati, and offered him insights into its behavior, he honored Hecox by naming this new variety of the slug after her (*Ariolimax columbiana* var. *hecoxi*).

Yet Hecox's interests extended well beyond just shells, and she amassed a spectacular collection of fossils, rocks, bird eggs, crustaceans, Native American baskets, Eskimo artifacts, coral, and coins, as well as many other natural and human-made objects, which she artfully displayed in cabinets in the keeper's quarters. Viewing her private museum was a high point of every lighthouse tour at Santa Cruz. In 1905 Hecox donated her collections to the Santa Cruz Public Library, which opened the Hecox Museum in its basement, making it the first public museum in the city. After being moved to various locations, the Hecox Museum finally became the founding collection of the Santa Cruz Museum of Natural History, where it remains today.

Another daughter who followed in her father's footsteps was Thelma Austin. In 1917 her father was appointed keeper at Point Fermin Lighthouse, an elegant Victorian-style structure in Los Angeles overlooking San Pedro Bay. He and his wife promptly moved into the lighthouse, with Thelma and her six siblings. Eight years later Thelma's mother died, and her grieving father followed soon thereafter. Thelma applied for the keeper's job, pleading her case in a letter to the service. "Why, the sea and this lighthouse seem to me like a holy shrine," she wrote, "and I'm afraid it would break my heart to give it up. But no matter what happens, I will accept my fate with a brave heart, and just as cheerfully as my parents would have done. When you have been raised in the lighthouse atmosphere, as I have been, it is mighty difficult to change your mode of living and accept any other line of endeavor which does not offer romance and adventure." Persuaded by her passion, the service

Biloxi Lighthouse, 1901.

appointed Austin keeper in 1925, and she stayed there until just two days before the Japanese bombed Pearl Harbor, when the U.S. Coast Guard decommissioned the lighthouse, replacing the Fresnel lens with a radar antenna.

Though it was less common was for a daughter to succeed her mother as principal keeper, it did happen on occasion. Maria Younghans served as keeper of the Biloxi, Mississippi, Lighthouse from 1867 to 1918, taking over the post upon the death of her husband, Perry. Maria's daughter, Miranda, had long assisted her mother with her lighthouse duties, and when Maria retired, Miranda got her job.

A FEW WOMEN BECAME principal keepers outright, and not as a result of succeeding their husband, father, or mother. Emily Maitland Fish's story is one of the most unusual, for she was far more sophisticated, worldly, and wealthy than the typical keeper. She was born Emily A. Maitland in 1843, in the small town of Albion, Michigan. The marriage of her older sister Juliet, to Dr. Melancthon Fish in the early 1850s precipitated a series of events that would ultimately lead to Emily's appointment as keeper of the Point Pinos Lighthouse in Monterey, California.

Instead of practicing medicine right away, Melancthon took his new bride, Juliet, on a tour of Europe, Africa, and Asia, finally settling in Shanghai, where for six years he served as inspector of the imperial Chinese customs. In 1859 Juliet died while giving birth to a daughter, who was named after her. Whether Emily arrived in China before or after her sister died is unknown, but in 1860 she married Melancthon, and two years later they returned to the United States with baby Juliet and a Chinese servant named Que.

With the Civil War raging, Melancthon joined the Union army as medical director of the Sixteenth Army Corps. Emily followed him while he traveled with the troops from Virginia to Georgia, working just behind the front lines for the U.S. Sanitary Commission, a precursor of the American Red Cross. After the war Melancthon was transferred to the Army Arsenal in Benicia, California, where he stayed for a time

Emily Fish, the "Socialite Keeper," circa 1890.

before setting up a private practice in Oakland, and also joining the medical faculty at the University of California at Berkeley. The Fishes became prominent members of the local high society, and their magnificent home in Oakland "was one of the social centers, famous for the good taste and austere exclusiveness of its mistress, for the epicurean perfection of its dinners, and the social irreproachability of its company." Emily's comfortable life with Melancthon, however, came to an end on March 23, 1891, when he died of heart disease at the age of sixty-three.

Financially independent as a result of her husband's pension and income from her property, Fish spent the next couple of years in mourning and living quietly with Que by her side. Then, after a visit from Juliet and her husband, Lt. Cdr. Henry E. Nichols, Fish's life veered in a different direction. Henry, who was the lighthouse inspector for the twelfth district, which encompassed California, mentioned to his mother-in-law that the keeper at Point Pinos Lighthouse was retiring soon. Intrigued,

Fish peppered her son-in-law with questions about the lighthouse and what was required of the keeper, and his answers were alluring enough for her to apply for the position. With Henry's recommendation, she got the job, and in 1893, at the age of fifty, Fish moved into the lighthouse, with Que, and remained there until 1914, when she retired at the age of seventy-one.

Like the other California lighthouses built in the 1850s by Gibbons and Kelly, Point Pinos consisted of a modest keeper's house with a tower rising from its center, which in this case displayed a third-order Fresnel lens. Fish transformed the house with elegant furniture, paintings, silverware, and china, all taken from her opulent Oakland home. With Que's help she planted beautiful gardens, trees, and lawns, and also turned the ninety-four-acre lighthouse reservation into a menagerie of sorts, populated with Thoroughbred horses, Holstein cows, white Leghorn chickens, and a small army of black standard French poodles.

The lighthouse historian Clifford Gallant labeled Emily Fish the "Socialite Keeper," and she certainly lived up to that title. Like her Oakland home, her new abode at the lighthouse became a hub of social activity, with Fish holding high teas and intimate (albeit sumptuous) dinners for friends, artists, military officers, and local dignitaries. She still

Point Pinos Lighthouse in Monterey, California, circa 1857. The drawing was rendered by T. E. Sandgren, based on a sketch by Maj. Hartman Bache.

was, as one contemporary noted, "an elegant and hospitable lady of the finest character." Despite her busy calendar, and the time she and Que spent taking care of the animals and the gardens, Fish did not neglect the lighthouse, and she consistently received high ratings from lighthouse inspectors.

Interestingly enough, Fish's stepdaughter, Juliet Nichols, continued the family tradition, also becoming a lighthouse keeper. In 1902, four years after her husband, Henry, died in the Philippines during the Spanish-American War, she was appointed keeper at the Angel Island Lighthouse in San Francisco Bay. The station's fifth-order Fresnel lens was paired with a three-thousand-pound bronze bell, which served as the fog signal and was operated by a wind-up clockwork mechanism that automatically rang the bell by striking it with a hammer. Nichols's finest hours as keeper came in early July 1906. On the second day of the month, just as a thick fog was rolling in, she started the fog signal, but after a few minutes it broke down. She knew that mariners were counting on that bell to warn them of danger, so she used the disabled hammer to continue manually hitting the bell for twenty hours and thirty-five minutes—at the same frequency as that produced by the automatic mechanism, twice every fifteen seconds—until the fog lifted. After this grueling ordeal, her arms were throbbing, her body exhausted, and her ears ringing. A workman came out on July 3 and made some repairs, but he did a poor job, for on the evening of July 4 the mechanism failed again. This time, however, the signal's hammer was stuck, so Juliet grabbed a nail hammer instead and wearily started swinging away until the weather cleared the next morning. For these two nights of near-constant hammer-swinging and quick-thinking improvisation, Nichols received a commendation from the board for her exemplary actions.

IN ADDITION TO THE 140 women who became principal keepers, more than 240 served as assistant keepers. All of them worked under their husbands, fathers, or mothers, and a few were ultimately promoted to head keeper upon their relative's death. Women keepers, both principals and assistants, were typically paid the same as their male counterparts, and by all accounts were no less competent in the performance of their duties.

Considered within the context of the larger society, women lighthouse keepers were something of an anomaly. In the nineteenth century and on into the early twentieth, most women didn't have formal jobs but rather stayed home and performed unpaid domestic labor. Women who did work outside the home rarely had jobs that were as important, responsible, or independent as that of a keeper. But before women keepers are held aloft as a shining example of progress in the battle for equality of women in the workplace, it should be borne in mind how and why women keepers got their positions. Almost all of them were appointed because they were part of the keeper's family and, by virtue of that association, already had the requisite—and generally unpaid—skills to run a lighthouse. Furthermore both the board and the service were well aware that if a keeper's widow wasn't given the job, she would likely face grave financial difficulties supporting herself and her family. This was especially the case before keepers were offered pensions in 1918, which could be transferred to widows upon the death of the keeper. Appointing the widow was thus a compassionate way to avert a cruel financial blow, while at the same time ensuring that the lighthouse was in good hands. Appointing a keeper's daughter similarly guaranteed the same continuity of competence. As for the few women who got the keeper's job because of political or governmental connections, that had more to do with nepotism and power than the fight for parity. Still, even though the appointment of women keepers was driven by unique circumstances, it remained a positive sign in the march toward workplace equality. Each time a woman keeper performed admirably offered one more argument in favor of the notion that women could do the same jobs as men—and just as well.

WHILE WOMEN MADE SIGNIFICANT advances as lighthouse keepers, prevailing against the strong headwinds of the society in which they lived, African Americans did not find the same opportunities or representation within the lighthouse establishment. When Francis Ross Holland, Jr., wrote his extensive history of American lighthouses in 1972, he found no examples of black keepers, and only a few instances of their employment on lightships. Thus, Holland concluded, "The present evidence indicates . . . that throughout the nineteenth and early twentieth [centuries], the lighthouse establishment was pretty much a lily-white organization."* In subsequent years Holland, as well as a few other researchers, dug more deeply into the records and uncovered examples of black keepers, but still the numbers are small. The lighthouse historian and genealogist, Sandra MacLean Clunies, for example, identified roughly thirty black men who served either as the primary or assistant keeper at lighthouses in Maryland and Virginia between 1870 and 1900. It is possible that further research in this area will cause the numbers of black keepers to grow, but it is unlikely that they will rise enough to contradict Holland's basic conclusion that the lighthouse establishment was overwhelmingly white. And that should come as little surprise, given the extreme prejudice against blacks that existed during the nineteenth and early twentieth centuries, and the difficulties they often faced in gaining employment in a wide range of professions.

FOR MANY, LIGHTHOUSE KEEPING became a family business of sorts, with the torch being handed down through multiple generations. One of the best examples of this is the Garraty clan, which produced a veritable dynasty of keepers who worked at a variety of lighthouses on Lakes Huron and Superior between 1864 and 1926. All told, the patriarch, Patrick Garraty, and four of his children—three sons and a daughter—operated lighthouses for an impressive 184 years.

Lighthouse families often intermarried, and here again Abbie Burgess provides an interesting example. In 1861 Samuel Burgess was fired from his job as keeper of Matinicus Rock Lighthouse, one of many keep-

---

* It should be pointed out, however, that many blacks, either as slaves or freemen, worked as laborers, building many of the nation's lighthouses, and many slaves served as unpaid "assistant keepers," helping their masters, as was the case for Shadwell, the slave kept by George Worthylake at Boston Lighthouse.

ers purged for political reasons during President Lincoln's first term. Burgess was replaced by one of his friends, John Grant. Abbie stayed on to show Grant what was required to run the lighthouse, and before long she fell in love with Grant's son Isaac, and they soon married. Isaac was appointed assistant keeper of Matinicus Rock in 1864, with Abbie becoming third assistant keeper six years later. In 1875 the couple left the Rock with their four children and settled at the White Head Lighthouse, near Spruce Head, Maine, where the two of them became keeper and assistant keeper. In 1890 they both resigned on account of Abbie's deteriorating health.

Not long after this she wrote a letter to a friend, in which she reflected on her lighthouse life, and what she knew was her fast-approaching death: "Sometimes I think the time is not far distant when I shall climb these lighthouse stairs no more. It has almost seemed to me that the light was a part of myself." Abbie said she often dreamed about hurrying between Matinicus and White Head to make sure that the lamps were lit. "I must always see the lights burning in both places before I wake . . . I feel a great deal more worried in my dreams than when I am awake." In concluding her letter, she mused, "I wonder if the care of the lighthouse will follow my soul after it has left this worn-out body! If I ever have a gravestone, I would like it to be in the form of a lighthouse or beacon."

Abbie Burgess died in 1892, but it wasn't until 1945 that she got her wish. That is when the famed New England maritime author and lecturer, Edward Rowe Snow, who had been inspired by Abbie's story, decided to honor her request. To that end he organized an intimate gathering at the Forest Hill Cemetery, in South Thomaston, Maine, and placed at the foot of Abbie's grave a small metal lighthouse, which stands watch there to this day.

OPERATING AND MAINTAINING A lighthouse was arduous work, but keepers still had time for other pursuits. Some engaged in hobbies, such as whittling, painting, or stamp collecting. Keepers could also take on additional jobs as long as they didn't interfere with their lighthouse responsibil-

The metal lighthouse at the foot of Abbie Burgess's grave.

ities, and many keepers took advantage of this option to supplement their government income. Keepers moonlighted as cobblers, tailors, fishermen, harbor pilots, justices of the peace, and, in at least one instance, as a dental hygienist (Thelma Austin, when she was the keeper at Point Fermin Lighthouse). Robert Israel, the head keeper at Point Loma Lighthouse, at the mouth of San Diego Bay, from 1873 to 1892, and his wife, Mary, who served as assistant keeper for a few years, made hefty profits speculating in San Diego real estate, and Mrs. Israel also produced beautiful frames decorated with seashells, which she sold to tourists.

Many lighthouse keepers were avid gardeners, for practical and aesthetic reasons. Growing vegetables and fruits enabled them to supplement their food supplies, which was especially important at remote lighthouses where the rations provided by the government were often insufficient to meet a family's needs. Planting flowers and ornamental shrubs and trees helped beautify a lighthouse's grounds. Even at offshore lighthouses that were devoid of any natural soil, the impulse to garden was strong. A keeper in the late 1800s at Saddleback Ledge Lighthouse, a barren granite rock about a quarter acre in size, located near the entrance to East Penobscot Bay in Maine, was clearly an optimistic man. With

1. *Beavertail Lighthouse, at the tip of Jamestown, Rhode Island, painted sometime in the second half of the nineteenth century, artist unknown. The lighthouse shown, completed in 1856, is the third and last one built at this location. It replaced an earlier stone tower from the mid-1700s.*

2. The Lighthouse at Two Lights, *by Edward Hopper, 1929. This painting shows the east tower of twin lights at the Cape Elizabeth Lighthouse, in Maine.*

3. The Long Leg, *by Edward Hopper, 1935. Long Point Lighthouse, located in Provincetown, Massachusetts, can be seen in the distance. This image appeared on a U.S. postage stamp in 2011 as part of the postal service's American Treasures series.*

Studebaker Commander 4-door sedan

This Studebaker's "next look" is a years-ahead look !

4. Detail of a magazine advertisement for the 1950 Studebaker, using the Piedras Blancas Lighthouse, in San Simeon, California, as a background motif.

5. The beams emanating from the lantern room at Pigeon Point Lighthouse during the annual celebration of the first lighting of the lighthouse in 1872. The lighthouse station, located in Pescadero, California, is now open to the public as a hostel.

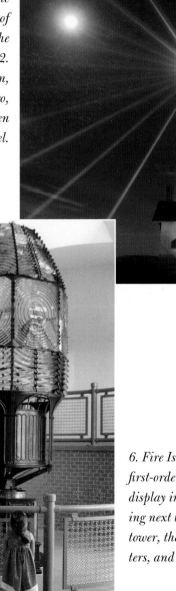

6. Fire Island Lighthouse's first-order Fresnel lens on display in its own building next to the lighthouse tower, the keeper's quarters, and visitor center.

7. Sunrise at Marblehead Lighthouse, in Marblehead, Ohio, overlooking Lake Erie.

8. Cape Neddick "Nubble" Lighthouse, in York, Maine, lit up for the holidays.

9. Michigan's St. Joseph Pier Lighthouse, outer-range light, in December 2010, covered by a thick layer of twisted ice following a winter storm that created twenty-foot waves on Lake Michigan.

10. The Borden Flats Lighthouse, at the mouth of the Taunton River in Fall River, Massachusetts. The lighthouse is privately owned, and is rented out for overnight stays.

11. Lighthouse Dandelions, *by Jamie Wyeth, 1997. The painting depicts Tenants Harbor Lighthouse in Maine, which overlooks Penobscot Bay. Wyeth uses the lighthouse both as a residence and a studio.*

12. *Ponce de Leon Inlet Lighthouse, Ponce Inlet, Florida.*

13. *Cape Hatteras Lighthouse on the Cape Hatteras National Seashore.*

14. *Point Vicente Lighthouse, Rancho Palos Verdes, California.*

15. *The tower at Heceta Head Lighthouse, Yachats, Oregon.*

16. *Stormy sunset at Portland Head Lighthouse, in Cape Elizabeth, Maine. Barely visible on the far right of the image is the Ram Island Ledge Lighthouse.*

17. *Sunset at Michigan City East Pierhead Lighthouse, in Indiana, overlooking Lake Michigan.*

18. *A stunning thirty-second time-exposure image of the Ludington North Breakwater Lighthouse, in Ludington, Michigan.*

19. *Lily Dolin's painting of the Edgartown Lighthouse, on Martha's Vineyard, Massachusetts. Lily is the author's teenage daughter, and she did this painting to inspire her dad to finish the book!*

little more than faith and constant tending, one year he managed to grow "three sickly pea-vines, two hills of potatoes, and a dozen spears of oats," all rising from the pile of trash that had accumulated next to the lighthouse tower.

At Mount Desert Rock, another of Maine's many granitic islands, the lighthouse garden was an act of inspired improvisation. Every spring either the keeper or a kindly fisherman from one of the nearby towns would bring barrels of soil to the lighthouse from the mainland, which the keeper and his family tenderly spread into cracks and crevices on the island, and then planted with flowers. The splashes of color that soon appeared brightened an otherwise grim and gray landscape, and delighted mariners as they sailed by what many called "God's Rock Garden." This brilliant display, of course, was only ephemeral. The first major storm would generate waves that breached the island, scouring its surface and washing away the garden. But, for as long as it lasted, it was a magnificently beautiful sight.

Keepers looking to fill their larder could also turn to the water, which offered a plenitude of fish. And in the saltier realms, keepers gathered

Keeper Elson Small milking his cow at the St. Croix River Lighthouse in Maine.

oysters, clams, mussels, and lobsters to make for a satisfying repast. Many keepers also raised animals for food, including chickens, cows, and goats. In addition to providing sustenance the livestock often lent a helping hand, or hoof as the case may be. Oxen, horses, and mules were extremely useful in hauling supplies, and the latter two beasts of burden could also transport people. When the Farallon Island Lighthouse mule, named Patty, died in 1913, one of the keepers resorted to verse to honor Patty's yeoman service over the years:

> *Mule Patty, always good*
> *Caused no trouble where she stood*
> *Always ready and seldom sick*
> *Died of old age without a kick.*

Pets were quite common at lighthouses, especially dogs and cats, which not only provided loving companionship but also served other valuable purposes. Cats killed rats and mice that might otherwise have raided the lighthouse's pantry, and dogs provided protection and kept a watchful eye on their owners. In performing this last task, a dog at Mount Desert Rock Lighthouse became a lifesaver. One sunny summer's day in 1896, the keeper's son went outside to play, and soon wandered off without his mother noticing. A half hour later, the family dog ran into house, sopping wet and barking wildly. The keeper's wife, thinking that the dog had dragged another piece of driftwood from the surf and wanted to show her his find, shooed him back outside to dry off. But when he returned moments later and dropped the boy's drenched hat at her feet, she knew something was terribly wrong. She bolted from the house, following the dog to the shoreline, where she found her son lying unconscious on the rocks, his clothes in tatters and his body bruised. It became clear to her what had happened: Her boy had fallen in, and the dog had rescued him, dragging his body over the rocks onto the shore. According to a contemporary account, he "soon recovered from the effects of the accident that had so nearly turned the lonely light station into a place of mourning."

One dog rumored to have saved numerous children from drowning

He Is Saved, a late-nineteenth-century Currier & Ives print based on Edwin Henry Landseer's painting of the Newfoundland Milo, saving the son of the keeper at Egg Rock Lighthouse. (In the fashion of the day, the little boy is dressed in girl's clothes.)

was Milo, a large Newfoundland who was owned by keeper George B. Taylor, and lived in the late 1850s at Egg Rock Lighthouse, located about a mile off Nahant, Massachusetts. Tales of Milo's lifesaving actions were told far and wide, and even crossed the Atlantic, catching the attention of the popular English artist Edwin Henry Landseer, who was best known for his often oversentimental paintings of animals. In this vein, Landseer produced two paintings of Milo, the more dramatic of which is titled *He Is Saved*. It shows an exhausted Milo resting on some rocks, cradling in his hefty paws the keeper's young son, Fred, who is unconscious, having just been dragged not a moment too soon from the ocean's clutches. The painting became famous throughout America, and beyond, and was reproduced in multiple prints by Currier & Ives, all of which only added to Milo's legend, and to the general romanticized view of lighthouse keepers' lives.

At least one dog, whose heroics have been described in language suitable for young-adult fiction, is credited with saving a vessel from disaster. Spot was a Springer spaniel owned by the family of the keeper Augustus B. Hamor, who was stationed at the Owl's Head Lighthouse, near Rockland, Maine, from 1930 to 1941. Hamor's children taught Spot to ring the fog bell by using his mouth to pull the rope attached to the bell's clapper. When vessels passed by the lighthouse, Spot would often run out and yank the bell. Spot grew most attached to one vessel in particular—the daily mail boat to Matinicus Island, captained by Stuart Ames. When-

Owl's Head Lighthouse, circa 1890s.

ever Ames passed by the lighthouse he would blast the ship's whistle, and Spot would ring the bell in return.

One day a driving snowstorm hit the area, and Ames was late returning to Rockland Harbor. Gravely concerned about her husband, Mrs. Ames telephoned Hamor. "My husband speaks so often of your dog, Spot," she said. "Do you think that he might be able to hear the mail boat's whistle?" Hamor let Spot out of the house, but the dog soon

Memorial marker for Spot, the Lighthouse Dog, at Owl's Head Lighthouse.

returned and curled up on his blanket. A few minutes later, however, he sprang up and rushed to the door, barking violently. Thinking that Spot must have heard the whistle, Hamor opened the door again, and out flew Spot. The snowdrifts were so high that he could not reach the bell. Instead he ran to the edge of the cliff and stood there barking. In the meantime, Captain Ames, nearly blinded by the snow, kept blasting his whistle, hoping to hear something in return that might give him his bearings. As the mail boat crept perilously closer to the rocky promontory upon which the lighthouse stood, Ames finally heard Spot's barking and adjusted his course to avoid the rocks. The captain then blew the boat's whistle three times, acknowledging the dog's assistance, and continued on safely into port. A few hours later, a much-relieved Mrs. Ames called Hamor to express her gratitude for Spot's vigilance.

GIVEN THEIR CLOSE QUARTERS, daily routine, and relative isolation, it was important that the people living in a lighthouse got along. Keepers' quarters were hardly palatial, and in most instances quite cramped. If one didn't like, or at least respect or tolerate, the people one lived and worked with in such close proximity for twenty-four hours a day, seven days a week, then things could pretty quickly devolve into misery, and given the vagaries of human nature and stresses of the job, there were more than a few lighthouses where conflict erupted.

Sometimes it didn't take much to set people off. At Cape Hinchinbrook Lighthouse in Alaska, a stag station with three keepers on at a time, a fight over food got things rolling. The two assistant keepers stopped speaking to each other because one liked his potatoes mashed, the other fried. Finding this behavior childish, the head keeper tried to get his two hostile colleagues to see the error of their ways. He had almost succeeded when another dispute threw the entire station into a tizzy. A ring owned by one of the assistant keepers went missing, and he accused the other assistant of taking it. The head keeper again tried to play peacemaker, but instead was drawn into the fray, thereby becoming the third combatant in a trilateral cold war, and for the next six months all communication between the keepers ceased. In complete silence the men continued standing their watches and cooked their own meals (presumably preparing their potatoes however they liked), all while living under the same roof and trying their best to avoid one another. This petty quarrel finally ended when the lighthouse tender dropped off a relief keeper.

Under duress even good buddies could turn on one another. St. George Reef Lighthouse is located about six miles off the coast of Crescent City California, and stands on North West Seal Rock, the barren basaltic tip of an ancient volcano. The lighthouse's inherent isolation was tough for many of its keepers to handle, but when nature transformed it into a temporary prison, the situation could get much worse. A bout of particularly nasty weather in 1937 cut off the lighthouse from contact with the outside world for fifty-nine days. For that entire time the churning seas and blasting winds made it impossible for the lighthouse tender to get to the rock to deliver supplies and mail. During the first month of their enforced isolation, the four men at this stag station grew increasingly irritable, and the level of their discourse slowly deteriorated as cabin fever set in. According to the head keeper, George Roux, "After the first four weeks, we were so talked out and thought out that just to say 'please pass the salt' or 'lousy day today, ain't it?' became a serious personal affront. It got so bad that we would try to ignore the presence of each other to avoid scraps. This despite our being solid friends for years. Toward the end, when we opened a can of beans or some kind of can and ate it cold, we would face away from each other—not looking, not talking, just so fed up with each other's company that it was almost unbearable. I've heard of men going stir crazy in prison, well, that's just what almost happened to us." When the weather cleared on the sixtieth day, and the supply ship was finally able to land, Roux said, "Life in the tower returned to normal. . . . We were friends again. Talked our heads off."

On rare occasions, conflict might spawn violence. In August 1897, Whale Rock Lighthouse, a spark-plug-type caisson lighthouse located at the mouth of the West Passage of Narragansett Bay, was the scene of a near-fatal battle between the head keeper, Judson Allen, and assistant keeper, Henry Nygren. Allen had had trouble with Nygren in the past on account of his benders on the mainland, after which he would return to the lighthouse stinking drunk and accordingly irascible. But on the evening of August 12 the inebriated Nygren got back to the lighthouse long after he was due, in a particularly agitated state. Allen tried to calm him down, but this only enraged Nygren, who grabbed Allen by the throat. Although Nygren was a much larger and brawnier man, Allen wrenched himself free, but then Nyrgren hit him with an oar and threw a bucket at his head. In the melee that followed, Allen knocked Nygren to the floor, but the assistant keeper sprang up, seized a butcher's knife, and began chasing Allen around the lighthouse, slashing away. Allen rushed into his room and barricaded the door, which Nygren threatened to knock down. When Nygren went to grab an ax, the head keeper made a break for it. He rushed out of the lighthouse, jumped into one of the rowboats, and began pulling furiously for the mainland through the rough seas under a moonlit sky.

Nygren pursued Allen in the other boat, and at one point screamed, "Oh, I'll murder you; I'm after you!" Allen reached shore first, and ran barefoot over the rocks and macadam roads as fast as he could. Nygren continued his mad pursuit, but the chase ended when Allen eluded his assailant by hiding in a cornfield. While Nygren returned to the lighthouse, Allen crawled on his hands and knees to a nearby farmhouse, where he commandeered a horse and rode it to the Narragansett Pier Life Saving Station. When Allen arrived, the *Boston Globe* reported, "He was almost naked. His feet were bloody and he had a knife wound in the back."

The following evening, two men from the lifesaving station went to the lighthouse to see if they could talk to Nygren, and perhaps take him in, but his behavior put an end to that plan. According to the *Globe*, while the men watched from the safety of their boat, Nygren, still apparently drunk, "smashed crockery, threw the utensils for housekeeping overboard and danced wildly." The next day a government vessel from Newport arrived with armed men, clapped Nygren into irons, and took him into custody. Soon thereafter the board fired him.

———

THE AFFAIR AT WHALE Rock provides an instance in which a keeper posed the threat, but there were also times when the peril came from strangers, and there is no more dramatic example of this than what transpired at the Ship Shoal Lighthouse, a screw-pile structure in the Gulf of Mexico, located about four miles off the Louisiana coast. As reported in the local press, and by newspapers as far away as New York City, on Wednesday, February 22, 1882, the head keeper, Edward Dunn, and the third assistant keeper, Fred Leach, were coal-tarring the roof of the keeper's dwelling when they saw a small sailboat about three

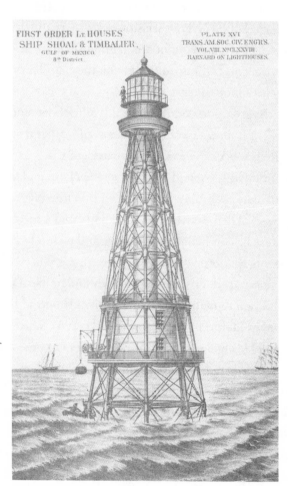

Drawing of Ship Shoal Lighthouse, off the Louisiana coast, the site of a vicious attack on the keepers in 1882.

miles away, bestilled by the dead calm, and floating lazily on the Gulf's glassy surface. After peering through a spyglass, they realized it was the lighthouse boat, which the two other assistant keepers had taken about a week earlier to Morgan City, Louisiana, to pick up supplies. Instead of two people in the boat, there was only one. Dunn thought that his assistants might have had an accident, so he sent Leach in the other lighthouse boat to investigate.

As Leach came closer to the boat, he realized its occupant was a stranger, and when he was within hailing distance, he asked him where he was going and how he acquired the boat. The stranger, a fifty-one-year-old man named James Woods, said he bought the boat from three men in Morgan City for one hundred dollars, and that he was bound for Pascagoula, on the Mississippi Gulf Coast. Leach, barely maintaining his composure, told Woods that the boat belonged to the lighthouse, and that he was going to take it back there. Woods protested, but as there was no wind and he wasn't going anywhere, he relented. Leach attached a line to the sailboat and rowed back to the lighthouse.

When Dunn saw that Woods had no other clothes with him, or any provisions, he became convinced that he had stolen the boat. Dunn wanted to get Woods to the collector of customs in Morgan City as soon as possible for questioning. He would have had Leach take him if he had been able to spare him, but felt that he couldn't run the lighthouse on his own. So Dunn reluctantly invited Woods into the lighthouse, his plan being to flag down a passing vessel to take Woods in.

For three days no vessels came close enough to be signaled, and the situation remained very tense. The keepers and Woods eyed each other warily, stayed on their guard, and spoke little. On Saturday evening at six, Dunn ascended the spiral stairway to begin his six-hour watch.

At about nine o'clock, while Leach was sleeping, Woods grabbed the revolver he had hidden under his clothes, and a hatchet he found in the lighthouse, and crept into the assistant keeper's room. As Woods was readying to strike, Leach woke up, saw the intruder, and jumped from bed. Woods swung the hatchet twice, each time missing his mark. While dodging the hatchet's blade, Leach screamed "Help!" and "Murder!" to alert Dunn. With his third swing, Woods connected with a vicious blow to the side of Leach's face, knocking him down.

Hearing the screams, Dunn rushed down the stairs, but by the time he reached the upper part of the dwelling, it was quiet and dark. Dunn grabbed his revolver and went to get a lamp. Before Dunn made it to the room where the lamps were stored, Woods shot him in the shoulder. Dunn fired in the direction of the flash, and was then hit a second time in the same shoulder. Dunn fired three more times and was hit with another ball, this time on his right side. Sometime during this skirmish, Woods also sent three shots in Leach's direction, hitting him in the back and arm. Woods, however, did not escape unscathed. One of Dunn's bullets had gone clear through Woods's right leg, just below the kneecap.

Everything was quiet once more. Dunn lit a lamp and descended to the lower part of the dwelling, where he found Leach staggering about, covered in blood. One side of Leach's face was cut away, exposing his jawbone and teeth. While the keepers were looking for Woods, they heard the iron trap door to the lantern room shut, and instantly knew where their attacker had gone.

For the next two nights the lighthouse was cloaked in darkness. The two keepers did their best to dress each other's wounds, and they took turns standing watch at the base of the stairs in case Woods came down. Since Dunn was out of ammunition, the two keepers armed themselves with a carving knife and a boat scraper.

On Monday, Woods yelled down from the lantern room, offering to relinquish his weapons and give himself up. He had lost a lot of blood, was in great pain and, without water or food for two days, on the verge of passing out. The keepers accepted his surrender, ending the grisly standoff, and even tended to their attacker's wounds, feeding him when he came down, before locking him in one of the bedrooms and nailing the window shut so he couldn't escape.

Two more days passed, and still Dunn had no success flagging down a ship. By that time Leach had decided he could not wait any longer for medical help. A very large and muscular man, he thought he was still capable of making it to Morgan City by boat despite all his wounds. He reluctantly agreed to take Woods with him.

On Thursday, March 2, Leach left the lighthouse with his prisoner, and upon arriving in Morgan City handed Woods over to the authorities and then went into surgery. As it turned out, Woods had indeed stolen the boat from the assistant keepers (where those keepers went or what they did in the ensuing days remains a mystery). Woods was tried for his crimes and sentenced to fourteen years in jail. Dunn and Leach ultimately recovered from their injuries, and returned to their jobs at the lighthouse.

MOST LIGHTHOUSES UP THROUGH the early twentieth century were especially isolated, and this created many difficulties, one of which involved education. At lighthouses relatively close to a town or city, keepers at least had the option of sending their children to the local school, not that this was always easy. For example, children who lived on islands within rowing distance of a school still had to get there and back, usually with one of their parents or an older sibling providing the transportation. In good weather this could be a pleasant, if not tiring, trip, but in stormy conditions it became a harrowing expedition. And when the weather was truly horrific, school was canceled.

In contrast, keepers who lived too far from civilization to transport their children to school on a daily basis had to explore other ways of educating them. Some keepers shipped their children off to boarding schools, or sent their wives to live in a town or city where the children could attend school. Other children were home-schooled, and in a few instances keepers even pooled their money to hire a teacher to live at the lighthouse.

The board and service were sympathetic to the educational needs of lighthouse children, whenever possible transferring keepers with children to lighthouses that were relatively close to schools. For a brief time the service offered limited financial aid to help defray some of the keepers' educational expenses, but beyond that most keepers were pretty much on their own—except in Maine. In the early 1900s the Maine Seacoast Missionary Society became quite concerned that children at the state's numerous far-flung lighthouses were "growing up without school privileges, some of them in lamentable ignorance." The society tried but failed to enlist the federal government to address this problem. So it pressured state officials to fill the void, and in 1916 Maine began funding teachers to travel by boat to many of the state's isolated offshore lighthouses (the society also pitched in by sending volunteer teachers to a number of lighthouses). These teachers stayed a few weeks at each lighthouse, providing books, outlining study plans, giving assignments, and then heading off to the next lighthouse. It was then up to the parents to make sure their children finished the assignments before the teacher's next scheduled visit. According to a lighthouse child who was taught by one of these itinerant teachers, "It was a hit-or-miss kind of schooling that depended greatly on the seriousness of the parents in wanting their children to have a good education."

ANOTHER MAJOR DIFFICULTY FACED by those living at isolated lighthouses was illness and injury. Like education and other resources, doctors were far away and difficult to reach, making keepers and their families their own first line of defense in confronting health problems, relying primarily on the rudimentary medicine chest and instructions provided by the government. When the situation grew dire, however, keepers turned to others for help. By flagging down a passing vessel, a keeper could get word to the nearest doctor to come quickly, or could have the vessel transport the patient to the doctor. Sometimes this was not an option, forcing the keeper to take drastic action, as happened at the Farallon Island Lighthouse in 1898.

On Christmas Day eleven-year-old Royal Beeman became violently ill, alarming his parents—the head keeper, William Beeman, and his wife, Wilhelmina (Minnie). Administering Dover's Powder, a popular opium-based remedy, had no effect, and the next day Royal's condition worsened. He desperately needed to see a doctor, but there seemed to be no way to get him to the nearest hospital in San Francisco, thirty miles away. A raging storm pounding the coast meant that there was virtually no hope of a ship passing by, and the Lighthouse Board tender wasn't scheduled to visit the island anytime soon. The only form of transportation off the island was a fourteen-foot dory with a crude sail, which the keepers used for fishing. While this vessel was seaworthy under calm conditions, it likely would not stand a chance against the tempest blowing offshore.

For three days the Beemans tended to Royal as best they could, but he was slowly slipping away. "He was in constant pain," Minnie Beeman recalled, "moaning and crying pitifully until I could hardly stand it." Finally, on December 29, the boy's parents decided that despite the continuing storm, they had no choice than to risk all in an attempt to get their son to a hospital. If they stayed on the island, he would surely die.

Wrapping Royal in a blanket and oilskins, his parents then laid him on a mattress in the bottom of the dory. The first assistant keeper, Louis Engelbrecht, volunteered to help William row and sail the boat. The final passenger was Royal's two-month-old sister, Isabel, who could not be left behind because she was still breast-feeding. While Beeman and Engelbrecht were gone, the two other assistant keepers were put in charge of the lighthouse.

The men headed toward the San Francisco lightship, which was moored about twenty-two miles from the Farallons. It was an agonizing journey to say the least. Waves washed over the dory's side drenching everyone, rain and hail pelted them, and the men's arms grew weary from the strain. Amazingly, some eight hours after their bold, if desperate, voyage had begun, and without the aid of any navigational equipment, they reached their destination.

The lightship, however, was of no help, since it had to stay on station and could not take them to shore. Beeman and Engelbrecht battled on for another hour, and just as they were about cross the treacherous San Francisco Bar, still a few miles from the Golden Gate, the pilot ship *America* arrived. It took all five passengers, as well as the dory, on board, and then sped to the San Francisco docks, from which Royal was quickly whisked to a hospital.

Local newspapers got wind of the story and presented Minnie as a hero who had risked her life to try to save her son's. Using the melodramatic language that typified reportage of the period, an article about the ordeal in the *San Francisco Examiner* was headlined, "She Proved That There Is No Love Like a Mother's Love." And indeed, not just Minnie's but also her husband's and Engelbrecht's determination and bravery in the face of real danger were truly heroic. Unfortunately, the story had a heartbreaking outcome. Despite the valiant efforts of a team of doctors, Royal died on January 3. This painful loss helped persuade the Beeman family to transfer to the California mainland, where William worked first at the Point Arguello Lighthouse, just south of Lompoc, and then at Point Loma.

IN ADDITION TO PHYSICAL ILLNESSES, lighthouse keepers also had to contend with psychological issues not so easily cured by recourse to the medicine chest or a trip to town. Lighthouse keepers were no exception to the obvious rule that isolation often fosters loneliness and depression. Oscar Daniels, assistant keeper at the Cherrystone Bar Lighthouse in the Chesapeake Bay, wrote in his log one day in 1909, "A man had just as well die and be done with the world at once as to spend his days here," signing this entry, "All Alone." One of the keepers at Washington State's Cape Flattery Lighthouse in the late 1800s became so overwhelmed by the loneliness of his situation that he tried to commit suicide by flinging himself off a cliff near the lighthouse. Despite plummeting almost one hundred feet into the rocky surf below, he survived, albeit with serious injuries. His fellow keepers found him mangled and unconscious, and brought him back to the keeper's house. Soon thereafter he was sent off-island for treatment, and with that his career as a keeper came to an end.

Loneliness and depression were hardly unique to keepers; their families were also afflicted. Anna Marie Carlson, whose husband was the assistant keeper at the Outer Island Lighthouse in the remote Apostle Islands of Lake Superior in the early 1890s, once told a reporter that during her first year at the lighthouse she only had three people to talk to—her husband, the head keeper, and a fisherman who lived in a shack on the shore during the summer. "Oh! The loneliness of those days on Outer Island! There was nothing to see but water with the dim outline of the Apostle's group behind the haze, and an occasional steamer way out on the lake." The only reason that she could endure the isolation, Mrs. Carlson said, was that she loved her husband.

In one particularly heartrending case, the terrible solitude proved too much for a keeper's wife to bear. On the morning of June 9, 1922, Ellsworth Smith, the keeper at Conimicut Lighthouse, a spark-plug beacon in Narragansett Bay, said good-bye to his wife, Nellie, and his two sons, five-year-old Robert and two-year-old Russell, before heading to Providence on business. "When I left," Ellsworth later recalled, "Nellie seemed to be happy. She was playing with the children. She kissed me goodbye and waved to me as I steered for the shore." Seeing his wife this way reassured Ellsworth, since she was usually in a much darker mood. During the year he and Nellie had lived at the lighthouse, she "had grown morose and despondent as a result of her isolation." Her extreme loneliness had led her to beg Ellsworth to take her away from the lighthouse, and many times she had threatened to kill herself unless he did.

Soon after Ellsworth left that morning, Nellie followed through on this threat, giving her children poisonous mercury bichloride pills before taking a fatal dose herself. By the time Ellsworth returned in the afternoon, his wife and younger son were dead, and Robert was quickly fading. Ellsworth laid his surviving son in the dory and rowed him to the mainland, where a doctor was able to save his life. Despite this terrible misfortune, whose memories clung to the lighthouse, Ellsworth returned to his post, with young Robert at his side.

The pangs of loneliness were by no means limited to adults. In 1876 fourteen-year-old Annie Bell Hobbs, the daughter of one of the assistant keepers at Maine's Boon Island Lighthouse, sent a letter to *The Nursery*, a popular publication for young readers, in which she recounted her perspective on the place she called home. "Out at sea . . . is Boon Island," Annie wrote, "upon which I have been a prisoner, with the privilege of the yard, the past two years. . . . The broad Atlantic Ocean lies before and all around us. Now and then sails dot the wide expanse, reminding me that there is a world besides the little one I dwell in." After her parents finished the school lessons for the day, Annie said she would turn her "eyes and thoughts towards the mainland, and think how I should like to be there, and enjoy some of those delightful sleigh-rides which I am deprived of while I am shut out here from the world."

In addition to loneliness, simple boredom and monotony were equally implacable enemies. Nancy Rose, the keeper at the Stony Point Lighthouse on the Hudson River for forty-seven years, when asked by a reporter if anything interesting happened to her, responded, "Nothing ever happens up here. One year is exactly like another, and except the weather nothing changes." A keeper at the wave-swept Minot's Lighthouse, off the coast of Massachusetts near Boston, reflecting on the dullness of his days, said, "The trouble with our life out here is that we have too much time to think."

While seclusion drove some to depression, alcoholism, madness, or worse, others—usually from the outside looking in—continued to believe in the long-romanticized simple routine and quiet afforded by the life of a lighthouse keeper. The physicist and Nobel laureate Albert Einstein viewed the keeper's "time to think" as a golden opportunity. In 1933 the great scientist, a newly arrived émigré fleeing Nazi Germany, proposed an alternative use for America's lighthouses. "When I was living in solitude in the country," Einstein wrote, "I noticed how the monotony of a quiet life stimulates the creative mind." After observing—with perhaps pardonable naïveté—that "there are certain occupations . . . which entail living in isolation," such as working in lighthouses, he wondered, "Would it not be possible to place young people who wish to think about scientific problems . . . in such occupations?"

Although there is no evidence that any keepers used their time to solve scientific problems, some keepers did take advantage of the "quiet life" to engage in intellectual pursuits. Thoreau spoke of a classmate of his "who fitted for college by the lamps of a light-house, which was more light, we think, than the University afforded." And when William Hunt Harris became second assistant keeper at the Carysfort Reef Lighthouse in 1889, he brought with him a stack of law books, which he studied each day upon completing his lighthouse duties. Three months later he was transferred to Northwest Passage Lighthouse, off Key West, bringing his books with him, and following the same routine. This worked out well, for within a year's time he left the lighthouse, passed the bar, and soon became a prominent lawyer, later serving in both houses of the Florida legislature.

THE BOARD AND THE SERVICE were keenly aware that loneliness and monotony often affected lighthouse life. The traveling libraries that made the rounds of more remote lighthouses were one attempt to help alleviate these twin difficulties, with the books providing an absorbing diversion for many keepers. However, the single greatest weapon in the fight against these problems came in the 1920s, with the widespread introduction of radios, which put the world at people's fingertips.

George Rockwell Putnam realized that radios could improve the quality of life at isolated stations, but since virtually the service's entire budget was being funneled into modernizing equipment and expanding aids to navigation, he didn't have the resources to buy radios for keepers. In 1925, however, a New York woman who was moved by stories of lonely keepers donated twenty-five radios to various lighthouses. This benevolent act intrigued Putnam's boss, Secretary of Commerce Herbert Hoover, who thought that there might be other equally generous individuals. So in 1926 Hoover, a great believer in personal charity as opposed to government spending, issued a public appeal for people to donate radios to the service. "I don't know of any other class of shut-ins," Hoover wrote, "who are more entitled to such aid. The Government does not pay them any too well, and the instruments which they can hardly afford are in many cases the only means of keeping in touch with the world." And if this didn't compel people to step up, Hoover tugged a little harder on their heartstrings. "At best," he wrote, "many of these men are forced to lead a dreary, lonely existence, shut off from practically all the ordinary amusements of the average citizen. They are faithful servants of the

American Government employed in most necessary work wherein inattention to duty might end in serious disaster." Radios, Hoover argued, would help ease their burden.

The response was phenomenal. Nearly three hundred radios were donated and distributed to lighthouses nationwide. Now the lucky recipients could not only listen to entertaining shows, but they could also keep up with the news and obtain weather reports that enabled them to better prepare for storms, and warn ships of deteriorating conditions.

A keeper at Florida's American Shoal Lighthouse marveled at the changes the new radio had wrought. "At other times when a president was elected," he wrote, "sometimes it has been one month before we knew who was elected; this time when Secretary Hoover was elected [on November 6, 1928] and was announced to the world we heard it as soon as anybody else. The last two big fights when it was announced who was champion we heard it. We listen also to ministers preaching, and there is singing; it is almost the same as being in church."

Christmas could be a particularly lonely time of the year for keepers and their families, since it often had to be celebrated without the comforting presence of relatives and friends. Here too it was not the government, but private citizens who took action to make keepers' lives a little brighter during the holiday. In 1929 Capt. William "Bill" H. Wincapaw decided that he wanted to give something back to the lighthouse keepers who had helped him so much over the years. As a pilot of seaplanes and other aircraft operating out of Rockland, Maine, Wincapaw had many times rescued fishermen in distress, and safely transported injured or sick islanders to the mainland for treatment, saving numerous lives. He often relied on lighthouse beacons to help him find his way, especially during bad weather. Without their guidance, he knew that his job would be far more difficult and dangerous than it already was. As a result of his great respect for keepers and their families, and his gratitude for the service they provided, Wincapaw expressed his appreciation in an unusual way. On Christmas Day 1929 he loaded his plane with a dozen "care packages" full of candy, magazines, newspapers, coffee, and other small items, and then flew over lighthouses in the vicinity of Rockland,

The Flying Santa plane passing by Boston Lighthouse in 1947.

jettisoning the packages as he passed by, and timing it so that they landed as close to the lighthouse as possible. The beneficiaries of Wincapaw's flight of joy were thrilled with by his kindly gesture, and Wincapaw was equally thrilled by the response. So much so, that he made the flight an annual affair. Thus was born the tradition of the Flying Santa. Over time the reach of Flying Santa expanded dramatically. By the mid-1930s Wincapaw, with the help of his son, Bill junior, were visiting nearly one hundred lighthouses and Coast Guard stations up and down the New England coast. In 1936 the historian Edward Rowe Snow was enlisted to help out, and his involvement continued, remarkably, for nearly fifty years, long after the Wincapaws had performed their last flights in 1946.

Snow wasn't a pilot, so at first he flew with Bill junior at the controls, and then, after 1946, he hired a pilot and a plane, while he played the role of Flying Santa, dressing appropriately for the part and often bringing his wife and daughter along to share in the fun of dropping the packages to the lighthouses below. Although Snow received contributions to fill the packages with goodies—everything from cigarettes, razors, and gum to

The Snow family—Edward, his wife, Anna-Myrle, and daughter,
Dorothy ("Dolly")—loading the Flying Santa plane in 1963.

dolls, jigsaw puzzles, and balls—he paid for more than 90 percent of the
cost of the flights out of his own pocket. As an author and a high school
teacher, Snow was hardly wealthy, but he was happy to fund the trips. "I
have been more than repaid for the expense," Snow wrote, "by the pleasure I have received from the waving of the lighthouse keepers at their
lonely stations and the letters they later send to me."

By the mid-1950s Snow was visiting as many as 250 lighthouses and
Coast Guard stations up and down the east coast, from Sable Island, off
Nova Scotia, all the way to Florida. There were a few years when he went
farther afield, to the Great Lakes, Bermuda, and even the west coast.
However, Snow suffered a stroke in 1981, and died the following year
at the age of seventy-nine. But the Flying Santa tradition lived on, first
being sponsored by the Hull Lifesaving Museum, and more recently by
the nonprofit group Friends of Flying Santa, which still annually visits
lighthouses and Coast Guard stations in New England, but by helicopter
rather than plane.

———

ALTHOUGH LONELINESS AFFLICTED MANY keepers, and while some level of monotony was an inevitable part of the job, most keepers were satisfied with, if not enamored of, their chosen profession. This was particularly evidenced by the fact that so many remained keepers for decades, with few complaints, rather than resign and find another line of work. After being keeper of Indiana's Michigan City Lighthouse for forty-three years, Harriet Colfax told a reporter shortly before her retirement, "I love the lamps, the old lighthouse, and the work. They are the habit, the home, everything dear I have known for so long." And for every keeper's wife or child who bemoaned the lighthouse life, there were many more who enjoyed it. For example, when a reporter in the early 1930s asked the wife of the keeper at Split Rock Lighthouse, on Lake Superior, for her thoughts on living at the lighthouse, she responded, "I'm happy here. I've got a good husband. We have everything we need. It's nice up here. We like it." As for a child's perspective, Marion Humphries provides the perfect counterpoint to the melancholy musings of Boon Island's Annie Bell Hobbs. Marion's father was keeper at the Piney Point Lighthouse, located on the Maryland side of the Potomac River, and she lived there in the early 1900s, from the age of seven to twelve. "You ever see Piney Point?" she told an interviewer later in life. "God, how I loved that place when I was a kid. I didn't have to go to school, cause there wasn't any! There was no schools anywhere near Piney Point! My mother was my teacher. . . . I loved to help my dad with the light."

At a deeper level, many keepers, realizing just how rarefied their profession was, were especially proud of their job, and extremely dedicated to the central mission of the lighthouse establishment—keeping the mariner safe. In carrying out this mission, keepers rightfully believed they were doing something noble, something that was bigger than themselves, something that truly mattered. Connie Small, whose husband, Elson, served as keeper at a number of Maine lighthouses from the 1920s to the 1940s, spoke for many keepers and their families when she said, "When we were on the light, we didn't think of it as a job. We thought of it as a calling." John J. Cook, the keeper of Stamford Harbor Lighthouse, in Connecticut, eloquently captured this almost religious sense of a higher purpose when he responded to an interviewer in 1908, who asked him how he could take pleasure in the Christmas holiday when he had to spend it stuck in the lighthouse, away from the joyous festivities taking place on the mainland:

> I dunno, it is pretty lonesome here sometimes, especially in winter, but we manage to enjoy our holidays. We can't go to church on Christmas and we miss the nice music and the fine sermons, but there is a compensation for that. What more soul-stirring music could there be than that of wind and wave as they whistle and roar or moan and swish past our little home? And that light aloft is a sermon in itself. Many a fervent 'Thank God,' many a heart-deep prayer has gone up, maybe from people who wouldn't be thinking of such things ashore, when the red gleam of Stamford Light was made out in a storm, or the bell heard in a fog. My little light has its mission just as your pulpit preacher has his; and no one who has watched it through the terrible winter storms can fail to appreciate this, and with it his responsibility. Human life, yes, human souls depend upon that light Christmas and every other night of the year, and I dare guess it's compensation for the loss of a Christmas sermon to keep the light burning steadily.

CHAPTER 11

LIGHTHOUSE HEROES

· · · · · · · · · · · · · · ·

"Miss Ida Lewis, the Heroine of Newport," on the cover of the July 31, 1869, issue of Harper's Weekly.

ALTHOUGH THE MAIN JOB OF LIGHTHOUSE KEEPERS WAS TO tend to the lighthouse, they were also supposed to render assistance to people involved in wrecks, or otherwise in distress on the water. In doing so, keepers, much like firemen, saved thousands of people, often at great risk to their own lives, and perhaps it is this selfless quality that has cast an almost romantic glow on the American lighthouse keeper, a loving image frozen nostalgically in time. While many keepers can be counted among those who engaged in rescues that were both thrilling and memorable, at the top of such a historical list must stand Ida Lewis and Marcus A. Hanna. Their stories illustrate how keepers, by performing their job with exemplary dedication and courage, could become heroes.

Born on February 25, 1842, Idawalley Zoradia Lewis was the child of Capt. Hosea Lewis and Idawalley Zoradia Willey. To avoid confusion between the two namesakes, the daughter was referred to simply as Ida, while the mother was called Zoradia. Hosea worked as a coast pilot and on a revenue cutter for many years before being appointed keeper of Lime Rock Lighthouse, in Newport, Rhode Island, in 1853. The lighthouse was a crude, short stone tower with a small lantern room on top. It stood about two hundred yards from the shore on a jumble of limestone ledges in Newport Harbor, known locally as Lime Rock. The lighthouse had no keeper's quarters, so Hosea and his family lived in town, and he commuted to work by boat.

Twice daily Hosea dutifully rowed to the lighthouse to tend the light, with Ida frequently at his side. She would often take up the oars, and with that practice she grew into a skilled rower who learned the many moods of the sea and could handle a skiff in all types of weather. According to Ida Lewis's biographer Lenore Skomal, Hosea would regale his daughter with stories of his seafaring past, and how he had risked his own life to save others'. Hosea also taught her how to rescue someone from the water, making sure to pull the drowning person over the stern rather than the side of the boat, to keep them from tipping the boat over. "It was her father," Skomal writes, "[who] instilled in Ida the seed of heroism."

After more than two years of making these taxing treks to the lighthouse every day in all types of weather, Hosea's health began to suffer. He pleaded with his superiors to build a keeper's house on Lime Rock, arguing that it made much more sense for him to live next to the light so that he could better perform his duties. The board agreed, and by 1857 it had constructed a two-story granite-and-brick house, which had built into its northwest corner a square brick column with a small lan-

*Engraving of the Lime Rock Lighthouse, off Newport, Rhode Island,
as depicted in the July 31, 1869, issue of Harper's Weekly.*

tern room on top. Hosea could now tend to the lighthouse's sixth-order Fresnel lens by simply accessing the lantern room via an alcove on the house's second floor.

The Lewis family moved in at the end of June, but calamity struck in October when Hosea suffered a crippling stroke that left him partially paralyzed and unable to perform his keeper's duties. As a result, Ida, now fifteen, and Zoradia took on the responsibility of running the lighthouse, with Ida shouldering most of the load. In addition to her lighthouse duties, she also ferried her two younger siblings to and from school in Newport, and did supply runs to and from town, all the while strengthening her body and improving her boat-handling skills.

One year later, in September 1858, those skills were put to the test. Early that day four boys who attended a private school in Newport decided to take a catboat—a small, shallow-draft, wide-beamed sailing vessel with the mast near the bow—across the harbor for an island picnic. After eating, they sailed about beyond the harbor's mouth, and then headed back. With the weather getting rougher, they lowered the sail, preferring to let tide carry them in. As they neared Lime Rock, Lewis could see them horsing around and hear them laughing. One of the party shimmied up the mast and began rocking back and forth, perhaps to amuse or scare his friends. This prank quickly backfired, as the boat capsized, pitching all four schoolboys into the water.

True to her training, Lewis reacted instantly, hopping into her skiff and quickly rowing to the boys. By the time she arrived, they were on the verge of drowning. The hull of the boat had sunk so low that it offered no purchase, forcing the boys to tread water. But being immersed had numbed their limbs, and the weight of their wet clothes was dragging them down. While the boys flailed about, struggling to keep their heads above water, Lewis, much as her father had instructed her, kept cool. Remembering Hosea's teaching, she pulled the boys in one by one, over the stern, and then rowed them back to the lighthouse, where Zoradia handed out warm blankets and hot drinks. One of the boys was "so far gone," teetering on the edge of consciousness, that he had to be revived with stimulants, possibly alcohol but most likely smelling salts. They all slowly came around, expressed their gratitude to Lewis, and went on their way.

Over the next decade Lewis continued to act as the keeper and lifeguard of Lime Rock, performing three more daring rescues in the harbor, including one that involved a sheep. On a particularly cold morning in January 1867, while a nor'easter was lashing Newport, three Irishmen who worked for a prominent local banker were herding one of his prize sheep down Main Street when it bolted toward the harbor. With the men in pursuit, the sheep jumped into the water and was soon swept farther offshore. The men ran along the harbor's edge for a short distance before reaching Jones Bridge Wharf, where they spied an empty skiff. Despite the treacherous conditions in the harbor and their lack of boating skills, the men crowded into the skiff and set off after the wayward sheep, fearing that if they failed to save it they would soon be unemployed.

As related in a biography locally published two years later, lashing winter waves swamped the boat, which was rapidly drifting seaward, and when it capsized, the men found themselves in need of rescue. Ida had been sewing near a window when she heard the men's piercing screams, and upon looking out she saw their predicament. She ran to her boat and expertly negotiated the rough seas to reach the skiff. As she got closer she could hear the men's heavy Irish brogue as they prayed to God for deliverance. Upon seeing Lewis, one of the men reportedly exclaimed, "Oh Holy Vargin, and be jabbers, have you come to save me?" "(Such stereotypical language was fairly typical of the mid-nineteenth century, when the concept of political correctness lay more than one hundred years in the future.) After pulling the men on board, Lewis deposited them on Jones Bridge Wharf. Not done yet, seeing the sheep floating farther out to sea, she raced after it, tied a lasso around its neck, and rowed back to shore with the sheep in tow behind. The overjoyed Irishmen thanked Lewis, and left with their lives, their prize, and their jobs.

By early 1869 Lewis had saved nine people and one runaway ovine from the waters around Lime Rock, yet few beyond her family and those she had saved even knew that the rescues had taken place. Although a couple of them generated cursory mentions in the local newspapers, Lewis's heroics remained largely unknown to the general public. Her next rescue that would change all that.

EARLY ONE EVENING IN March 1869, on her way to tend to the light, Zoradia Lewis looked out the window and screamed, "Ida, oh my God, Ida run quick, a boat capsized and men drowning, run quick, Ida!" About halfway between the lighthouse and Goat Island, Sgt. James Adams and Pvt. John McLoughlin, soldiers from Fort Adams, which sat on a peninsula to the west of Lime Rock, were desperately clinging to the hull of a boat. Earlier in the day, they had engaged the services of a fourteen-year-old boy, who boasted that despite the stormy conditions, he could safely ferry them from town to the fort for a small fee. The boy's confidence, however, proved greater than his abilities, and when the boat capsized, he paid for his foolishness with his life. He had neither the strength to hold on to the boat's hull nor the ability to tread water, and he soon sank beneath the waves, his body never to be found.

According to Mrs. Lewis it was "blowing a living gale and raining torrents" when she saw the men in distress, but that didn't deter her daughter. Still battling a lingering cold, and without taking the time to

Coast Guard commissioned painting of Ida Lewis rescuing soldiers
James Adams and John McLoughlin, by John Witt, 1989.

put on shoes or a coat, Ida ran out of the house in her stockinged feet, with only a towel tied loosely around her neck for extra protection. Asking her younger brother, Hosea, to accompany her to help haul the men in, she was soon rowing to the rescue with him by her side.

Powering through the whitecapped waves that slammed into the skiff and threatened to swamp it, Lewis and her brother finally reached the stricken soldiers, and with great difficulty dragged them onto the boat. Weary from the strain, and now hauling more than twice as much weight, she leaned into the oars and returned to Lime Rock. By the time the skiff pulled in, Adams, drenched and shivering uncontrollably, was "barely able to totter up to the house," while McLoughlin, who had passed out, had to be carried in.

Her feet nearly frostbitten, her aching muscles protesting her efforts, Ida warmed herself by the fire as her family cared for the soldiers, who slowly recovered. According to Ida's older brother, Rudolph, Adams said, "When I saw the boat approaching and a woman rowing, I thought, she's only a woman and she will never reach us. But soon I changed my mind." The soldiers stayed overnight, and the next morning Ida, still exhausted from her earlier exertions, rowed them back to the fort.

UNLIKE HER PAST RESCUES, this one didn't remain hidden from view. Exactly how word of the rescue spread is not clear, but soon papers in Newport and Providence ran stories detailing the event, and when one of those stories landed on the desk of an editor with the *New-York Tribune*, he immediately sent a reporter to Lime Rock to interview the young "good Samaritan." The article that resulted ran on April 12, 1869, and detailed not only her most recent rescue but also the four that preceded it. The article dwelled on Lewis's bravery and portrayed her as a hero, labeling her the "Guardian Angel of Newport Harbor" and the "Grace Darling of America."

This last comparison was high praise indeed. Grace Horsley Darling had been hailed the world over for her part in a dramatic rescue off the Northumberland coast of England in 1838. Twenty-two years old at the time, the daughter of the keeper of Longstone Lighthouse, in the early

Engraving of Ida Lewis (center), and her mother and father, inside the keeper's quarters at Lime Rock Lighthouse, as depicted in the July 31, 1869, issue of Harper's Weekly.

morning of September 7 she was looking toward the ocean and the storm that was blowing when she saw a ship wrecked on Big Harcar Rock, an island about a mile from the lighthouse. It was the steamer *Forfarshire*, which had been bound for Dundee, Scotland. Grace alerted her father, William, who grabbed his telescope to look for survivors. They saw none at first, but a while later, as the sky lightened, they noticed movement on the rock. As the story is most often told, Grace urged her father to go with her to attempt a rescue, but he resisted at first, fearing that the seas were too rough, before finally agreeing to join her. Whether or not William was in on the decision from the start, the record is clear that both he and Grace soon shoved off in the lighthouse's twenty-foot rowboat and headed for the rock. When they arrived they were able to take aboard only five of the nine survivors. After returning to the lighthouse, and dropping off his daughter and three of the survivors, William and two of the rescued men returned to the rock to collect the other four.

News of the rescue soon filtered out, and Grace's role in it catapulted her into the maws of the tabloid press that had recently come of age in early Victorian England. No longer was she just the keeper's daughter, she had become a national hero, lionized for her bravery. She received an admiring letter from Queen Victoria, who was three years younger and only one year into her nearly sixty-four-year reign, the second longest of any British monarch. Darling was also awarded a gold medal by the Humane Society, entertained by nobility, and given a £750 purse, which was collected through a public subscription. Poems were written about her, portraits were painted of the winsome brunette, marriage proposals flooded in, and many people even requested locks of her hair as a memento of her daring deed. Just four years after the rescue, in 1842, the fearless Darling—who never sought and didn't enjoy her sudden celebrity—died of tuberculosis at the age of twenty-six.

As it turns out, Ida Lewis, who was twenty-seven, was about to experience a celebrity quite similar to Grace Darling's. The glowing article in the *Tribune* set off a media feeding frenzy, and was soon followed by others in *Harper's Weekly* and *Frank Leslie's Illustrated Newspaper*, which were equally effusive about Lewis's actions, with the *Harper's* piece claiming that one of her earlier rescues of a soldier who was in danger of drowning "was a most daring feat, and required courage and perseverance such as few of the male sex even are possessed of." These articles also included engravings depicting the heroine of Lime Rock. Many of the readers no doubt were surprised by the images, which showed a woman of average height and slender build (she weighed just over 100 pounds). As Skomal notes, "Her size alone made the stories of her rescues even more sensational."

The coverage in major national magazine and newspapers, which was echoed in hundreds of smaller publications from coast to coast, made Lewis by far the most famous lighthouse keeper in America, and also one of the most famous women in the nation, up there with the likes of such historical heavyweights as Clara Barton, the pioneering nurse who was christened the "Angel of the Battlefield" for her heroic work during the Civil War, and the novelist Louisa May Alcott, most famous for penning *Little Women*. Throughout the spring and summer of 1869, Lewis was showered with awards, gifts, and adulation, of which only a partial accounting is offered here. In May the Lifesaving Benevolent Association of New York gave her a silver medal and $100, and the Rhode Island General Assembly passed a resolution in her honor, recognizing her heroism. Soon thereafter the officers and soldiers of Fort Adams collected $218 and gave it to Lewis as a token of their thanks, this on the heels of a gold pocket watch that Adams and McLoughlin had bestowed upon Lewis for saving them. Newport declared July 4, 1869, Ida Lewis Day, and four thousand people gathered to pay her tribute and watch her receive a brand-new rowboat, appropriately named *Rescue*, which was funded by public donations. Photographers besieged her, and the cartes-de-visite images that resulted were sold far and wide, further cementing her celebrity status. Again similar to Grace Darling, many a suitor wrote to Lewis, asking for her hand in marriage.

By her father's count, between nine and ten thousand people came to visit America's new star that summer. Many of them were famous, including Gen. William Tecumseh Sherman, the Union general who was reviled in the South and revered in the North for his scorched-earth tactics during the Civil War, and the suffragettes Elizabeth Cady Stanton and Susan B. Anthony, who had earlier that year launched the National Woman Suffrage Association, whose main goal was the passage of a constitutional amendment giving women the right to vote. Stanton and Anthony held Lewis up as an example of the great achievements women were capable of, and used her public acclaim and heroism as yet another argument in favor of granting women more equality with men, including, most especially, the right to participate fully in elections. President Ulysses S. Grant also stopped by. According to legend, Grant was so determined to meet the young heroine that he purportedly said, "I have come to see Ida Lewis, and to see her I'd get wet up to my armpits if necessary." If he actually did say this, he needn't have worried about getting wet, for he ended up briefly chatting with Lewis at a prearranged meeting on Long Wharf in Newport, where he told her, "I am happy to meet you, Miss Lewis, as one of the heroic, noble women of the age."

Staying true to the humble dedication of her profession, Lewis didn't let all this recognition go to her head. In her mind the rescues were simply part of her job. "If there were some people out there who needed help," she told a reporter later in her life, "I would get into my boat and go to them even if I knew I couldn't get back. Wouldn't you?" After her almost unprecedented rendezvous with fame in the summer of 1869, life settled down for Lewis, and that is how she liked it, much preferring tending to the light than being treated as a celebrity, caught in its beam. She remained at Lime Rock until October 23, 1870, when she married a mariner from Bridgeport, Connecticut, one William Heard Wilson, whom she had known for three years. However, the marriage was a fleeting and unhappy one, and after only two years of residing in Connecticut, she left her husband—again defying the conventions of the time—and returned to the lighthouse at Lime Rock.

It was during this time that Lewis's father died, and her mother was appointed keeper, following the board's custom of having widows succeed their husbands. It was Lewis, however, who did most of the work in the lighthouse, and she felt slighted by not being chosen keeper. Finally, in 1879 Ida took over from her mother and remained keeper until her death in 1911, thirty-two years later. Lewis's famous rescue in March 1869, however, was not her last. In 1877 she saved three drunken soldiers who capsized their boat while trying to cross the harbor from the town to Fort Adams. Four years later she performed another rescue that would garner her one of the most prestigious awards of her life.

Late on the afternoon of February 4, 1881, Frederick O. Tucker and Giuseppe Gianetti, both members of the military band at Fort Adams, were in town when they decided to stroll back to the fort *over* the frozen harbor. Walking side by side, they reached a point called Brenton's Cove, about halfway between the lighthouse and the fort, where the ice began to get mushy and thin. It had been common knowledge at the fort that the ice in this part of the harbor was dangerous, but either the men were unaware of this or they didn't care (one observer later claimed that the bandmates were drunk). A few steps further, and both of them plunged through the ice into the freezing water below.

Mother and daughter had been watching the soldiers' progress from their kitchen window, and when the two men fell through and began screaming, Zoradia allegedly fainted. While Ida's sister Harriet, tended to their mother, Ida grabbed a clothesline and raced out onto the ice, followed soon thereafter by Rudolph. Reaching the drowning men first, she stood on firmer ice and tossed them the line. Tucker grabbed it, and Lewis, using all her strength to keep from slipping and being pulled in, dragged him onto the ice. By that time Rudolph had arrived, and together he and his sister pulled Gianetti to safety. Neither of the men was able to stand on his own, so the siblings carried them back to the lighthouse, where they recuperated for a while before being taken to the fort's hospital for treatment.

This rescue received widespread press attention, but more than that, it won Lewis a gold medal for lifesaving from the U.S. Government. The award had been established by an act of Congress in 1874, and was to be given to persons who "endanger their own lives in saving, or endeavoring to save lives from perils of the sea," with the gold medal being "confined to cases of extreme and heroic daring." Lewis was the first woman thus honored. Likely just as meaningful as the award was the letter she received from Tucker's mother a week after the rescue. "Dear good brave woman," the letter began. "What can I say. What can I do for I cannot thank you half enough on paper for saving the life of my Dear Boy."

Lewis's last documented rescue came in 1906, when she was sixty-three. Two of her friends were rowing out to visit her at the lighthouse when one of them stood up and fell in. In what must by then have been pure reflex for her, Lewis immediately got into her skiff and plucked the woman from the water. By the end of her career Lewis was officially credited with rescuing eighteen people from drowning. When she died on October 24, 1911, at the age of sixty-nine, many tributes were offered to her selflessness and bravery. One of the most rousing and patriotic came from a *New York Times* article, published a week after her death, which used the occasion to set the record straight on a transatlantic rivalry. "The Grace Darling of America? Why do they call Ida Lewis that?" the *Times* wondered. "Grace Darling is the Ida Lewis of England. . . . Grace Darling never had a record like this. . . . The Grace Darling of America? Nonsense. Whom has England, or for that matter, any other country, to show that can match our Ida Lewis?"

More than fourteen hundred people attended Lewis's funeral. She was buried in Newport's Common Burying Ground, and despite the incisive pronouncement of the *New York Times*, when her friends and admirers erected a tombstone in her honor the epitaph read, "Ida Lewis, The Grace Darling of America, Keeper of Lime Rock Lighthouse." The building Lewis loved so much was renamed the "Ida Lewis Lighthouse" in her honor in 1924, making it the only American lighthouse to ever be named after a keeper. The board decommissioned the lighthouse three years later, replacing it with an automatic beacon atop a metal tower. And in 1928 the lighthouse became the clubhouse for Newport's Ida Lewis Yacht Club, which is connected to shore by a wooden walkway. Appropriately enough, the club's triangular burgee, or flag, depicts a lighthouse bracketed by eighteen stars, one for each of the lives Ida Lewis saved.

IF IDA LEWIS BECAME FAMOUS in part for the sheer number of rescues she carried out, Marcus A. Hanna distinguished himself among keepers for just one incredible rescue that became a brutal struggle against the elements. Hanna's story begins with the schooner *Australia* tied at a wharf in Boothbay, Maine, in the late afternoon of January 28, 1885, waiting to start a scheduled trip to Boston. The cargo consisted of mackerel, dried fish, and guano (seabird droppings, which farmers used as fertilizer). At five o'clock, under fair skies and a light easterly wind, the *Australia* shoved off, with its three-man crew consisting of Capt. J. W. Lewis, and seamen Irving Pierce and William Kellar. By eleven the *Australia* was off Halfway Rock, so named because it is halfway between Cape Small and Cape Elizabeth, in Casco Bay. If Lewis took any comfort in seeing the beam of the Halfway Rock Lighthouse, it was overshadowed by his growing concern about the wind-whipped snowstorm that had overtaken his ship.

Lewis decided to take shelter in Portland Harbor, which lay about ten miles northwest of Cape Elizabeth. But as the January weather worsened and the seas mounted, Pierce told Lewis he thought that plan too dangerous, and recommended that they ride out the storm offshore. No sooner had Lewis agreed to this and shifted direction than a mighty gust blew the mainsail to shreds. Lewis reduced the area of the foresail, and began repeatedly sailing the ship closer, and then farther away from the coastline, hoping to roughly maintain the ship's position until the morning light.

As the crippled ship battled with the elements on the open seas, the temperature, already a frigid four degrees, dropped to ten below. With waves breaking over the bulwarks and flooding the hold, and an ever-thickening layer of ice coating every exposed surface, the men feared that the ship would founder, so they began pitching overboard everything that wasn't fastened to the deck to lighten its load. Not long after midnight Lewis heard over the roar of the storm the shrill whistle of the fog signal coming from the Cape Elizabeth Lighthouse. Located on a large, rocky headland just southeast of Portland, the lighthouse consisted of two identical sixty-seven-foot cast-iron towers, each housing a second-order Fresnel lens. The station's steam-powered fog signal was housed in its own building near the shore.

All through the night Lewis and his men struggled to keep the *Aus-*

tralia within hearing range of the fog signal. Shortly after dawn on the morning of January 29, they spotted land and the lighthouse's eastern tower close by. They tried to sail the ship around the cape, but the wind and waves were driving them ever closer to the shore, so they decided that their best chance of surviving was to strand the ship intentionally. A few minutes later the *Australia* plowed into the rocks near the lighthouse.

BETWEEN MIDNIGHT AND 6:00 A.M., Cape Elizabeth's head keeper, Marcus A. Hanna, had been on duty running the fog signal. Forty-three years old at the time, Hanna was no newcomer to lighthouses. His grandfather was one of the first keepers at Boon Island, and Hanna spent his first few years of his life at the Franklin Island Lighthouse, in Muscongus Bay, just offshore from Bristol, Maine, where his father had been the keeper. Hanna followed in his father's and grandfather's footsteps in 1869, becoming the keeper at Pemaquid Point Lighthouse, at the western entrance to Muscongus Bay, and perched on the edge of exquisitely scenic rock ledges made of finely layered gneiss, with alternating black, white, gray, and rust-colored bands that plunge into the sea at gently sloping angles. Four years later, in 1873, Hanna was transferred to Cape Elizabeth Lighthouse.

Of the weather raging outside on that miserable January night, Hanna would later say that it was "one of the coldest and most violent storms of snow, wind, and vapor" he had ever experienced. After being relieved by the second assistant keeper, Hiram Staples, Hanna trudged and at times crawled through the prodigious snowdrifts to get to his quarters, where his wife—and longtime assistant keeper—Louise, was waiting for him. Hanna was suffering from a severe cold, and the six-hour watch combined with his exposure to the storm had left him "weak and exhausted." All he wanted to do was rest. He put his wife in charge of dousing the lights at sunrise, and then fell into a deep sleep.

At 8:40, after opening the side door to the keeper's house, Mrs. Hanna saw the *Australia*'s stationary and tilting masts in the distance. Hurrying back inside, she yelled to her husband, "There is a vessel ashore near the fog signal!" Hanna jumped up, put on his hat, coat, and boots, and rushed as fast as he could through the drifts, heading toward the wreck. On the way he stopped at the fog-signal house, where he found, to his utter amazement, that Staples was unaware of the wreck even though it was barely two hundred yards away.

Staples followed Hanna to the surf's edge, where they came upon a horrific scene. Pierce and Kellar were in the fore rigging, almost frozen in place. One of them feebly raised his arm, and both cried out for help. As for Captain Lewis, he had been swept overboard soon after the ship stranded, and his mangled body would be found in the surf days later. Hanna recalled that upon seeing Pierce and Kellar, "I felt that there was a terrible responsibility thrust upon me, and I resolved to attempt the rescue at any hazard."

It was not the first time that Hanna's sense of duty compelled him to risk all on behalf of his fellow man. During the Civil War, some twenty-two years earlier, Hanna was a sergeant in Company B, Fiftieth Massachusetts Infantry. From late May through early July 1863, Hanna's unit was part of the Union forces laying siege to the Confederate stronghold at Port Hudson, Louisiana, located on the Mississippi River about twenty miles above Baton Rouge. On the morning of July 4, Company B was ordered into a

Marcus A. Hanna.

rifle pit—a shallow trench affording cover for infantry firing at the enemy—to support a battery of soldiers from New York.

The men from Company B had already been engaged in an action earlier that day, and hadn't had time to refill their canteens. As a result they went into the rifle pit with very little water. Since the July weather was sweltering, by afternoon the Massachusetts soldiers were becoming dangerously dehydrated, prompting their lieutenant to give them permission to go on a water run to replenish their canteens. With the nearest spring five hundred yards away, and the enemy in control of the higher ground, such a dash would expose a runner to a veritable turkey shoot of enemy fire. Despite the extreme danger Hanna volunteered to go, but when he asked for assistance, no one stepped forward. Undeterred, Hanna took off with fifteen canteens draped about his body, and notwithstanding the hail of bullets coming from the Confederate lines, he made it to the spring and back unscathed. For this valorous feat, Hanna was awarded the Congressional Medal of Honor.

SINCE THE WRECK OF the *Australia* was many yards from the shore, Hanna thought that the only way to rescue the men was by throwing them a line. Not having a suitable rope at the lighthouse, Hanna grabbed an ax from the fog-signal building and slogged his way through three hundred yards of deep snow to a pilothouse, planning to hack his way in and retrieve a rope he knew was there. Finding the pilothouse door completely blocked by a huge snowdrift, Hanna ran back to the fog-signal building and told Staples to follow him with a shovel. Staples dug a path to the door, and Hanna broke through with the ax, grabbed the rope, and raced back to scene of the disaster. By this time Nathaniel Staples, Hiram's fifteen-year old son, had arrived, and Hanna immediately sent him to the closest neighbor's home to summon help.

Hanna tied a piece of metal to the end of the rope, climbed over the ice-covered rocks into the roiling surf, and repeatedly pitched the rope toward the wreck, while Hiram Staples stood by ready to assist. Every toss landed about ten feet short, and each time Hanna pulled the rope back in, it would begin to freeze and stiffen in his hands, making it even more difficult to use. After nearly twenty attempts Hanna was so numb that he had to retreat to a sheltered area nearby, where he stomped his feet and shook his hands to warm them. He also unraveled and twisted the rope to dislodge its coating of ice. Dismayed by the failure to get the rope to the men, the shivering Staples returned to the fog-signal building, leaving Hanna alone.

As Hanna headed back toward the wreck, a prodigious wave lifted the *Australia*, hurling it closer to the shore, where, Hanna said, "she came down with a thunderous crash, staving in her whole port side [and] careening her on her beam ends." Amazingly Pierce and Kellar still clung to the rigging, but their situation was now even more precarious than before. Hanna threw the line, and it landed on the deck between the men, but they couldn't grab it before it slid into the water. Hanna waded deeper into the frigid surf and threw the line again. This time it hit its mark, and the men secured it around Pierce's waist. The nearly spent Hanna climbed out of the water and up the icy bank, screaming for help, but nobody heard his cries.

Plunging back into the water, Hanna labored mightily to haul Pierce to shore and up the bank. According to Hanna, "Pierce's jaws were set, he was totally blind from exposure to the cold, and the expression on his face I shall not soon forget." Hanna turned his attention to Kellar.

After a couple of failed attempts, Hanna got the line to Kellar, who tied it around his waist and signaled to be pulled in. But Hanna was exhausted. Thoroughly soaked, with hypothermia setting in and his body aching from his exertions and his illness, he doubted he had the strength to drag another man to shore. Still, Hanna began reeling in the line, and just when his endurance was giving out, Nathaniel Staples and two neighbors arrived and helped Hanna pull Kellar in and carry him to the signal house. A few minutes later a towering wave destroyed what was left of the *Australia*, littering the coast with debris.

The rescuers stripped Pierce's and Kellar's frozen clothes, and then gave them dry flannels, hot liquids, and food. Hanna, too, was similarly cared for. With the storm raging yet, and snowdrifts blocking the way,

Hanna and the others weren't able to get Pierce and Kellar to the keeper's house until the following day, where Hanna and his wife continued nursing them. It was another two days before the roads were cleared enough for Hanna and his assistants to make their way to Portland, the largest city in the state. They returned with doctors from the U.S. Marine Hospital, who transported Pierce and Kellar back to the city, where they were successfully treated for severe frostbite and shock.

On April 29, 1885, less than two months before the Statue of Liberty arrived with great fanfare in New York Harbor on board the French naval ship *Isère*, the government awarded Hanna a Gold Lifesaving Medal, the same honor Ida Lewis had received, for his heroic conduct on that storm-lashed January day. Thus Marcus A. Hanna became the only person in American history ever to have won both the Congressional Medal of Honor and its civilian counterpart.

THE EXTENT TO WHICH KEEPERS rendered assistance to people in distress on the water became much clearer with the advent of the Lighthouse Service. Each year the *Lighthouse Service Bulletin* briefly detailed incidents in which lighthouse service employees, mainly keepers, saved lives or property. In the service's first decade alone, more than 1,234 such incidents were recorded. But it wasn't only keepers who came to the rescue. Sometimes lighthouses did too, as was the case at Bolivar Point in Texas and Kilauea Point in Hawaii.

Just after sunrise on Saturday, September 8, 1900, a real-estate agent and insurance broker named Buford T. Morris awoke in his weekend home in Galveston, Texas, looked out the window, and was greeted by a wondrous sight. "The sky seemed to be made of mother of pearl," he later recalled. "Gloriously pink, yet containing a fish-scale-effect which reflected all the colors of the rainbow. Never have I seen such a beautiful sky." This surreal morning scene would prove a potent and ominous sign, as a short while later these brilliant colors faded, the sky darkened, and rain began to fall. A killer of massive proportions was on the way.

Nobody in Galveston was particularly worried about the weather that morning. Although a major storm had dumped more than two feet of rain in Cuba over the past week, roared over the tip of Florida, and then planted itself in the Gulf of Mexico, causing widespread damage along the Louisiana and Mississippi coasts, the U.S. Weather Bureau's forecasters didn't think the storm was worthy of being called a hurricane, nor did they think Galveston would be hit too hard. Minor flooding and strong winds, perhaps, but nothing the city hadn't handled before.

By late morning, however, the weather had gotten much worse. People living on Bolivar Peninsula, a long, slender ribbon of sand that lies directly across a ship channel from Galveston, were growing quite concerned. With winds gusting up to fifty miles per hour, and the Gulf waters, which had already swept over some low-lying areas, rising fast, some residents who had been displaced from their homes went to the Bolivar Point Lighthouse at the peninsula's tip seeking refuge. If any structure in the area could withstand the storm's fury, they thought, it would be the lighthouse.

Built in 1872 to replace the tower that had been torn down during the Civil War, the new Bolivar Point Lighthouse rose 117 feet above sea level and had a cast-iron shell with a brick-lined interior. By noon the head keeper, Harry C. Claiborne, and his assistants had welcomed more than one hundred storm refugees into the lighthouse and closed the door. The water at the base of the tower was already a few feet deep, and the new occupants spread themselves out on the iron stairs that wound up the center of the lighthouse, sitting on alternating steps.

Around the time Claiborne closed the lighthouse door, another drama was playing out nearby. The train coming from Beaumont, Texas, on its way to Galveston was creeping slowly over the flooded tracks as it approached the end of the line, about a quarter mile from the lighthouse. At that point the locomotive and its two coaches, filled with ninety-five passengers, were supposed to be loaded onto the *Charlotte M. Allen*, a ferry that would take them the two miles across the ship channel to Galveston. As the passengers watched with growing apprehension, the *Charlotte M. Allen* tried to battle its way from Galveston to the boat slip at Bolivar Point, but was having no luck fighting the storm. Towering swells

Bolivar Point Lighthouse, circa early twentieth century.

broke over the ferry's bow, and the whipping winds blew it off course. Finally the ferry captain gave up, turned the *Charlotte M. Allen* around, and headed back to Galveston.

The water on the tracks had continued rising and was now near the top of the train's wheels. Hoping to return to Beaumont, the conductor ordered the engineer to reverse engines, but as the train began moving backward, water rushed into the coach compartments. When the train briefly stopped, ten passengers jumped off. They had been looking at the sturdy lighthouse in the distance and thought they would be safer in there than on the train. As they waded through the rushing water toward what they hoped would be their tower of salvation, the train began moving again and was soon out of sight. Upon reaching the lighthouse, the passengers yelled and knocked on its door, and Claiborne let them in. They would be the last people to enter.

THE WEATHER BUREAU HAD been drastically wrong. The storm that hit the Galveston area was what would register today as a category 4 hurricane on the Saffir-Sampson Scale (developed in the late 1960s), with sustained winds of more than 130 mph, and gusts reaching as high as 200 mph, strong enough to rip the bark off trees. The bureau's mistake was not all that surprising, however, given the rudimentary nature of weather forecasting in 1900, in addition to the fact that hurricanes are notoriously fickle, and have since time immemorial, and right up to the present, thwarted people's ability to predict their violent course. The failed forecast only added to the frustrations and fears of the 125 people crammed into the lighthouse, who would have to ride out the hurricane together.

That night, as the tower swayed from side to side, Claiborne tended to the light, for even in this calamitous weather he thought there might be mariners on the water who needed the beacon's aid. Holding onto the iron handgrips in the lantern room to keep from being thrown off his feet, he kept the light burning. Claiborne had stocked up on supplies just before the storm in case the flooding was worse than anticipated, so he was able to feed the refugees. Providing fresh water, however, proved more of a challenge. Volunteers leaned out onto the catwalk surrounding the lantern room, holding buckets aloft to catch the rain, yet the spume of the waves crashing into the tower rose so high that the first few bucketfuls were salty, not fresh. After more attempts, however, drinkable water was obtained, and the buckets were passed to the thirsty people below.

The next day, when the floodwaters receded and the lighthouse's iron door was finally opened, the people streamed gratefully out into the bright sunshine only to be greeted by a gruesome sight. Strewn around the tower's base were a dozen corpses. In fact, death was everywhere. The Great Galveston Hurricane had leveled thousands of buildings and claimed at least six thousand lives, with some estimates rising as high as ten thousand. It remains the worst natural disaster in American history. Among the dead were the eighty-five passengers who remained on the train instead of heading to the lighthouse. Somewhere along its way back to Beaumont, the train and everyone on board had been engulfed by the hurricane.

Fifteen years later the Bolivar Point Lighthouse would again live up to its reputation as a savior. On the afternoon of August 16, 1915, as another hurricane bore down on the Texas coast, sixty people who lived in the vicinity of Bolivar Point rushed to the lighthouse to find refuge. Claiborne, who was still the head keeper, welcomed them in. That night, according to the assistant keeper, James P. Brooks, "The big tower shook and swayed in the wind like a giant reed." A little after nine, the tower's violent motion damaged the mechanism that rotated the lens, forcing Brooks to turn the lens by hand. By ten o'clock the tower was vibrating so wildly that even this was impossible, so Brooks secured the lens to keep it from falling off its pedestal and left the light burning. When he climbed down the stairs, he confronted another problem. Wind had blown open the iron door, allowing water to rush in and fill the bottom of the tower to a height of five feet. Brooks grabbed a rope and jumped in, and despite being thrown about and badly bruised, he managed to fasten the door shut.

The water receded slowly the following day, and the wind was still blowing hard, forcing people to stay in the tower another night. Because there was no more kerosene, the lighthouse was dark for the first time since it was built. Finally, on the morning of August 18, their ordeal over, the sixty famished refugees emerged from the lighthouse.

IN THE CASE OF the Kilauea Point Lighthouse twelve years later, it wasn't refugees from a hurricane who were saved, but rather a plane and its two-man crew. Just before 7:00 a.m. on June 27, 1927, U.S. Army lieutenants Lester J. Maitland and Albert F. Hegenberger climbed into their new Fokker C-2 Wright 220-horsepower trimotor transport plane, named the *Bird of Paradise*, hoping to become the first aviators to fly nonstop from California to Hawaii. Their attempt meshed perfectly with the tenor of the times. This was an era early in the evolution of manned flight when pilots and plane manufacturers were constantly pushing themselves to fly farther and faster, to prove to the public at large the great military and commercial potential of aviation. A little more than a month before the *Bird of Paradise*'s flight, Charles Lindbergh had made his own bit of history when he flew the single engine 220-horsepower *Spirit of St. Louis* 3,600 miles from Roosevelt Field on Long Island to Le Bourget Field in Paris, thus completing the first solo transatlantic flight and earning the moniker "Lucky Lindy"—although luck in fact had little to do with it, since his preparation and training for the flight had been meticulous.

The *Bird of Paradise* had a wingspan of seventy-two feet, and on that June morning it carried 1,120 gallons of gasoline and tipped the scales at fourteen thousand pounds, including all the equipment on board and the weight of its two occupants. The plane took off from Oakland airport at 7:09, with Maitland as pilot and Hegenberger as navigator. Their flight plan had them covering roughly 2,400 miles of ocean, and landing at Wheeler Field on the island of Oahu sometime in the early morning hours of the following day. Critical to their success would be Hegenberger's ability to keep them on course, because if they drifted more than 3.5 degrees off course in either direction, they would completely miss the islands.

Unfortunately the so-called Murphy's law came into play: Almost everything that could go wrong did. Within an hour and a half of taking off, all their fancy navigational equipment failed, including the radio beacon receiver and the induction compass, which uses the earth's magnetic fields to determine direction. The smoke bombs they had brought with them to measure drift couldn't be used because of the high winds and rough seas. Rather than despair, however, Hegenberger, who was considered one of the army's best navigators, improvised. To measure drift he used an ordinary compass and tracked the movement of the whitecaps on the waves, which he could see out of the trapdoor in the floor of the plane. He also relied on dead reckoning to determine the plane's location.

At 10:00 p.m. Maitland and Hegenberger decided to get above the heavy cloud cover to use celestial navigation, which led to another problem. As they approached eleven thousand feet, the center engine's cylinders and carburetor intake iced over, causing the center engine to cut out. It wasn't until the plane descended to three thousand feet that the engine revived, restoring the plane's full power. Still wanting to use the stars to navigate, Maitland took the plane slowly up to seven thousand feet, as high as he could go and avoid icing. This allowed Hegenberger to locate Polaris, the North Star, giving him added confidence that they were on course.

The Bird of Paradise *coming in for a landing at Wheeler Field in the early morning hours of June 28, 1927.*

A little after 3:00 a.m. on June 28, Maitland said he "saw a light which was more yellow than a star," far off in the distance, to the left of the plane. At first he thought it was a steamer, but then, with a profound sense of relief, he realized that it was the beam from the Kilauea Point Lighthouse, a fifty-two-foot-tall steel-reinforced concrete tower located near the edge of a lofty promontory on Kauai, the northernmost island in the Hawaiian chain. Kauai was only about seventy-five miles from their destination on Oahu, but because of the rain, and his concern about flying over the mountains of Oahu in the dark, Maitland circled Kauai until the sun rose and then finally headed to Wheeler Field. Nearly out of fuel, the *Bird of Paradise* landed at 6:29 a.m.

There is no way of knowing what would have happened if Maitland hadn't seen the lighthouse's beam. Beyond Kauai there is nothing but ocean for thousands of miles. Had they flown past Kauai in the darkness and kept going, the plane would have run out of fuel and plunged into the water. According to some accounts Maitland and Hegenberger realized that they were north of their course, and had they not seen the lighthouse about when they did, they were planning to circle around to the south, which might or might not have resulted in them sighting one of the islands, and ultimately finding Wheeler Field.

These what-ifs notwithstanding, there is no doubt that the lighthouse's beam was instrumental in the success of the flight. As the August 1, 1927, issue of the *Lighthouse Service Bulletin* noted, "These aviators picked up the light at a distance of about 90 miles, soon recognizing it as a lighthouse and subsequently identifying it by its flashes. If Lieutenants Maitland and Hegenberger had not picked up Kilauea Point Light, they might have passed the Hawaiian Islands, missing them entirely." In a private conversation Maitland assigned the lighthouse a more definitive starring role. At a reception held for the aviators shortly after they landed, he told a high-ranking Lighthouse Service official that "the Kilauea Lighthouse had saved his life."

CHAPTER 12

MARVELS OF ENGINEERING AND CONSTRUCTION

· · · · · · · · · · · · · ·

Scaffolding around the St. George Reef Lighthouse toward the end of construction, 1891.

EVERY LIGHTHOUSE POSES A UNIQUE CHALLENGE TO ITS ARCHITECTS and builders. The design must be sound, the site properly prepared, the materials of high quality, environmental obstacles overcome, and the engineers and workmen up to the task of executing the job skillfully. But not all lighthouses are equal. Some posed challenges so great that the resulting structures can truly be considered marvels of engineering and construction. Minot's Ledge, Tillamook Rock, and St. George Reef are three American lighthouses deserving that appellation.

In fact there were actually two Minot's Ledge Lighthouses, one completed in 1849 and the other—the true marvel—only eleven years later, in 1860, when Lincoln was first elected. But to understand how the second one came to be built, it is necessary tell the story of the first, as well. That tale begins, as so many lighthouse stories do, with disasters at sea.

About two miles off the coast of Cohasset, Massachusetts, and nine miles southeast of the mouth of Boston Harbor, lies a cluster of rock ledges that had terrorized mariners for hundreds of years. The most notorious of these so-called Cohasset Rocks is Minot's Ledge, named after the prominent Boston merchant George Minot, who lost a ship there in the mid-1700s. Minot's Ledge was particularly treacherous because most of the time it was completely submerged. Only at low tide could it be seen, and then only a small part of the ledge was visible just above the surface.

In 1838 the Boston Marine Society became gravely concerned about the many ships and lives claimed by Minot's. Accordingly, its leaders began lobbying the federal government to build a lighthouse on the ledge, but their pleas to Congress, then bent on retrenchment and more interested in westward expansion, fell on deaf ears. Then IWP Lewis, the reformer who led the charge against the continued use of Winslow Lewis's mediocre "magnifying and reflecting lantern" and for the adoption of Fresnel lenses, joined the discourse. In his scathing 1843 report on the lighthouses of Maine, New Hampshire, and Massachusetts, IWP echoed the society's call for action. After listing forty shipwrecks that had occurred in the vicinity of Minot's Ledge in just the previous nine years, Lewis argued that a lighthouse "is more required [there] than on any part of the seaboard of New England." As for the feasibility of building a lighthouse in such an exposed, wave-swept location, Lewis was confident it could be done. "Though formidable difficulties would embarrass the undertaking," he concluded, "they were not greater than such as were successfully triumphed over by a 'Smeaton' or a 'Stevenson.' "

The Smeaton to whom IWP referred was the British engineer John

Smeaton, a legend in the world of lighthouse construction for having built the third Eddystone Lighthouse, located off Plymouth, England, in the late 1750s. The first Eddystone Lighthouse—Henry Winstanley's creation—was destroyed by the "Great Storm" in 1703, and the second burned to the ground in 1755. This set the stage for the third effort, spearheaded by Smeaton, who decided to build his lighthouse out of stone. The resulting edifice was a tour-de-force of eighteenth-century engineering, unlike any structure that had come before. Smeaton had designed the stone blocks in each layer, or course, of the tower to be cut so that they dovetailed with one another, essentially fitting them together like a jigsaw puzzle. Then, to connect each course with the ones above and below, he inserted oak pins into holes drilled in the blocks. Finally, instead of employing a conical tower, he designed it to resemble an oak tree, which, he noted, is "broad at its base, curves inward at its waist, [and] becomes narrower towards the top." Smeaton's rationale, based on a solid understanding of nature, was simple: "The English oak tree withstands the most violent weather conditions," he said, and "we seldom hear of a mature oak being uprooted." All these features helped to create an astonishingly sturdy structure that could survive not only the fiercest pummeling from the sea, but also wind gusts from the most vicious storms. Upon its completion in 1759, Smeaton's triumph, hailed throughout the European and colonial worlds of the mid-eighteenth century, became the model for anyone building a lighthouse in a wave-swept location.

One such inspired individual was the Scottish engineer Robert Stevenson, patriarch of the famed lighthouse Stevensons. In the early 1800s Britain's Northern Lighthouse Board tasked him with building a lighthouse on Bell Rock, a sandstone reef located about eleven miles off Scotland's craggy east coast and completely submerged most of the time. Stevenson closely followed Smeaton's design, and the Bell Rock Lighthouse, first lit on February 1, 1811, in the waning years of the Napoleonic era, ranks as one of his masterpieces.

By referring to "a Smeaton or a Stevenson," IWP was thus throwing down the gauntlet to the American congressmen who were the target audience for his report, by playing to their patriotism. If these British fellows could build lighthouses on wave-swept locations, why, wondered Lewis, couldn't American engineers do the same at Minot's Ledge?

It wasn't until March 1847 that Congress, largely preoccupied with the war against Mexico, was convinced, and ordered the U.S. Army Corps of Topographical Engineers to build a lighthouse on the ledge. The corps immediately sent an engineer, forty-six-year-old Capt. William Henry Swift, to Cohasset to evaluate the site and propose a plan. Swift, who was born in Taunton, Massachusetts, and already had a fairly distinguished career as a surveyor, coastal engineer, and canal builder, first had to decide where to put the lighthouse. There is both an inner and an outer Minot's Ledge, separated by about three hundred feet, and Swift chose the outer because the rock at that location was much more solid and had fewer seams than the one at inner Minot's.

Swift now had to decide what type of lighthouse to build. He didn't have much space. At low tide the only visible part of the ledge was roughly twenty-five feet in diameter. While Swift believed it would be possible to build a stone tower on such a slender foundation, he estimated that it would cost between $250,000 and $500,000. Given the great expense, he didn't think a stone tower like Smeaton's or Stevenson's was a viable option. But that didn't concern him because he had a much cheaper alternative in mind, which he thought would work just as well.

His plan at its most basic called for placing the keeper's quarters and the lantern room far above the waves, supported by stiltlike iron piles embedded in the ledge. Not only would an iron-pile lighthouse be more economical, costing between twenty and fifty thousand dollars, but Swift also believed that it could withstand the elements as well as a lighthouse made of stone. Here he used the same argument that American engineers would use in later years to support the construction of iron skeleton lighthouses offshore; namely, that the lighthouse's open structure offered little resistance to wind and waves, which could pass right through and around the piles. Swift's bosses at the corps approved his plan and told him to proceed.

The main obstacle to the project was time. Construction could only take place from spring to early fall, since the months of Massachusetts's

Drawing of the first
Minot's Ledge
Lighthouse,
circa 1849.

winter were far too cold and stormy. Within that span, work could only proceed when the ledge was exposed around low tide—a mere two to three hours a day. And even that was contingent upon the vagaries of the Atlantic, with its ever-shifting mood. If the waves were too high or, worse, a storm was closing in, work quickly derailed. To maximize the amount of work time, the contractor moored a schooner near the site, weather permitting, and had his men sleep on board so that they could reach the ledge immediately when the conditions were right.

Work commenced in July 1847 and finished just over two years later in October 1849. The resulting lighthouse cost $39,500 and was seventy feet high. The keeper's quarters sat on a fourteen-foot-wide iron platform fifty-five feet above the ledge. Nine iron piles held the platform aloft, and each pile was cemented into five-foot-deep holes drilled into the rock. For added stability the piles were braced horizontally and diagonally with iron rods. The lantern room sat on top of the keeper's quarters, and beneath the quarters, enclosed within the piles, was a storeroom for oil, provisions, and other supplies.

Henry David Thoreau, while a passenger on a sailboat heading from Provincetown to Boston, first saw the lighthouse in the summer of 1849, a few months before its completion. "Here was the new iron lighthouse," he wrote, "then unfinished, in the shape of an egg-shell painted red, and placed high on iron pillars, like the ovum of a sea monster floating on the waves,—destined to be phosphorescent. As we passed it at half-tide we saw the spray tossed up nearly to the shell. A man was to live in that egg-shell day and night." Actually three men would live at the lighthouse—Isaac Dunham, who was appointed keeper in late 1849, and his two assistants. The men rotated, with two being on duty while the third was ashore.

Dunham lit the lighthouse's lamps for the first time on January 1, 1850, and soon thereafter his worries began. "A tremendous gale of wind," he wrote in his log on January 8, came over the water, and "it seems as though the lighthouse would go from the rock." From here on out Dunham's log is punctuated by entries that show a man increasingly in fear for his life. On March 31, after enduring numerous bouts of bad weather, Dunham thought it a miracle that he had survived the winter: "For this month ends, and I thank God that I am yet in the Land of the Living." But April storms brought renewed terror. Early on April 6 Dunham wrote that another gale produced "an ugly sea which makes the lighthouse reel like a drunken man—I hope God will in mercy still the raging sea—or we must perish." Later that same day he added, "We cannot survive the night—if it is to be so—O God receive my unworthy soul for Christ sake for in him I put my trust." Yet the gale ended, and Dunham lived another day.

Even the kitten Dunham brought as a companion was rattled by the storms, driven mad by the precarious conditions in the lighthouse, skittering about the watch room in a panic when the tower shook. The kitten's tenure didn't last long. On a day when the seas were calm and the sun was shining brilliantly in a cloudless sky, Dunham thought the frightened feline's frayed nerves would be soothed by a walk around the gallery platform outside the watch room, where it could get some fresh air. Dunham opened the door to the gallery and called to the kitten, which promptly raced up the ladder into the watch room, then circled the room twice, each time passing right by the open door. On its third circuit, the clearly addled kitten rushed out the door and kept going, across the platform and then over the edge into midair. When Dunham reached the gallery railing and looked down, he saw the kitten barely moving on the ledge far below. The next wave, however, swept it off the rock, thereby ending its short and frazzled life.

Having survived that most punishing winter, Dunham urged his superiors in the spring of 1850 to reinforce the lighthouse, claiming that if this were not done soon, the next major storm would surely be the end of it. Dunham's request was ignored, and Swift dismissed his concerns, reiterating his great faith in the ability of the lighthouse to handle the worst weather imaginable. Rebuffed, and unwilling to put his life on the line during what was sure to be another tempestuous New England winter, Dunham resigned his post on October 7, 1850, and his two assistants followed suit.

John W. Bennett replaced Dunham, and hired two new assistants, Joseph Wilson and Joseph Antoine. Prior to his departure Dunham shared his concerns about the lighthouse with a great number of people, and the safety of Minot's had become a lively topic of conversation in and around Boston and Cohasset. Bennett too had heard the scuttlebutt, but rather than take any heed of what Dunham said, he disparaged the former keeper as an alarmist.

All it took, however, was one good nor'easter in the late fall of 1850 for Bennett to aver that Dunham was right. As soon as the storm had passed, and lighthouse ceased its violent shaking, Bennett wrote to the customs collector in Boston, with a plea identical to Dunham's: Strengthen the lighthouse or else. Again no action was taken.

Three days before Christmas another gale walloped Minot's, sending Bennett into a tailspin. At the height of the two-day tempest he wrote an anguished letter to the editor of the *Boston Daily Journal* that he feared might be his last:

At intervals an appalling stillness prevails, creating an inconceivable dread, each [of us] gazing with breathless emotion at one another; but the next moment the deep roar of another roller is heard, seeming as if it would tear up the very rocks beneath as it burst upon us—the lighthouse, quivering and trembling to its very centre, recovers itself just in time to breast the fury of another and another as they roll in upon us with resistless force. . . . Our situation is perilous. If any thing happens ere day dawn upon us again, we have no hope of escape. But I shall, if it be God's will, die in the performance of my duty.

To make sure the letter got out, even if he didn't, he placed a copy of it in a bottle and threw it into the sea.

Like Dunham, Bennett survived, and when his letter appeared in the *Journal* a few days later, it precipitated a lengthy response from Swift, which appeared in the *Boston Daily Advertiser*. The captain defended the lighthouse both in terms of its economy as compared with a stone tower, and of its safety. In the end, he wrote, "Time, the great expounder of the truth or the fallacy of the question, will decide for or against the Minot; but inasmuch as the light has outlived nearly three winters, there is some reason to hope that it may survive one or two more." Swift was too optimistic or perhaps too prideful of his own creation, for the winter of 1850–51 would be the lighthouse's last.

From April 14–17, 1851, while Bennett was ashore, leaving Wilson and Antoine behind, a historic storm slammed the Massachusetts coast, generating some of the highest tides ever seen in the area, washing out train tracks, flooding buildings, sweeping away houses, and causing serious damage all along the shore. The worst time for Wilson and Antoine came on the evening of the sixteenth. Believing that the lighthouse would not make it through the storm, they put another note in a bottle, which was miraculously found by a Gloucester fisherman the next day. It read, "The lighthouse won't stand over to night. She shakes 2 feet each way now."

Exactly when the lighthouse lost its battle with the elements is not known. A few people on shore reported seeing the faint beams of light as late at 10:00 p.m., and the lighthouse's six-hundred-pound fog bell could still be heard faintly ringing three hours later. Soon thereafter, however, Minot's Lighthouse was completely rent from the ledge and thrown like

Destruction of Minot's Lighthouse, from Gleason's Pictorial, *1851.*

a matchbox toy into sea, leaving behind only the bent stubs of the pilings, sheared off a few feet above the rock. When Bennett arrived at the beach at 4:00 a.m., evidence of the disaster was strewn about. He found remains of the keeper's quarters and the lantern room, as well as some of his own clothes. The battered bodies of the two assistant keepers were recovered later.

There were recriminations all around. Swift predictably blamed the keepers for modifications they had made to the lighthouse, including adding a platform beneath the storeroom to hold supplies, which he said only created another surface for the waves to pound against. Bennett, for his part, argued that the lighthouse was poorly designed, too heavy for the small base upon which it stood, and that the iron used in its construction was of inferior quality.

Regardless of who deserved blame, the lighthouse was irrevocably gone, and mariners were once again without a guiding light on the ledge, but not for long. A few weeks after the storm, a group of Boston insurance companies sent a steamship fitted out with a light to be moored off the ledge. That ship was soon replaced with a lightship supplied by the Department of the Treasury. Still, this was seen as a temporary fix. As the number of wrecks in the vicinity of Minot's continued to mount, the government decided that another lighthouse would have to be built on the same spot, this time out of stone.

GEN. JOSEPH G. TOTTEN, chief of the Army Corps of Engineers and a member of the Lighthouse Board, designed the new lighthouse after studying the work of Smeaton and Stevenson. But rather than propose a tapering tower shaped like an oak, Totten went with a conical form, believing it would be equally sturdy. He then tapped Capt. Barton S. Alexander, a seasoned engineer, to oversee construction. On June 20, 1855, Alexander sent men to Minot's to clear the rock of seaweed and mussels, and to remove the vestiges of the iron piles from their holes. On July 1 he and his construction team landed on the ledge for the first time. Before beginning to work, Alexander rallied his troops. He told them that the task ahead would be long and arduous, and full of unforeseen obstacles and delays, but he was confident that they would carry it through until the lighthouse was completed, "whether it be two years or ten."

As with the iron-pile lighthouse, construction took place from spring to early fall. The most difficult challenge was preparing the ledge. The base of the lighthouse was to be thirty feet across, but at low water only twenty-five feet of the ledge was exposed. This meant that some of the rock that had to be leveled was perpetually underwater, and the rest exposed so briefly that the men had only a very limited amount of time to accomplish their work. As Alexander noted, "There had to be a combination of favorable circumstances to enable us to land on the Minot rock at the beginning of that work—*a perfectly smooth sea, a dead calm, and low spring tides*. . . . Frequently, one or the other of the necessary conditions would fail, and there were at times months . . . when we could not land there at all."

Since the men could work on the ledge at most only a few days a month, Alexander had them do double duty to keep them busy. When they weren't on the ledge, they were on shore at Government Island, a staging area in Cohasset, painstakingly cutting, chiseling, drilling, and hammering the stone building blocks for the lighthouse, each of which weighed about two tons and were made from the finest-grained granite that had been quarried in nearby Quincy, Massachusetts, and then transported to Government Island by ship.*

Alexander employed two rowboats to get himself and his men to Minot's. According to one of the men, they remained vigilant to ensure that they lost no time on the rock. "We would watch the tide from the cove," he said, "and just as soon as the ebb had reached the proper stage we would start out with it, and at the moment a square yard of ledge was bare of water, out would jump a stone cutter and begin work. Soon another would follow, and as fast as they had elbow room others still, until the rock would resemble a carcass covered with a flock of crows."

In 1856 wrought-iron piles twenty feet long were inserted into holes formerly used by the iron-pile lighthouse. These would later be incorporated into the stone tower, serving to bolt it to the rock. The piles were bound together at the top by an iron frame, creating a scaffold from which ropes were strung to give the men something to grab onto when waves threatened to wash them off their feet. Even with the ropes, however, men were sometimes caught off guard and swept into the water. That is why Alexander hired the aptly named Michael Neptune Braddock to serve as a lifeguard, watching the men from a boat while they worked, and diving in to rescue them when necessary.

The difficult project was making good progress until it encountered a major setback on January 19, 1857. During a nor'easter the bark *New Empire* crashed into the outer ledges of Cohasset before running aground not far away. Once the storm died down, Alexander looked toward Minot's and was shocked by what he *didn't* see. His carefully crafted and, he thought, exceptionally strong iron scaffold, piles and all, was gone. He assumed it had been swept away by the storm, and for the first time he questioned the wisdom of the project. "If tough wrought iron won't stand it," he said, "I have my fears about a stone tower." But his despair evaporated when it was determined that the *New Empire*, not the weather, had dislodged the scaffold when it struck the ledge.

* Government Island is now connected to the mainland.

With renewed confidence Alexander sent his men to Minot's in the spring of 1857. They reinserted iron piles into the ledge and recut some of the rock that was damaged during the collision. By the end of that season the men had laid the first four foundation stones, each of which was affixed to the rock with long iron bolts and the finest quality Portland cement. The following year the men finished the foundation and brought the tower up to its sixth course.

The tower's granite blocks were cut to exacting specifications. Each one was dovetailed to fit snugly into the blocks on either side of it, and holes were drilled into the top and bottom of the blocks, into which were inserted galvanized iron bolts that firmly held the different courses together. To ensure that everything fit together perfectly, Alexander had his men assemble the courses at Government Island before ferrying the blocks to the ledge, where they were lowered into place by a derrick attached to an iron mast running up through the center of the structure. To further bind the blocks to one another, and the iron bolts to their holes, cement was used throughout.

Much of the early work on the ledge was done beneath the level of the lowest low tide, but Alexander devised a creative way to do some of this under relatively dry conditions. He had his men use hundreds of sandbags to build temporary cofferdams surrounding the work area. Once the sandbags were in place, the water within was bailed out and large sponges were employed to mop up any seepage. In this manner a small area would be exposed for a short period, during which time the men could level the uneven rocky ledge and put the stones in place.

This method, however, could not be used all the time, and some of the leveling work was done with specially designed hammers and chisels when the ledge was covered with as much as three feet of water. By the same token, some of the lowest stones in the tower had to be laid in the water. This posed a problem, since the water swirling around the stones would wash away the cement before it could properly set. To overcome this difficulty another creative technique was developed. A large piece of thin muslin was laid out on a platform on the ledge. The muslin was slathered with cement, and then the stone was placed on top. Cement was then spread on the sides of the stone, and the remaining cloth was folded up to cover the cement. After about ten minutes the cement began to set, and then the stone was lowered into position. The muslin envelope not only shielded the cement from being washed away by the water, but it was also thin and porous enough so that the cement could ooze through the cloth, allowing the stone to bond to those below and next to it.

On October 2, 1858, a grand ceremony held in Cohasset commemorated the laying of the lighthouse's cornerstone. The illustrious crowd—diverted from the pre–Civil War tensions that already consumed Boston—included the city's mayor, many city officials, presidents of insurance companies, and shipowners. To assure the audience that history would not be repeating itself, Alexander told them that there was no comparing the lighthouse then being built on the ledge with the earlier one. "A light-house of iron was erected here some years ago," he said,

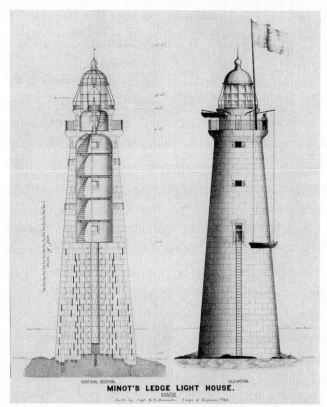

Schematic of second Minot's Ledge Lighthouse.

"whose fearful fate all may remember. Now again we are erecting a lighthouse here, but this time of granite, granite piled on granite, granite to build upon, the earth's substructure; granite engrafted and dovetailed in the foundation, and granite the whole."

The final speaker of the day was the famed orator Edward Everett, a former secretary of state and Massachusetts governor, representative and senator, who took this opportunity to use the lighthouse as a metaphor for the Union he so desperately wanted to keep together, but which was already exhibiting the severe political strains that would ultimately tear it asunder during the Civil War. "Let us remember," he said, "that in the event of [the rupture of the Union] . . . the protecting power which now spreads its aegis over us, East and West, North and South, will be forever gone;—and as you have told us, sir, that the solid foundations of the structure you are rearing are linked and bolted together with dove-tailed blocks of granite and bars of galvanized iron, so as never to be moved, so may the sister States of this Union be forever bound together, by the stronger ties of common language, kindred blood, and mutual affection."

By the end of the 1859 season the men laid stone up to the thirty-second course, sixty-two feet above low water. On June 29, 1860, almost exactly five years to the day from when construction had commenced, the last of the 1,079 granite blocks was added to the tower. The following months were spent putting up and fitting out the lantern room, and on November 15, less than two weeks after Lincoln was elected president, the lighthouse was illuminated for the first time.

The impressive structure soared 114 feet from the ledge to the top of the lantern. The bottom forty feet were comprised of solid granite, with the exception of a three-foot-wide cistern for potable water. Higher up in the tower were the storeroom, keepers' quarters, workroom, watch room, and finally the lantern room, which originally housed a second-order Fresnel lens exhibiting a fixed white light. Costing three hundred thousand dollars, Minot's was the most expensive lighthouse built in the United States up to that point.

Totten and Alexander had lived up to the standards set by Smeaton

Clement Drew's painting, titled Ship Passing Minot's Light, *circa 1860–80.*

and Stevenson. As the highly respected nineteenth-century Army engineer John Gross Barnard observed, Minot's Ledge Lighthouse "ranks, by the engineering difficulties surmounted in its erection, and by the skill and science shown in the details of its construction, among the chief of the great *sea-rock* lighthouses of the world." Completed in the waning months of peace before the outbreak of the Civil War, Minot's Ledge Lighthouse became both a symbol and a dramatic sight on its own. Henry Wadsworth Longfellow, observing it for the first time, said that it "rises out of the sea like a beautiful stone cannon, mouth upward, belching forth only friendly fires."

Long after the Civil War had run its bloody course, in 1894, the Lighthouse Board introduced a new system for identifying lighthouses, in which each lighthouse was given a distinctive numerical flash pattern. Minot's was one of the first to be changed. That year a new second-order rotating Fresnel lens with multiple panels was installed in the lantern room, and instead of exhibiting a fixed white light, Minot's now showed a 1–4–3 flash; that is, a single flash of light, followed by an interval of darkness, then four quick flashes, followed by another interval, then finally three more flashes.

Wave breaking on Minot's Ledge.

Not long after this new pattern went into effect, a romantically inclined observer saw in it something more than mere flashes: The 1-4-3 pattern corresponded numerically to the one of the most cherished phrases in the English language—"I Love You." And from that point forward, Minot's Lighthouse was known as the "I Love You Light." Never mind that the staid government officials who made the switch certainly didn't have amore on their minds.

A CONTINENT AWAY FROM Minot's Ledge, in the Pacific Northwest, lies the Columbia River valley. The area had a booming economy in the 1870s, with commodities such as salmon, grain, timber, and gold fueling the region's rapid growth. The main highway for commerce into and out of the valley was, of course, the Columbia River, which, at more than 1,200 miles long, was the longest river in the Pacific Northwest, and the fourth largest river in North America based on flow. Numerous ships had wrecked trying to negotiate the treacherous currents, towering waves, and hidden sandbars guarding the river's mouth, a record of destruction that had contributed mightily to the sobriquet later given to this dangerous stretch of coast—the Graveyard of the Pacific. While the lighthouse established at Cape Disappointment in 1856, and another one built on nearby Point Adams in 1875, helped ships navigate the river's mouth, commercial and shipping interests up and down the west coast were urging the government by the late 1870s to erect another lighthouse in the area to provide mariners an added measure of safety as they approached the river. Congress responded on June 20, 1878, ordering the board to build a beacon on Tillamook Head, a prominent headland twenty miles south of the Columbia.

However, the man tapped to investigate the proposed site, the army engineer G. L. Gillespie, believed that Congress had made a mistake. He argued that Tillamook Head, which rose well over one thousand feet above sea level, was a wrong if not outright dangerous place for a lighthouse. Not only was the headland too high, thereby ensuring that a lighthouse placed at or near the summit would often be shrouded in fog, but also just to get to the top of Tillamook Head would require building a road twenty miles through heavily wooded terrain, a daunting and very expensive prospect. As for building a lighthouse lower down on the face of Tillamook Head, Gillespie thought that was an equally impractical idea since the area was prone to frequent landslides.

Rather than give up, Gillespie recommended an alternate site—Tillamook Rock. Located a little more than a mile off of Tillamook Head, the rock was a foreboding mass of basalt only an acre in size that jutted 120 feet out of the sea and was split into two unequal parts by a deep chasm. The surrounding waters ranged from 100 to 240 feet deep, and when the full fury of the Pacific was unleashed, tremendous waves battered the rock and often completely enveloped it in the incredible force of its violent embrace.

Gillespie's proposal to place a lighthouse on the rock was met with ridicule and disbelief. As far as anyone knew, no one had ever set foot on the rock, not even the local Tillamook Indians, who thought it was cursed by the gods. And the logistics of landing work crews and building a lighthouse on such an exposed and wave-swept site, which was more than twenty miles from the nearest port at Astoria, Oregon,* seemed insurmountable, notwithstanding the board's earlier success at Minot's. Despite the logistical difficulties inherent in the project, the board trusted its engineer's judgment and ordered him to devise a plan for conquering the fearsome rock. Gillespie, in turn, tasked the district superintendent of lighthouse construction, H. S. Wheeler, with the job.

On June 17, 1879, Gillespie sent Wheeler to Astoria, ordering him not to come back until he had landed on Tillamook Rock and taken measurements. Less than a week later the revenue cutter *Thomas Corwin* steamed to the rock with Wheeler and a few of his men on board. Although the seas were moderate, the waves breaking on the edge of Tillamook looked menacing as they clawed their way up the rock and fell back on themselves in a mass of seething white foam. The *Corwin*'s surfboat was gingerly maneuvered close to the rock at a spot where the seas were a bit calmer. Still, getting onto the rock was tricky. Since each passing swell caused the boat to rise and fall quickly, the men had to time their jumps perfectly or risk falling into the water. After a number of false starts, two of Wheeler's men, crouching like tigers ready to pounce, leaped from the boat and landed successfully. Now all they needed were their surveying instruments, but before that transfer could be achieved, the seas became rougher, and the boat had to back off to avoid being smashed into the rocks. Panicked by the prospect of being marooned, the two men launched themselves into the water and were rescued by lifelines thrown from the boat.

Wheeler returned to the rock four days later, and this time he made the leap but wasn't able to land his instruments. Instead he used a hand tape to make rough measurements, which were enough for him to submit a general plan to the board. Determining where to situate the lighthouse

---

* Astoria was named after the fur merchant John Jacob Astor, and America's first multimillionaire, who unsuccessfully attempted to create a fur-trading empire on the banks of the Columbia River.

Profile of Tillamook Rock before the lighthouse was built.

was paramount, posing more than just a bit of a problem, since the crest of Tillamook Rock consisted of "a large rounded knob resembling the burl of a tree," and was neither large nor flat enough to serve as an adequate base for the lighthouse. So Wheeler proposed having a work crew blast away the top thirty feet of the rock to create a flat platform about ninety feet above the water, upon which the lighthouse could sit. Once the platform was ready, construction of the lighthouse could begin, with all the building materials prepared on shore and ferried to the rock. The board approved the plan on September 11, 1879, and Congress consented to the changed location.

To handle this monumentally tricky job, Wheeler appointed John R. Trewavas as superintendent of construction. Born in England, Trewavas had in the 1860s helped build the Wolf Rock Lighthouse, a hulking granite tower more than 115 feet high, located nine miles off Land's End in Cornwall, England, on a wave-swept rock that measured roughly 130 by 100 feet. When Wheeler tapped Trewavas he was living in Portland, Oregon, and was considered one of the finest stonemasons on the West Coast. His first task was to thoroughly survey the rock, which he attempted to do on September 18. When the *Corwin*'s surfboat backed up to the rock, Trewavas steadied himself and then jumped. He made it to the rock but then slipped and fell, and was washed into the sea by a wave. A sailor dived in with a lifeline, but before he could effect a rescue, the gifted Englishman disappeared beneath the surface.

News of Trewavas's death generated a strong backlash on the mainland. When the project was first announced, most area residents found the idea of building a lighthouse on Tillamook Rock foolhardy. Now that a death had occurred, many of them thought the undertaking so danger-ous that it should be abandoned. If talk like this went on too long, the board feared it wouldn't be able to hire local laborers because their minds would be poisoned against the project. To avoid this the board immedi-ately appointed Alexander Ballantyne to replace Trewavas, and ordered him to hire a crew of quarrymen and head to Astoria right away, where a boat would be waiting to take him and his men directly to the rock.

Appointing Ballantyne, a heavily muscled bulldog of a man in his fifties, who was just below average height and sported a neat Vandyke beard, made good sense. Like Trewavas he hailed from Britain, but in his case from Scotland, and he had befriended Trewavas when they worked together at Wolf Rock. Soon after Trewavas headed to America, Ballan-tyne followed, and by the late 1870s the two of them had a thriving stone-mason business operating out of Portland. Not only was Ballantyne an exceptionally talented mason, he was also a natural leader who inspired confidence and led by example.

Ballantyne soon had eight men under contract, but when he arrived in Astoria on September 23, the board's plan for a quick getaway hit a snag. The fall gales had predictably descended on the coast, making the ocean conditions too rough for the *Corwin* to leave. Ballantyne had no way of knowing how long these conditions would last, and that worried him. If his men were stuck in Astoria for an extended period, he would not be able to keep them from frequenting local establishments where they would be exposed to the "idle talk of the town," which might scare them off with lurid tales of Trewavas's death and of the many dangers awaiting anyone who ventured to Tillamook Rock. Ballantyne couldn't risk losing any of his men this way, so he moved them to the old keeper's quarters at Cape Disappointment, which was across from Astoria on the Washington side of the river.

This isolation lasted until October 21, when the weather suddenly improved and the *Corwin* headed out. Ballantyne knew he had to devise a better method of getting men and materials onto the rock than jump-ing from a heaving surfboat, which had already claimed one life. His clever alternative was to create an aerial tramway of sorts. He ran a heavy rope from the mast of a moored ship to a point high on the rock, then rigged the rope with a traveler—a large block with a hook beneath it—that could be moved back and forth along the rope's entire length by a continuous line attached to the shank of the traveler's hook and looped around a pair of pulleys. Drawing the line in one direction brought the traveler to the ship, while drawing it in the other took it to Tillamook. Thus anything hung from the traveler's hook could be transported on and off the rock.

To transport his men, Ballantyne employed a breeches buoy, which was simply a circular rubber life preserver attached to a pair of breeches (pants) cut off at the knees. The men slipped into the buoy, which was then suspended from the traveler's hook, and off they went on what was invariably a wild and turbulent ride. Each passing wave rocked the boat, causing the rope to rise and fall quickly, alternately flinging the buoy's passenger high into the air and then plunging him seaward. On any but extremely calm days, which were painfully rare, the rope's gyrations were so great that the men were repeatedly dunked in the chilly water, and sometimes completely submerged for a few moments, arriving at their destination soaking wet, where the only thing that could help warm them up was the meager heat thrown off by the diminutive cookstove.

Most of the men braved the transit to the rock with good humor, or at least without much complaint, but there was one notable exception, a corpulent quarryman named Gruber who weighed three hundred pounds.

Drawing of the breeches buoy and traveler used to transport workers onto and off Tillamook Rock.

He simply didn't fit into the breeches buoy. Ballantyne proposed lashing the large man to the top of the buoy, a plan to which Gruber strenuously objected. The forceful Ballantyne would not give up, and he sent Gruber back to Astoria on the steamer and ordered him to be fitted out with a larger breeches buoy and return to the rock when it was ready.

When Gruber returned with the king-size buoy, however, he was overcome by paroxysms of fear and refused to get in. Hoping to allay Gruber's concerns, Ballantyne climbed into the roomy buoy and told his men to haul away. Certainly, Ballantyne thought, once Gruber saw how safe and easy this was, he would acquiesce. But things didn't work out as Ballantyne had hoped, and the "curse of the rock" asserted itself once again. The rope was so slack that Ballantyne was dragged through the water much of the way, only scaring Gruber more. Finally, after some not-so-gentle persuasion on Ballantyne's part, Gruber reluctantly agreed to go across using a bosun's chair—basically, a wooden plank supported by multiple ropes—while wearing a life preserver, since this mode of transportation gave him a little more freedom of movement than the buoy. To his great relief Gruber made it without even touching the water, becoming the first man to reach the rock completely dry.

The sea was not the only fear-inducing element, for the men were greeted by the bellowing of thousands of sea lions, which covered the rock like a writhing brown carpet and were not at all pleased by this invasion of their domain. Aggressive if approached, the sea lions at first stood their ground, forcing the men to be on their guard at all times while walking around the rock. Not long after the blasting began, however, the sea lions departed en masse for another haunt further to the south, as yet untrammeled by man.

The most immediate task the men faced upon landing was providing shelter for themselves and their supplies. Crude A-frame tents were fashioned from cut-up canvas and lashed with ropes to ringbolts inserted into the rock. It was "rather disagreeable" in the tent, according to Ballantyne, with the canvas flapping violently in the wind, and the rain and the sea spray drenching the men and their belongings. The tents, however, could be only temporary. With winter coming on, they needed something sturdier, and after leveling off an area about ninety feet above the water, they built a small wooden frame house to serve as their quarters.

While they were settling in, the blasting commenced. At first the men rappelled down the sides of the rock, suspended from ropes attached to ringbolts hammered into the summit. Some of the men sat in bosun's chairs, while others tied the ropes loosely around their bodies. Dangling precariously nearly one hundred feet above the water, often buffeted by biting winds that caused them to sway ominously from side to side, the men drilled relatively shallow holes in the rock, plugged them with cartridges containing one pound of black powder, and then got out of the way before lighting the fuse. The explosions sent shards of rock into the air and plummeting into the water below. (No wonder, then, that the sea lions had wisely chosen to escape to a more serene location).

The goal of this work, soon achieved, was to create narrow benches upon which the men could stand so that they could increase the blasting intensity. The outer layer of the rock, which had been weathered and lashed by storms and waves for eons, was flaky and brittle, and as a result had been relatively easy to remove. But farther in the rock was denser and more difficult to dislodge. Now the men drilled larger and deeper holes that they filled with as much as one hundred pounds of black powder, generating increasingly powerful explosions that blew away up to 250 cubic yards of rock at a time.

As the men slowly blasted their way from the outer edges of the rock toward the center, weather remained their most persistent foe. Days of calm and good working conditions alternated with gale-force winds and pelting rains that made blasting difficult and at times impossible, not only threatening to blow the men off the rock but also soaking the powder so as to render it useless. Nothing, however, prepared them for the tempest that visited them in the New Year, as if to demarcate the 1880s with a most violent inauguration.

The storm began on January 2, 1880, and for the next four days the rain didn't stop, the waves continued to mount, and the wind was so strong that the men could barely hold on to their tools. Nevertheless, they worked through the pain in their benumbed hands, and the increasing fatigue spreading through their bodies. On January 6, when the storm turned even more savage, Ballantyne halted work and told his men to batten down everything they could before retreating to their quarters.

That evening the storm morphed into a rare West Coast hurricane. By midnight heavy salt spray and fist-size chunks of rock were flying over the top of Tillamook. Ballantyne ordered his men to brace the roof and walls of their wooden house with drills and steel bars. Two hours later a tremendous sea rose out of the darkness, its swirling wind-driven whorls of spume mashing into the makeshift quarters, which barely withstood the assault. The blacksmith shop next to it, however, did not, and its roof was torn apart.

The men panicked, but Ballantyne, the resilient Scotsman, remained calm, and with his steely resolve he stopped them from fleeing the quarters to get to higher ground, a move that likely would have been their last, given the howling winds and the repeated blows from the sea. At four in the morning Ballantyne tentatively ventured outside, hoping to discover what had happened to the storehouse, located farther down the rock's slope, a mere thirty-five feet above the water. Nearly blind in the inky darkness, he groped around for about half an hour, battered by the wind and waves, before returning to the quarters. With the coming of dawn he got his answer: The storehouse was destroyed, and everything in it was gone. Fortunately Ballantyne had stockpiled plenty of water and about three months' worth of bread, bacon, beans, and tea in the quarters themselves, so he and his men were in no danger of starving.

For two more days the storm would not relent, the men remaining disagreeably cooped up, and when they finally emerged, continuing bad weather made it nearly impossible to work. In the meantime people on shore had become concerned about the men's fate. Some of the materials washed from the rock during the storm had been found on nearby beaches, leading many to assume the worst. It wasn't until January 18, almost two weeks later, that coastal waters were calm enough for relief ships to get to the rock with fresh provisions, and bring word back to the mainland that the men were in satisfactory shape.

From this point forward operations progressed smoothly, with only

Drawing of construction at Tillamook Rock Lighthouse, 1881.

minor weather-related interruptions. Quarrymen were added to the work crew, and every week more of Tillamook Rock was blasted away. The most welcome change as far as the men were concerned was the erection of a steam-powered derrick fitted with a large boom, which eliminated the need to use the breeches buoy. Instead a cable lowered from the boom to the steamer's deck and attached to a steel cage transported workers on and off the rock without getting them wet. The boom also made it much easier to land supplies.

By the end of May the platform for the lighthouse was complete. Roughly 4,700 cubic yards of rock had been removed, reducing the height of Tillamook from 120 to 91 feet. Ballantyne inspected the work, and, in his characteristically crisp fashion, pronounced it a job well done. Soon thereafter a much larger steam-powered derrick with an extremely long boom was secured to the rock and put to work lifting the heavy materials needed to build the lighthouse. The most important of these was the fine-grained basalt blocks quarried at Mount Tabor, a long-dormant volcanic cinder cone outside of Portland, which would form the structure's shell.

The lighthouse's cornerstone was laid on June 22, and by the end of the year the building was nearly finished. On January 3, 1881, however, a disaster occurred that was a reminder of why a lighthouse on Tillamook was so desperately needed. The wind had been blowing hard all day, and visibility was extremely limited due to thick fog and driving rain. At eight that night, workers on Tillamook heard shouting in the distance, and soon after they emerged from their quarters they saw faint lights through the murk, followed immediately by the unmistakable command "Hard aport," the order for turning a vessel sharply to the left. Wheeler, who was on Tillamook at the time, ordered the men to put out lanterns to warn the oncoming vessel away from the rock. The men could hear the ship's masts and rigging creaking, and about two hundred yards off they saw the faint outlines of the ship before it disappeared into the night.

All they could do was hope that the ship had survived, but when the fog lifted in the morning, the tragic reality said otherwise. Near the base of the soaring cliffs of Tillamook Head, they could make out the ship's masts peeking above the waves. As they would later learn, it was the British-flagged bark *Lupatia*, which had been heading from Japan to the Columbia River to pick up a cargo of wheat. Sixteen men were on board, but the sole survivor was the ship's dog, an Australian shepherd, which was found whimpering on the rocks soon after the crash.

The accident weighed heavily on the minds of the Tillamook work-

Tillamook Rock Lighthouse, 1891.

ers, who could not help but wonder if things might have turned out differently had the lighthouse been operational. One of them later remarked, "From that hour on, finishing the tower to get the light lit and the fog horn going was more than just a job." Less than three weeks later, on January 21, the lighthouse cast its beam over the water for the first time.

The lighthouse consisted of the keeper's quarters and the fog-signal building, both one story high, connected to each other, and encased in two-foot-thick granite walls. The square tower, sixteen feet a side, was two stories high and rose out of the center of the dwelling. The lantern room sitting atop the tower housed a first-order Fresnel lens that displayed a white flash every five seconds. It had taken 575 days to build Tillamook Rock Lighthouse, at a cost of $123,493, and one brilliant life.

THE MISERABLE WEATHER AND dangerous conditions that plagued the Tillamook Lighthouse led mariners and its keepers to refer to it as Terrible Tilly. The storm that struck the lighthouse in October 1934 is just one of many, though arguably the worst, that helped forge this most fitting nickname. In the early morning hours of October 21, it slammed into the coast with wind gusts as high as 109 miles per hour. The unrelenting noise outside, however, would not deter assistant keeper Henry Jenkins from getting some well-deserved sleep after a long night tending to the light. But soon after dozing off around nine thirty in the morning, he awoke gasping for air. A wave breaking on the top of Tillamook had smashed open the storm shutters, flooding his room with the icy waters of the Pacific, washing him out of bed, and unceremoniously depositing him in a heap in the closet.

The lighthouse was under attack. Immense waves repeatedly engulfed the entire station, topping the lantern room that stood 133 feet above normal high tide. The sledgehammer-like walls of water ripped away a twenty-five-ton chunk of the rock, obliterated the station's sizable derrick and severed the undersea telephone cable connecting Tillamook with the mainland.

The four keepers fought their way through swirling waters to the lantern room, where they were greeted with a scene of devastation. Flying debris and rocks—one weighing sixty pounds—had shattered sixteen of the lantern's glass panels, and cracked or chipped many of the first-order Fresnel lens's prisms. The oil vapor lamp was severely damaged and the lens's revolving mechanism disabled. Glass shards, seaweed, and even small fish lay scattered about the room.

Working in water often up to their necks, the keepers struggled most of the day to clamp the lantern room's storm shutters into place to protect against further aerial assaults. That night the lighthouse was dark, but by the next evening the men had rigged a small emergency lantern that sent forth a fixed white light. And Jenkins had cobbled together a shortwave radio set that enabled him to contact amateur radio operators on shore, who got word to the local superintendent of lighthouses about what was transpiring on the rock.

The storm raged until the twenty-fifth, and it was two more days before the seas calmed down enough for the tender *Manzanita* to arrive, providing relief and initiating repairs. Throughout their ordeal the keepers had no heat, little sleep, and they had to use a blowtorch to warm up their canned food. But every night with the exception of the first, they kept the emergency light burning. When the head of the Mexican lighthouse service read an article about this dramatic event in the *Lighthouse Service Bulletin*, he had it translated into Spanish and sent to all the keepers in his country "as an example of courageous performance of duty."

SOON AFTER FINISHING THE Tillamook Rock Lighthouse, Ballantyne headed more than three hundred miles south to take on an even bigger challenge—the building of the St. George Reef Lighthouse. The reef is a chain of visible as well as submerged rocks located about six miles off Point St. George on the coast of Northern California, not far from the Oregon border. When the British naval officer and explorer George Vancouver encountered these rocks during his expedition to the Pacific Northwest in 1792, he said they were "very dangerous," and christened them "Dragon Rocks." And in fact the reef had long been a threat to shipping, but it wasn't until an accident in 1865 that the idea of building a lighthouse in the area was first broached publicly.

During a gale on July 30, 1865, only months after the end of the Civil War, the *Brother Jonathan*, a 220-foot-long steam-powered sidewheeler, carrying 244 people and a shipment of gold, foundered on one of the rocks of St. George Reef. The ship sank within forty-five minutes, and all but nineteen of the people on board perished, making it the West Coast's worst peacetime maritime disaster to date. The accident was widely covered by news outlets nationwide, and the desire to avoid future disasters spurred calls to build a lighthouse on the reef to warn of the danger.

The Lighthouse Board thought this an excellent idea, and within two years of the accident asked Congress to fund the project. Congress balked, in part because it was directing so much money to rebuilding what the Civil War had destroyed, including numerous eastern and southern lighthouses. Congress was also wary of placing a lighthouse on one of the reef's wave-swept rocks. Despite the success at Minot's Ledge, Congress was not convinced of the economic or engineering feasibility of building a lighthouse on a spot so fully exposed to the wrath of the often tempestuous Pacific.

Throughout the 1870s the board continued lobbying Congress to fund the lighthouse, to no avail. During this time the board considered two possible locations for the lighthouse—either on one of the reef's rocks or on Point St. George, finally deciding against the latter, arguing that it would be too far away from the reef to serve as an effective warning. Instead the board concluded that the lighthouse should be built on Northwest Seal Rock, the part of St. George Reef farthest from the coast and closest to shipping lanes, and near where the *Brother Jonathan* had hurled its human cargo into a vengeful sea. The rock was roughly an acre in size, barely three hundred feet in diameter, and rose only fifty-four feet above the water.

The board approached Congress yet again in 1881, a propitious time because it was right after Ballantyne had conquered Tillamook, a project many had deemed impossible. If Tillamook could be tamed, Congress concluded, then so too could North West Seal Rock. As a result, in 1882, seventeen years after the *Brother Jonathan* disaster, Congress gave the board the go-ahead and the initial funding to begin building what would come to be known as the St. George Reef Lighthouse. The board, in turn, appointed Ballantyne to oversee construction.

THE ST. GEORGE REEF LIGHTHOUSE would be quite different from the one at Tillamook. Instead of blasting off the top of the rock to make a platform for the lighthouse, the plan was to incorporate part of North West Seal Rock into the lighthouse's foundation, thereby more securely anchoring the structure so that it could withstand the relentless hammering of ocean waves. A central column of rock would be blasted and chiseled down into a series of benches or terraces. Around and on this column an oval pier, or caisson, ninety feet in diameter and made of granite blocks would be built up to a height of nearly fifty feet. Much of the space between the outer caisson and the inner column of rock would be filled with rubble and concrete, but enough space would be left toward the top of the caisson to build a number of rooms, including the engine room, coal room, and storerooms. The top of the caisson would be covered with stone flagging, and the seven-story lighthouse would rise from there.

One of the first things the indefatigable Ballantyne had to decide was where to house his workers. The nearest port, Crescent City, was thirteen miles from North West Seal Rock. Lodging the men there would result in too much valuable time being lost in transport to and from the rock. Having the men stay on the rock was also not a viable option during the early stages of the project, when so much blasting would be going on in such a confined space. His answer was to moor a ship near the rock where his men would stay during the May-to-September work season.

A former sealing schooner, *La Ninfa*, was hired to serve as the workmen's quarters. On April 3, 1883, the steamer *Whitelaw* took *La Ninfa* in tow and headed out from San Francisco to North West Seal Rock. The work party on *La Ninfa* numbered twenty-five, including the crew, quarrymen, stonecutters, and a blacksmith. Also on board were explosives, provisions, and tools. Stormy weather forced the *Whitelaw* to turn back twice before finally making it to the rock on April 9.

The immediate task was to moor *La Ninfa* about 350 feet away from the rock by securing it to four spar buoys that were in turn chained to mushroom sinkers—so named for their shape—that anchored the buoys in place. One sinker weighed six tons, while the other three were four tons. The *Whitelaw* was only able to lower the six-ton sinker and attach *La Ninfa* to its buoy before the seas got too rough, forcing the *Whitelaw* to steam off to wait out the storm. It wasn't until a week later that the *Whitelaw* was able to return, but when the men tried to position the remaining moorings, they discovered that the water was far deeper than expected. As a result the spar buoys were not big or buoyant enough to stay much above the water, given the great weight of the extra chain hanging beneath them.

Ballantyne transferred all the men on *La Ninfa* to the *Whitelaw*, and then headed to Humboldt Bay, about seventy-five miles away, to procure larger buoys. The empty *La Ninfa* remained behind. Difficulties in obtaining the buoys and a stretch of nasty weather delayed the *Whitelaw's* return to the rock until April 28. There was one major problem, though—*La Ninfa* was nowhere in sight, and neither was the buoy to which it had been attached.

A little more than a week later the missing schooner was found floating offshore not far from Crescent City. Ballantyne concluded that the same storm that had delayed his return to the rock with the new buoys had caused the eight-inch hawser that had been holding *La Ninfa* to its mooring to part, setting the ship adrift. The *Whitelaw* towed *La Ninfa* back to the rock, where the men secured it to four moorings; for additional stability it was also connected to the rock by two cables.

The men first set foot on the rock in early May, and over the next couple of days they landed drilling and stonecutting tools, blasting powder, and other supplies and provisions. These first landings were accomplished by rowing surfboats close in, whereupon the men jumped to the rock—a system that worked well as long the seas were relatively calm. But Ballantyne needed to be able to get his men on and off the rock even when conditions were rougher, and just as important, he needed a way to evacuate his men from the rock quickly when a storm blew in and waves threatened to wash over it, as they often did.

Ballantyne's transport solution built upon what he had learned at Tillamook Rock. He ran a wire cable from *La Ninfa*'s masts to the top of North West Seal Rock, and then attached a traveler to the cable that was quite different from the one used at Tillamook. Instead of a block with a hook underneath, the traveler to North West Seal Rock was "made of two pieces of boiler plate, bolted together and forming the bearings for the axles of 4 grooved gun-metal wheels which just held the cable between the upper and lower pairs." A four-foot-diameter horizontal iron ring with wooden planking affixed to it was suspended from this traveler, creating a cage in which four to six men could stand. The cage was moved to and from the rock by an endless line of cable attached to the traveler.

A donkey engine, or steam-powered winch, was soon employed, which propelled the men from the ship to the top of the rock. The engine's services were not required on the return trip, because the steep descent from the top of the rock allowed the cage to travel down the cable at great speed, giving the men a thrilling ride, akin to today's ziplining. While the men worked, Ballantyne kept an eye on the extremely mercurial weather. When waves started climbing up the sides of the rock, he would yell for the men to stop working, lash their tools to ringbolts embedded in the rock, and run for the cage. It took less than half an hour to evacuate all the men from the rock to the safety of the ship.

Severe storms delayed the work during that first season on the rock, but by July the summer weather moderated conditions, and blasting began in earnest. The process was similar to that used at Tillamook. Just before the fuses were lit the men would run for safety. As Ballantyne later recalled, "At my cry of 'fire in the hole' they would have to hunt for their holes like crabs." But safety was only a relative concept, considering the shower of rock shrapnel the blasts sent flying in every direction, which bruised and bloodied many of the men. Some of the blasts were so powerful that they sent large chunks of rock raining down on *La Ninfa* more

Drawing of construction proceeding on St. George Reef Lighthouse,
showing the method of landing the men from La Ninfa.

than three hundred feet away, leaving numerous scars on the ship's exterior, but no major damage.

In addition to dodging stone projectiles, the men had to contend with the persistently violent seas. Much of the time they were drenched in salt spray coming from waves breaking on the rock, and on September 10 two quarryman working near the top of the rock were hit by a huge wave that washed them thirty feet down the slope, where they landed on a flat surface, bruised but otherwise uninjured.

By the end of September 1883 the blasting had been completed, and the stage was set for building the masonry caisson. During the fall and spring of 1884, the project moved ahead on a number of fronts. Specifications detailed the exact size, shape, and ultimate location of all the stone blocks that would be used to build the caisson. Soon after these specifications were drawn up, a quarry along the Mad River, not far from Humboldt Bay, was contracted to provide the granite for the project. At the same time an extensive work area and depot were built on the north spit of Humboldt Bay, where stonecutters took the rough blocks and worked them into their final shapes. A wharf was also built at the spit to serve as a staging area for shipping the finished blocks to the rock.

Just when Ballantyne was looking forward to beginning work on the caisson, the project stalled. In three consecutive years—1884, 1885, and 1886—the board asked Congress for $150,000 to continue work on the lighthouse. But the United States, deep in the throes of a sustained depression, was economically ailing, and the situation was exacerbated by a panic that hit Wall Street in 1884, when a number of banks collapsed. With business failures on the rise and government revenues falling, Congress kept a tight rein on spending. As a result it appropriated only $30,000 for the lighthouse in 1884, $40,000 the next year, and nothing in 1886.

Since the board estimated that a single season of work on the rock cost at least $75,000, virtually all activity on the reef was halted during these three years. The modest funds that were available mostly went to keep the quarrymen and stonecutters on the mainland employed, but even their work in 1884 and 1885 was limited, while in 1886 it stopped altogether. This led Ballantyne to observe ruefully, "In four years only one working season of about one hundred days was utilized advantageously on the rock."

With the economy rebounding, Congress appropriated $120,000 for the project in 1887, and work on the caisson commenced. Finished blocks, some weighing as much as six tons, were soon streaming to the rock by ship, where they were lifted in nets onto a pier by large boom derricks. Smaller derricks then helped the men maneuver the heavy stones into place. The blocks were numbered so that the men knew exactly where they should go. For added strength, each block was connected to its neighbor by a mortise-and-tenon joint, with the tenon (projection) being inserted into the mortise (cavity) to make a tight fit. To connect each course of blocks to the ones above and below, bronze dowels were inserted into precut holes. All the blocks were cemented together, with only three-sixteenths of an inch separating them. By the end of the 1887 season the caisson was twenty-two feet high.

The 1887 season, predictably, was not devoid of drama. A series of heavy gales added to the difficulty and danger of the work, as the men labored to move the huge blocks into their preassigned locations. Almost daily the men were forced to race to the cage to be taken off the rock to avoid being washed into the sea by gargantuan waves. The awesome power of

Workers who built the St. George Reef Lighthouse, circa 1888.

these waves was on display during a storm in June when a 3.5-ton granite block that had been set into place thirty feet above the sea was lifted and thrown onto a higher bench cut into the reef, where it broke apart.

Over the next two years Congress provided a total of $350,000, enabling work to progress at a fast clip. Bigger derricks were employed, a larger pier was built on the rock for offloading materials, and in 1888 Ballantyne had his men build permanent quarters on the rock, which had room for the fifty-two men who were now laboring on the project. The men had already been sleeping high up on the rock in temporary structures, but when conditions became rough they still had to use the cage to rush back to the ship moored offshore. The permanent quarters eliminated the need for the cage and the ship, and allowed the men to increase their efficiency by spending more time working; and in bad weather they could get to safety much faster. But in reality no place on the rock could truly be considered safe at this time, especially when the Pacific became cantankerous. In May 1889, a ferocious storm hit the rock, with waves pounding the workmen's quarters, causing its two-foot thick wooden beams to pulsate. One particularly nasty breaker crashed open the doors, and filled the building with a swirling maelstrom of salt water, which sucked a few of the men right outside, leaving them clinging to the rocks lest they be swept into the sea. Ballantyne, ever the unflappable Scot, tersely recorded the event in his journal, noting, "The men's quarters, although strongly built, were smashed in during a gale about 2 o'clock one morning in May. No one was injured, but some of the men were washed out of their bunks."

By 1889 the caisson, comprising 1,339 granite blocks, was essentially complete, with only a minor amount of paving yet to be done at the top. Due to a delay in funding in 1890, work on the lighthouse tower didn't begin until 1891. The first stone of the square tower was laid on May 13, and the last was lowered into place on August 23. The only fatality of the entire project occurred during this time, when a workman holding a rope attached to a cargo net moving overhead failed to let go of the rope in time and was dragged over the edge of the caisson, falling to his death on the rocks below. Given the extreme weather, the crashing waves, the blasting, the precipitous flights on the aerial tramway, and the huge number of unwieldy granite blocks that had to be raised, moved, and lowered into place, it is a testament to late-nineteenth-century American engineering, as well as Ballantyne's oversight and his men's skill, that only one person died during the project.

At last, on October 29, the men, having topped the tower with its iron lantern room and put the finishing touches on the lighthouse, were done. It was an engineering feat worthy of a mythological fable. But just when the workers were ready to leave, St. George Reef, as if in a scene scripted by Homer, would not let them go. For more than a week a tremendous storm, producing thunderous waves that caused the caisson and tower to shudder, imprisoned the men in their own creation. On November 8, after the storm ended and the waves died down, the relieved workmen finally departed the rock, more confident than ever that the lighthouse could withstand whatever the unruly Pacific had to offer.

On December 1, 1891, the station's fog whistles began sounding, but it would be almost another year before the custom-made first-order Fresnel lens arrived from France and was installed in the tower. When the lighthouse began shining on October 20, 1892, its intense light streamed

St. George Reef Lighthouse, circa 1963.

from the lantern room at 146 feet above the water and could be seen up to twenty miles away.

The entire endeavor had taken roughly a decade from start to finish, and had cost $752,000, making St. George Reef far and away the most expensive lighthouse ever built in the United States. To put that in perspective, consider that the Statue of Liberty, which was finished in 1886, is estimated to have cost around $600,000 to build, pedestal and all.

CHAPTER 13

OF BIRDS AND EGGS

. . . .

Engraving of birds about to crash into the lantern room of a lighthouse, circa 1870.

I T WAS A NOISE THE KEEPER HAD HEARD MANY TIMES BEFORE: wild geese honking as they flew near the lighthouse. But in the early evening of February 22, 1900, the keeper on duty at the Hog Island Lighthouse suddenly realized that this was no ordinary flyby. As he sat in the watch room of the 150-foot-tall iron skeleton tower located on Virginia's Eastern Shore, a verdant peninsula separating Chesapeake Bay from the Atlantic, the honking grew louder, then deafening, before all at once the lighthouse was under siege, the sounds of breaking glass filling the air. When the keeper rushed up the stairs to see what was happening, a scene of pandemonium greeted him, as wave after wave of geese and ducks crashed through the windows of the lantern room.

The man on watch alerted his fellow keepers, who came running with their shotguns. For one and a half hours the keepers blasted away to fend off this aerial bombardment, stopping only when their ammunition ran out. The next morning the lighthouse resembled a battlefield, with spent shells littering the floor and the carcasses of some sixty-eight birds scattered around the base of the tower and along the lantern room's deck. Many of them died from blunt-force trauma upon smashing into the lantern room's glass or the metal parts of the tower. Others had been fatally cut when they shattered the glass, and still others were brought down by gunfire.

No sooner had the keepers collected and disposed of all the carcasses than another assault commenced, three nights later. Having used all their ammunition warding off the first attack, the keepers resorted to waving sticks from the lighthouse's deck to try to beat the birds off, but they kept on coming. The onslaught grew so intense that the keepers were forced to retreat into the tower to protect themselves from the avian missiles hurtling in their direction. When they emerged from their makeshift bunker this time, the carnage was even more astounding, with 150 broken, dead birds strewn about the lighthouse.

What caused these birds to act in such a catastrophic way remained a mystery at the time. Some suggested that they had been blinded or disoriented by the light, causing them to fly into it, or perhaps they had been drawn to the light like a moth to a flame. Or, was it possible, given the great duration and sustained nature of the attacks, that the birds had targeted the lighthouse for some unknown reason? The truth is that nobody knew the reason for this bizarre avian assault, and these many years later we still do not know for certain why birds of all types so often collide with lighthouses.

Certainly proximity plays a key role. Virtually all of the nation's lighthouses are located in the path of one of the four major North American migration flyways—the so-called Pacific, Central, Mississippi, and Atlantic Flyways (Hawaii and its lighthouses are in the Central Pacific

Flyway). These are the aerial routes that birds tend to take in their migrations to and from the summer breeding and winter feeding grounds. As a result untold numbers of birds fly over and around lighthouses, and feed or nest on lands surrounding them. Although the vast majority of these birds have no trouble avoiding lighthouses as they go on their way, a significant number smash into them, often with fatal results. To protect against dive-bombing birds, the board and the service often placed protective wire-mesh screens around the lantern rooms at particularly susceptible lighthouses, but still the birds kept on coming.

Many observers over the years have commented on this strange and disturbing behavior. The poet and essayist Celia Thaxter, a great lover of both lighthouses and birds, wrote despairingly about the too-often-fatal attraction between the two. "The lighthouse, so beneficent to mankind, is the destroyer of birds," she wrote in her 1873 book, *Among the Isle of Shoals*. "Sometimes in autumn, always in spring, when birds are migrating, they are destroyed in such quantities [as a result of flying into the glass panes]. . . that it is painful to reflect upon."

When the famed scientist and later secretary of the Smithsonian Institution, Spencer Fullerton Baird, climbed into the lantern room of the Cape Hatteras Lighthouse one windy October night in 1876, he witnessed a rather dramatic display of the kind Thaxter wrote about. "As soon as it was fairly dark," Baird wrote, "I could see thousands of small birds flying around the leeward of the tower. It was a grand sight, as the lens of the light would perform its steady revolution, throwing its dazzling rays upon them while seeking shelter by hovering close up under the lee of the tower. As soon as the light would fall upon them, they would fly from it and come in contact with the lantern with such force that they were instantly killed. At one time the whole element was ablaze with them, shining in the rays of light like myriads of little stars or meteors." Baird's tally for the night—nearly five hundred birds dead.

It was keepers, of course, who had the most intimate connection with these misguided flights of doom, and their logs and letters are filled with comments about birds striking their lighthouses. For example, in December 1920 the keeper at Thacher Island Lighthouse reported that a flock

The cover of the October 15, 1887, issue of Frank Leslie's Illustrated Newspaper, *showing the avian carnage created by the Statue of Liberty's illuminated torch. The caption claims that 1,375 birds died in one night.*

of geese had plowed into one of the towers, with five of the birds dying on impact and three crashing through two of the glass panels, severely chipping a few of the Fresnel lens's precious prisms. Such events were almost always traumatic and unwelcome, since they usually required not only cleaning up the remains of the battered and bloodied victims but also performing time-consuming and sometimes quite expensive repairs. There were, however, instances in which keepers viewed bird collisions in a much more favorable light, as was the case for William C. Williams, a keeper at Maine's Boon Island Lighthouse in the late nineteenth and early twentieth centuries.

A few days before Thanksgiving one year in the late 1800s, Williams had been worrying about what to prepare for the upcoming holiday dinner, seeing as neither he nor his assistants had been able to get ashore for the past couple of weeks, and the pantry was looking downright anemic. While pondering his options one evening during his turn in the watch room, Williams heard a crashing noise outside, as if something had just slammed into the building. Opening the door to investigate, there on the deck he saw four lifeless black ducks. But surely, he thought, four ducks alone couldn't have made such a horrific racket, so he walked down to the base of the tower, where he found four more. With this very literal gift from above that year's Thanksgiving on Boon Island was one of the most delicious and bountiful in years.

KEEPERS WERE UNIQUELY PLACED not just to witness these collisions but also to help scientists investigate bird behavior and collect specimens. Ornithologists were well aware of the lighthouses' role in avian mortality, and as a result some of them worked with keepers to obtain useful data. William Dutcher, who would later help found the National Audubon Society and serve as its first president, had a keen interest in the birds of Long Island, and during the 1880s, while he was an officer of the American Ornithologists' Union (AOU), he cultivated relationships with a few keepers in the area. That is how he learned of the tremendous bird kill at the Fire Island Lighthouse on September 23, 1887. The lighthouse's keeper, E. J. Udall, wrote to Dutcher telling him how "a great bird wave . . .,rolling southward along the Atlantic" had crossed paths with the lighthouse that night, leaving 595 birds dead at the foot of the tower. Udall went one step further and shipped all the birds to Dutcher in New York City so he could study them. Dutcher discovered twenty-five species in the lot, including the western form of a female palm warbler, the first ever recorded on Long Island.

In 1904 Wells Woodbridge Cooke, an ornithologist working at the United States Biological Survey, who was famed for his studies of bird migration and distribution, gave full credit to lighthouse keepers in South Florida for their valuable contributions to his work. "The largest single addition to the knowledge of movements of birds along the southern border of the United States," Cooke concluded, "is due to records of species striking the lighthouses off the south coast of Florida." One of the keepers at the Sombrero Key Lighthouse, located on a mostly submerged reef in the mid–Florida Keys, was a particularly exemplary cataloger and correspondent. He spent numerous hours counting and identifying birds that struck the skeleton tower, forwarding his reports to Washington for analysis. Over one five-year period, this keeper provided an astounding 1,816 reports, which included 2,011 bird fatalities. Not all strikes, however, were fatal. The keeper also noted that just over ten thousand birds that had collided with the tower were only temporarily knocked out and were able to resume their flight after coming to. When, in later years, the Biological Survey supplemented its migration studies by banding birds to track their movements, keepers contributed to this effort by inspecting the birds killed or injured at lighthouses for bands and then sending them to the survey.

SOME KEEPERS WENT BEYOND collecting dead birds to protecting live ones. The nineteenth century, especially the latter half, has been called the Age of Extermination, sadly for good reason. An astonishing number of animals, including tens of millions of buffalo alone, were slaughtered to feed the growing population, respond to the demands of fashion, and for what was still considered sport. Birds suffered mightily, especially from the depredations of market hunters, who traded in wildlife for a living. These men killed ducks, geese, and other game birds with reckless abandon to supply shops and restaurants with meat. In a particularly horrific example, a lone gunner on a single day in 1893 shot more that five thousand ducks on Chesapeake Bay. Market hunters also killed vast quantities of birds for their beautiful feathers, which were used to adorn women's hats, a fashion craze at the time. On a stroll through one of New York's toniest shopping districts in 1886, Frank Chapman, an ornithologist with the American Museum of Natural History, counted 700 hats, of which 542 were festooned with feathers of an amazing variety, representing at least forty species. Birds were also under serious threat from eggers who collected eggs for sale, and some birds, such as the Atlantic puffin, were under siege from all directions—killed for their meat and feathers, and also pillaged for their eggs.

The late 1800s being the era of the emerging conservation movement in America, when wildlife was finally deemed worth defending, many states, spurred on by the grassroots lobbying of local Audubon societies, the AOU, and other birding organizations, reacted to this wholesale slaughter by adopting bird-protection laws. The federal government gave these laws an added boost on May 25, 1900, when it passed the Lacey Act, which prohibited the shipment across state lines of wildlife, including birds, killed in violation of state laws. These laws, however, suffered from a lack of enforcement. Although a number of states hired game wardens, there were still many areas where enforcement was minimal or non-existent. Private birding organizations stepped in to try to fill that void, with a crucial assist from lighthouse keepers.

In 1900 Dutcher, a dedicated conservationist and inspiring leader, spearheaded a program sponsored by the AOU that used privately raised funds to hire wardens to protect seabirds during the breeding season along the East Coast, especially terns and gulls whose feathers were prized in the millinery trade. Most of these wardens had no connection to lighthouses, but a few did. Since many of the rookeries for terns and gulls were in the vicinity of lighthouses, Dutcher approached the Lighthouse Board with the idea of having keepers serve as wardens. The board approved, and over the next few years a handful of keepers became paid wardens, while others volunteered their services. The only restriction the board placed on them was that they could not allow their bird-related work to interfere with their lighthouse-keeping duties.

The results were quite encouraging. In the first year of the program, for example, George Pottle, the keeper of Maine's Franklin Island Lighthouse, a forty-five foot tall round brick structure located about midway between Pemaquid Point and Port Clyde, kept a close eye on the tern colonies located on three neighboring islands. He reported to Dutcher that one time he stopped a hunter from shooting birds, and that on ten occasions he kept people from taking eggs. Better yet, he estimated that by the end of the season the number of breeding pairs at the three colonies had risen by one thousand over previous years. The success of the AOU's warden program led a number of state Audubon societies to follow suit, and some of them employed keepers as well.

Not only did the board heartily support the idea of keepers becoming wardens, but it also encouraged all of its keepers to do their part to protect birds. In 1900 the board had the officers in the various lighthouse districts send a circular to all lighthouse keepers that warned them to comply with state game laws and tried to imbue them with a "spirit of protection, not only of the game birds, but of song birds, and of all bird life." Two years later the board formalized this directive to protect birds by including it in the official instructions to lighthouse keepers, and adding that if the keepers saw anyone violating a game law, they should report them immediately.

When the National Audubon Society was founded in 1905, Dutcher became its first president, and he brought with him the warden program he had started at the AOU. In subsequent years quite a few Audubon wardens were lighthouse keepers who worked not only along the East Coast but also the Gulf Coast as well as the Great Lakes, protecting a great variety of birds, especially those sought for the plume and egg trade. As more bird protection laws were passed, and the states and the federal government invested more heavily in enforcement, the need for Audubon wardens diminished, and they were eventually replaced by government game wardens. Exactly when lighthouse keepers stopped serving as wardens is not known, but as late as 1930, the keeper at Matinicus Rock Lighthouse was still in the Audubon Society's employ.

ARGUABLY THE MOST DRAMATIC story concerning lighthouses and birds took place at California's Farallon Island Lighthouse, and it revolved around eggs. Throughout the late 1850s and early 1860s the battle lines were being drawn in the fight over who would control the lucrative trade in common murre eggs taken from Southeast Farallon Island, where the lighthouse was located.* The Pacific Egg Company continued to act as if it owned the island, and in fact claimed it had a grant from the state government to confirm that status. The company believed it had sole rights to collect the eggs, and to establish its operations on a firmer footing it built landing facilities and roads on the island, as well as quarters to

---

*For the background to this fight and the trade in common murre eggs, see chapter 7.

house its employees. Although rival groups would often land on the island to pilfer eggs, sometimes resulting in violent fights with company employees, Pacific Egg maintained its iron grip on the bulk of the egging business. This was fine with Nerva Wines, the head lighthouse keeper from 1855 to 1858, "who was," as a contemporary observer noted, "a stockholder in the company, and as long as he received his dividend that was all he cared for."

The situation became more complicated in the summer of 1859, when President James Buchanan issued an executive order that declared the Farallon Islands federal property to be used solely for lighthouse purposes. Despite this assertion of power, the government took no immediate action to evict the egg company or restrict its business. However, Amos Clift, the head keeper who replaced Wines, viewed the federal claim of ownership as a personal call to action. Since the federal government owned the islands, Clift assumed that as a federal employee he was entitled to take over the lucrative egg trade. Writing to his brother in Connecticut in November 1859, Clift said that he hoped that the company would soon be driven from the island, and he would get what he justly deserved. "If I could have the privilege of this egg business for one season," he wrote, "it is all I would ask and the government might 'kiss my foot and go up along.'"

At the same time that Clift was writing to his brother, things were becoming more fractious on the island. San Francisco's *Daily Alta California* reported that a rival group of eggers had seized control of part of Southeast Farallon, ripped up government roads, and "drawn lines and posted up notices warning the keepers not to pass them on pain of death." During the next egging season, in 1860, tensions continued to escalate. Pacific Egg and its rivals were, the paper said, "armed to the teeth and breathing defiance against each other." At one point gun-toting egg company employees even ordered the keepers to leave the island, but either out of a sense of duty or in the hopes of profiting from the eggs themselves, they stayed put and refused to be intimidated.

In the midst of this Clift wrote to his brother that the "egg co. and the lighthouse keepers are at war. . . . They have tried every means in their power to effect my removal, but up to this point they have failed and now I have made up my mind that if I stay here I will see that the co. is 'cleaned out.'" Instead of the egg company, however, it was Clift who was driven from the island. In June the board fired him for "the undue . . . assumption to monopolize and farm out the valuable privilege of collecting eggs."

The egg imbroglio came to a head in the late spring of 1863, when a rival group launched a major attack on the island. On the evening of June 3, three boats filled with twenty-seven armed Italian fishermen, led by one David Batchelder, moored in Southeast Farallon Island's Fisherman's Bay. The company men armed themselves and went down to confront the interlopers. Isaac Harrington, the Pacific Egg foreman, warned Batchelder and his men to leave, and told them if they tried to land it would be "at their peril." Batchelder replied that "in spite of hell he would go ashore in the morning."

Batchelder's three boats made their move shortly after daybreak. As they came closer to the island, someone in Batchelder's group yelled, "God damn you, don't shoot!" Exactly what happened next is contested. Both sides claimed the other fired first. Regardless of how it started, the battle was brief, fierce, and deadly. Within about fifteen minutes, company employee Edward Perkins lay lifeless, shot through the stomach, and five of the men on the boats were wounded. This carnage was enough for Batchelder to give up the fight and sail back to San Francisco, where one of his men, who had been shot in the throat, later died in a local hospital.

The egg war of 1863 was over. Batchelder was convicted of manslaughter and spent time in jail before being freed after the conviction was overturned on appeal. As for the egg company, its aggressive defense of its position scared off other rivals, securing it the monopoly over egging, which it held until May 1881. In the end it was the company's arrogance and its unwavering belief that it owned the island and could do what it pleased that brought about its downfall.

By the late 1870s the company's profits from egging were only a fraction of what they had been in earlier years. Part of the problem was that the common murre population had plummeted due to decades of relentless egging, and the annual haul of eggs had fallen from roughly a million per year to fewer than two hundred thousand. Not only had the number of eggs dropped dramatically, but so too had the demand for them, since the West Coast chicken population was on the rise, providing an increasing number of eggs much more pleasing to the discerning palate. Thus instead getting a dollar a dozen for common murre eggs, the company was lucky to get a quarter. With profits declining, the company decided to explore other business opportunities. To that end, in 1879 it leased to another company the right to hunt seals and sea lions at the Farallons and to set up facilities to render their blubber into oil.

This move infuriated the board. It had long contended that Southeast Farallon was government property, and that Pacific Egg had no right to be there. Now that the company had leased part of the island it had gone too far. How could it lease what it did not own? The board became even more enraged in 1880, when rendering operations got under way. The stench of decaying seal carcasses and burning flesh was nauseating, but of far greater concern was the smoke, which the keepers complained obscured the light. At the same time the egg company took other actions that further exacerbated the situation. Although keepers had traditionally collected eggs for their own use, the company put a halt to that practice, and when one of the assistant keepers tried to gather eggs, company employees attacked him. The company even demanded that the keepers silence the foghorn so it would not scare away the birds.

All of these insults spurred the government to legally evict the egg company, and on May 23, 1881, U.S. Marshal A. W. Poole, backed up by twenty-one well-armed soldiers, arrived on the lighthouse tender *Manzanita* to deliver the eviction notice. Only one egg company employee was reluctant to go: Luff Wood, the company's caretaker, who had lived on the island for more than a decade and considered it his home, begged to stay but was politely rebuffed. According to one of the other eggers, the general feeling among the men was relief: "We steamed away from the windy rocks, the howling caverns, the seething waves, the frightful chasms, the seabirds, the abalones, the rabbits, the gloomy cabins. . . . Joyfully we bounded over the glassy waves, that grew beautiful as the

Farallons faded in the misty distance. . . . Thus ended the last siege of the Farallons by the egg-pickers of San Francisco. (Profits *nil.*)"

The egg company was gone, but egging did not stop. Fishermen and lighthouse keepers, often working in tandem, continued to gather and sell common murre eggs. Although the price of the eggs fell even further, the keepers nevertheless found this moonlighting to be an excellent way to supplement their government salaries. The board finally put a halt to their activities at the urging of scientists at the California Academy of Sciences and the AOU, who were gravely concerned about the alarming drop in the number of seabirds nesting on the Farallons, which had been brought about decades of rapacious egging, especially of common murre eggs, but also those of other bird species. In December 1896 the board issued an order prohibiting keepers from "engaging in the business of collecting or selling wild birds' eggs on these islands, in any form." While this stopped keepers from selling eggs, for many years they still collected them for their own use. Eventually all commercial egging on the islands stopped as the price of eggs continued to fall and the federal government further restricted access to nesting areas. Today the Farallon Island Lighthouse, as well as all of the Farallon Islands, are part of the Farallon National Wildlife Refuge, administered by the U.S. Fish and Wildlife Service. Fully protected now, the islands are home to the largest seabird breeding colony south of Alaska, including a healthy and growing population of common murres.

The ugly behavior of a few keepers at the Farallon Island Lighthouse notwithstanding, during the late nineteenth and early twentieth centuries, birds and lighthouse keepers typically lived in relative harmony with one another, even though the relationship between birds and the lighthouses themselves was often quite devastating to the former. Thus in a small but meaningful way, lighthouse keepers, particularly those enlisted as bird wardens, contributed to the growth of the conservation ethos in the United States, which not only benefited the birds and the broader environment of which they were an integral part, but also the character and well-being of the society at large.

CHAPTER 14

A CRUEL WIND

· · · · · · · · · · · · · ·

Waves batter a seawall in Woods Hole, Massachusetts,
during the Great Hurricane of 1938.

Hurricanes are an occupational hazard for lighthouse keepers, especially on the East and Gulf Coasts. Some hurricanes are particularly noteworthy in the annals of lighthouse history because of the devastation they wrought. One of the earliest to achieve this negative distinction hit the Florida Keys on October 10, 1846, obliterating the Key West and Sand Key Lighthouses and killing twenty people who were at the lighthouses when they were washed away. The hurricane that roared onto the Gulf Coast in September 1906 destroyed the Lake Borgne and Horn Island Lighthouses in Mississippi, and gravely damaged others, including Alabama's Sand Island Lighthouse. The storm also killed two keepers, along with three of their family members. The hurricane that blasted the northeastern United States in 1938, however, ranks at the top of the list of memorable "lighthouse" hurricanes, not only because of the extent of the damage but because of its impact on the people who survived—and those who did not.

EDWIN S. BABCOCK, better known as Babbie to his friends, was tired and he wanted to go home. In addition to running a combination grocery, gas station, restaurant, and cabin rental business called Babbie's on the mainland, he also served as a substitute keeper at the Plum Beach Lighthouse. This iron spark-plug lighthouse, completed in 1899, was located in the center of Narragansett Bay's West Passage, between North Kingstown and Jamestown, Rhode Island. Babbie had already been at the lighthouse for three days, so on the afternoon of September 21, 1938, it was time for him to leave. At about two thirty he said good-bye to the assistant keeper, John Ganze, got into the lighthouse dory, and began rowing to shore about a half mile away.

Determined though he was to get back to his wife and daughter and his business, Babbie was no match for the whipping winds and choppy seas buffeting the dory. A short time after starting out, he turned around and headed back to the lighthouse, making it only after considerable effort. Ganze and Babbie lashed the dory to the iron railing on the lighthouse dock, then looked south toward the mouth of the bay, where they saw the three o'clock ferry heading from Jamestown to Saunderstown. But rather than motoring ahead at a respectable speed, the ferry was barely moving.

Concerned about the rapidly worsening weather, Ganze and Babbie battened down the lighthouse, shutting the windows and portholes while locking the doors. The next time they looked down the bay, visibility was so low that the ferry had disappeared from view. Had they in fact been able to see the vessel, it would have presented a strange sight. The ferry was turning around. Less than halfway across the nearly two-mile passage, the captain realized that the weather was too rough to proceed, so he headed back to Jamestown.

———

WHAT GANZE, BABBIE, AND the ferry captain didn't know at the time was that the Great Hurricane of 1938 was bearing down on them. In fact, nobody along the coasts of New York or southern New England knew about the hurricane before it hit, and by then it was too late to get out of its way. As the hurricane barreled northward off the Eastern Seaboard, the U.S. Weather Bureau (which later became the National Weather Service), still quite limited in its forecasting abilities, had actually predicted that it would lose strength and veer out into the colder waters of the North Atlantic without making landfall. Just before the hurricane slammed into the Northeast, gale warnings were issued for the area, but gales were relatively common and were no cause for alarm. People were not being told to prepare for the worst.

The hurricane, however, defied predictions. Instead of heading safely out to sea, it suddenly swerved toward the coast, racing at a blistering 60 to 70 mph—faster than any hurricane before it—coming ashore in Suffolk County, Long Island, and then picking up strength and blasting into southern New England with unimaginable force, packing sustained winds of up to 121 mph, with gusts hitting 186. It could not have come at a worse time. Not only was it high tide, but it was also the autumnal equinox, when the moon passes closest to the earth, generating especially strong gravitational forces that produced some of the highest high tides of the year—which, when combined with the driving wind, caused monumental storm surges. The hurricane destroyed so much of the local communications systems, including phone and telegraph lines, that places that were hit first had no way of alerting those who were next in line, so they were equally unprepared for the maelstrom that suddenly enveloped them.

AFTER SECURING THINGS AS best they could, Ganze and Babbie retreated to the kitchen, which was on the same level as the deck encircling the lighthouse. But soon the waves were crashing over the deck, a full ten feet above the level of the normal high tide. To escape the rising waters they climbed up the iron spiral staircase to one of the keeper's rooms on the next level, taking with them a bottle of water, a radio, and a flask of whiskey, from which they soon took a few swigs to help take the edge off their fast-fraying nerves. But as the hurricane intensified, the ocean rose even more rapidly. When the waves began crashing into the windows of the room they were in, they ascended one more flight to Ganze's quarters.

Babbie was terrified. Severe storms had ravaged the area before, but this one seemed more threatening than any he had ever experienced. Ganze was less concerned. Although he was only twenty-nine, he had been a keeper for more than ten years, his most recent posting being at Rhode Island's Sakonnet Point Lighthouse, another caisson-style spark-plug lighthouse surrounded by water. Ganze reassured Babbie that he had survived more severe storms at Sakonnet. Before the day was over, however, he would change his mind.

Increasingly the two men felt the lighthouse shake as it was battered by the relentless wind and waves. Through the portholes they saw the remains of houses, boats, and trees zoom by. They heard more ominous sounds below, as the kitchen door and the windows in the lower quarters blew open, allowing tons of water to rush in. Then out of the portholes they saw their two boats floating away, quickly disappearing from sight.

Ganze and Babbie were running out of options. The water was coming up fast, and the waves were breaking ever higher outside. There were only two more levels above them—the room with the fog-bell machinery, and the lantern room at the very top of the lighthouse. They decided that they could not go to the lantern room because it was too exposed, so they climbed up to the fog-bell room to make their last stand. There Ganze bolted shut the iron trapdoor that led to the lantern room, and—in what was at once an act of resignation and desperation—he and Babbie stood back-to-back and tied themselves to the metal column in the center of the room, which housed the weights that powered the revolving mechanism for the lighthouse's fourth-order Fresnel lens. According to the historian Lawrence H. Bradner, who interviewed Ganze years later, the two keepers were thinking, "If the lighthouse went over, as they feared it would, they would at least be found together."

As the winds grew ever more powerful and the waves rose even higher, reaching nearly to the top of the fifty-four-foot structure, the lighthouse was suddenly struck by a massive wall of water, causing the building to shudder violently. At the same instant the air pressure in the lighthouse dropped drastically, and according to Ganze, the cement walls lining the inside of the building began to crack "like an eggshell." Fearing that the lighthouse might actually implode, the men untied themselves and opened the portholes in the room below to equalize the pressure inside and out. They then went back to the fog-bell room, but instead of tying themselves up again, they grabbed hold of what they could while the lighthouse continued to tremble and groan with each new assault. Recalling this moment many years later, Ganze said, "If it had gone on ten minutes longer we'd a been gone!"

Unbeknownst to them, the worst had passed. By early evening on the twenty-first, the winds and waves had diminished, and the waters in the swollen bay started to recede. The next morning the extent of the damage became clear. All the rooms were in a shambles, and most of the keepers' belongings had been washed into the bay. The iron coal stove had been pitched across the room, railings on the main deck twisted or ripped away, and much of the concrete that made up the deck's flooring was gone. Boulders weighing as much as four tons, which formed the riprap, or girdle of stones, protecting the lighthouse, had been shifted or completely swept into the water. And there were numerous visible cracks in the lighthouse's iron shell.

Though Babbie and Ganze survived the hurricane itself, their ordeal was not over. Throughout that day and into the evening, the two of them waited in vain, without water or food, for someone to rescue them. Certainly, they thought, the Lighthouse Board or the Coast Guard would send a boat to pick them up, but none ever came. On the mainland Babbie's wife and daughter, fearing the worst, begged the police to send a boat to check the lighthouse to see if the men had survived, yet despite assurances the police didn't follow through. Instead it was two local men, the Cook brothers, Jim and Charlie, both in their early twenties, who stepped up, after Babbie's wife and daughter told them of their predicament. The brothers rowed their fourteen-foot crabbing skiff to the light-house that evening, and just after eleven, more than twenty-four hours after the hurricane had swept by, they brought Babbie safely back to shore; Ganze decided to stay behind until more help arrived the next day.

WALTER EBERLE WOULD NOT be so lucky. He was one of the assistant keepers at Whale Rock Lighthouse, another spark-plug structure located near the mouth of Narragansett Bay, not too far from the Plum Beach Lighthouse. While Babbie and Ganze were surveying the damage to their lighthouse early on the morning of September 22, they glanced down the bay and saw a shocking sight. The entire iron structure of the Whale Rock Lighthouse was gone, and all that remained was the caisson upon which the tower had stood, looking very much like the stump of a mighty tree that had been cut down near its base.

Eberle, a twenty-year veteran of the navy, had been appointed assistant keeper at Whale Rock only one year earlier, in 1937, and his wife and six children lived nearby in Newport. On the morning of September 21, Eberle sensed that the weather was changing for the worse, so he headed out to the lighthouse a little earlier than normal to relieve the head keeper, Dan Sullivan. Exactly when the Whale Rock Lighthouse lost its battle

Whale Rock Lighthouse, after the Great Hurricane of 1938.

with the hurricane will always remain unknown, but it was most likely around the same time that the Plum Beach Lighthouse was hit by the massive wall of water, for Ganze and Babbie later recalled that right after the storm had passed, no light shone anymore from Whale Rock. After a long, agonizing night of waiting and worrying in the Eberle household, the phone rang at five thirty in the morning, and Walter's wife, Agnes, answered it. "The light is gone," Sullivan told her. Walter Eberle's body was never found.

FARTHER UP NARRAGANSETT BAY, another drama was playing out at the Prudence Island Lighthouse, an octagonal granite structure in the center of the bay, which was established in 1852. George T. Gustavus, a longtime veteran of the service, had served at six lighthouses before being appointed keeper at Prudence Island in 1937. In midafternoon on September 21 he was in the lighthouse residence with his wife and their fourteen-year-old son, Eddie, when they heard frantic knocking at the front door. Gustavus opened the door, and in rushed Martin Thompson, the former keeper of the lighthouse. Thompson, who lived just a short distance away in a cottage he christened the Snug Harbor, had brought with him a Mr. and Mrs. Lynch, who summered on the island. They were all looking for a safe place to ride out the storm, and Martin believed the keeper's house was the most secure building around. He had lived in that house for twenty-five years and was convinced that "it would stand any blow that would strike."

The waves were soon crashing against the outside of the house, and everyone climbed to the second story to escape the water that was flooding the first. A little while later two towering waves combined with tremendous wind gusts demolished the house. "We were caught like rats in a trap," Gustavus later recalled, and everyone was thrown into the debris-choked waters. The next thing Gustavus remembered was being rescued about a half mile from the lighthouse. A teenage boy walking along the beach had spotted him among the wreckage and extended a plank, which Gustavus said he clamped onto with a "death grip." He was then hauled out of the water and taken to a nearby cottage.

*Martin Thompson,
former keeper of the
Prudence Island
Lighthouse.*

Even though Gustavus had no idea what had happened to his wife and son, his first thought was to tend to his keeper's duties. Since the lighthouse's electricity had been cut off, Gustavus and a few other men rigged a wire from the nearby electrical plant to get the light going again. Only then did he start searching for his loved ones. His neighbors tried to assure him that his family had survived and were being cared for, but "I knew better," Gustavus remembered thinking. Two more days passed before they discovered the remains of his wife on a beach near Newport.

*Prudence Island
Lighthouse, after the
Great Hurricane
of 1938*

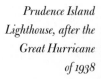

The bodies of Thompson and the Lynches washed up on Prudence Island almost a week later. Like Walter Eberle's, the body of Gustavus's son, Eddie, was never recovered.

SIMILAR LIGHTHOUSE STORIES PLAYED out up and down the New England coast. Earlier that day, as the hurricane churned its way toward them, there had been an air of excited anticipation among the residents at the Dumpling Rock Lighthouse, located on the west side of the entrance to Buzzards Bay, just off the coast of Dartmouth, Massachusetts. The head keeper, Octave Ponsart, was getting ready to take his family on its first vacation in many years. The Depression had exacted a punishing toll on the Ponsarts, but they had saved enough money to buy a new car and some new clothes, and now Octave—along with his wife, Emma, their daughter, Bette, and Bette's cousin Connie—were ready to go. Their suitcases were packed and loaded in the dory. But before they could leave the island the hurricane blew in, trapping them.

Ponsart and the assistant keeper, Henry Fontenot, immediately sent Emma, Bette, Connie, and Fontenot's wife, May, into the two-story wooden keeper's quarters attached to the wooden lighthouse tower. The

Dumpling Rock Lighthouse, circa 1889.

men then went to secure the dory, but the wind and the waves were too much for them, and the dory was swept out to sea. After a quick check to make sure the doors to the tower and the oil house were bolted shut, the two men joined the others in the house, whose first floor was already filling with water. The women and children were sent to the assistant keeper's room on the second floor, which was on the lee side of the house, farthest from the punishing winds. Looking out toward the water from the first floor, the two keepers could scarcely believe what they were seeing through the rain and heavy salt spray. A succession of enormous waves—each appearing bigger than the last—was heading in their direction. Fontenot told Ponsart, "I think we're going to lose the light."

The keepers raced up the stairs to join the others. Since the men had been doing work on the assistant keeper's room, boards and nails lay scattered about, and they made good use of them, hammering the planks over the windows to reinforce them and driving nails into the floorboards for extra bracing. As the hurricane intensified, the building began falling apart. Roof tiles and clapboards flew into the air, windows shattered, and one side of the house partially caved in. As Emma Ponsart later recalled, "We really thought we were going to die. In a few minutes, even."

Then they heard a tremendous noise, which she said was "like a freight train or what an earthquake must sound like." Immediately thereafter the house shuddered so violently that the three people sitting on the bed were thrown to the floor. When the keepers opened the bedroom door, they saw what had caused the jarring impact. There, in the almost completely submerged living room, suddenly presided an enormous boulder, which had been flung into the side of the house by the furious seas. That rock might very well have saved all of their lives, according to Seamond Ponsart Roberts, the Ponsarts' daughter, who was born two years after the hurricane and often listened to her parents tell the story of that dramatic event. The rock, Roberts said, "opened up a channel through the house, easing the flow of water entering and exiting the building," and it also anchored "the house and the lighthouse to Dumpling Rock."

Huddling together in the assistant keeper's room, the six survivors slept fitfully through the night. The next morning they went downstairs only to find that very little of the first floor was left, virtually all of its contents washed away, yet Rexena, the lighthouse dog, had miraculously survived, and was found on the top shelf of what remained of the linen closet. Keeper Ponsart's brand-new car, which had been parked on the mainland, had been lifted by the surging waters and deposited somewhere in the murky depths offshore. The family's vacation money had also disappeared. Ponsart had given it to his wife for her to put into a pocket, but she had tucked the cash into one of the suitcases to keep it dry. The suitcases were in the dory, so when it was swept out to sea, the Ponsarts' savings were too.

EVERYONE WHO LIVED THROUGH the hurricane of 1938 experienced how incredibly fast the weather conditions changed, including Sidney Z. Gross, the head keeper at the Saybrook Breakwater Lighthouse, a sparkplug structure in Old Saybrook, Connecticut, at the mouth of the Connecticut River where it flows into Long Island Sound. Just before two in the afternoon on September 21, Gross was looking out on the perfectly calm waters of the river and the Sound. At two a slight southeast breeze picked up, and within fifteen minutes it became so hazy that Gross and the assistant keeper, S. L. Bennett, turned on the fog signals. Forty-five minutes later, at three, the wind was blowing so hard that neither Gross nor Bennett could open the door and go outside to secure items around the lighthouse. Each time they attempted to venture out, the wind forced them back in.

By three thirty the churning waters had almost reached the platform surrounding the tower's main level, and they had already washed away the metal bridge to the breakwater. At four the entire platform was ripped from the tower, carrying off the lighthouse's rowboat. At four thirty, one tank holding fifteen hundred gallons of kerosene, and another with six hundred gallons of oil, both went sailing into the abyss. Thirty minutes later a wave crashed through one of the windows of the engine room and sent glass flying, a shard of which left a gash on one of Bennett's hands. When the engines, which powered the fog signal, were doused with tons of water, they shorted out and the signals' horns were silenced. Gross hooked a battery up to the signal, but no sooner had the signal started blaring again than the battery switch burst into flames, forcing him to disconnect the battery and put out the fire. The horns fell silent once more. An hour later, at six, the battery storage shed broke open, and all the batteries inside, as well as an outboard motor, disappeared into the ocean's maw. By this time the water had risen to the second level of the tower and was flooding into the hall through a broken window. Gross later recalled, "I certainly did not expect to see another sunrise, as the whole structure was shaking under the violent pounding."

At dusk Gross entered the lantern room to light the light, but since there was no electricity, he disconnected the electric lamp, and replaced it with an IOV lamp. The fourth-order Fresnel lens was shaking so violently that Gross thought it would fall to the floor and shatter at any moment. The lens held, but it was only as good as its light source, and here Gross faced another problem. Each time he put a new mantle into the lamp, it collapsed due to the vibrations. So he went back another generation in lighting technology and swapped out the IOV lamp for one

The power of the Great Hurricane of 1938 can be seen in this picture,
which shows the Lighthouse Service tender Tulip *thrown up on the tracks*
of the New Haven Railroad in New London, Connecticut.

that used a wick and burned kerosene. He nursed the lamp all night to make sure it didn't go out. "When daylight came at last, what we saw," Gross said, "seemed more like a bad dream than reality. There was nothing around the tower. Everything was gone except the battery house and even that was badly out of shape."

ABOUT EIGHTY MILES FARTHER up the coast from the Saybrook Breakwater Lighthouse, the Palmer Island Lighthouse in New Bedford Harbor didn't escape the hurricane's wrath. Its keeper, Arthur Small, was a seasoned mariner, having been a commercial fisherman, served on merchant ships, and, in the navy, sailed around the world as part of President Theodore Roosevelt's "Great White Fleet," an armada of sixteen battleships whose mission was to spread goodwill and also impress other countries with America's vast sea power. On September 21 Small's keen understanding of maritime weather, developed over his many years at sea, told him that a storm was coming. How bad he did not know, but the thick mugginess of the air and the yellowish-green tinge of the sky were clear signs that he had better be prepared. He spent much of the day securing things around the lighthouse and hauling extra kerosene and lamp equipment to the tower.

Palmer Island was barely six acres in size, and sat near the mouth of New Bedford Harbor. In addition to the twenty-four-foot-tall conical stone tower, other structures on the island included the keeper's quarters, an oil house, and a boathouse. Small had been keeper for nineteen years, and at the time of the hurricane he was living on the island with his wife, Mabel, and their beloved cats.

Small was a painter of some renown, specializing in maritime themes, especially meticulously researched and detailed images of ships. He was very proud of being a keeper, and thought people should be more respectful of the importance and responsibility of the keeper's job. One day Small shared his frustrations with Edward Rowe Snow. "It is a popular idea that there is very little to do except for striking a match once a day to light the lamp," Small said. "Few of these landlubbers realize that

Palmer's Island Lighthouse, circa 1919.

if a fog comes in during the middle of the night the keeper must be ready
to turn on the fog signal at once, for if the fog bell is silent for a moment,
even then a great vessel may be feeling her way into the harbor, depending on the ringing of the fog signal bell for her safety." Small pointed out
that if even a single large ship went down in the harbor's narrow channel,
"all shipping in or out of the harbor would be at a standstill. . . . In a
short time all the city would be seriously crippled. That is what makes
me angry when I hear of the easy job of a lighthouse keeper, as described
by some fair weather sailor or inland resident."

Small was not looking for adulation. In fact he laughed at the idea
of keepers being considered heroic for just doing their job. "Whenever
they say anything about a lighthouse keeper," Small told a reporter,
"they always act as if he were some kind of hero. We're not heroes. Here
I am on this island, perfectly safe, working and painting pictures, while
you wander around New Bedford, crossing the streets with automobile
and trolley cars whizzing by, just missing you by a few feet. Why, you
people take more chances in a week than I do in ten years." But on September 21 Palmer Island would become anything but a "perfectly safe"
place to be.

By late afternoon the island was completely covered in water, prompting Small to take his wife to the oil house, the highest point on the island, where he thought she would be protected. Small was heading for the lighthouse, battling his way through the raging waters, when he was swept off his feet and hit by floating debris. Mrs. Small had been watching from the oil house, and when she saw that her husband had been injured and was struggling in the water, she rushed to the boathouse to grab the dory to rescue him. Small regained his footing in time to see her enter the boathouse, but no sooner had she gone inside than a crushing wave flattened the building, trapping her. The following wave washed what was left of the boathouse off the island.

In recounting this horrific episode later, Small said, "I was hurt and she knew it. Seeing the wave hit the boathouse was about the last thing I remember. I must have been hit by a piece of timber and knocked unconscious. I came to some hours later, but all I remember was that I was in the middle of some wreckage. Then I must have lost my senses, for I remember nothing more." Astonishingly, despite his injuries and the shock of having witnessed the almost certain death of his wife, Small managed to get back to the tower, where he kept the light burning and the fog signal going through the night.

Arthur and Mabel Small with a few of their cats.

The tower and the oil house were the only structures still standing on Palmer Island the next morning—the rest had been swept away. When two of Small's friends in New Bedford saw the devastation, they rowed to the island and took him to a hospital on the mainland, where he was treated for exhaustion and exposure. Before leaving the island, however, Small had to obtain permission from his superiors, since there was a service rule stating, "No keeper may leave his post until relieved, if he is able to walk." One of Small's friends made the call, and a relief keeper was sent, allowing Small to depart.

Small had lost virtually all his worldly possessions during the hurricane, including many of his paintings and sketches, his sizable library,

Hurricane damage to Bullocks Point Lighthouse in East Providence, Rhode Island.

and between seven and eight thousand dollars in savings. But the most tragic loss of course was his wife, his loving companion for thirty years, whose body was found later washed up in Fairhaven. On September 26, Lighthouse Service Commissioner Harold D. King honored Small, stating that his actions during the hurricane represented "one of the most outstanding cases of loyalty and devotion that has come to the attention of this office." After recuperating in the hospital, and an extended leave with full pay, Small was appointed keeper of the Hospital Point Lighthouse, in Beverly, Massachusetts, where he stayed until retiring in 1945.

ALL TOLD, MORE THAN twenty-five lighthouses were significantly damaged during the hurricane of 1938—Whale Rock being the only one completely obliterated—and seven people lost their lives. The trail of destruction ranged from the eastern portions of Long Island and Connecticut all the way to Gloucester, Massachusetts. The service received numerous reports of railings and decks torn away, boats lost, foundations cracked, windows and doors broken, walls collapsed, and personal belongings washed out to sea.

The losses sustained by the Lighthouse Service, however, were only a small part of a much larger canvas of catastrophe and devastation. By the time it was over, the Great Hurricane of 1938 had killed 682 people, seriously injured 1,754, and damaged or completely demolished roughly 20,000 homes, and more than 3,000 boats (another 2,500 were lost at sea). It ranks as the most destructive natural disaster ever to strike New England, and one of the worst storms in American history.

CHAPTER 15

THE NEW KEEPERS

· · · · · · · · · · · · · ·

*The Hooper Strait Lighthouse on display at the Chesapeake Bay
Maritime Museum, in St. Michaels, Maryland.*

THERE WAS GREAT EXCITEMENT THROUGHOUT THE RANKS OF the Lighthouse Service in the spring of 1939. All eyes were focused on the fast-approaching date of August 7, marking the 150th anniversary of President George Washington's signing the bill that gave the federal government control over the nation's lighthouses. Harold King, George Putnam's successor at the service, had been working with Congress to have the government publicly recognize this milestone, and he succeeded on

May 15, 1939, when President Franklin Delano Roosevelt signed a joint resolution of Congress, designating the week of August 7, 1939, as "Lighthouse Week." It was to be a nationwide celebration, when Americans could show their appreciation for the "devoted, efficient, faithful, and splendid work" of the lighthouse establishment since 1789.

The celebration, however, turned into a requiem of sorts on July 1, 1939, when Congress passed Roosevelt's Reorganization Plan II, which disbanded the Lighthouse Service and summarily transferred its employees and all its responsibilities to the U.S. Coast Guard. Touted as a sensible move since both organizations' missions involved ensuring the safety of the nation's waters, the reorganization was intended to promote administrative and economic efficiency through consolidation.

The reorganization, however, came as quite a shock to the service's employees, especially since it was announced, paradoxically, just as they were preparing to celebrate the service's illustrious history. While some keepers resigned rather than make the switch, the rest were given the option of retaining their civilian status or converting to positions within the Coast Guard's military hierarchy. About half chose to remain civilians, while the rest joined the military ranks, with most becoming chief or first-class petty officers.

Many keepers who had spent their careers working for a civilian service they respected and oftentimes loved were at best unsettled, or more likely traumatized, by the move. Now they were thrown into a highly structured military organization, with different rules and procedures and a new pecking order. It was inevitable that there would be a certain amount of dislocation, and there was considerable friction between the often-idiosyncratic keepers and the more-regimented Coast Guard personnel. Some keepers bristled at having to take orders from young Coast Guard officers, whom they felt didn't know much about running lighthouses. Grumbling notwithstanding, the reorganization was quickly completed, and America's lighthouses continued to operate smoothly.

In the process the reorganization also created a new kind of lighthouse keeper. When keepers who had been part of the service retired or resigned, their places were taken by Coast Guard servicemen who were usually stationed at lighthouses for relatively short stints, often just a couple of years, before being sent off to other assignments. Thus, slowly over time, temporary keepers replaced those who had chosen to make a career of lighthouse work.

Roosevelt's hopes for increased economic efficiency were quickly realized, however. In its first year the reorganization resulted in savings of a million dollars, nearly 10 percent of the old Lighthouse Service's annual budget. Despite the bittersweet end to the service's 150 years of relative autonomy, this new efficiency and military structure would prove useful a little more than a year later, when the Japanese bombed Pearl Harbor, turning the naval port into a glowing fireball of death and destruction, and the United States entered World War II. Once again lighthouses were drawn into the fray.

Many lighthouses, as in the past, were blacked out or dimmed, and communications plans were put in place so that keepers could quickly be alerted to extinguish the lights if necessary. Lighthouse keepers participated in coastal patrols and kept on the lookout for enemy ships, planes, or submarines. A few lighthouses were painted with camouflage colors to blend into their surroundings, and troops and artillery were deployed at some lighthouses to guard against invasion. Lighthouses resumed their normal operations toward the end of the war as threats to the coast diminished. Then, seven months after the war ended, the Coast Guard was rocked by one of the worst lighthouse disasters in American history.

THE ORIGINAL SCOTCH CAP Lighthouse was made of wood and built on the side of a cliff on Unimak Island, Alaska, in 1903. It was replaced in 1940 by a steel-reinforced concrete building sixty feet tall, whose beacon shone ninety-two feet above the high-water mark. The new fortress-like lighthouse seemed impregnable. But on the morning of April 1, 1946, a force of nature proved that it was not.

Five Coast Guard keepers ran the lighthouse, behind which, farther up the cliff, stood a radio-direction-finding station (DF) also manned by the Coast Guard. The first hour and twenty-nine minutes of the mid-

Scotch Cap Lighthouse, before the seismic wave destroyed it in April 1946.

night watch at the lighthouse on April 1 passed uneventfully. A minute later, however, the earth began to tremble. The watch at the DF station noted in the log: "0130—severe earthquake felt. Building rocked severely. Objects shaken from the shelves. Duration approximately 30–40 seconds. Building creaked and groaned but no apparent damage. Weather, clear, calm." The watch then used the radiophone to contact his counterpart at the lighthouse, who was equally shaken up but okay.

The earthquake had originated ninety miles from the lighthouse in the Aleutian Trench, about eighteen thousand feet beneath the ocean's surface, when two immense tectonic plates collided, one grinding its way under the other. At 1:57 a.m. the plates collided again, spawning another earthquake, shorter in duration but considerably stronger than the earlier one. The DF station and the lighthouse shuddered violently but survived intact. What the men on watch had no way of knowing, however, was that a killer was bearing down on them with astonishing speed.

The second earthquake triggered a tsunami, or seismic wave, that raced outward in all directions at many hundreds of miles per hour. Approaching the shallower waters around Unimak Island, the tsunami

The remains of Scotch Cap Lighthouse after the seismic wave hit.

slowed dramatically, but as it encountered the sea floor it quickly soared out of the depths into a towering wall of water one hundred feet high.

At 2:18 the DF station watch heard a great roaring outside, immediately followed by a "terrific sea" that crashed into the station, flooding the lower part of the building and causing extensive damage. The station's senior officer immediately ordered the six men who were off duty at the time to retreat to higher ground in case another great wave hit. As they were clambering up the rocky hillside in the dim moonlight, one of them looked back toward the water and yelled, "The light!—The Scotch Cap Light! It's gone out."

Minutes later the DF station's senior officer sent a radio message, which read in part: "Tidal wave–may have to abandon this place X believe NNHK [Scotch Cap Lighthouse] lost." At 3:00, after the seas moderated, the officer called his men back to the station. There was still no light shining down below, and upon further investigation it became clear that the worst had happened. At 3:45 the log recorded the fateful conclusion, "Light station total loss, all hands." A few hours later the black of night receded, and dawn revealed the grisly scene of destruction. The crew of the DF station searched through the debris, finding only a human foot, what appeared to be a small piece of human intestine, and a kneecap.

Tremors continued for a few weeks, as did the search for the remains of the five keepers. While many body parts were found, including a headless, disemboweled corpse, only one of the dead men was positively identified. Never before or since have so many lighthouse keepers been killed in a single disaster. The keepers, however, were not the only victims. When the tsunami hit Hawaii, about five hours after the second earthquake struck, it devastated the islands, killing 159 people.

A temporary light was quickly established at Scotch Cap, which was replaced in 1950 by a new reinforced-concrete lighthouse located much higher up the slope—it was hoped far enough from the sea to be beyond the reach of even the most gigantic wave.

IN THE DECADES AFTER the war the Coast Guard built few new lighthouses. One of the last and most unusual was the South Carolina's Charleston Lighthouse, located on Sullivan's Island, on the north side of the entrance to Charleston Harbor. It was a replacement for the Morris Island Lighthouse, which was threatened by erosion, and located just south of the entrance to Charleston Harbor. Built in 1962, during the Kennedy administration, the Charleston Lighthouse is 140 feet tall, has a triangular profile, and is made out of steel and concrete, with an aluminum outer skin. In addition to its nontraditional design, it is also the only lighthouse in the United States with both an elevator and air-conditioning. The lighthouse's carbon arc lamps originally produced a blistering 28 million candlepower, making it one of the brightest lighthouses in the world—so hot that when the light was on, keepers had to put on asbestos welding suits to protect themselves before entering the lantern room. After much complaining from the locals, and continuing concerns about the safety of the keepers, the light's power was reduced to 1.5 million candlepower, which can still be seen twenty-seven miles out to sea.

While the Coast Guard built a few new lighthouses, it decommissioned many more. The spread of radio beacons, as well as shoran (short-range navigation) and loran (long-range navigation) radar systems, which were developed during World War II, spelled the end of an era and made some lighthouses unnecessary, since these new technologies gave vessels a more accurate means of pinpointing their position and finding their way along the coast. Many decommissioned lighthouses were simply demolished, their physical history eradicated rather than preserved. Others were abandoned, and still others were sold to private individuals or transferred to local governments or other federal agencies, such as the National Park Service. And quite a few lighthouses were decommissioned not because they were unneccessary, but rather because they could be easily replaced by less-expensive, easier-to-maintain high-tech buoys or metal poles mounted with a light and, if necessary, a fog signal.

Beyond building new lighthouses and decommissioning old ones, the Coast Guard—bound by financial exigencies—focused most of it energy on automation. In 1946, 468 lighthouses in the United States still had at least one keeper. The Coast Guard had compelling reasons for wanting

Charleston Lighthouse, on Sullivan's Island, in Charleston, South Carolina.

to automate these lighthouses as quickly as possible. The cost savings that resulted from automation were particularly attractive, given budgetary constraints and the need to fund other facets of its mission, including search and rescue, boating safety, and national security. And by eliminating the need for keepers, automation freed up Coast Guard personnel to perform other critical jobs.

Progress was steady up through the mid-1960s, at which point the number of lighthouses with keepers had dwindled to around three hundred. Although this was a significant reduction, the Coast Guard was not happy with the pace of automation. As a result, in 1968 it launched the Lighthouse Automation and Modernization Program (LAMP) to accelerate the process. By 1990 every American lighthouse had been automated, save for the Boston Lighthouse, which was finally automated in 1998.

Automation, during these postwar years, was not without controversy, however. Many people feared that removing the human element would make the lighthouses less effective and dependable. The Coast Guard tried to allay such concerns by pointing out that automation technologies were trustworthy, and redundancies were built in to increase reliability. Precision timers, sensitive fog sensors, light-activated switches, remote-control systems for operation, and automatic bulb changers all ensured consistent performance. For lighthouses off the grid, power was provided by heavy-duty generators with backup units, or state-of-the-art solar-powered systems. And where electricity was available, auxiliary generators were on hand to kick in when the electrical lines failed. The Coast Guard also argued that even if the automated lighthouses were slightly less effective in serving mariners' needs than those manned by keepers, the considerable savings more than justified this very small loss in performance. While automating a station cost roughly $100,000, it resulted in $25,000 worth of savings, enabling the project to be paid off within four years.

Yet another change that came along with automation was the retirement of most of the classic Fresnel lenses. Bulky and expensive to maintain, these marvels of engineering were increasingly replaced with newer optics. One that is widely used today combines tungsten-halogen lamps

A modern optic, the Vega light (VRB-25), at the Rockland Breakwater Lighthouse, in Rockland, Maine.

with acrylic lens panels, which rely on the same prism technology that Fresnel invented, to produce intense beams of light visible over great distances. And many offshore lighthouses now employ solar-powered LED lights, with accompanying acrylic lenses, which are fairly inexpensive, efficient, and require little maintenance. Sadly, some retired Fresnel lenses were discarded and ultimately destroyed. Many others, however, were saved and are now in museums or in storage facilities maintained by the Coast Guard.

As AUTOMATION MOVED AHEAD and the number of keepers dwindled, a shift took place within their ranks, with young Coast Guard personnel replacing civilian keepers who had begun their career with the service. Some Coast Guard keepers were not enamored of the job. When those on duty at the New London Ledge Lighthouse, a stately mansion of a lighthouse perched on a human-made island at the mouth of the Connecticut's Thames River, were interviewed in 1987 about their feelings regarding the posting, their comments were unequivocal. The choicest cuts included:

"This place is worse than a prison"; "I don't ever want to be a lighthouse keeper again"; and "Pardon me, lady, but I [gotta] tell you this place stinks!" There were, however, also Coast Guard keepers who appreciated the work and the venerable history of their predecessors. Such was the case for Tony Tuliano, a Coast Guard fireman apprentice, who was in 1977 stationed at Plum Island Lighthouse, a gray granite, two-story dwelling with a cast-iron tower and lantern room rising from its pitched roof, built in 1869 and located at the tip of Long Island's North Fork. Although initially disappointed with his posting, Tuliano soon changed his mind. "When I had the evening watch," he wrote,

> I would enjoy climbing up to the light tower early and spend time sitting out on the catwalk with my legs hanging over the edge. The solitude and scenic beauty was soothing to the soul. Time seemed to slow down up there. Passing mariners would wave and it was like I could sense them saying "thank you for being there." It was not so much them saying it to me, but to the institution of the manned lighthouse, whose unfailing sole purpose was to guide them safely home. It was times like this that would help me come to realize the true tradition of this lighthouse and the keepers before me.

By 1989 THERE WAS just one civilian keeper left, and that was Frank Schubert, who tended the Coney Island Lighthouse, a sixty-eight-foot-tall cast-iron skeleton tower, with an adjoining seven-room brick keeper's cottage, nestled in the private residential community of Sea Gate, Brooklyn, at the west end of Coney Island. Tall and lean, with the weathered countenance of a man who had spent his much of his life braving the elements on or near the sea, Schubert began his career with the Lighthouse Service more than fifty years earlier, in 1937, serving as a seaman on the lighthouse tender *Tulip*. When the Coast Guard took over, Schubert opted to remain a civilian and was made keeper at the Old Orchard Shoal Lighthouse, a spark-plug-style caisson structure near Staten Island, and then he worked for a while maintaining various navigational aids on Governors Island,

Coney Island Lighthouse, with the keeper's quarters to the right of the tower.

Frank Schubert polishes the fourth-order Fresnel lens at the Coney Island Lighthouse in 1961.

just off the tip of Manhattan, before being drafted into the army in 1942. After the war Schubert worked again at Governors Island, followed by the appointment in 1960 as keeper at Coney Island.

Besides his wife, Marie, and his three children, who were raised in the keeper's cottage, Schubert loved nothing more than tending the lighthouse and being near the ocean's salt spray. So devoted were he and his wife to the keeper's life, that, when interviewed by a reporter in 1986, he confessed that they hadn't gone to see a movie since 1946, and hadn't taken a vacation for twenty years, at which point Marie piped up, gently pointing out that it had actually been twenty-five.

While the Coast Guard automated the lighthouse in 1989, it kept the seventy-three-year-old Schubert on as keeper, even though he was more of a caretaker than a traditional keeper, since the light no longer needed continual tending. Nevertheless Schubert did maintain the property, and every day he would climb the tower's eighty-seven steps to check on the light and fog signal.

Starting in the late 1980s and running until the early twenty-first century, Schubert got plentiful press coverage as the last civilian lighthouse keeper. On the two-hundredth anniversary of the lighthouse system in 1989, he was invited to meet President George H. W. Bush in the Oval Office, commenting later that the president "was nuts about lighthouses." (Bush's reaction is hardly surprising given the many summers he spent at the family compound on Walker's Point, in Kennebunkport, Maine, pursuing his passions for fishing and boating along the area's rugged coastline, so famed for its many picturesque beacons.) But it was Schubert's interview on National Public Radio's *All Things Considered* in February 2002 that made him a national celebrity.

Titled "The Last Lighthouse Keeper," the interview was part of a larger series meant to pay homage to jobs that were on the verge of disappearing. During the interview Schubert said that the Coast Guard kept him around "because of public relations, that's it, because we do get a lot of visitors." But if that was indeed the sole reason, his bosses must have blanched at what he said next: "Visitors, visitors, visitors—it drives me crazy. I've had people . . . want to spend weekends out here. They want to pay me to put them up. They want to spend weekends just hanging around the lighthouse. I don't know why they like lighthouses. When was the last time you were on a lighthouse? To you it's romantic, but when you see it every day, day after day, it's not romantic anymore."

Unfortunately for Schubert, the situation degenerated after his decidedly frank interview. Everyone, it seemed, wanted to talk to him and see him, as if he were a rare exhibit in a zoo. His phone rang incessantly, and hordes of visitors, ranging from documentarians and reporters to lighthouse lovers and the simply curious, came by the lighthouse at all times of day. "My head's going to explode," he told a reporter. "I don't have anything interesting to tell." But in fact Schubert *did* have plenty of stories to tell, including his being credited with rescuing fifteen people over the years.

Despite some crustiness—perhaps brought out late in his life in the wake of all the unwanted attention—Schubert had always been a faithful public servant, and a gracious host to the thousands of schoolkids, lighthouse buffs, and others who visited the lighthouse over the years. And after he died on December 11, 2003, at the age of eighty-eight, in the keeper's quarters he had for so long called home, he was given a fitting tribute by the region's Coast Guard commander: "The Coast Guard mourns the loss of its most courageous sentry of the sea. His devotion to duty and courage are unequaled."

Although Schubert was the last of the civilian keepers with ties to the Lighthouse Service, he was not the country's last keeper. That honor goes to the keeper at the Boston Lighthouse. Federal legislation spearheaded by the late senator Edward Kennedy in 1989 requires the lighthouse to have a keeper to maintain its historic character, and to serve as a living museum that educates the public about the essential role of lighthouses in the nation's development. And to this day, a civilian keeper employed by the Coast Guard performs this important duty.

WHILE AUTOMATION SAVED THE Coast Guard tens of millions of dollars and freed up personnel for other assignments, it also created serious problems for the lighthouses themselves. Without keepers to care for the property on a daily basis, lighthouse buildings, including keeper's quarters, the towers themselves, and associated structures, began inexorably to deteriorate. Peeling paint, loose shingles, rotting wood, cracked masonry, as well as other signs of decay became commonplace. Vandals made their terrible mark too, defacing and stealing property. Although the Coast

Guard periodically serviced automated lighthouses, its main mission was to maintain the navigational aids—the light and the fog signal—not the buildings themselves, though so many were already historic structures. The Coast Guard did its best to reverse the ravages of time, shore up buildings where the need was critical, and deal with damage done by trespassers and thieves, but with limited resources it could do only so much. At decommissioned lighthouses that were abandoned and, therefore, did not benefit from periodic Coast Guard visits, the situation bordered on the catastrophic.

For the nation's coastal sentinels—with their long careers of service—in danger of being allowed to molder and rot away, forgotten, help was soon on the way. Starting in the mid-1960s and continuing up to the present, a great array of nonprofit and government organizations concerned about the fate of lighthouses, and reflecting the growing public fascination with these beacons of American history, have taken action to preserve them. Such groups have become the new keepers or stewards of the lighthouses, their work aimed at ensuring that lighthouses are not only saved from deterioration or destruction but also brought back to life for the benefit of present and future generations.

There is precedent for such action. Prior to the mid-1960s a number of nonprofit or government entities got involved in lighthouse preservation. For example, in 1925 the well-heeled and civic-minded members of the Stonington Historical Society, in Stonington, Connecticut, not far from the Rhode Island border, bought the decommissioned Stonington Harbor Lighthouse from the government, turning it into the Old Lighthouse Museum in 1927. Six years later, in 1933, the National Park Service assumed control of the Old Point Loma Lighthouse, located at the entrance to San Diego Bay, and after refurbishing it, opened it up to visitors. And in 1946 the Fairport Historical Society transformed the Fairport Harbor Lighthouse, in Fairport Harbor, Ohio, on the edge of Lake Erie, into the Fairport Harbor Museum and Lighthouse.

The pace at which lighthouses were saved from ruin for the public benefit increased dramatically in the mid-1960s, spurred on in part by the passage of the National Historic Preservation Act of 1966, which focused attention on the urgent need to preserve America's historically significant sites. Long-neglected lighthouses ranked very high on the list of structures desperately in need of preservation, and most of them were ultimately added to the National Register of Historic Places established by the act.

The Chesapeake Bay Maritime Museum in St. Michaels, Maryland, which showcases the region's rich nautical heritage, was one of the first of the new keepers to step forward. By 1966 many of the Chesapeake's iconic cottage-style, screw-pile lighthouses had already been razed and replaced by simple beacons, often nothing more than a light on a sturdy metal pole. The Hooper Strait Lighthouse was up next on the chopping block when the museum, driven by the desire to preserve an important piece of the bay's history, bought the lighthouse from a demolition contractor for a thousand dollars. The new owners cut the lighthouse in two, put both pieces on a barge, and transported them sixty miles to St. Michaels, where the lighthouse was put back together and set on its new foundation, instantly becoming one of the museum's prime attractions.

Another preservation effort took place at California's East Brother Lighthouse, located on East Brother Island in San Pablo Strait, which

The Old Stone Lighthouse Museum, in Stonington, Connecticut.

Hooper Strait
Lighthouse,
circa 1916.

connects San Francisco Bay to San Pablo Bay. Built in 1874, the light-house consisted of an attractive Victorian-style keeper's quarters and attached tower. The Coast Guard automated the lighthouse in 1969, and had planned to replace it with a steel tower or a simple concrete structure. But the idea of demolishing this magnificent lighthouse was strongly opposed by local citizens and other groups who thought it had too much history and charm to be torn down. Local civic organizations pleaded with the Coast Guard to reconsider its decision, which it did, expressing its willingness to donate or lease the island and the lighthouse to a gov-ernment agency that would preserve it as a historic landmark.

Bolstering the case for preservation, the Contra Costa Shoreline Parks Committee succeeded in having the lighthouse placed on the National Register of Historic Places in 1971. But although numerous agencies expressed interest in taking on the project, they all found the costs prohibitive. As the years dragged on, the lighthouse buildings, rav-aged by the weather and vandalism, continued to decay, and the only regular visitors were the Coast Guard personnel who maintained the light and fog signal.

East Brother Lighthouse, now serving as a Victorian bed-and-breakfast.

Finally in 1979, a group of local residents formed East Brother Light Station, Inc., a nonprofit whose sole goal was to restore the lighthouse and make it accessible to the public. The Coast Guard granted the group a twenty-year, no-fee renewable lease, and it immediately began fixing up the island and transforming the lighthouse into a deluxe bed and breakfast, the profits from which were to be used to cover the costs of restoration and upkeep. With the help of a major federal grant and significant individual, business, and local government support, as well as the sweat equity of more than three hundred hardworking volunteers, the restoration was completed within a year, and in November 1980 the lighthouse bed-and-breakfast welcomed its first paying guests.

The outside of the lighthouse is painted as it would have appeared in 1874, and the inside reflects the layout as it was in the early twentieth century. Guests have the option of choosing among five rooms, some costing more than four hundred dollars a night. In return they get the incomparable experience of staying in an exquisitely appointed and historically important lighthouse, and are also are provided with a boat ride to and from the island, complimentary champagne, a full breakfast, a four-course dinner, and best of all, a lighthouse tour.

———

ABOUT THE SAME TIME that East Brother Lighthouse was being rescued, another group of people across the country banded together to save
their treasured icon—the Fire Island Lighthouse, a magnificent 168-foot-
tall tower, painted with alternating black and white bands, located just to
the south of mainland Long Island on a long, thin barrier island comprising ever-shifting sand dunes, beaches, and scrub woodlands. The Coast
Guard decommissioned the lighthouse in 1973, replacing it with a small
strobe light placed on a water tower in nearby Robert Moses State Park.
When word got out that the Coast Guard was thinking of demolishing the
lighthouse, Thomas Roberts III, a prominent banker who had grown up
and lived across from Fire Island, in Bayshore, sprang into action. Unable
to bear the thought of losing such and important piece of Long Island's
history, in 1979 he founded the Fire Island Lighthouse Preservation Society, whose goal was to save the lighthouse from destruction and return it
to its former glory. Since the lighthouse lay within the boundaries of the
Fire Island National Seashore, the society worked with the Coast Guard to
transfer ownership of the lighthouse to the National Park Service, which
was done in 1981. But with the National Park Service's budget as tight as
the Coast Guard's, it could not fund the necessary repairs to the tower,
which had deteriorated considerably during nearly a decade of neglect.

In 1982 the society launched a major fund-raising drive to restore the
lighthouse. They sponsored black-tie dinners, runs, clambakes, and con-
certs. A single cocktail party raised thirteen thousand dollars. Children
scoured area beaches for redeemable aluminum cans, generating $186 for
the cause. The Seventh Avenue fashion designer Liz Claiborne, and her
husband and business partner, Arthur Ortenberg, who summered near
the lighthouse, encouraged—and then matched—corporate donations.
In a few years the society raised more than $1.3 million from thousands of
contributors, and in another positive sign, the lighthouse was placed on
the National Register of Historic Places in 1984.

The grand moment for the society came on the night of May 28, 1986,
when thousands of spectators, as if attending a swank gala, only on a

The Fire Island Lighthouse, showing the lens room in the foreground
and the tower and keeper's quarters behind.

sandbar and nearby boats, watched the Coast Guard relight the fully restored tower, once again making it an official aid to navigation. For the next ten years the National Park Service ran the visitor center and conducted tours of the keeper's quarters and the lighthouse, with continued financial support from the society. In 1996 sole responsibility for operating the site was transferred to the society, and a decade later the society also assumed the task of maintaining the beacon, which is now a private aid to navigation.

Today the society keeps the lighthouse open year-round and relies on two paid staff members and 120 enthusiastic volunteers to guide and delight the roughly 110,000 annual visitors. One of the highlights of the tour is the lighthouse's original first-order Fresnel lens, which the society, with the cooperation of the Coast Guard and National Park Service, was able to retrieve from the Franklin Institute in Philadelphia, where it had been displayed for many years. The lens sits in its own building, which of course was built by the society, with the help of hundreds of thousands of dollars' worth of donated materials and labor, as well as funding from New York State and the society.

FARTHER UP THE EAST coast, in Newport, Rhode Island, the fabled summer resort and home to many Gilded Age mansions, such as Cornelius Vanderbilt's The Breakers, the Rose Island Lighthouse Foundation pursued a slightly different approach to preservation. The Coast Guard decommissioned the circa-1870 lighthouse in 1970, right after the Newport Bridge, which spans the east passage of Narragansett Bay, was completed, since the bridge's bright lights rendered the lighthouse unnecessary. The lighthouse thus sat abandoned for fourteen years and was routinely vandalized, which took a ruinous toll on the historic edifice with its mansard roof and octagonal lighthouse tower rising from one end. In 1984 a group of concerned citizens formed the Rose Island Lighthouse Foundation, determined to restore and maintain the lighthouse. When the federal government transferred the dilapidated lighthouse to Newport at no cost the following year, the foundation, with the city's blessing, got to work.

Over the next eight years, with the support of grants and the labor of numerous volunteers, the lighthouse was handsomely restored to reflect its turn-of-the-century 1912 appearance. The total cost of the res-

Rose Island Lighthouse.

toration, including in-kind contributions, was roughly $1.2 million and on August 7, 1993, the lighthouse was relighted as a private aid to navigation. For a while, the foundation relied on volunteer resident keepers to operate the lighthouse and welcome visitors, but then it came up with a creative alternative management plan. It began renting rooms in the lighthouse to people who wanted to be keepers for a night or a week, thereby creating what is called a "keeper-vacation" experience. The keepers not only pay for the privilege of being keeper, they also spend at least one hour a day doing the keeper's chores, including monitoring marine weather forecasts, greeting visitors, and performing special projects. The program is immensely successful, contributing significantly to covering lighthouse costs.

EFFORTS TO PRESERVE LIGHTHOUSES received a big boost in extreme northern climes from the Maine Lights Program. Established by federal legislation in 1996, this innovative program resulted in the no-cost transfer of ownership of twenty-eight Maine light stations—the buildings and land associated with the lighthouses—from the Coast Guard to governmental and nonprofit entities. The new owners, in turn, are required to preserve the light stations and ensure public access, while the Coast Guard is responsible for maintaining the lights and fog signals at those stations that remain active aids to navigation.

It may seem anachronistic that any lighthouses need to remain active given the widespread use of GPS and radar, which can determine a vessel's position with astonishing accuracy. But many mariners, especially local commercial and recreational boaters, still rely on lighthouses for guidance. High-tech navigational equipment notwithstanding, lighthouses provide a helpful and familiar, if redundant, means of determining one's location. And if the equipment fails, it's reassuring to know that lighthouses are still there.

In 1998, while thanking Maine's then-senator Olympia Snowe for her efforts to pass the Maine Lights legislation, the former commandant of the Coast Guard, Adm. James M. Loy, captured the essence of why this

*Marshall Point Lighthouse, in Port Clyde, Maine. This scene will be familiar
to viewers of* Forrest Gump. *In the movie Tom Hanks, as the protagonist, runs
up and down this ramp as part of his cross-country marathon.
The lighthouse was the eastern terminus of Gump's run.*

program was so important. "You solved a problem for the Coast Guard
and for Maine," he said. "We have a commitment to keep the lights burning as long as mariners need them. But the austerity of our budget does
not allow us to make a commitment to the preservation of historic structures at a time that we're running a fleet of ships whose own antiquity
rivals that of some of these lighthouses."

THE MAINE LIGHTS PROGRAM helped inspire the passage of the
National Historic Lighthouse Preservation Act of 2000 (NHLPA), which
in large part did for the country as a whole what the Maine Lights Program
had done for the Pine Tree State. Under the NHLPA, light stations that the
Coast Guard determines are no longer necessary to accomplish its mission
are made available for transfer at no cost to federal agencies, state and local

governments, and nonprofit organizations.* A number of restrictions are placed on such transfers, however. Only light stations on the National Register of Historic Places or those eligible for listing can be considered for transfer. Before a government entity or nonprofit organization is chosen to receive a light station, it must have an approved plan in place that ensures it will preserve the property's historic features and also make the station available to the public at reasonable times. And if the light station is to remain an active aid to navigation, the Coast Guard is guaranteed access to the station to perform necessary maintenance.

Once the Coast Guard identifies a list of eligible light stations, it passes it on to the General Services Administration (GSA), the federal government's real-estate arm. The GSA then advertises the availability of the stations to the public, and conducts tours for interested parties. The National Park Service evaluates applications, and the GSA transfers ownership of the light stations to the approved new keepers. In the event that there are no applicants, or if all the applications are deemed unsuitable, the light stations are sold through an online public auction to the highest bidder, with the proceeds going to the Coast Guard to support its lighthouse-related work. Private buyers of light stations are also required to preserve the property's historic features and allow the Coast Guard access if the lighthouse is still active.

As of 2015 the NHLPA has resulted in seventy-three lighthouse transfers to government or nonprofit keepers. Most of these transfers were to organizations that were already involved in preservation efforts. For example, Georgia's Tybee Island Lighthouse and Museum had been managing the lighthouse under a lease from the Coast Guard for well over a decade when it was awarded ownership of the lighthouse in 2002. At the same time the NHLPA has led to the sale of forty-one lighthouses to the public via auctions, which have netted more than four million dollars. With prices varying widely, the least expensive sale thus far is the

---

*Although other federal agencies, such as the National Park Service and the Bureau of Land Management, own lighthouses and can participate in the NHLPA, the Coast Guard owns the vast majority of the eligible lighthouses, and it is those that form the bulk of the transfers.

Cleveland Harbor East Breakwater Lighthouse, on Lake Erie, which was sold for $10,000. The Graves Lighthouse, at the mouth of Boston Harbor, is at the other extreme, garnering an impressive $933,888.

But the actual price paid is only the beginning of the cost of owning a lighthouse. Many of these properties have been abandoned for years, requiring a huge investment of time and money to refurbish them. The work, which can run into the hundreds of thousands, if not millions, of dollars, may include everything from installing plumbing and heating to scraping off thick layers of rust, repairing floors, and repainting. As one architect who has restored lighthouses observed, "It's said you can't build a submarine with bake sales—well, you can't restore a lighthouse with bake sales, either."

Even beyond the financial concerns, owning a lighthouse is not for the faint of heart. Most of those sold to date are offshore spark-plug lighthouses or are on small islands; others are located at the end of rocky piers. Access often requires a boat, and getting on and off the boat and into the lighthouse can be quite a tricky feat. In some cases there is no dock, necessitating a precarious climb up a ladder (at the Graves Lighthouse the ladder is a hair-raising forty feet long). Once in the lighthouse, the adventures often continue, especially when a punishing storm rolls in, offering a thrilling if not outright terrifying experience. And at lighthouses with active fog signals, the owners must contend with them blaring away when visibility drops.

MANY OWNERS TRANSFORM THEIR lighthouse into a private getaway. That is what the Billingsley and Gonsoulin families did with the Middle Ground Lighthouse, a fifty-six-foot-tall spark-plug lighthouse built in 1891, which peaks above the water in Hampton Roads, just offshore from Newport News, Virginia. They purchased the lighthouse in 2006 for $31,000, and then worked for five summers renovating it with the help of friends and family. Now the owners spend long weekends at the place, often with guests, savoring the spectacular 360-degree view, which Dan Billingsley says is "like nothing else in the world."

The Graves Lighthouse, circa 1956.

Lynn and Dave Waller were also looking for an escape when, in 2013, they bought the 113-foot-tall Graves Lighthouse, a conical granite tower topped with a bronze-and-glass lantern room, which bears a strong resemblance to the Minot's Ledge Lighthouse a bit farther down the Massachusetts coast. Dave, who owns a special-effects company, and Lynn, a graphic designer, are used to fixer-uppers, having purchased a rundown firehouse in Malden, Massachusetts, which they lovingly restored and now serves as their home. When Waller first heard that the lighthouse was for sale he remembers thinking it "an enormously cool thing and also a fun challenge." Since becoming the owners, he says, he and his wife feel like "we are on a journey, but are not exactly sure where we're going." They have done their research, hired contractors, and renovations are ongoing. While they plan to use the lighthouse as a vacation home, inviting friends and family, they are also thinking of other creative uses, one of which has already borne fruit. In August 2014 they auctioned a weekend at the lighthouse as a fund-raiser for a local school some of their children attended, generating a whopping $8,500. The Wallers envision doing similar fund-raisers, and are also exploring the possibility of involving local groups in weather-, science-, and marine-related projects that center around the lighthouse. Opening the lighthouse to the public on certain days or making it available for overnight stays is also under consideration.

Other buyers, true to the American entrepreneurial tradition, are looking primarily for an investment. Nick Korstad, who admits that he has "always been obsessed" with lighthouses, and jokes that in a past life he might have been a keeper, purchased the Borden Flats Lighthouse, a spark-plug structure at the mouth of the Taunton River in Massachusetts, in 2010 for $56,000. After two years of hard work Korstad opened the lighthouse for overnight stays. It operates like a bed-and-breakfast without the breakfast part—guests have to bring their own food. Enamored of his current job, Korstad avers that "there is nothing else I would rather do," and he is hoping to purchase other lighthouses to add to his collection of lighthouse inns.

Some preservationist purists still balk at the notion of selling Ameri-

Sleeping quarters in the Borden Flats Lighthouse.

ca's historic lighthouses to private individuals, fearing that they will not be properly restored and maintained. But such sales nonetheless serve a very valuable purpose. As Bob Trapani, the executive director of the nonprofit American Lighthouse Foundation, points out, "Nonprofit groups and government agencies cannot possibly care for all the lighthouses out there, so the private sector has become our last line of defense. Without it, who knows what would happen to these historic structures?" And thus far, in fact, private owners have proved themselves to be good stewards. When they buy a lighthouse, the deed includes preservation requirements to which they must adhere, and if the owners fail to meet them, the government can take the lighthouse back. To date there has been no need to activate this reversionary clause because the owners have been committed to the proper preservation of their lighthouses. One such owner is Pete Jurewicz, who bought the Thimble Shoal Lighthouse, off Hampton, Virginia, in 2005 for $65,000. "It burns me up," Jurewicz said, "when people say that these lights are going into private hands and being lost. They're not being lost, they're just being put into the hands of somebody that's going to take care of them." In a 2013 article in the *Wall Street Journal* on individual ownership of lighthouses, the reporter commented, "One part unique retreat, one part folly, the private lighthouse may be the ultimate status symbol for those in search of a great place on the water." While a certain cachet undeniably comes with owning a lighthouse, the broader public is fortunate that so far the owners of private lighthouses have much loftier goals than mere status on their minds.

The Coast Guard hopes to make many more lighthouses available through the NHLPA in the coming years. Although there is no way of knowing what will happen to these lighthouses, if past is prologue, there is good reason to believe that many of them will be cared for by responsible public and private stewards. For some lighthouses, however, the future is bleak. Since 1993 *Lighthouse Digest* has maintained a "Doomsday List" of lighthouses that are in danger of being lost forever. Some are so decrepit that it is not feasible to restore them, and others are so remote that there is little interest in doing so. And while still others can

City seal for Fernandina Beach, Florida, with an image of the Amelia Island Lighthouse at its center. Many cities and towns incorporate a local lighthouse into their official seals.

be saved, their rescue would require a substantial infusion of cash. The Coast Guard owns most of these lighthouses, and when they are offered through the NHLPA, it is likely that many of them will find no takers, thereby leaving them to an uncertain fate. Ultimately most, if not all of these orphaned lighthouses will, indeed, be lost forever. Even those that are successfully matched with public and private stewards are not guaranteed a bright future. While many organizations and individuals have found creative ways to raise the necessary funds to operate and maintain lighthouses, there will be those who fall short of their goals, despite the best of intentions.

NEGLECT AND DECAY ARE not the only forces threatening to destroy lighthouses. The wind and the waves also conspire to pose a significant risk. Coastal erosion is an irresistible and awesome force of nature that has caused more than a few lighthouses to tumble into the surf, the most famous example being Delaware's Cape Henlopen Lighthouse, which finally toppled in the spring of 1926, after battling nearly 140 years of shifting sands and encroachment by the ocean. Some lighthouses threatened by erosion, however, have not succumbed to this fate but instead have been moved out of harm's way. Such was the case for Block Island's Southeast Lighthouse and the Highland Lighthouse in Truro, Massachusetts, both of which were relocated in the 1990s, well back from the fast-eroding sand cliffs that were threatening to send them plummeting into the sea.

The most challenging move of all involved the Cape Hatteras Light-house, a National Historic Landmark operated and maintained by the National Park Service as part of the Cape Hatteras National Seashore. When the third Cape Hatteras Lighthouse was completed in 1870, it stood fifteen hundred feet from the high-tide mark. But every year there-after the ocean crept closer to the lighthouse, to the point that by 1919 there was only a three-hundred-foot buffer between it and the waves. In subsequent decades many strategies were employed to keep the ocean at bay, including planting grasses and shrubs, replenishing the beach, and building artificial dunes and groins, structures designed to trap sand as it moves down the shoreline. Although there were periods when the erosion slowed, and even years when the beach in front of the lighthouse grew considerably wider, by the early 1980s the situation was dire, the water having closed to within fifty to seventy feet of the tower. As debate heated up over whether or not to take action to save the lighthouse, addi-tional erosion control measures were employed, such as piling up sand-bags and improving the groin nearest to the tower. Finally, in 1989, the

Cape Henlopen Lighthouse, its foundation undermined by erosion, is on the verge of falling over in 1925.

The Cape Hatteras Lighthouse in mid-move.

National Park Service decided to move the lighthouse, but it would be another ten years—and many studies, debates, and appropriations battles later—before the move commenced.

The twelve-million-dollar project began on June 17, 1999, and concluded less than a month later, during which time the nearly five-thousand-ton lighthouse was transported more than half a mile, in increments of between 10 and 355 feet per day, to a site roughly 1,500 feet from the ocean's edge—the very same distance that the 1870 tower was from the ocean when it was built. This technically complex process, which was witnessed by throngs of people who gathered to watch the spectacle, required constructing a steel support platform for the lighthouse, and then employing heavy-duty hydraulic jacks to lift the lighthouse and move it on rollers over a track made of steel beams. Numerous sensors were placed throughout the tower to ensure that it remained level throughout the move, and to alert the work crews to any unusual stresses and strains.

The lead contractor on the project was International Chimney Corporation, out of Williamsville, New York, and their main partner in this endeavor was Expert House Movers, based in Sharptown, Maryland.

These two companies have developed a sterling track record for moves of this type, having successfully relocated six lighthouses since 1992, the most recent of which involved the Gay Head Lighthouse on Martha's Vineyard, which was transported a little more than 130 feet back from the crumbling cliffs of Gay Head. But the Cape Hatteras project stands out from the rest, as it is the tallest masonry structure ever moved, and it earned the Opal Award for Outstanding Civil Engineering Achievement, presented by the American Society of Civil Engineers in 2000. Although erosion continues to eat away at Cape Hatteras, in its new location the lighthouse should be safe from being swallowed up by the ocean until the end of this century.

Erosion will continue to undermine lighthouses, and there will no doubt be a need for other dramatic moves. It is also likely that the considerable costs involved will force people to abandon some lighthouses as lost causes, in effect, giving in to the elements. But whatever happens, one thing is certain. Global climate change, and the resulting rise in sea level, will place our most vulnerable lighthouses, the ones closest to the ocean's edge, increasingly in peril.

THOUGH WE WILL NEVER return to a time when new lighthouses will be built, there is an inherent drama in the ongoing story of America's lighthouses, which all Americans can experience. Of the nearly seven hundred lighthouses still standing in the United States, around half of them are owned and/or operated by nonprofit groups or government agencies, and are open to the public in one form or another. The public has access to a small number of privately owned lighthouses as well. Quite a few lighthouses have small exhibits, and in some cases, sizable museums that document the lighthouse's unique history, and display lighthouse-related objects, sometimes including a Fresnel lens. Organizations in a number of states sponsor "Lighthouse Challenges" once a year, giving people the opportunity over a weekend to visit area lighthouses, the goal being to make it to as many of them as possible in the time allotted. And there is a growing number of lighthouse festivals around the nation, where people can spend days celebrating and learning about the lighthouse while listening to great music, eating regional food, and perusing the offerings of local craftspeople.

Each year millions of people visit America's lighthouses to take in their beauty, learn about their often romantic and always fascinating history, and marvel at their design and construction. Some even come for the ghosts. It seems that nearly every lighthouse has a ghost, or more than one, who makes appearances from time to time, according to those who believe in such apparitions. One of the earliest ghost sightings occurred at the Concord Point Lighthouse, in Havre de Grace, Maryland. A newspaper article from 1889 tells of the keeper having seen "the head, of a man, devil, woman, or whatever," with eyes as "big as those of a cow," and sparkling "just like two big diamonds." The ghost would rest "against the wire frame around the lantern," and whenever it appeared it left behind a wonderful smell, that filled the lantern room "with a perfume like a flower garden." Many lighthouse ghosts are purported to be former keepers, invariably involved in some nefarious, melancholy, or gruesome incident that becomes part of their enduring story. St. Simons Lighthouse, a 104-foot brick tower with a handsome adjoining Victorian-style keeper's house, located on St. Simons Island, Georgia, provides an excellent example of this. In 1880 assistant keeper John Stephens shot and killed head keeper Frederick Osborne after the two had become embroiled in a heated argument. What precipitated the dispute is not known, but Stephens was ultimately acquitted of murder. Not long after the event, stories began circulating of Osborne haunting the lighthouse, still performing his keeper's duties, and occasionally being seen in the lantern room or being heard, his footfalls on the spiral stairs echoing through the tower.

Those who want to dig a little deeper into lighthouse history have a number of options. A visit to the Maine Lighthouse Museum in Rockland, Maine, places one in the midst of the single largest collection of lighthouse artifacts and Fresnel lenses in the nation. The recently opened National Lighthouse Museum, located in the old U.S. Lighthouse Bureau's main depot station, on Staten Island, New York, has ambitious expansion plans that will transform it into the country's largest and most comprehensive lighthouse museum, its goal being not only to educate people about the critical role of lighthouses in shaping America's history, but also to get them excited about visiting lighthouses nationwide. And many other museums around the country, especially those that focus on maritime history, have wonderful lighthouse exhibits, often with one or more glistening Fresnel lenses serving as the star attraction.

Beyond visiting lighthouses and lighthouse museums, people in search of lighthouse history and lore have a wide array of popular books to choose from, most of which focus on a particular region or a single lighthouse. There are also two exceptional magazines that produce a remarkable range of articles, covering lighthouses from almost every angle imaginable. One is the *Keeper's Log*, a quarterly that has been published by the U.S. Lighthouse Society since 1984. The other is *Lighthouse Digest*, a bimonthly that originated in 1992. And if one's goal is greater involvement in the world of lighthouses, there is a host of national, regional, and local lighthouse organizations to join.

FOR THREE CENTURIES LIGHTHOUSES have illuminated America's shores. They, and their dependable keepers, have performed spectacularly well, protecting mariners as well as the passengers and cargoes traveling on their ships. The success and growth of the American economy could not have been achieved without the help of these brilliant beacons. It seems only appropriate, therefore, that after all those years of valuable service directed at saving others, lighthouses themselves are now being saved in increasing numbers so that they will endure as monuments to America's great maritime tradition, delighting us not only with their breathtaking beauty but with the instantaneous sense of history they convey. It is equally fitting that so many Americans have fallen in love with lighthouses. They truly are national treasures worthy of awe and admiration.

EPILOGUE

. . . .

*Boston Lighthouse in 2015, after extensive renovations and repairs
in advance of the lighthouse's tricentennial celebration in 2016.*

ON ONE OF THOSE QUINTESSENTIALLY HOT BUT EVER SO BREEZY
days in early July, I decided to take a break from my research and go on
a brief journey through America's lighthouse history. Early that morning I drove from my house in Marblehead to Boston to visit the Boston
Lighthouse, where that history dramatically begins. But first I had to get
there. I bought a ticket to take the boat tour to Little Brewster Island,

which is one of thirty-four islands that form the Boston Harbor Islands National Recreation Area, managed by the National Park Service.*

During the forty-five-minute trip to the island, a National Park Service ranger regaled the passengers, most decked in shorts and sun visors, with captivating stories about the harbor's history, heavy emphasis being placed on the harbor's polluted past and the multibillion-dollar cleanup effort that brought it back to life. Toward the end of our short voyage, the Boston Lighthouse, a bright white sentinel standing watch over the harbor's mouth, loomed ever larger, until it dominated the scene and commanded the attention of all on board.

The boat docked, we got off, and were warmly welcomed by a woman wearing a long dress and a bonnet, such as would have been worn by the keeper's wife in 1783, when the current lighthouse was built. This vision from the past was Dr. Sally Snowman, a historian and Coast Guard auxiliarist, who has been the lighthouse's keeper since 2003. She presented a fascinating introduction to the island and the lighthouse's history, and then sent us on our way to explore.

I immediately walked to the lighthouse tower, eagerly anticipating the climb to the lantern room, which houses a second-order Fresnel lens. Along the way a jumble of complicated thoughts and images flooded into my mind. I wondered what George Worthylake, the first keeper, looked like, and how indescribably stricken his daughter Ann must have been when she saw her father drown on that chilly November day in 1718. Aware of our Revolutionary history, I tried to envision Maj. Benjamin Tupper leading three hundred patriots on their daring raid on the lighthouse in the summer of 1775, getting the best of the inebriated British marines who boasted that they would have no trouble defending the lighthouse against an even larger force. And I thought about the fury that Bostonians must have felt in the spring of 1776 upon learning that the

*The Boston Light tours are a collaborative effort between National Park Service, the Coast Guard, Boston Harbor Island Alliance, University of Massachusetts Boston, and the Friends of the Boston Harbor Islands.

British fleet had blown up their lighthouse before retreating north to the Tory-favorable community in Halifax, Nova Scotia.

The lantern room did not disappoint. The eleven-foot-tall two-ton lens, with its 336 glistening prisms and twelve bull's-eyes, was dazzling, spectacularly gorgeous. I marveled at Fresnel's genius and reflected on how his invention revolutionized lighthouse illumination. Through the lantern room's glass panes, I could see the harbor's entrance and the Atlantic beyond. I could only imagine how many millions of mariners had sailed or motored into the harbor over the years, heaving a sigh of relief when they saw the lighthouse's gleam or heard the fog signal blaring in the distance.

After exiting the tower, I wandered the grounds, looking at the cannon that served as the country's first fog signal, as well as the keeper's quarters. Given my background in marine biology, I could not resist a trip to the edge of the island, where I found a few tide pools teeming with life. With time for the tour over, I boarded the boat for the return trip to Boston, and the next stage in my journey, which took me back to Marblehead and the stately colonial house where Elbridge Gerry was born.

In the summer of 1789, when the inaugural federal Congress met in New York City, it was Gerry who introduced the first draft of the bill that would ultimately result in the federal government's taking control of the nation's lighthouses. Standing in front of his family's house, I felt a twinge of pride knowing that a longtime resident of the town I call home played such a seminal role in the history I was writing about.

My next and final stop was just a short drive away, at the tip of a rocky peninsula called Marblehead Neck, where the Marblehead Lighthouse stands on a promontory next to the entrance to the town's deep and inviting harbor. There, instead of admiring the lighthouse, I tried to conjure a ghost. The current lighthouse is the second one built on this spot, but I was thinking about the first, finished in 1835 after the citizens of Marblehead had pleaded with the government to build a beacon on this rocky headland to make their "good harbor . . . easy of access to the care and weather beaten mariner."

The original lighthouse consisted of a modest two-story keeper's

Marblehead Lighthouse,
in Marblehead,
Massachusetts,
circa 1890s.

dwelling and a detached masonry tower that was only twenty-three feet tall, but because of the headland's elevation, the top of the tower soared nearly sixty feet above mean high water. Ezekiel Darling, the first keeper, enjoyed some local renown, starting with his role as one of the gunners on the USS *Constitution* during the War of 1812.

Darling, a relatively short, wiry man, served as keeper until 1860, when he was about seventy years old and nearly blind. Like so many other keepers, he is credited with multiple rescues, the most famous being the time that he and four other "gallant Marblehead men"—as a contemporary newspaper account called them—"put off in a tremendous sea, and brought ashore the officers and crew of the brig *John Hancock*, which was dashed to pieces on Tinker's Island in a violent easterly storm, when the snow drifted eight to ten feet deep."

Darling's replacement was Jane C. Martin, who had learned her lighthouse-tending skills assisting her father, the keeper at Baker's Island Lighthouse in the neighboring town of Salem. Martin's tenure lasted but three years, and soon after she left, the Neck—long thinly settled and used primarily for farming, pasturage, and as a place to dry fish—began changing in ways that would greatly affect the lighthouse's future. Starting in the late 1860s and accelerating thereafter, wealthy people from Boston and other nearby places began building large summer homes in the area.

By the early 1880s the conspicuously large and often lavish new homes were already overshadowing the diminutive lighthouse. Local mariners complained vociferously that they could no longer see the light on their approach to the harbor. To remedy this problem, in 1883 the Lighthouse Board erected a tall mast next to the lighthouse, which exhibited a lantern that was hoisted into position each night by means of a rope. This temporary beacon served for a decade before the board decided to replace it with something much more effective and substantial. At first the board thought of building a 100-foot-tall brick lighthouse, but instead opted for economy, ordering the construction of a much cheaper, 105-foot-tall cast-iron skeleton tower, which was first lit in 1896.

Present-day Marblehead Lighthouse.

That lighthouse was the one that stood before me now, in the midst of one of Marblehead's beautiful parks. The tower is painted a dull brown, while the lantern room and surrounding gallery are black. The lighthouse was automated in 1960, when its sixth-order Fresnel lens was replaced with a modern optic, which emits a fixed green light. The lighthouse is still active, and the Coast Guard maintains the light while the town of Marblehead maintains the tower itself.

With this visit to Marblehead Neck, I had come to the end of my daylong journey. It had taken me from the colonial origins of America's lighthouse history up through the present. And as I sat on one of the park benches and gazed up at the tower, I pondered the profoundly consequential role that this local lighthouse—and all the others ever built in America—played in the nation's development. They quite literally lit the way for the United States.

ACKNOWLEDGMENTS

. . . .

Wʜɪʟᴇ ᴡʀɪᴛɪɴɢ ɪs ᴀ sᴏʟɪᴛᴀʀʏ ᴘʀᴏᴄᴇss, ʏᴏᴜ ᴄᴀɴ'ᴛ ᴡʀɪᴛᴇ ᴀ book without a lot of help. Most of all I would like to thank Bill Rusin and Bob Weil, the sales director at W. W. Norton, and the editor in chief at Liveright, respectively, for suggesting I write a history of America's lighthouses. It was a great idea, and I thoroughly enjoyed researching and writing the book. Once I handed in the manuscript, Bob and his assistant editor, Will Menaker, did an excellent job editing, giving me valuable direction. With her "lapidary" cursor, my copy editor, Sue Llewellyn, also contributed significantly to the quality of the prose, and her sense of humor was much appreciated. Bob's, Will's, and Sue's dedication to their craft made me a better writer.

All of my books with Norton have been beautifully designed, a feast for the eyes. *Brilliant Beacons* continues this trend, due to the careful attention and creative touch of Anna Oler, Liveright's production direc-tor. Don Rifkin, associate managing editor at Norton/Liveright, was his usual tireless and keen-eyed self, repeatedly checking the text and layout for errors and inconsistencies. Kudos for the dramatic cover, which cap-tures the elemental majesty of lighthouses, goes to Steve Attardo, the art director at Liveright. Without dedicated people working to promote a new title to bookstores, online sellers, and potential readers, an author's work would fail to find a good audience, and for such promotion I am heavily indebted to Deirdre Dolan, assistant sales director at Norton; Peter Miller, director of publicity at Liveright; Cordelia Calvert, Peter's assistant; and Phil Marino, who handles social media. And an author couldn't ask for a more enthusiastic booster than Bill Rusin, who mightily supported the book from its inception, and made sure that it had an excellent launch at publication.

My agent, Russ Galen, as always, provided encouragement, sage advice, and perspective. I couldn't imagine having a better partner in the writing business, and I am extremely grateful that he agreed to be my agent more than a decade ago. This is our fourth book together, and I hope there are many more.

Early reviewers of the manuscript include Jeremy D'Entremont, Sarah Gleason, Tim Harrison, Theresa Levitt, and Bruce Roberts. Their comments were invaluable, but of course any errors in the book are solely my responsibility. Jeremy deserves an additional thank-you for taking me on my first few lighthouse tours, and for being gracious enough to answer the many e-mail queries I sent, asking him for additional information.

Many dedicated individuals who love lighthouses have written wonderful books and articles on these iconic structures. Without their work I couldn't have written this book, and my debt to them is reflected in the notes.

Other people whom I would like to thank include Kevin Abbing, John Babin, Charlene Bangs Bickford, Dolly Bicknell, Al Bina, Dot Black, Michael Blanchette, Lawrence H. Bradner, Tiffany Brevard, Robert Browning, Craig Bruce, Ken Carlson, Marion Chandler, James W. Claflin, Sandra MacLean Clunies, Lorna Condon, Tony Connors, Alfred J. Delaposta, Linda C. Dianto, Mike DiRenzo, Bill Dulmaine, Jeanne Gamble, Joanie Gearin, Tom Gill, Christopher Havern, Selden B. Hill, Al Hitchcock, Thomas Hoffman, Cathy Horridge, Joe Jakubik, Sarah Jones, Varoujan Karentz, Andrew Knight, Nick Korstad, Jami Lanier, Robert LaRosa, Mary E. Linne, Bert Lippincott, Valerie Lutz, Ronald Marcus, Gerry McChesney, Mark C. Mollan, Jane Porter Molloy, Art Noble, Edward Nunez, Lori Osborne, Henry Osmers, Jim Patterson, Peter E. Randall, Todd Reed, Clara Scarborough, Steve Schiffer, Doug Smith, Patrick Scalfani, Annie Schmidt, Scott Schubert, Alisa Scott, Ellen Schockro, Sally Snowman, Patti Stanton, Jeff Stephens, Brian Tague, Albert E. Theberge, Marie Thomas, Jr., Ashley Trujillo, Hilary Wall, Dave Waller, Tom Warren, Elizabeth Wood, and Jamie Wyeth.

The librarians at both the Abbot Public Library, in my hometown, and Harvard's Widener Library were also very helpful, as were the staff at the National Archives in Washington, DC; College Park, Maryland; and Waltham, Massachusetts.

I am most grateful for the support of my family. My parents, Stan and Ruth Dolin, and my sister, Penny, were always there for me when I wanted to talk, and my father and sister were also early reviewers of the manuscript. My in-laws, George and Ruth Rooks, to whom this book is dedicated, have been equally supportive, and Ruth's comments on the manuscript were quite helpful. My children, Lily and Harry, encouraged me throughout the writing process, asking how my book was going and when I was going to be done! Lily's beautiful painting of a lighthouse, which appears in the color insert, hung in my office while I worked, and looking at it not only brought a smile to my face, but it also spurred me on.

Of all the people who helped me along the way, none was more important than my wife, Jennifer. She was my first reviewer, and in so many ways, she makes everything I do possible. Without her, my best friend, I simply couldn't have written this book.

LIGHTHOUSE
ORGANIZATIONS

. . . .

IN ADDITION TO NAMES AND ADDRESSES, THIS LIST INCLUDES an excerpt from the organization's bio or mission statement, and its website, if available.*

ALABAMA LIGHTHOUSE ASSOCIATION

The mission of the Alabama Lighthouse Association is the historic preservation of lighthouses in Alabama.

P.O. Box 250
Mobile, AL 36601
alabamalighthouses.com

AMERICAN LIGHTHOUSE COUNCIL

The American Lighthouse Council is a nonprofit corporation composed of a consortium of lighthouse organizations, stewards, and other practitioners dedicated to the preservation, restoration, and interpretation of American lighthouses.

americanlighthousecouncil.org

AMERICAN LIGHTHOUSE FOUNDATION

The mission of the American Lighthouse Foundation is to save and preserve our nation's historic light stations and their rich heritage. This will be accomplished through the restoration, promotion, and adaptive reuse

* This list does not claim to be comprehensive.

of America's historic light stations, as well as educational initiatives that foster the sustainable preservation of lighthouses and perpetuate the legacy of the men and women who have tended them.

Owls Head Light Station
186 Lighthouse Road
Owls Head, ME 04854
(207) 594-4174
lighthousefoundation.org

The American Lighthouse Foundation chapters include:

AVERY POINT LIGHTHOUSE SOCIETY

P.O. Box 1552
Groton, CT 06340
averypointlight.com

CAPE COD CHAPTER

P.O. Box 565
Rockland, ME 04841
855-722-3959
racepointlighthouse.org

FRIENDS OF LITTLE RIVER LIGHTHOUSE

P.O. Box 565
Rockland, ME 04841
(877) 276-4682
littleriverlight.org

FRIENDS OF PEMAQUID POINT LIGHTHOUSE

c/o Caren Clark
954 Dutch Neck Road
Waldoboro, ME 04572

FRIENDS OF POMHAM ROCKS LIGHTHOUSE

P.O. Box 15121
East Providence, RI 02915

FRIENDS OF PORTSMOUTH HARBOR LIGHTHOUSES

P.O. Box 8232
Portsmouth, NH 03802–5092
(603) 828–9243
portsmouthharborlighthouse.org

FRIENDS OF ROCKLAND HARBOR LIGHTHOUSES

P.O. Box 741
Rockland, ME 04841
(207) 542–7574
rocklandharborlights.org

FRIENDS OF WOOD ISLAND LIGHTHOUSE

P.O. Box 26
Biddeford Pool, ME 04006
woodislandlighthouse.org

NEW ENGLAND LIGHTHOUSE LOVERS

38 Lime Kiln Road
Tuckahoe, NY 10707
newenglandlighthouselovers.org

DELAWARE RIVER & BAY LIGHTHOUSE FOUNDATION

The Delaware River & Bay Lighthouse Foundation is an all-volunteer organization that serves as the caretaker for two of Delaware's nine remaining historic lighthouses—Harbor of Refuge Lighthouse and Delaware Breakwater East End.

P.O. Box 708
Lewes, DE 19958

(302) 644-7046

delawarebaylights.org

FLORIDA LIGHTHOUSE ASSOCIATION

The Florida Lighthouse Association is a nonprofit group of citizen activists dedicated to the preservation of the thirty remaining historic lighthouses that line Florida's 1,350-mile coastline.

P.O. Box 1676

St. Petersburg, FL 33731

(727) 667-7775

floridalighthouses.org

FRIENDS OF FLYING SANTA

Friends of Flying Santa was formed in 1997 to help ensure the future of the annual Christmas flights to New England lighthouses.

P.O. Box 80047

Stoneham, MA 02180-0001

(781) 438-4587

flyingsanta.com

GREAT LAKES LIGHTHOUSE KEEPERS ASSOCIATION

Originally consisting of an informal gathering of retired lighthouse keepers, their families and friends, the Great Lakes Lighthouse Keepers Association was officially incorporated as a nonprofit organization in 1983, making it one of the nation's longest-lived lighthouse preservation groups.

707 North Huron Avenue

P.O. Box 219

Mackinaw City, MI 49701

(231) 436-5580

gllka.com

Lighthouse Friends.com

This extensive website, with individual pages for each lighthouse, is run by Kraig Anderson and Marilyn Stiborek, and includes photographs, directions, histories, and GPS coordinates garnered during their personal visits to every lighthouse in the United States and a growing number in Canada.

lighthousefriends.com

The Lighthouse Preservation Society

The Lighthouse Preservation Society's mission is to preserve historic lighthouse structures for future generations, to open them up to public use and enjoyment, and to document their history and that of their keepers.

11 Seaborne Drive
Dover, NH 03820
(603) 740-0055
lighthousepreservation.org

Michigan Lighthouse Alliance

The alliance includes more than fifty nonprofit organizations of lighthouse preservation groups and lighthouse stakeholders from around the state of Michigan.

P.O. Box 141
Drummond Island, MI 49726
michiganlighthousealliance.org

New Jersey Lighthouse Society

The New Jersey Lighthouse Society is a nonprofit educational corporation dedicated to the history and preservation of lighthouses everywhere, but particularly in the New Jersey region, including Delaware Bay and New York Harbor.

P.O. Box 332

Navesink, NJ 07752–0332

(732) 291–4777

njlhs.org

Outer Banks Lighthouse Society

The Outer Banks Lighthouse Society actively supports all North Carolina lighthouses.

P.O. Box 1005

Morehead City, NC 28557

outerbankslighthousesociety.org

Sable Points Lighthouse Keepers Association

The mission of the Sable Points Lighthouse Keepers Association is to preserve, promote, and educate the public and make its lighthouses accessible to all. Its lighthouses are on the east coast of Lake Michigan: Big Sable, Ludington North Breakwater, Little Sable, and White River.

P.O. Box 673

Ludington, MI 49431

(231) 845–7417

splka.org

United States LighthouseSociety

The United States Lighthouse Society is a nonprofit historical and educational organization incorporated to educate, inform, and entertain those who are interested in lighthouses, past and present.

Point No Point Lighthouse

9005 Point No Point Road NE

Hansville, WA 98340

(415) 362–7255

uslhs.org

The United States Lighthouse Society chapters include:

Long Island Chapter

lilighthousesociety.org

Chesapeake Chapter

cheslights.org

Pacific Northwest Lighthouse Group

pnwlg2014.org

Point No Point Chapter

pnplighthouse.com

LIGHTHOUSE MUSEUMS

· · · · · · · · · · · · · · ·

THIS LIST INCLUDES A RANGE OF LIGHTHOUSE MUSEUMS IN the United States, from small to large. Most of these museums are connected to or incorporated within lighthouses.*

ABSECON LIGHTHOUSE MUSEUM

31 S. Rhode Island Avenue
Atlantic City, NJ 08401
(609) 449–1360
abseconlighthouse.org

ANNAPOLIS MARITIME MUSEUM/THOMAS POINT SHOAL LIGHTHOUSE

723 Second Street
Annapolis, MD 21403
(410) 295–0104
thomaspointlighthouse.org

BARNEGAT LIGHTHOUSE

P.O. Box 167
Barnegat Light, NJ 08006
(609) 494–2016
www.state.nj.us/dep/parksandforests/parks/barnlig.html

*This list does not claim to be comprehensive.

BATTERY POINT LIGHTHOUSE AT THE DEL NORTE COUNTY HISTORICAL SOCIETY

577 H Street
Crescent City, CA 95531
(707) 464-3922
delnortehistory.org/lighthouse

BEAVERTAIL LIGHTHOUSE MUSEUM ASSOCIATION

P.O. Box 83
Jamestown, RI 02835
(401) 423-3270
beavertaillight.org

BLOCK ISLAND SOUTHEAST LIGHTHOUSE

18 Old Town Road
Block Island, RI 02807
(401) 864-4357
blockislandhistorical.org

BODIE ISLAND LIGHTHOUSE

Cape Hatteras National Seashore
8210 Bodie Island Lighthouse Road
Nags Head, North Carolina 27959
(252) 473-2111
nps.gov/caha/planyourvisit/bils.htm

BOCA GRANDE LIGHTHOUSE & MUSEUM

Barrier Island Parks Society, Inc.
P.O. Box 637
Boca Grande, FL 33921
(941) 964-0060
barrierislandparkssociety.org/
port-boca-grande-lighthouse-museum

Boston Lighthouse

Little Brewster Island
Boston, MA 02109
(617) 223-8666
bostonharborislands.org/events_bostonlight.html

Cana Island Lighthouse at the Door County Maritime Museum

120 North Madison Avenue
Sturgeon Bay, WI 54235-3416
(920) 743-5958
dcmm.org

Cape Hatteras National Seashore

1401 National Park Drive
Manteo, NC 27954
(252) 473-2111
nps.gov/caha/planyourvisit/visitor-centers.htm

Cape May Lighthouse & Museum

215 Lighthouse Avenue
Cape May, NJ
(609) 884-8656
capemaymac.org/attractions/capemaylighthouse.html

Charlotte-Genesee Lighthouse Historical Society

70 Lighthouse Street
Rochester, NY 14612
(585) 621-6179
geneseelighthouse.org

Chesapeake Bay Maritime Museum

213 North Talbot Street
St. Michaels, MD 21663

(410) 745-2916

cbmm.org

CHOPTANK RIVER LIGHTHOUSE

Long Wharf Park

High and Water Streets

Cambridge, MD 21613

(410) 463-2653

choosecambridge.com/index.php/choptank-river-lighthouse/

COLCHESTER REEF LIGHTHOUSE AT THE SHELBURNE MUSEUM

6000 Shelburne Road

P.O. Box 10

Shelburne, VT 05482

(802) 985-3346

shelburnemuseum.org/explore/buildings/galleries/lighthouse

CONCORD POINT LIGHTHOUSE

Corner of Concord & Lafayette Streets

Havre de Grace, MD 21078

(410) 939-3213

concordpointlighthouse.org

COPPER HARBOR LIGHTHOUSE

14447 Highway M26

Copper Harbor, MI 49918

(906) 289-4966

copperharborlighthousetours.com

CURRITUCK BEACH LIGHTHOUSE

Outer Banks Conservationists, Inc.

P.O. Box 970

Manteo, NC 27954

(252) 473–5440
currituckbeachlight.com

CUSTOM HOUSE MARITIME MUSEUM

150 Bank Street
New London, CT 06320
(860) 447–2501
nlmaritimesociety.org

DRUM POINT LIGHTHOUSE AT THE CALVERT MARINE MUSEUM

14200 Solomons Island Road
Solomons, MD 20688
(410) 326–2042
calvertmarinemuseum.com/199/Drum-Point-Lighthouse

DUNKIRK LIGHTHOUSE & VETERANS PARK MUSEUM

P.O. Box 69 - 1 Lighthouse Point Drive
Dunkirk, NY 14048
(716) 366–5050
dunkirklighthouse.com

EAGLE BLUFF LIGHTHOUSE

Peninsula State Park
9462 Shore Road
Fish Creek, WI 54212
(920) 421–3636
eagleblufflighthouse.doorcountyhistoricalsociety.org

EAGLE HARBOR LIGHTHOUSE COMPLEX AND MUSEUM

Keweenaw County Historical Society
670 Lighthouse Road
Eagle Harbor, MI 49950
keweenawhistory.org/sites/lighthouse.html

EAST END SEAPORT MARITIME MUSEUM

Greenport, NY 11944
(631) 477-2100
eastendseaport.org

1860 LIGHTHOUSE & LIGHT STATION MUSEUM

311 Johnson Street
Port Washington, WI 53074
(262) 268-9150
portwashingtonhistoricalsociety.org

FAIRPORT HARBOR MARINE MUSEUM

129 Second Street
Fairport Harbor, OH 44077
(440) 354-4825.
fairportharborlighthouse.org

FIRE ISLAND LIGHTHOUSE PRESERVATION SOCIETY

4640 Captree Island
Captree Island, NY 11702-4601
(631) 661-4876
fireislandlighthouse.com

GRAND TRAVERSE LIGHTHOUSE MUSEUM

15500 North Lighthouse Point Road
Northport, MI 49670
(231) 386-7195
grandtraverselighthouse.com

GREAT LAKES SHIPWRECK MUSEUM

18335 North Whitefish Point Road
Paradise, MI 49768
(888) 492-3747
shipwreckmuseum.com

GROSSE POINT LIGHTHOUSE MUSEUM

Lighthouse Park District
2601 Sheridan Road
Evanston, IL 60201-1752
(847) 328-6961
grossepointlighthouse.net

HARBOR TOWN LIGHTHOUSE MUSEUM

149 Lighthouse Road
Hilton Head Island, SC 29928
(866) 305-9814
harbourtownlighthouse.com

HECETA HEAD LIGHTHOUSE

P.O. Box 250
Yachats, OR 97498
(866) 547-3696
hecetalighthouse.com

HEREFORD INLET LIGHTHOUSE AND MUSEUM

P.O. Box 784
Rio Grande, NJ 08242
(609) 522-4520
herefordlighthouse.org

HIGHLAND LIGHTHOUSE

27 Highland Light Road
North Truro, MA 02652
(508) 487-1121
highlandlighthouse.org

HILLSBORO LIGHTHOUSE PRESERVATION SOCIETY MUSEUM

Hillsboro Inlet Park
A1A at 2700 N. Ocean Boulevard

Pompano Beach, FL, 33062

(954) 609-7974

hillsborolighthouse.org

HORTON POINT LIGHTHOUSE

Southold Historical Society

P.O. Box 1

Southold, NY 11971

(631) 765-5500

southoldhistoricalsociety.org/lighthouse.htm

JUPITER INLET LIGHTHOUSE & MUSEUM

500 Captain Armour's Way

Jupiter, FL 33469

(561) 747-8380

jupiterlighthouse.org

KEY WEST LIGHTHOUSE & KEEPER'S QUARTERS AT THE KEY WEST ART & HISTORICAL SOCIETY

938 Whitehead Street

Key West, FL 33040

(305) 294-0012

kwahs.org/visit/lighthouse-keepers-quarters/

OLD POINT LOMA LIGHTHOUSE/CABRILLO NATIONAL MONUMENT

1800 Cabrillo Memorial Drive

San Diego, CA 92106-3601

(619) 557-5450

nps.gov/cabr/learn/historyculture/old-point-loma-lighthouse

MAINE LIGHTHOUSE MUSEUM

One Park Drive

Rockland, ME 04841

(207) 594-3301

mainelighthousemuseum.org

Marblehead Lighthouse Historical Society Museum

110 Lighthouse Drive

Marblehead, OH 43440

(419) 798-2094

marbleheadlighthouseohio.org

Mariners' Museum and Park

100 Museum Drive

Newport News, VA 23606

(757)596-2222

marinersmuseum.org

Marquette Maritime Museum and Lighthouse

300 North Lakeshore Boulevard

Marquette, MI 49855

(906) 226-2006

mqtmaritimemuseum.com

Marshall Pont Lighthouse and Museum

P.O. Box 247

Port Clyde, ME 04855

marshallpoint.org/index.php

Martha's Vineyard Museum

59 School Street

Martha's Vineyard, MA 02539

(508) 627-4441

mvmuseum.org

McGulpin Point Lighthouse Museum & Old Mackinac Point Lighthouse

mightymac.org

Michigan City Historical Society, Old Lighthouse Museum

Heisman Harbor Road, Washington Park
P.O. Box 512
Michigan City, IN 46361–0512
(219) 872-6133
oldlighthousemuseum.org

Monhegan Museum of Art & History

(housed in the Monhegan Light Station)
1 Lighthouse Hill
Monhegan, ME 04852
(207) 596-7003
monheganmuseum.org

Montauk Point Lighthouse Museum & Gift Shop

2000 Montauk Highway
Montauk, NY 11954
(631) 668-2544
montauklighthouse.com

Mukilteo Lighthouse

Mukilteo Historical Society
304 Lincoln Avenue, Suite 101
Mukilteo, WA 98275
mukilteohistorical.org

National Lighthouse Museum

200 Promenade at Lighthouse Point
P.O. Box 10296

Staten Island, NY 10301–0296

(718) 390–0040

lighthousemuseum.org

NAVESINK TWIN LIGHTS MUSEUM

Lighthouse Road

Highlands, NJ 07732

(732) 872–1814

twinlightslighthouse.com

NEW CANAL LIGHTHOUSE MUSEUM AND EDUCATION CENTER

8001 Lakeshore Drive

New Orleans, LA 70124

(504) 836–2215

saveourlake.org

NEW DUNGENESS LIGHTHOUSE

P.O. Box 1283

Sequim, WA 98382

(360) 683-6638

newdungenesslighthouse.com

NORTH POINT LIGHTHOUSE MUSEUM

2650 North Wahl Avenue

Milwaukee, WI 53211

(414) 332–6754

northpointlighthouse.org

OLD BALDY LIGHTHOUSE & SMITH ISLAND MUSEUM OF HISTORY

101 Lighthouse Wynd

Bald Head Island, NC 28461

(910) 457–7481

oldbaldy.org

OLD MACKINAC POINT LIGHTHOUSE

526 North Huron Avenue
Mackinaw City, MI 49701
(906) 847-3328
mackinacparks.com

OLD POINT LOMA LIGHTHOUSE

Cabrillo National Monument
1800 Cabrillo Memorial Drive
San Diego, CA 92106-3601
(619) 557-5450
nps.gov/cabr/learn/historyculture/old-point-loma-lighthouse.htm

ONTONAGON LIGHTHOUSE MUSEUM

422 River Street
Ontonagon, Michigan 49953
(906) 884-6165
ontonagonmuseum.org

PEMAQUID POINT LIGHTHOUSE AND MUSEUM

3119 Bristol Road
New Harbor, ME 04554
(207) 677-2492
bristolparks.org/lighthouse.htm

PENSACOLA LIGHTHOUSE & MUSEUM

2081 Radford Boulevard
Pensacola, Fl 32508
(850) 393-1561
pensacolalighthouse.org

PINEY POINT LIGHTHOUSE, MUSEUM, AND HISTORIC PARK

44720 Lighthouse Road
Piney Point, MD 20674

(301) 994–1471

www.stmarysmd.com

Pointe aux Barques Lighthouse Society

8114 Rubicon Road

Port Hope, MI 48468

(989) 428–2010

pointeauxbarqueslighthouse.org

Point Cabrillo Lighthouse and Museum

45300 Lighthouse Road

Mendocino, CA 95460

(707) 937–6123

pointcabrillo.org

Point Fermin Lighthouse Historic Site and Museum

807 West Paseo Del Mar

San Pedro, CA 90731

(310) 241–0684

pointferminlighthouse.org

Point Isabel Lighthouse and Keeper's Cottage

421 East Queen Isabella Boulevard

Port Isabel, TX 78578

(956) 943–7602

portisabelmuseums.com

Point Pinos Lighthouse

80 Asilomar Avenue

Pacific Grove, CA 93950

(831) 648–3176

pointpinoslighthouse.org

POINT REYES LIGHTHOUSE

Point Reyes National Seashore
1 Bear Valley Road
Point Reyes Station, CA 94956
(415) 464-5100
nps.gov/pore/learn/historyculture/people_maritime_lighthouse
.htm

POINT SAN LUIS LIGHTHOUSE

P.O. Box 308
Avila Beach, CA 93424
(855) 533-7843
sanluislighthouse.org

POINT SUR HISTORIC PARK & LIGHTHOUSE

Big Sur, CA 93920
(831) 625-4419
pointsur.org

POINT VICENTE LIGHTHOUSE AND MUSEUM

31550 Palos Verdes Drive West
Rancho Palos Verdes, CA 90275
(310) 541-0334.
palosverdes.com/pvlight

PONCE DE LEON LIGHTHOUSE AND MUSEUM

4931 South Peninsula Drive
Ponce Inlet, FL 32127
(386) 761-1821
ponceinlet.org

PORT BOCA GRANDE LIGHTHOUSE AND MUSEUM

880 Belcher Road
Boca Grande, FL 33921

(941) 964-0060
barrierislandparkssociety.org/
port-boca-grande-lighthouse-museum

PORTLAND HEAD LIGHTHOUSE AND MUSEUM

1000 Shore Road
Cape Elizabeth, ME 04107
(207) 799-2661
portlandheadlight.com

PRESQUE ISLE TOWNSHIP MUSEUM SOCIETY

P.O. Box 208
Presque Isle, MI 49777
(989) 595-9917
presqueislelighthouses.org

ROANOKE RIVER LIGHTOUSE & MARITIME MUSEUM

West Water Street
Downtown Plymouth, NC 27962
(252) 217-2204
roanokeriverlighthouse.org

RONDOUT LIGHTHOUSE AT THE HUDSON RIVER MARITIME MUSEUM

Hudson River Maritime Museum
50 Rondout Landing
Kingston, NY 12401
(845) 338-0071
hrmm.org/rondout-lighthouse.html

ROSE ISLAND LIGHTHOUSE FOUNDATION

P.O. Box 1419
Newport, RI 02840
(401) 847-4242
roseislandlighthouse.org

St. Augustine Lighthouse & Museum

100 Red Cox Road
St. Augustine, FL 32080
(904) 829-0745
staugustinelighthouse.com

St. George Lighthouse Museum

2B East Gulf Beach Drive
St. George Island, FL 32328
(850) 927-7745
stgeorgelight.org

St. Simons Island Lighthouse Museum and Keeper's Dwelling

610 Beachview Drive
St. Simons Island, GA 31522
(912) 638-4666
saintsimonslighthouse.org

Sand Point Lighthouse

Delta County Historical Society
16 Water Plant Road
Escanaba, MI 49829
(906) 789-6790
deltahistorical.org

Saugerties Lighthouse Museum

Saugerties Lighthouse Conservancy
PO Box 654
Saugerties, NY 12477
(845) 247-0656
saugertieslighthouse.com

Scituate Lighthouse at the Scituate Historical Society

43 Cudworth Road
Scituate MA 02066
(781) 545-1083
scituatehistoricalsociety.org/light

Sea Girt Lighthouse

9 Ocean Avenue
Sea Girt, NJ 08750
(732) 974-0514
seagirtlighthouse.com

Seguin Island Light Station and Museum

72 Front Street, Suite 3
Bath, ME 04530
(207) 443-4808
seguinisland.org

Seul Choix Lighthouse Museum

Gulliver Historical Society
672 North West Gulliver Lake Road
Gulliver, MI 49840
(906) 283-3317
greatlakelighthouse.com

Sodus Bay Lighthouse Museum

7606 North Ontario Street
Sodus Point, NY 14555-9536
(315) 483-4936
sodusbaylighthouse.org

Southport Light Station Museum

Kenosha History Center
220 51st Place

Kenosha, WI 53140

(262) 654-5770

kenoshahistorycenter.org

SPLIT ROCK LIGHTHOUSE

3713 Split Rock Lighthouse Road

Two Harbors, MN 55616

(218) 226-6372

sites.mnhs.org/historic-sites/split-rock-lighthouse

STONINGTON HISTORICAL SOCIETY OLD LIGHTHOUSE MUSEUM

7 Water Street

Stonington, CT 06378

(860) 535-1440

stoningtonhistory.org

STURGEON POINT LIGHTHOUSE AND MUSEUM

Alcona Historical Society

P.O. Box 174

Harrisville, MI 48740

(989) 724-6297

alconahistoricalsociety.com

TAWAS POINT LIGHTHOUSE

686 Tawas Beach Road

East Tawas, MI 48730

(989) 362-5658

michigan.gov/mhc/0,4726,7-282-61080_62661---,00.html

TWO HARBORS LIGHTHOUSE

520 South Avenue

Two Harbors, MN 55616

(218) 834-4898

lakecountyhistoricalsociety.org/museums/view/
two-harbors-light-station

Tybee Island Lighthouse and Museum

30 Meddin Avenue
Tybee Island,GA 31328–9733
(912) 786–5801
tybeelighthouse.org

Umpqua River Lighthouse and Museum

1020 Lighthouse Road
Winchester Bay, OR 97467
(541) 271–4631
umpquavalleymuseums.org

United States Coast Guard Museum
(in 2018 a new national Coast Guard Museum is
due to open in downtown New London)

Waesche Hall
U.S. Coast Guard Academy
15 Mohegan Avenue
New London, CT 06320–8511
(860) 444–8511
uscg.mil/hq/cg092/museum/museumhours.asp

Watch Hill Lighthouse

Watch Hill Lighthouse Keepers Association
P.O. Box 1511
Westerly, RI 02891
www.watchhilllighthousekeepers.org

Westport Maritime Museum

Grays Harbor Lighthouse
1020 West Ocean Avenue

Westport, WA 98595

(360) 268-0078

westportmaritimemuseum.com

West Quoddy Head Lighthouse

973 South Lubec Road

Lubec, Maine 04652

(207) 733-2180

westquoddy.com

White River Light Station and Museum

6199 Murray Road

Whitehall, MI 49461

(231) 894-8265

whiteriverlightstation.org

Wind Point Lighthouse Fog Horn Building Museum

P.O. Box 44067

Racine, WI 53404-7001

(262) 880-8266

windpointlighthouse.com

Yaquina Bay Lighthouse

Friends of Yaquina Lighthouses

750 Lighthouse Drive #7

PO Box 410

Newport, OR 97365

(541) 574-3100

yaquinalights.org

NOTES

. . . .

ARCL	*Annual Report of the Commissioner of Lighthouses to the Secretary of Commerce, for the Year Ending ___*
ARLHB	*Annual Report of the Lighthouse Board, for the Year Ending ___*
LSB	*Lighthouse Service Bulletin*
NAB	National Archives Building, Washington, DC
NACP	National Archives at College Park, MD
NDAR	*Naval Documents of the American Revolution*
ORUCN	*Official Records of the Union and Confederate Navies in the War of the Rebellion*
Report of the Officers	*Report of the Officers Constituting the Light-House Board* (Washington: A. Boyd Hamilton, 1852)
RG	Record Group
RLHB	*Report of the Lighthouse Board, in the Annual Report of the Secretary of the Treasury, on the State of the Finances for the Year Ending ___*
TDCCR	Treasury Department Collection of Confederate Records, Records Relating to Lighthouse Establishment
USLB	United States Lighthouse Board

INTRODUCTION

xii **the *Union***: "Loss of Ship Union," *Salem Gazette* (February 28, 1817); "Shipwreck" *National Advocate* (March 1, 1817); and James Duncan Phillips, *Pepper and Pirates: Adventures in the Sumatra Pepper Trade of Salem* (Boston: Houghton Mifflin Company, 1949), 63–65.

xv **"Among all the hosts"**: William S. Pelletreau, *A History of Long Island From Its Earliest Settlement To The Present Time*, vol. 2 (New York: Lewis Publishing Company, 1905), 28.

CHAPTER 1: COLONIAL LIGHTS

1 **"Now a new . . . these coasts?"**: Samuel Clough, *The New England Almanack for the Year of 1701* (Boston: R. Green and J. Allen, 1701), 2–3.

2 **magnificent Pharos**: Alan Stevenson, *A Rudimentary Treatise on the History, Construction, and Illumination of Lighthouses* (London: John Weale, 1850), 1–6; Judith McKenzie, *The Architecture of Alexandria and Egypt: c. 300 BC to AD 700* (New Haven: Yale University Press, 2007), 41–45; and David Abulafia, *The Great Sea: A Human History of the Mediterranean* (London: Oxford University Press, 2011), 155.

2 **"to the safety"**: Peter A. Clayton, "The Pharos at Alexandria," in *The Seven Wonders of the Ancient World*, edited by Peter A. Clayton and Martin J. Price (New York: Routledge, 1988), 143.

2 **"like a star"**: Twelfth-century Arabian geographer Edrisi, quoted in William Henry Davenport Adams, *Lighthouses and Lightships: A Descriptive and Historical Account of Their Mode of Construction and Organization* (London: T. Nelson and Sons, 1870), 25.

2 **"a mountain"**: Achilles Tatius, *Achilles Tatius*, translated by S. Gaselee (London: William Heinemann, 1917), 249.

3 **nearly seventy**: D. Alan Stevenson, *The World's Lighthouses Before 1820* (London: Oxford University Press, 1959), 8–12, 17–37, 46, 86–87, 97–109.

4 **"ragged stones"**: Julian Stockwin, *Stockwin's Maritime Miscellany: A Ditty Bag of Wonders from the Golden Age of Sail* (New York: Random House, 2001), 58.

4 **Henry Winstanley . . . the least**: The background for the Eddystone Lighthouse comes from Fred Majdalany, *The Eddystone Lighthouse* (Boston: Houghton Mifflin Company, 1960), 23–72.

5 **"the greatest"**: Ibid., 57.

6 **"fier-bales"**: Arnold Burges Johnson, *The Modern Light-House Service* (Washington: Government Printing Office, 1890), 13.

7 **age-old problem**: Francis Ross Holland, Jr., *America's Lighthouses: Their Illustrated History Since 1716* (Brattleboro, VT: Stephen Greene Press, 1972), 8.

7 **"one continued"**: John F. Campbell, *History and Bibliography of* The New American Practical Navigator *and* The American Coast Pilot (Salem, MA: Peabody Museum, 1964), 29.

7 **"at some headland"**: "Note on Boston Light," in *Publications of the*

Colonial Society of Massachusetts, Transactions, 1899–1900, vol. 6 (Boston: The Colonial Society, 1904), 278–79.

8 **"the want of"**: "An Act for Building and Maintaining a Light-House Upon Great Brewster (Called Beacon-Island) at the Entrance of the Harbour of Boston," in *Acts and Laws, of His Majesty's Province of the Massachusetts-Bay in New-England* (Boston: S. Kneeland, 1759), 184–85.

9 **Boston Lighthouse was lit**: "Boston," *Boston News Letter* (September 10–17, 1716).

9 **Judging by . . . light itself**: Thomas Knox, "Boston Light House," *Massachusetts Magazine* (February 1789), 71; "Resolve Directing Richard Devens, Esq., Commissary General to Build and Compleat a Light House and Other Buildings at the Entrance of Boston Harbour . . ." (July 2, 1783), in *Acts and Laws of the Commonwealth of Massachusetts* (Boston: Wright & Potter Printing Company, 1890), 711; and Sally R. Snowman and James G. Thompson, *Boston Light: A Historical Perspective* (North Andover, MA: Flagship Press, 1999), 7.

9 **George Worthylake**: Background on Worthylake comes from Nathaniel B. Shurtleff, *A Topographical and Historical Description of Boston* (Boston: Boston City Council, 1871), 570; and Edward Rowe Snow, *The Lighthouses of New England*, updated by Jeremy D'Entremont (Beverly, MA: Commonwealth Editions, 2002), 177.

9 **"kindling the"**: "An Act for Building and Maintaining a Light-House," 185.

9 **Worthylake, his wife**: "Boston," *Boston News-Letter* (November 3–10, 1718).

10 **"tarried on board"**: Contemporary source quoted by Snow, *The Lighthouses*, 177.

10 **Between ten . . . for burial**: Ibid., 177–79.

11 **"Providence Asserted"**: Richard C. Fyffe, "Providence Asserted and Adored: A Cotton Mather Text Rediscovered," in *Essex Institute Historical Collections* (July 1989), 201–38.

11 **"inexpressible horror"**: Ibid., 209–10.

11 **Whereas Mather . . . the drownings**: Benjamin Franklin, *The Autobiography of Benjamin Franklin* (Boston: Houghton, Mifflin and Company, 1886), 19–20; Walter Isaacson, *Benjamin Franklin: An American Life* (New York: Simon & Schuster, 2003), 20–21; and H. W. Brands, *The*

First American: The Life and Times of Benjamin Franklin (New York: Anchor Books, 212), 20.

12 **"The Lighthouse Tragedy"... "very bad one"**: Franklin, *The Autobiography*, 20.

13 **"as large ... a *lighthouse*"**: Benjamin Franklin, *Memoirs of the Life and Writings of Benjamin Franklin, Written by Himself to a Late Period, and Continued to the Time of his Death*, edited by William Temple Franklin (London: Henry Colburn, 1818), 132–33.

13 **With Worthylake ... the surface**: "Boston," *Boston News-Letter* (November 10–17, 1718); and "Boston," *Boston News-Letter* (November 17–24, 1718).

14 **"great gun"**: Snow, *The Lighthouses*, 180.

14 **fires gutted**: Fitz-Henry Smith, Jr., *The Story of Boston Light, With Some Accounts of the Beacons in Boston Harbor* (Boston: Privately printed, 1911), 22–24.

15 **Clergymen had ... blasphemous act**: Isaacson, *Benjamin Franklin*, 137–44; and Bertrand Russell, *Russell: The Basic Writings of Bertrand Russell* (New York: Routledge Classics, 2009), 47.

15 **"thought it"**: Knox, *Boston Light House*, 70.

15 **colonies' economy grow faster**: John J. McCusker, "Colonial Statistics," in *Historical Statistics of the United States: Earliest Times to the Present, Millennial Edition*, vol. 5, part E, edited by Susan B. Carter et al. (Cambridge: Cambridge University Press, 216), 5-627–36.

16 **"the faraway"**: R. A. Douglas-Lithgow, *Nantucket, A History* (New York: G. P. Putnam & Sons, 1914), 25.

16 **"Take out"**: Herman Melville, *Moby-Dick or the White Whale* (Boston: St. Botolph Society, 1892), 63.

16 **voted two hundred pounds**: Karen T. Butler, *Nantucket Lights: An Illustrated History of the Island's Legendary Beacons* (Nantucket: Mill Hill Press, 1996), 9–12, 19.

17 **"the most violent"**: "Extract of a Letter from Nantucket, March 9, 1774," *Essex Journal and Merrimack Packet* (March 23, 1774).

17 **Rhode Island followed suit**: Background for Rhode Island's first lighthouse comes from Richard L. Champlin, "Rhode Island's First Lighthouse," *Newport History* (Summer 1970), 49–64; Susan B. Franklin, "The Beavertail Lighthouse," *Rhode Island History* (October 1951), 97–101; Varoujan Karentz, *Beavertail Light Station on Conanicut Island: Its Use, Development and History from 1749* (Charleston, SC: BookSurge Publishing, 2008), 31–43; and Sarah C. Gleason, *Kindly Lights: A His-*

tory of the Lighthouses of Southern New England (Boston: Beacon Press, 1991), 16–19.

17 **"for the preservation"**: Gleason, *Kindly Lights*, 16.

18 **lighthouse goes dark**: Background for this section comes from "Newport, November 10," *Newport Mercury* (November 3–10, 1766); "Jamestown, November 14, 1766," *Newport Mercury* (November 10–17, 1766); and "Newport, November 22, 1766," *Newport Mercury* (November 17–24, 1766).

19 **"sporting with"**: "Newport, November 22, 1766," *Newport Mercury*.

19 **"private fortune . . . blame"**: "Jamestown, Nov. 28, 1766," *Newport Mercury* (November 24–December 1, 1766).

19 **"contempt . . . to determine"**: "Josiah Arnold on Beaver Tail Light" (February 1767), Petitions to the General Assembly, vol. 13, no. 53, Rhode Island State Archives.

19 **awarded him**: "General Treasurer—Accounts Allowed, Arnold with the Colony," June 1767, Second Session, Rhode Island State Archives.

20 **New London was next**: Background for the New London Lighthouse comes from Charles J. Hoadly, *Public Records of the Colony of Connecticut, From May, 1757, to March, 1762, Inclusive* (Hartford: Case, Lockwood & Brainerd Co., 1880), 468–69; and Edward Rowe Snow, *Famous Lighthouses of America* (New York: Dodd, Mead & Company, 1955), 88–89.

20 **New Yorkers forged**: Background for New York's lighthouse comes from Kenneth Scott, "The Sandy Hook Lighthouse," *American Neptune* (April 1965), 123–25; Edmund Andros to Philip Carteret (March 7, 1680), in *The Andros Papers, 1679–1680*, edited by Peter R, Christoph and Florence A. Christoph (Syracuse: Syracuse University Press, 1989), 238–39; "Scheme of a Lottery," *New-York Gazette* (July 6, 1761); Julia Bricklin, "The Colonial Public Lottery: A Beacon Light for New Yorkers," *Financial History* (Summer 2013), 12–15; and "Scheme of the New-York Light-House and Publick Lottery," *New-York Mercury* (April 25, 1763).

21 **"It is surprising"**: "New-York, Dec. 19," *New-York Mercury* (December 19, 1757).

21 **"an object so"**: Cadwallader Colden, "The Light House on Sandy Hook," *Colonial Records of the New York Chamber of Commerce, 1768–1784*, edited by John Austin Stevens, Jr. (New York: John F. Trow, 1867), 320.

21 **sixty pounds per year:** Ed Crews, "How Much Is That in Today's Money?" *Colonial Williamsburg* (Summer 2002), accessed on May 29, 2015, at http://www.history.org/foundation/journal/Summer02/money2.cfm.

22 **"judged to be":** "New-York, June 18," *New-York Mercury* (June 18, 1764).

22 **Philadelphia had:** Background for Pennsylvania's lighthouse come from John W. Beach, *The Cape Henlopen Lighthouse* (Dover, MD: Henlopen Publishing, 1970), 10–24; Bob Trapani, Jr., *Delaware Lights: A History of Lighthouses in the First State* (Charleston, SC: History Press, 2007), 13–14; Douglas J. Evans, *The History of Cape Henlopen Lighthouse, 1764–1926* (Senior thesis, University of Delaware, Newark, 1958); and "Scheme," *Pennsylvania Gazette* (November 12, 1761).

22 **And given Pennsylvania's:** David McCullough, *John Adams* (New York: Simon & Schuster, 2001), 79.

22 **"the wrecks":** Evans, *History of Cape Henlopen Lighthouse*, 5.

23 **"that the elegant":** Harold E. Gillingham, "Lotteries in Philadelphia Prior to 1776," *Pennsylvania History* (April 1938), 94.

23 **notice to all:** "To All Masters of Vessels," *Pennsylvania Gazette* (December 5, 1765).

23 **led by Charleston:** Background for Charleston's lighthouse comes from Douglas W. Bostick, *The Morris Island Lighthouse: Charleston's Maritime Beacon* (Charleston, SC: History Press, 2008), 13–19; Suzannah Smith Miles, *Writing of the Islands: Sullivan's Island and the Isle of Palms* (Charleston, SC: History Press, 2004), 64–65; "Charles-Town, June 1," *South Carolina Gazette* (June 28, 1768); "Charles-Town, June 16," *The South Carolina Gazette* (June 16, 1767); and "Charles-Town, December 2," *South Carolina Gazette* (December 2, 1766).

24 **one at Gurnet Point:** Jeremy D'Entremont, *The Lighthouses of Massachusetts* (Beverly, MA: Commonwealth Editions, 2007), 245–46.

24 **"by directing":** "An Act for the Building and Maintaining a Lighthouse on the East End of the Gurnet, at the Entrance of the Harbor of Plymouth," in *Acts and Resolves, Public and Private, of the Province of the Massachusetts Bay*, vol. 4 (Boston: Wright & Potter, 1890), 992.

25 **Portsmouth, New Hampshire:** Background for Portsmouth's lighthouse comes from Jane Molloy Porter, *Friendly Edifices: Piscataqua Lighthouses and Other Aids to Navigation, 1771–1939* (Portsmouth: Portsmouth Marine Society, 2006), 21–38.

25 **"King's Broad Arrow":** Eric Rutkow, *American Canopy: Trees, Forests, and the Making of a Nation* (New York: Scribner, 2012), 28–32.

25 **"If such a"**: Porter, *Friendly*, 23.

26 **"It is to"**: "Portsmouth, Dec. 16," *New-Hampshire Gazette* (December 16, 1768).

26 **"Many valuable . . . unfeeling recusant"**: Porter, *Friendly*, 28.

26 **"the most likely explanation"**: Ibid, 30.

27 **"been the"**: Ibid., 38.

27 **crash of the *Watch and Wait***: The background and all the quotes relating to the *Watch and Wait* come from Anthony Thacher, "Anthony Thacher's Narrative of His Shipwreck," in *Chronicles of the First Planters of the Colony of Massachusetts Bay, From 1623 to 1636*, edited by Alexander Young (Boston: Charles C. Little and James Brown, 1846), 485–86.

29 **"forty marks"**: John R. Totten, *Thacher Genealogy*, part 1 (New York: New York Genealogical and Biographical Society, 1910), 74.

29 **the Londoner**: Lemuel Gott, "Centennial Address," in *History of the Town of Rockport*, compiled by John W. Marshall, et al. (Rockport, MA: Rockport Review Office, 1888), 27.

30 **Marblehead merchants petitioned**: Petition by Jeremiah Lee, Ben Marston, and Azor Orne (April 2, 1771), in *The Acts and Resolves, Public and Private, of the Province of the Massachusetts Bay*, vol. 5 (Boston: Wright & Potter, 1886), 149–50.

30 **The legislature appointed**: "An Act for Building and Maintaining a Lighthouse or Houses on Thacher's Island or on the Mainland of Cape Ann," (April 26, 1771), in *Proceedings in the North Atlantic Coast Fisheries Arbitration Before the Permanent Court of Arbitration at the Hague*, vol. 5 (Washington: Government Printing Office, 1912), 1313–14.

31 **"Ann's Eyes"**: Eleanor C. Parsons, *Thachers: Island of the Twin Lights* (Canaan, NH: Phoenix Publishing, 1985), 17.

CHAPTER 2: CASUALTIES OF WAR

32 **"public humiliation . . . of blood"**: Continental Congress, "Proclamation for a Day of Fasting and Prayer," in *Documents and Records Relating to the Province of New Hampshire, From 1764 to 1776*, vol. 7, edited by Nathaniel Bouton (Nashua: Orren C. Moore, 1873), 545.

33 **On July 2**: "order," July 2, 1775, in *The Journals of Each Provincial Congress of Massachusetts in 1774 and 1775, and of the Committee of Safety*, edited by William Lincoln (Boston: Dutton and Wentworth, 1838), 441–42.

33 **already extinguished**: "Feb. 2, 1778," in *The Acts and Resolves, Public and Private, of the Province of Massachusetts Bay*, vol. 4 (Boston: Wright & Potter, 1890), 1005.

33 **Thacher Island Lighthouse was the next**: Joseph E. Garland, *The Fish and the Falcon: Gloucester's Resolute Role in America's Fight for Freedom* (Charleston, SC: History Press, 2006), 88–89; and Parsons, *Thachers*, 18–19.

34 **"to shift"**: "British Report of Destruction of Lighthouse on Thacher's Island," (July 6, 1775) in *NDAR*, vol. 1, edited by William Bell Clark (Washington: U.S. Government Printing Office, 1964), 828.

34 **"Liberty's Exiles"**: Maya Jasanoff, *Liberty's Exiles: American Loyalists in the Revolutionary World* (New York: Alfred A. Knopf, 2011), 6.

34 **ordered Major Vose**: For background on Vose's attack see "To George Washington from Brigadier General William Heath, 21 July 1775," *The Papers of George Washington, Revolutionary War Series*, vol. 1, *16 June 1775–15 September 1775*, edited by Philander D. Chase (Charlottesville: University Press of Virginia, 1985), 151–52; William Heath, *Memoirs of Major-General William Heath*, edited by William Abbatt (New York: William Abbatt, 1901), 18; "Richard Cranch to John Adams, 24 July 1775," *Adams Family Correspondence, December 1761–May 1776*, vol. 1, edited by Lyman H. Butterfield (Cambridge, MA: Harvard University Press, 1963), 258–60; "Extract of a Genuine Letter from Boston, Dated July 25, 1775," in *NDAR*, vol. 1, edited by William Bell Clark (Washington: U.S. Government Printing Office, 1964), 971; "Journal of His Majesty's Ship, Lively, Captain Thomas Bishop, Commanding" (July 20, 1775), *NDAR*, vol. 1, 935; and Elias Nason, *A Memoir of Mrs. Susanna Rowson* (Albany, NY: Joel Munsell, 1870), 19–20.

35 **"saw the flames"**: "Extract of a Letter From the Camp at Cambridge, July 24, 1775," in *NDAR*, vol. 1, 956.

35 **"these little"**: Abigail Adams to John Adams (July 25, 1775), in *Letters of Mrs. Adams, The Wife of John Adams*, edited by Charles Francis Adams (Boston: Wilkins, Carter, and Company, 1848), 45.

35 **"It is said"**: "James Warren to John Adams, extract" (July 20, 1775), in *NDAR*, vol. 1, 934.

35 **"To all Seafaring"**: "From the Massachusetts Gazette of July 20," in *The Remembrancer, or Impartial Repository of Public Events* (London: J. Almon, 1775), 151.

36 **"With this party"**: "Narrative of Vice Admiral Samuel Graves" (July 22, 1775), in *NDAR*, vol. 1, 950.

36 **by July 29**: "To John Adams from James Warren, 31 July 1775," *Papers of John Adams, May 1775–January 1776*, vol. 3, ed. Robert J. Taylor (Cambridge, MA: Harvard University Press, 1979), 110.

36 **ordering a second attack**: George Washington to Congress, July 21, 1775, *Official Letters to the Honorable American Congress, Written During the War Between the United Colonies and Great Britain, by His Excellency, George Washington*, vol. 1(London: G. G. and J. Robinson, 1795), 15.

36 **Benjamin Tupper**: For background on Tupper's raid see "From George Washington to John Hancock, 4–5 August 1775," *The Papers of George Washington*, vol. 1, 223–39; "To John Adams from William Tudor, 31 July 1775," *Papers of John Adams*, vol. 3, 107–8; "To John Adams from William Tudor, 31 July 1775," *Papers of John Adams*, vol. 3, 107–8; "To John Adams from James Warren, 31 July 1775," *The Adams Papers*, Papers of John Adams, vol. 3, *May 1775–January 1776*, edited by Robert J. Taylor. Cambridge, MA: Harvard University Press, 1979, pp. 108–12; "Major Benjamin Tupper to Brigadier General Horatio Gates, Cambridge," in *NDAR*, vol. 1, 1030; and Nason, *A Memoir*, 21–22.

36 **"If there is"**: D. Hamilton Hurd, *History of Norfolk County, Massachusetts, With Biographical Sketches of Many of its Pioneers and Prominent Men* (Philadelphia: J. W. Lewis, 1884), 469.

36 **"The whaleboats"**: "Narrative of Midshipman Christopher Hele, R.N." in *NDAR*, vol. 1, 1011.

36 **"in the liquor"**: Ibid.

38 **"it was very unhappy"**: "Abigail Adams to John Adams, 31 July 1775," *Adams Family Correspondence*, vol. 1, 270–71.

38 **"their gallant"**: "General Orders, 1 August 1775," *The Papers of George Washington*, vol. 1, 205–8.

38 **"Poetical Remarks"**: Elisha Rich, *Poetical Remarks Upon the Fight at the Boston Light-House* (Chelmsford, MA: Broadside, 1775).

39 **"rabble in"**: George Otto Trevelyan, *The American Revolution*, part 1, 1766–1776 (New York: Longmans, Green, and Co., 1899), 319.

39 **criticism rained**: "Lord Rochford to Lord Sandwich," in *NDAR*, vol. 2, edited by William Bell Clark (Washington: U.S. Government Printing Office, 1966), 708–9; and Nathaniel Philbrick, *Bunker Hill: A City, A Siege, A Revolution* (New York: Viking, 2013), 256–58.

39 **"It may perhaps"**: "Major General John Burgoyne to Lord George Germain," (August 20, 1775), in *NDAR*, vol. 1, 1190.

40 **Work crews . . . at night**: "Vice Admiral Samuel Graves to Philip Stevens," in *NDAR*, vol. 2, 1203.

40 **"so necessary"**: "Major General William Howe to Lord Dartmouth," in *NDAR*, vol. 2, 1155.

40 **British troops**: "Captain Francis Hutcheson to Major Frederick Haldimand," (December 25, 1775), in *NDAR*, vol. 3, edited by William Bell Clark (Washington: U.S. Government Printing Office, 1968), 238.

40 **The continued British . . . lighthouse guards**: "Joseph Ward to John Adams (June 16, 1776)," *Papers of John Adams*, vol. 4, 318; "Watertown, June 17," *Pennsylvania Evening Post* (June 25, 1776); and "Ezekiel Price, Diary of Ezekiel Price, 1775–76," in *Proceedings of the Massachusetts Historical Society, 1863–1864* (Boston: John Wilson and Son, 1864), 257.

40 **"a heap"**: "To John Adams from Josiah Quincy, 13–25 June 1776," *Papers of John Adams*, vol. 4, 308. See also "Master Log of the H.M.S. Milford," (June 14, 1776), in *NDAR*, vol. 5, edited by William James Morgan (Washington: U.S. Government Printing Office, 1970), 526.

41 **"the birthday"**: Thomas Paine, *Common Sense* (Philadelphia: W. and T. Bradford, 1776), 43.

41 **As early as**: David McCullough, *1776* (New York: Simon & Schuster, 2005), 80–81.

41 **be dismantled**: *Journal of the New York Provincial Congress* (March 4, 1776), in *NDAR*, vol. 4, edited by William Bell Clark (Washington: U.S. Government Printing Office, 1969), 162.

41 **"important enterprise . . . entirely useless"**: *Journal of the New York Provincial Congress* (March 6, 1776), in *NDAR*, vol. 4, 195.

42 **The party . . . the lighthouse**: *Journal of the New York Provincial Congress* (March 12, 1776), in *NDAR*, vol. 4, 310.

42 **Facing no . . . guarding the lighthouse**: "Captain Hyde Parker , Jr., R.N., to Vice Admiral Molyneux Shuldham," April 29, 1776), in *NDAR*, vol. 4, 1310–1313; Michael S. Adelberg, " 'So Dangerous a Quarter:' The Sandy Hook Lighthouse During the American Revolution," *The Keeper's Log* (Spring 1995), 11–12; "Ship Dutchess of Gordon, Sandy Hook, April 19, 1776," *Pennsylvania Journal* (May 1, 1776); and Michael S. Adelberg, *The American Revolution in Monmouth County: The Theatre of Spoil and Destruction* (Charleston, SC: History Press, 2010), 97.

43 **Tupper's force** : Solomon Nash, *Journal of Solomon Nash, A Soldier of*

the Revolution, 1776–1777, edited by Charles L. Bushnell (New York: privately printed, 1861), 20.

43 **"tho . . . little strange"**: "Lieutenant Colonel Benjamin Tupper to George Washington," (June 21, 1776), in *NDAR*, vol. 5, 663.

43 **But New Jersey . . . Malcolm's escort**: William Scudder Stryker, *"The New Jersey Volunteers" (Loyalists) in the Revolutionary War* (Trenton: Naar, Day & Naar, 1867), 4–11; and Adelberg, *The American Revolution*, 51–53, 98.

43 **Spermaceti Cove**: Nash, *Journal*, 20. See also Eric Jay Dolin, *Leviathan: The History of Whaling in America* (New York: W. W. Norton, 2007), 399, n39.

43 **"high spirits"**: Nash, *Journal*, 20.

44 **"artillery to play . . . not provoke them"**: "Lieutenant Colonel Benjamin Tupper to George Washington," (June 21, 1776), 663. See also Nash, *Journal*, 21.

44 **Tupper wrote**: "Lieutenant Colonel Benjamin Tupper to George Washington," (June 21, 1776), 663.

45 **"desist from"**: Ibid.

45 **Penning those . . . was canceled**: "General Orders, 20 June 1776," *The Papers of George Washington, Revolutionary War Series*, vol. 5, 52–53.

45 **"sent out"**: *"New-York Journal*, Thursday, July 4, 1776," in *NDAR*, vol. 5, 918–19.

45 **"We are in"**: Charles Francis Adams, *The Works of John Adams, Second President of the United States, With a Life of the Author*, vol. 1 (Boston: Little, Brown and Company, 1856), 223.

45 **To consolidate . . . burned homes**: David J. Fowler, " 'Loyalty is Now Bleeding in New Jersey': Motivations and Mentalities of the Disaffected," in *The Other Loyalties*, edited by Joseph S. Tiedermann, Eugene R. Fingerhut, and Robert W. Venables (Albany: State University of New York Press, 2009), 59–60; and Adelberg, " 'So Dangerous a Quarter," 13–15.

47 **"I'll give"**: Thomas Hill, "Sea Conquers Henlopen Light at Last," *New York Times Magazine* (March 21, 1926), 15.

47 **It's a wonderful . . . of the war**: "Cape Henlopen Light-House," *Register of Pennsylvania* (March 22, 1828), 191; J. Thomas Scharf, *History of Delaware, 1609–1888*, vol. 2 (Philadelphia: L. J. Richards & Co., 1888), 1236; and Trapani, *Delaware Lights*, 15.

48 **October 24, 1779**: "Boston, October 28" *New-Jersey Gazette* (November 10, 1779); and Samuel Greene Arnold, *History of the State of Rhode Island*

and Providence Plantations, vol. 2 (New York: D. Appleton & Company, 1860), 446.

48 **The extreme heat:** Champlin, "Rhode Island's," 51.

CHAPTER 3: LIGHTS OF A NEW NATION

49 **"We are in a wilderness . . . easier task":** James Madison to Thomas Jefferson (June 30, 1789), in *Letters and Other Writings of James Madison*, vol. 1 (Philadelphia: J. B. Lippincott, 1865), 480.

50 **main justifications:** David P. Currie, *The Constitution in Congress: The Federalist Period, 1789–1801* (Chicago: University of Chicago Press, 1997), 55–56; and Charlene Bangs Bickford and Kenneth R. Bowling, *Birth of the Nation: The First Federal Congress, 1789–1791* (Madison: Madison House Publishing, 1989), 29–31.

50 **Having stripped . . . commercial system:** Walter J. Stewart, *The Lighthouse Act of 1789* (Washington: U.S. Senate Historical Office, 1991), 2–5; Adam S. Grace, "From the Lighthouses: How the First Federal Internal Improvement Projects Created Precedent That Broadened the Commerce Clause, Shrunk the Takings Clause, and Affected Early Nineteenth Century Constitutional Debate," *Albany Law Review* (2004), 98–148; and Currie, *The Constitution in Congress*, 69–70.

51 **Antifederalists in particular:** Stewart, *The Lighthouse Act of 1789*, 4–5.

51 **But they were outvoted . . . nation's lighthouses:** Congress, *Laws of the United States of America*, vol. 1, 63–64; and *The Documentary History of the First Federal Congress of the United States of America, March 4, 1789–March 3, 1791, Legislative Histories*, vol. 5, edited by Charlene Bangs Bickford and Helen E. Veit (Baltimore: Johns Hopkins University Press, 1986), 1245–48.

52 **Appropriately enough:** United States Constitution Sesquicentennial Commission, *History of the Formation of the Union Under the Constitution* (Washington: U.S. Government Printing Office, 1941), 451–53.

52 **If the federal government failed:** Asaheli Stearns and Lemuel Shaw, *The General Laws of Massachusetts, From the Adoption of the Constitution, to February 1822*, vol. 1 (Boston: Wells & Lilly and Cummings & Hilliard, 1823), 384.

53 **Portland Head:** Jeremy D'Entremont, *The Lighthouses of Maine* (Beverly, MA: Commonwealth Editions, 2009), 83–84.

53 **"Does not this":** Christiane Mathan and William D. Barry, "Portland Head," *The Keeper's Log* (Summer 1991), 3.

53 **Some sixty . . . the keepers:** Charles C. Calhoun, *Longfellow: A Redis-covered Life* (Boston: Beacon Press, 2004), 172–73; and personal commu-nication with John Babin, Visiting Service Manager, Maine Historical Society, April 19, 2014.

54 **"The rocky ledge":** Henry Wadsworth Longfellow, *The Seaside and the Fireside* (Boston: Ticknor, Reed, and Fields, 1850), 41, 44.

54 **Georgia's Tybee Lighthouse:** Milton B. Smith, "The Lighthouse on Tybee Island," *Georgia Historical Quarterly* (September 1965), 245–63; and Cullen G. Chambers, *A Brief History of the Tybee Island Light Sta-tion, 1732–1999* (Tybee Island: Tybee Island Historical Society, 1999), 1–14.

54 **"a tower of":** Smith, "The Lighthouse," 246.

54 **Cape Henry Lighthouse:** Background for the Cape Henry Lighthouse comes from Arthur Pierce Middleton, "The Struggle for the Cape Henry Lighthouse, 1721–1791," *American Neptune* (January 1948), 26–36; and George Rockwell Putnam, *Lighthouses and Lightships of the United States* (Boston: Houghton Mifflin Company, 1917), 20–21.

55 **"obvious":** Middleton, "The Struggle," 26.

56 **thirty-four more lighthouses:** Stevenson, *Lighthouses Before 1820*, 181, 248; Winslow Lewis, *Description of the Light Houses on the Coast of the United States* (Boston: Thomas Bangs, 1817); Holland, *America's Light-houses*, 82–85, 111–19; and Richard W. Updike, "Winslow Lewis and the Lighthouses," *American Neptune* (January 1968), 36.

56 **"without parallel":** Henry Carter Adams, "Taxation in the United States, 1789–1816, vols. 5–6," in *Johns Hopkins University Studies in Historical and Political Science*, edited by Herbert B. Adams (Baltimore: N. Murray,1884), 70.

56 **warship *Somerset*:** Background for the crash of the *Somerset* comes from Richard F. Whalen, *Truro: The Story of a Cape Cod Town* (Charleston, SC History Press, 2007), 86–87, 99; and Edward Rowe Snow, *Storms and Shipwrecks of New England*, updated by Jeremy D'Entremont (Car-lisle, MA: Commonwealth Editions, 2003), 4–9.

57 **to build a lighthouse:** D'Entremont, *The Lighthouses of Massachusetts*, 187–88; and "Valuable hints, respecting the erection of a light house at clay pounds," *Massachusetts Magazine* (January 1, 1791), 46.

57 **"That mountain":** Levi Whitman to James Freeman (October 26, 1794), in *Collections of the Massachusetts Historical Society for the Year 1795* (Boston: Samuel Hall, 1795), 42.

58   The *Nottingham Galley*: Background for the story of the *Nottingham Galley* comes from John Deane, "The Loss of the *Nottingham Galley*, of London," in Archibald Duncan, *The Mariner's Chronicle Being a Collection of the Most Interesting Narratives of Shipwrecks, Fires, Famines, and Other Calamaties Incident to a Life of Maritime Enterprise*, vol. 2 (London: James Cundee, 1804), 57–74 (all quotes come from this source); and Richard Warner, "Captain John Deane and the Wreck of the Nottingham Galley," in *Kenneth Roberts Boon Island*, edited by Jack Bales and Richard Warner (Hanover, NH: University Press of New England, 1996), 3–7.

60   Nearly a . . . room on top: D'Entremont, *The Lighthouses of Maine*, 17–18.

60   the one at Montauk Point: The background for the Montauk Point Lighthouse comes from Henry Osmers, *On Eagle's Beak: A History of the Montauk Point Lighthouse* (Denver: Outskirts Press, 2008), 19–51; and Robert J. Hefner, "Montauk Point Lighthouse: A History of New York's First Seamark," *Long Island Historical Journal* (Spring 1991), 205–9.

60   "Perhaps no building": Timothy Dwight, *Travels in New-England and New-York*, vol. – (London: Charles Wood, 1823), 296.

61   Cape Hatteras Lighthouse: The background for the Cape Hatteras Lighthouse comes from Dawson Carr, *The Cape Hatteras Lighthouse: Sentinel of the Shoals* (Chapel Hill: University of North Carolina Press, 262), 13–16, 26–35; and Holland, *America's Lighthouses*, 112–14.

62   "first rate": Alexander Hamilton, "Light-House on the Coast of North Carolina," in *American State Papers: Documents, Legislative and Executive, of the Congress of the United States*, vol. 7 (Washington: Gales and Seaton, 1832), 265.

62   Responsibility for . . . the president: Putnam, *Lighthouses and Lightships*, 33–34.

62   "If the person": George Washington to Alexander Hamilton, October 1, 1792, in *The Writings of George Washington From the Original Manuscript Sources, 1745–1799*, vol. 32 (Washington: U.S. Government Printing Office, 1939), 174.

63   "the keepers": Putnam, *Lighthouses and Lightships*, 34.

63   government defended: "Tench Coxe to Benjamin Lincoln" (March 16, 1796), Light-House Letters, 1792–1809, National Archives at Boston.

64   "tedious service . . . impediments": George R. Putnman, "Beacons of the Sea," *National Geographic* (January 1913), 11–12.

64 **How American lighthouses were illuminated evolved:** Thomas Tag, "From Braziers and Bougies to Xenon, Part I" *The Keeper's Log* (Fall 2002), 30; and Thomas Tag, "Early American Lighthouse Illumination," *The Keeper's Log* (Fall 1998), 16–17; and Connie Jo Kendall, "Let There Be Light: The History of Lighthouse Illumination," *The Keeper's Log* (Spring 1997), 22–29.

64 **The whale oil . . . warmer months:** Elmo Paul Hohman, *The American Whalemen* (New York: Longmans, Green and Co., 1928), 334–35; and Richard C. Kugler, "The Whale Oil Trade, 1750–1775," in *Seafaring in Colonial Massachusetts* (Boston: Colonial Society of Massachusetts, distributed by University Press of Virginia, 1980), 164.

66 **The distance . . . far off:** Stevenson, *Rudimentary Treatise*, 15961; U.S. Department of Commerce, *The United States Lighthouse Service, 1915* (Washington: U.S. Government Printing Office, 1916), 36–38; and Terry Pepper, "Visibility of Objects at a Distance," at http://www.terrypepper .com/Lights/lists/visibility.htm, accessed on September 11, 2014.

67 **Aimé Argand:** Background for Argand and his invention comes from "The Argand Lamp," *The Penny Magazine of the Society for the Diffusion of Useful Knowledge* (March 29, 1834), 119–20; Stevenson, *The World's*, 61–63; and Tag, "Early American," 18.

67 **"a broken-off":** "The Argand Lamp," 120.

68 **"it gives":** Thomas Jefferson to William Smith (February 19, 1791), in *The Writings of Thomas Jefferson*, edited by Paul Leicester Ford, vol. 5, 1788–1792 (New York: G. P. Putnam's Sons, 1895), 290–91.

68 **When a light . . . its own:** Stevenson, *A Rudimentary Treatise*, 90; Tom Tag, "The Mirror of Light, Part One," *The Keeper's Log* (Summer 2001), 16–17; and Theresa Levitt, *A Short, Bright Flash: Augustin Fresnel and the Birth of the Modern Lighthouse* (New York: W. W. Norton and Company, 2013), 56.

70 **employed parabolic:** Stevenson, *The World's*, 64–69, 231–44.

70 **Born in . . . and iron:** John H. Sheppard, "Genealogy of the Lewis Family," in *New England Historical and Genealogical Register, and Antiquarian Journal* (April 1863), 162–65; Updike, "Winslow," 31–32; and Winslow Lewis to Stephen Pleasonton (January 9, 1838), in U.S. Sen.. Doc. 138, January 26, 1838, 66.

70 **"tall, fine-looking":** John H. Sheppard, "Brief Memoir of Dr. Winslow Lewis," *New England Historical and Genealogical Register, for the Year 1863*, vol. 17 (Albany, NY: J. Munsell, 1863), 8–9.

71 **"magnifying and reflecting"**: U.S. H.R. Doc. 183, 1843, 51; and Tag, "Early American," 18–20.

71 **While some accused**: Winslow Lewis, *Review of the Report of I.W.P. Lewis on the State of Light Houses on the Coasts of Maine and Massachusetts* (Boston: Tuttle and Dennett, 1843), 21–22; U.S. H.R.,Doc. 183, 51; and Winslow Lewis to Stephen Pleasonton, April 6, 1842, RG26 17E, Letters Received from Winslow Lewis (1826–1851), box 2, NAB.

72 **"reflectors came"**: Johnson, *The Modern*, 49.

72 **"had much the grain"**: Ibid., 49.

72 **And the glass . . . let through**: Lewis, *Review*, 4; Tag, "Early American," 18; and Tag, "The Mirror," 21.

73 **obtaining a patent**: Daniel Preston, "The Administration and Reform of the U. S. Patent Office, 1790–1836," *Journal of the Early Republic* (Autumn 1985), 331–35.

73 **patent number 1305**: Henry L. Ellsworth, *A Digest of Patents Issued by the United States, from 1790 to January 1, 1839* (Washington: Peter Force, 1840), 184.

74 **"It is to be"**: "Description of the Light-House at Sandy Hook," *New-York Magazine* (August 1, 1790), 438.

74 **"as great as"**: Lewis, *Review*, 23.

75 **"fully convinced . . . better lights"**: H. Dearborn to Albert Gallatin (December 20, 1810), in Lewis, *Review*, 24–25.

75 **Additional tests**: Ibid., 25–28.

75 **Congress concurred**: United States Congress, An Act to Authorize the Secretary of the Treasury, Under the Direction of the President of the United States, to Purchase of Winslow Lewis, his Patent Right to the New and Improved Method of Lighting Lighthouses, and for Other Purposes" (March 2, 1812), in *The Public Statutes at Large of the United States of America*, vol. 2, edited by Richard Peters (Boston: Charles C. Little and James Brown, 1845), 691.

75 **Later that . . . necessary supplies**: Lewis to Pleasonton, April 6, 1842; and Updike, "Winslow," 36.

75 **Federal Jack**: Updike, "Winslow," 36–37.

76 **forty lighthouses**: Ibid., 37.

76 **Their luck . . . in June**: Ibid.; and Winslow Lewis to Henry A. Dearborn (March 9, 1813), Light-House Letters, 1792–1809, National Archives at Boston.

76 "The enemy": James Scott, *Recollections of a Naval Life*, vol. 3 (London: Richard Bentley, 1834), 65.

77 "attacked the pantry": Ralph E. Eshelman, *A Travel Guide to the War of 1812 in the Chesapeake* (Baltimore: Johns Hopkins University Press, 2011), 192.

77 Another instance . . . rest of the war: Winslow Lewis to William Jones, August 15, 1813, RG26 17E, Letters Received from Winslow Lewis (1826–1851), box 1, NAB; Jacob E. Mallmann, *Historical Papers on Shelter Island and Its Presbyterian Church* (New York: A. M. Bustard Co., 1899), 84–85; and "British Naval Activity off Block Island," in *The Naval War of 1812: A Documentary History*, vol. 2 (Washington: U.S. Government Printing Office, 1985), 114.

77 most memorable story: "Along the South Shore," *Harper's New Monthly Magazine* (June 1878), 8–10; and D'Entremont, *The Lighthouses of Massachusetts*, 256–57.

77 "The old *La Hogue*": "Along the South Shore," 8.

79 another job: Updike, "Winslow," 39–40.

79 1816 alone: Ibid., 41.

79 "darkest period": Gleason, *Kindly*, 37.

CHAPTER 4: ECONOMY ABOVE ALL

80 On August 24, 1814: Stephen Pleasonton to William H. Winder (August 7, 1848), in Edward D. Ingraham, *A Sketch of the Events Which Preceded the Capture of Washington, by the British on the Twenty-Fourth of August, 1814* (Philadelphia: Carey and Hart, 1849), 47–49.

81 by appointing him: "New Treasury Offices," *The National Register* (March 8, 1817).

82 Pleasonton's responsibilities . . . superintendent of lighthouses": Robert Mayo, *The Treasury Department and its Various Fiscal Bureaus, Their Origin, Organization, and Practical Operations* (Washington: William Q. Force, 1847), 154–55.

82 "was a very": Charles Wilkes, *Autobiography of Rear Admiral Charles Wilkes, U.S. Navy, 1798–1877* (Washington: Naval History Division, Department of the Navy, 1978), 317–18.

82 In 1820: *RLHB*, June 30, 1857 (Washington: William A. Harris, 1858), 229.

82 After Congress . . . patent lamps: Holland, *America's Lighthouses*, 26–27, 30–31; and U.S., *Report of the Officers*, 525.

83   "unexampled": U.S. H.R. Doc. No. 38 (1844), 6.

83   Pleasonton relied most . . . by his office: Holland, *America's Light-houses*, 16–17; and U.S.H.R. Doc. No., 811, 1842, 98.

84   "would work": Holland, *America's Lighthouses*, 16.

84   "'hard' evidence": Ibid.

85   The opening up . . . the Great Lakes: Holland, *America's Lighthouses*, 176–84; and Todd R. Berger, *Lighthouses of the Great Lakes* (St. Paul: Voyageur Press, 2002), 21, 26.

85   The first one: Rick Tuers, *Lighthouses of New York* (Atglen, PA: Schiffer Publishing, 2007), 82–85.

85   along the Florida Keys: Love Dean, *Lighthouses of the Florida Keys* (Sarasota: Pineapple Press, 1998), 21–25; and Dorothy Dodd, "The Wrecking Business on the Florida Reef 1822–1860,"*Florida Historical Quarterly* (April 1944), 172–73.

86   "great want": Matthew C. Perry to Smith Thompson (March 28, 1822), in *Public Documents Printed by Order of the Senate of the United States, First Session of the Twenty-Fourth Congress, Begun and Held at the City of Washington, December 7, 1835*, vol. 5 (Washington: Gales & Seaton, 1836), 5–6.

86   were the wreckers: "Key West and Salvage in 1850," *Florida Historical Society Quarterly* (July 1929), 47; Jeremiah Digges, *Cape Cod Pilot: A Loquacious Guide* (Provincetown: Modern Pilgrim Press, 1937), 136–37; Rodney E. Dillon Jr., "South Florida in 1860," *Florida Historical Quarterly*, (April 1982), 453; Birse Shepard, *Lore of the Wreckers* (Boston: Beacon Press, 1961), 7–10; and Michael G. Schene, "The Early Florida Salvage Industry," *American Neptune* (October 1978), 270–71.

87   Ralph Waldo Emerson: Ralph Waldo Emerson, *Journals of Ralph Waldo Emerson*, edited by Edward Waldo Emerson and Waldo Emerson Forbes (Boston: Houghton Mifflin Company, 1912), 399.

87   "hold out": "An act more effectually to provide for the punishment of Act of 1790, certain crimes against the United States, and for other purposes," in *The Public and General Statutes Passed by the Congress of the United States of America, From 1789 to 1827 Inclusive*, edited by Joseph Story (Boston: Wells and Lilly, 1827), 2001.

87   Cape Florida Lighthouse . . . Thompson's slave: Dean, *Lighthouses of the Florida Keys*, 33–35.

88   At about four: The background and all the quotes for Thompson and Carter's ordeal at the lighthouse is based on John W. B. Thompson,

"Cape Florida Lighthouse," *Niles Weekly Register* (November 19, 1836), 181–82.

CHAPTER 5: EUROPEANS TAKE THE LEAD

92 **Unlike Lewis's . . . beam of light:** "Sea-Lights," *Encyclopaedia Britannica or Dictionary*, vol. 20 (Edinburgh: Adam and Charles Black, 1842), 19.

93 **Augustin-Jean Fresnel:** Background on Fresnel and his lens comes from François Arago, "Fresnel," in *Biographies of Distinguished Scientific Men* (London: Longman, Brown, Green, Longmans, & Roberts, 1857), 399–471; Levitt, *A Short*, 21–103; and Richard Updike, "Augustin Fresnel and His Lighthouse Lenses," *The Log of the Mystic Seaport* (Spring/Summer 1967), 35–39.

95 **"I find nothing":** Levitt, *A Short*, 28.

96 **"A lens, by":** Ibid., 56.

96 **"lenses by steps":** Arago, "Fresnel," 464.

97 **"Versailles of the Sea":** Levitt, *A Short*, 67.

97 **"King's Chamber":** Adams, *Lighthouses*, 216.

100 **Fresnel calculated:** Levitt, *A Short*, 76–77.

101 **"I could have":** Arago, "Fresnel," 470.

CHAPTER 6: THE "RULE OF IGNORANT AND INCOMPETENT MEN"

104 **After visiting France:** Levitt, *A Short*, 139.

104 **"the great deficiency":** U.S. Sen. Doc. 138, 1838, 21.

104 **"greatly inferior":** Ibid., 2.

104 **"nothing but the":** Ibid., 3.

104 **"cost to":** Ibid., 5.

105 **"the system which":** Ibid., 3.

105 **"enforced, our light":** Ibid, 6.

105 **"increased beyond the":** Ibid., 13.

106 **"either frivolous":** Ibid., 27.

106 **"were satisfactory":** Ibid., 32.

106 **"to whose experience":** Ibid., 34.

106 **"an unjustifiable":** Ibid., 37.

106 **"too complicated":** Ibid., 38.

106 **Blunts responded:** U.S. Sen. Doc. 258, 1838.

107 **"making common":** Ibid., 10.

108   board concluded: U.S. H.R. Doc. 811, 1842, 3; and U.S. H.R. Doc. 41, 1837.

108   his own investigation: U.S. Sen. Doc. 428, 1838.

108   40 percent: Holland, *America's Lighthouses*, 30.

109   "It cannot be": U.S. H.R. Doc. 24, 1838, 70.

109   "the aid of": Ibid., 72.

109   The reformers . . . the process: U.S. H.R. Doc. 811, 38; and Gleason, *Kindly*, 83–84.

109   "If well authenticated": U.S. Sen. Doc. 474, 1840, 1–2.

109   "the brilliancy . . . practical improvements": U.S. Sen. Doc. 619, 1840, 3–4.

110   "Mr. Pleasonton . . . utter worthlessness": John H. Schroeder, *Matthew Calbraith Perry: Antebellum Sailor and Diplomat* (Annapolis: Naval Institute Press, 2001), 85–86.

110   "The lenticular lights": Thomas R. Gedney to Messrs. Poindexter and Bradley (May 16, 1842), in *Report of the Officers*, 545.

110   "beauty and": U.S. H.R. Doc. 811, 39.

111   "are a brilliant": Winslow Lewis to Stephen Pleasonton, August 26, 1841, Miscellaneous Letters Received, RG 26, E17G, box 7, NAB.

111   After an early: F. W. D. Holbrook, "Memoir of Isaiah William Penn Lewis," in *Transactions, American Society of Civil Engineers* (December 1897), 453–54.

111   IWP's exposure . . . dried up: U.S. H.R. Doc. 183, 1843, annex, 6–19.

112   "Instead of order": Lewis, *Review*, 4.

113   "practical knowledge": U.S. H.R. Doc. 811, 99.

113   In contrast: U.S. H.R. Doc. 183, annex, 6–26.

113   "great zeal . . . much allowance": U.S. H.R. Doc. 811, 12.

113   "a practical knowledge": Ibid., 18.

114   "prevents any": U.S. H.R. Doc. 183, 20.

115   "calumnies:" U.S. H.R. Doc. 62, 1844, 1.

115   "the worst": Ibid., 58.

115   primarily owned: Porter, *Friendly*, 188.

115   "I do not": Stephen Pleasonton to Walter Forward, February 15, 1843, RG26, E35, Light-House Letters (1844), box 2, NAB.

115   "A talent": Lewis, *Review*, 5.

116   IWP's side: U.S. H.R. Doc. 183, 2.

116   "was a severe": "U.S. Lighthouse Service," *Appleton's Mechanics' Magazine and Engineers' Journal* (August 1852), 185.

117   "The interests of": U.S. Sen. Rep. 488, 1846, 14.

118 One reason: Porter, *Friendly*, 162; and Joel H. Silbey, *The American Nation, 1838–1893* (Redwood City, CA: Stanford University Press, 1991), 82.

118 "was not a bright": Wilkes, *Autobiography*, 317.

119 Facing political . . . build more: Levitt, *A Short*, 146; and Holbrook, "Memoir," 453.

119 four lighthouses: An Act Authorizing the Erection of Certain Lighthouses, and for other purposes (March 3, 1847), in *The Statutes at Large and Treaties of the United States of America from December 1, 1845, to March 3, 1851*, vol. 9, edited by George Minot (Boston: Charles C. Little and James Brown, 1851), 178.

119 One of these . . . Fresnel lens: Johnson, *The Modern*, 26; Holland, *America's Lighthouses*, 97–99; and David P. Heap, *Ancient and Modern Light-Houses* (Boston: Ticknor and Company, 1889), 62–63.

120 "fatal spot": U.S. H.R. Doc. 183, 13.

121 "rocket light . . . blazing star": W. R. Easton to Thornton Jenkins (August 3, 1851), in *Report of the Officers*, 338–39.

121 be widened: Edouard Stackpole, "The Saga of Sankaty," *Proceedings of the Nantucket Historical Association* (1950), 34–42.

121 Carysfort Reef Lighthouse: Dean, *Lighthouses of the Florida Keys*, 127–42; and Elinor De Wire, *Lighthouses of the South* (St. Paul: Voyageur Press, 2004), 64–65.

121 astonishing turn: William Allen Butler, *A Retrospect of Forty Years, 1825–1865*, edited by Harriet Allen Butler (New York: Charles Scribner's Sons, 1911), 198–202.

123 "Our whole": H. J. Raymond, "Our Lighthouse System," *American Review* (March 1845), 324.

124 Alexander Dallas Bache: Alexander Dallas Bache, *Dictionary of American Biography*, edited by Allen Johnson, vol. 1 (New York: Charles Scribner's Sons, 1928).

124 Every member: Levitt, *A Short*, 154–55.

125 "anything *but creditable*": *Report of the Officers*, 106. (Emphasis in original.)

125 "Our lighthouse ": Ibid., 107. (Emphasis in original.)

126 "Our light-houses as": David D. Porter to Thornton A. Jenkins (July 1851), ibid., 207.

126 "The lights on": H. J. Hartstene to Thornton A. Jenkins (July 18, 1851), ibid., 212.

126 **"not as efficient"**: Ibid., 8.

126 **"Nothing can"**: Alan Stevenson, *Account of the Skerryvore Lighthouse, With Notes on Illumination of Lighthouses* (London: Adam and Charles Black, 1848), 270.

126 **As for the . . . serve for perpetuity**: *Report of the Officers*, 22–24, 86, 121–22

127 **"furnished an"**: Ibid., 24.

127 **"compare, in point"**: Ibid., 62.

128 **In a letter**: U.S. H.R. Doc. 88, 1852, 1–6.

128 **"The great object"**: Gleason, *Kindly*, 91.

129 **"an unfair, unjust"**: U.S. Lighthouse Board, *Compilation of Public Documents and Extracts from Reports and Papers Relating to Light-Houses, Light-Vessels, and Illuminating Apparatus, and to Beacons, Buoys, and Fog Signals, 1789–1871* [hereafter, *Compilation*] (Washington: U.S. Government Printing Office, 1871), 576–77.

129 **"In 1852"**: Edmund M. Blunt, *The American Coast Pilot* (New York: George W. Blunt, 1867), v.

129 **"We are very"**: "The Light House System," *Vineyard Gazette* (September 10, 1852).

130 **"One wonders"**: Holland, *America's Lighthouses*, 28.

130 **"I feel under"**: Ted Nelson, "Stephen Pleasonton: The Rest of the Story," *The Keeper's Log* (Spring 2008), 26.

CHAPTER 7: BRIGHTER LIGHTS

133 **"I would not"**: Joseph Henry to Asa Gray (November 6, 1852), *The Papers of Joseph Henry*, edited by Marc Rothenberg, vol. 8 (Washington: Smithsonian Institution Press, 1998), 399.

133 **board's first task**: Background for this section on the management system and early reforms comes from U.S. Sen. Rep. 22, 1853, 108–10; Light-house Board, *List of Light-Houses, Lighted Beacons, and Floating Lights, of the United States* (Washington: A.O.P. Nicholson, 1856); Johnson, *The Modern*, 23, 102–3; Holland, *America's Lighthouses*, 36; and U.S. Lighthouse Board, *Organization and Duties of the Light-House Board: and Rules, Regulations, & Instructions of the Light-House Establishment of the United States* (Washington: U.S. Government Printing Office, 1864).

135 **"a light placed"**: *Report of the Officers*, 53.

135 **elevated to 150**: Holland, *America's Lighthouses*, 114.

135 **Originally built in 1826 . . . mountainous waves:** John Matteson, *The Lives of Margaret Fuller: A Biography* (New York: W. W. Norton, 2012), 417–18; Megan Marshall, *Margaret Fuller: A New American Life* (New York: Mariner Books, 2013), 371–84; "Shipwreck and Lost of Life," *Weekly Messenger* (July 24, 1850); and Holland, *America's Lighthouses*, 87–88.

136 **"America has produced":** Marshall, *Margaret Fuller*, 384.

137 **American pride . . . two years earlier:** Levitt, *A Short*, 166–68; and Cheryl Roberts, "Letters Reveal Last Journey of the Hatteras Lens But End in a Mystery," *Lighthouse Digest* (March 2000), 8–11.

138 **"This marvelous":** "The Fresnel Light," *Friend's Review* (October 22, 1853), 87.

138 **"in a few":** "The Crystal Palace—The Fresnel Light," *Daily Union* (September 27, 1853).

140 **Beyond this . . . weakening the beam:** Kendall, "Let There Be Light," 25–26; and Wayne Wheeler, "The Fresnel Lens," *The Keeper's Log* (Winter 1985), 12.

141 **"was a series":** James Woodward, "Lightening Lights: The Mercury Float Lighthouse Lens: Its Development, Use, and Decline," *The Keeper's Log* (Spring 2006), 30.

143 **Texas officials . . . Texas coast:** T. Lindsay Baker, *Lighthouses of Texas* (College Station: Texas A&M University, 2001), 3, 5, 28–31, 57–59; and David L. Cipra, *Lighthouses, Lightships, and the Gulf of Mexico* (Alexandria, VA: Cypress Communications, 1997), 177–78, 189–90.

145 **sixteen be built:** Background for the first sixteen lighthouses comes from Holland, *America's Lighthouses*, 153–57; "Report of the Secretary of the Treasury, in Compliance with a resolution of the Senate of January 10, 1855, calling for correspondence, etc., relative to the claim of Gibbons and Kelly, Senate Ex. Doc. 53, 33d Congress, 2d Sess.. (February 17, 1855); 1–178; Peter White, *The Farallon Islands: Sentinels of the Golden Gate* (San Francisco: Scottwall Associates, 1995), 26, 33–43; Randy Leffingwell, *Lighthouses of the Pacific Coast* (St. Paul: Voyageur Press, 2000), 24–37, 54; Levitt, *A Short*, 171–80; Hartman Bache to Edmund L. F. Hardcastle (July 11, 1855), in *RLHB*, June 30, 1855 (Washington: Beverly Tucker, 1856), 402–4; and Wayne Wheeler, "Alcatraz and the First West Coast Lighthouses," *The Keeper's Log* (Winter 1985), 2–6.

145 **"great and":** San Francisco merchants to Stephen Pleasonton, Septem-

ber 30, 1851, RG 26, E35, Light-House Letters, series P, Box 7 (1850–1851), NAB.

145 **"utterly destitute"**: William McKendree Gwin, *Congressional Globe* (March 23. 1852), 830.

146 **"rocky islet"**: Susan Casey, *The Devil's Teeth: A True Story of Obsession and Survival Among America's Great White Sharks* (New York: Henry Holt and Company, 2005), 6.

146 **"the Devil's Teeth"**: Ibid, 76.

147 **"rich, delicate"**: Charles S. Greene, "Los Farallones De Los Frayles," *Overland Monthly* (September 1892), 233.

147 **By the . . . as two hundred thousand dollars**: Leverett M. Loomis, "California Water Birds, No. III—South Farallon Island in July" in *Proceedings of the California Academy of Sciences, 1896* (San Francisco: California Academy of Sciences, 1897), 358; and John E. Bennett, "Our Seaboard Islands of the Pacific." *Harper's New Monthly Magazine* (November 1898), 861.

147 **The egging . . . their death**: Robin W. Doughty, "San Francisco's Nineteenth-Century Egg Basket: The Farallons," *Geographical Review* (October, 1971), 560–63; and White, *The Farallon*, 48.

150 **"however great . . . be exhibited"**: Hartman Bache to Edmund L. F. Hardcastle (July 11, 1855), 403–4.

151 **After the ship . . . steam-powered siren**: White, *The Farallon*, 39; and Charles Nordhoff, "The Farallon Islands," *Harper's New Monthly Magazine* (April 1874), 619.

152 **Tatoosh Island Lighthouse**: Background for this section comes from Jim A. Gibbs, *Lighthouses of the Pacific* (Atglen, PA: Schiffer Publications, 1986), 145–48; Alvin J. Ziontz, *A Lawyer in Indian Country* (Seattle: University of Washington Press, 2009), 73–74; *Report of the Commissioner of Indian Affairs Accompanying the Annual Report of the Secretary of the Interior for the Year 1858* (Washington: Wm. A. Harris, 1858), 237–38; and James G. McCurdy, "Cape Flattery and Its Light: Life on Tatoosh Island," *Overland Monthly* (April 1898), 345–47.

154 **"the vast . . . outermost peak"**: Richard Henry Dana, Jr. *Two Years Before the Mast, And Twenty-Four Years After, A Personal Narrative* (London: Sampson Low, Son, & Marston, 1869), 378–79, 388.

155 **In 1856 . . . had inherited**: "Our Light-house Establishment," *Putnam's Monthly* (June 1856), 658; and *RLHB*, June 30, 1860 (Washington: Thomas H. Ford, 1860), 363.

156 **"In a few short"**: Levitt, *A Short*, 180.

156 **"The prodigious"**: "Letter of Wm. B. Shubrick to S. P. Chase" (February 24, 1862), in *The Miscellaneous Documents of the Senate of the United States for the Second Session of the Thirty-Seventy Congress, 1861–62* (Washington: U.S. Government Printing Office, 1862), 16.

156 **1852 had predicted**: W. B. Shubrick to Howell Cobb, (March 13, 1858), in *RLHB*, June 30, 1858 (Washington: William A. Harris, 1858), 373.

CHAPTER 8: "EVERYTHING BEING RECKLESSLY BROKEN"

158 **he wrote to**: Thornton A. Jenkins to Salmon P. Chase, (November 26, 1861), in *RLHB*, June 30, 1861 (Washington: U.S. Government Printing Office, 1861), 203–6.

159 **"the coast of"**: Putnam, *Lighthouses and Lightships*, 100.

159 **Born in 1809 . . . around him**: Warren F. Spencer, *Raphael Semmes: The Philosophical Mariner* (Tuscaloosa: University of Alabama Press, 1997), 12; and Stephen Fox, *Wolf of the Deep: Raphael Semmes and the Notorious Confederate Raider CSS Alabama* (New York: Alfred A. Knopf, 2007), 11–12.

159 **"I am still"**: Raphael Semmes, *Memoirs of Service Afloat, During the War Between the States* (Baltimore: Kelly, Piet & Co., 1869), 75. See also Spencer, *Raphael Semmes*, 93–94.

159 **The situation in . . . loss of the lighthouses**: David Detzer, *Allegiance: Fort Sumter, Charleston, and the Beginning of the Civil War* (New York: Harcourt, 2001), 109–22, 147.

160 **The federal reinforcements . . . their approach**: "Star of the West Fired On," *Sacramento Daily Union* (February 11, 1861); and Detzer, *Allegiance*, 155–59.

160 **buried in**: Levitt, *A Short*, 187.

161 **"Here was . . . immediately"**: Semmes, *Memoirs*, 76.

161 **The next . . . of disdain**: Ibid, 76–78.

161 **Semmes said . . . own recommendation**: Spencer, *Raphael Semmes*, 99, 102; Semmes, *Memoirs*, 81–87; and Provisional Government of the Confederate States of America, "An Act to establish and organize a Bureau in connection with the Department of the Treasury, to be known as the Lighthouse Bureau," in *The Statutes at Large of the Provisional Government of the Confederate States of America* (Richmond: R. M. Smith, 1864), 47.

162 **"Fort Sumter"**: Semmes, *Memoirs*, 88.

162 **"power" to "hold"**: Abraham Lincoln, "Lincoln's First Inaugural Address"

(March 4, 1861), in *Political Speeches and Debates of Abraham Lincoln and Stephen A. Douglas, 1854–1861*, edited by Alonzo T. Jones (Battle Creek, MI: International Tract Society, 1895), 533.

162 **"The Confederacy could"**: James McPherson, *Ordeal by Fire: The Civil War and Reconstruction* (New York: Alfred A. Knopf, 1982), 145.

163 **"Light-House Bureau"**: Semmes, *Memoirs*, 91.

163 **The South responded . . . coast was dark**: Thornton A. Jenkins to Salmon P. Chase, (November 26, 1861), in *RLHB*, June 30, 1861 (Washington: U.S. Government Printing Office, 1861), 204; Kevin P. Duffus, *The Lost Light: The Mystery of the Missing Cape Hatteras Fresnel Lens* (Raleigh, NC: Looking Glass Productions, 2003), 7–13; and David L. Cipra, "The Confederate States Lighthouse Bureau: A Portrait in Blue and Gray," *The Keeper's Log* (Winter 1992), 9.

164 **"After the bombardment"**: "Hatteras Island and Its Lighthouse," *Frank Leslie's Illustrated Newspaper* (November 2, 1861).

164 **"The blackened coast"**: Levitt, *A Short*, 190.

164 **Not long . . . in riverbeds**: James T. Miller to Thomas E. Martin, November 23, 1861, RG365, E79, TDCCR (1860–1865) Box 2, NACP; George Wood to William Colcock, June 1861, RG 365, E79, TDCCR (1860–1865), Box 2, NACP; Cipra, *Lighthouses*, 12–14; and James Sorley to Louis Cruger, June 30, 1863, RG 365, E79, TDCCR, Box 2 (1860–1865), NACP.

165 **"a few more"**: Carr, *The Cape*, 46.

165 **"in consequence"**: Le Gyt Daniels to J. M. Mason (March 1, 1862), in *ORUCN*, series 2, vol. 2 (Washington: U.S. Government Printing Office, 1921), 161–62.

165 **Merchants and the companies . . . having surrendered**: David Stick, *The Outer Banks of North Carolina* (Chapel Hill: University of North Carolina Press, 1990), 117–26; Mallison, *The Civil*, 31; Thos. O. Selfridge to Hon. Gideon Welles, (August 10, 1861), *ORUCN*, series 1, vol. 6 (Washington D. C.: U.S. Government Printing Office, 1897), 72–73; and John G. Barrett, *The Civil War in North Carolina* (Chapel Hill: University of North Carolina Press, 1963), 33–34.

166 **"nests of pirates"**: Fred Mallison, *The Civil War on the Outer Banks* (Jefferson, NC: McFarland & Company, 1998), 31.

166 **danced a jig**: Ivan Musicant, *Divided Waters: The Naval History of the Civil War* (New York: HarperCollins, 1995), 85.

166 **"a place which"**: Duffus, *The Lost Light*, 48.

166 "I was desirous": S. C. Rowan to Gideon Welles (September 3, 1861), ORUCN, series 1, vol. 6, 160–61.

167 At the end of September . . . a strange chase ensued: Background for Chicamacomico races comes from Stick, *The Outer Banks*, 130–36; Duffus, *The Lost Light*, 58–61; and Carr, *The Cape Hatteras Lighthouse*, 47–49.

167 "The first ten": Stick, *The Outer Banks*, 134

168 "Here we found": Ibid., 135.

169 "a very important": Insurance company presidents to Thornton A. Jenkins (September 21, 1861), RG26, E35, Light-House Letters, Box 8 (1860–1861), 189.

169 including the board: William Shubrick to S. P. Chase (March 8, 1862), RG26, E35, Light House Letters, Box 8 (1862–1864), 4.

169 By the middle . . . from France: Duffus, *The Lost Light*, 97, 107–8; Peter H. Watson to Salmon P. Chase, April 5, 1862, Light House Letters, Box 8 (1862–1864), NAB, 26–27; and L. M. Goldsborough to Gideon Welles, (February 20, 1862), in *ORUCN*, series 1, vol. 6, 635.

169 searching for the missing lens: The background for this section on the pursuit and travels of the Cape Hatteras lens is based on Duffus, *The Lost Light*, 74–75, 82–96; George H. Brown to Thomas E. Martin, April 7, 1862, RG 365, E79, TDCCR, Box 2 (1860–1865), NACP; George H. Brown to Thomas E. Martin, April 9, 1862, RG 365, E79, TDCCR, Box 2 (1860–1865), NACP; George H. Brown to Thomas E. Martin, April 14, 1862, RG 365, E79, TDCCR, Box 2 (1860–1865,), NACP; Roberts, "Letters Reveal," 8–11; and Levitt, *A Short*, 192–93.

170 "hold the": S. C. Rowan to L. M. Goldsborough, March 27, 1862, in *Report of the Secretary of the Navy, With an Appendix, Containing Reports from Officers, December 1862* (Washington: U.S. Government Printing Office, 1863), 112–13.

170 "frighten[ing] the": S. C. Rowan to L. M. Goldsborough, March 29, 1862, in *ORUCN*, series 1, vol. 7 (Washington: U.S. Government Printing Office, 1898), 178.

170 "the destruction": George H. Brown to E. Farrand, March 23, 1861, RG 365, E79, TDCCR, Box 2 (1860–1865), NACP.

170 "very responsible": George H. Brown to Thomas E. Martin, April 1861, RG 365, E79, TDCCR, Box 2 (1860–1865), NACP.

171 loaded with: David T. Tayloe, list of materials received April, 13, 1862, RG 365, E79, TDCCR, Box 2 (1860–1865), NACP.

171   **"I have had"**: David T. Tayloe to Thomas E. Martin, April 20, 1862, RG 365, E79, TDCCR, Box 2 (1860–1865), NACP.

171   **another lighthouse drama**: Background for this drama comes from Dorothy Dodd, ed., " 'Volunteers' Report Destruction of Lighthouses," *Tequesta* 14 (1954), 67–70; Rodney E. Dillon, " 'A Gang of Pirates:' Confederate Lighthouse Raids in Southeast Florida, 1861," *Florida Historical Quarterly* (April 1989), 441–49; and Neil E. Hurley, *Florida's Lighthouses in the Civil War* (Oakland Park: Middle River Press, 2007), 63-67, 75-78.

171   **"a band of"**: Thornton A. Jenkins to Salmon P. Chase, (November 26, 1861), 204.

172   **"I informed him"**: Hurley, *Florida's Lighthouses*, 66.

172   **"we destroyed no"**: Dodd, " 'Volunteers,' " 68.

172   **"repeatedly boasted"**: Ibid., 69.

173   **"The light being"**: Ibid., 68.

173   **"endeavor at all"**: Jefferson B. Browne, *Key West: The Old and the New* (St. Augustine: Record Company, 1912), 91.

173   **When Florida . . . be protected**: Ibid., 91–92; and Gene M.Burnett, *Florida's Past: People & Events That Shaped the State*, vol. 2 (Sarasota: Pineapple Press, 1988), 120–24.

173   **remained lit**: Thornton A. Jenkins to Salmon P. Chase, November 26, 1861, 204.

174   **"shining as"**: John R. Goldsborough to Samuel F. Du Pont, February 11, 1862, in *ORUCN*, series 1, vol. 12 (Washington: U.S. Government Printing Office, 1901), 473.

174   **"ruthlessly destroyed . . . oil cans"**: S. F. Du Pont to Gideon Welles, April 1, 1862, in *Official Dispatches and Letters of Rear Admiral DuPont, U.S. Navy* (Wilmington: Ferris Bros., 1883). 143.

174   **"nothing save a heap"**: "Charleston Lighthouse Blown up and Destroyed," *Charleston Mercury* (December 20, 1861).

174   **"much injured"**: S. F. Du Pont to Gideon Welles, April 1, 1862, 144.

175   **"guerillas"**: *RLHB*, June 30, 1863 (Washington: U.S. Government Printing Office, 1863), 159–60. See also Holland, *America's Lighthouses*, 122.

175   **In May 1864 . . . further raids**: Foxhall A. Parker to Gideon Welles, May 21, 1864, RG 26, E35, Light House Letters, Box 8 (1862–64), NAB, 191–92; Blackistone Island at the following website accessed on June 23, 2014, http://www.lighthousefriends.com/light.asp?ID=1120; and Paul

E., Vandor, *History of Fresno California*, vol. 2 (Los Angeles: Historic Record Company, 1919), 1945.

176   **In September 1861**: Cipra, *Lighthouses*, 90–91.

176   **Sand Island Lighthouse**: Background for this section comes from Cipra, *Lighthouses*, 71–72; and Arthur Bergeron, Jr., *Confederate Mobile* (Baton Rouge: Louisiana State University Press, 2000), 63–66.

176   **"tumble the"**: Cipra, *Lighthouses*, 72.

177   **"There was"**: Ibid., 15–16.

177   **This was during . . . metal plates**: William B. Shubrick to W. P. Fessenden (October 5, 1864), *RLHB*, 1864 (Washington: U.S. Government Printing Office, 1864), 169; Cipra, *Lighthouses*, 189–99; and Wayne Wheeler, "Aransas Pass Lighthouse," *The Keeper's Log* (Winter 2005), 10–11.

177   **Using lighthouses as . . . a lookout**: Edward T. Cotham, Jr., *Sabine Pass: The Confederacy's Thermopylae* (Austin: University of Texas Press, 2004), 59–63.

178   **at least one**: Cipra, *Lighthouses*, 45–46; and *RLHB*, 1867 (Washington: U.S. Government Printing Office, 1868), 225.

179   **Next to . . . gaping holes**: Cipra, *Lighthouses*, 69.

179   **"Damn the torpedoes"**: Craig L. Symonds, *The Civil War at Sea* (Santa Barbara: Praeger, 2009), 154.

180   **One of . . . is unknown**: Cipra, *Lighthouses*, 179; and Baker, *Lighthouses*, 59.

180   **destroyed some 164**: William B. Shubrick to Hugh McCullough, October 16, 1866, in *RLHB*, September 30, 1866 (Washington: U.S. Government Printing Office, 1866), 227.

180   **This is what developed**: Background for Arnau and the St. Augustine Lighthouse comes from Hurley, *Florida Lighthouses*, 41–42, 47–49; and S. F. Du Pont to Gideon Welles, April 1, 1862, 144.

181   **Another case of retrieval**: *Report of the Secretary of the Navy, With an Appendix, Containing Reports from Officers, December 1862* (Washington: U.S. Government Printing Office, 1863), 140.

181   **"Immediately upon"**: C. K. Stribling to Salmon P. Chase, November 1, 1862, *RLHB*, June 30, 1862 (Washington: U.S. Government Printing Office, 1863), 149.

181   **After the South's . . . during the war**: B. Rush Hornsby to Samuel P. Chase, May 6, 1863, RG 365, E79, TDCCR, Box 2 (1860–1865), NACP; Cipra, *Lighthouses*, 18–19, 113–14; and Levitt, *A Short*, 208.

182   **"it was visited"**: William B. Shubrick to Salmon P. Chase, October 31,

1863, *RLHB*, June 30, 1863 (Washington: U.S. Government Printing Office, 1863), 156, 160.

182 **"They are amenable"**: J. Candace Clifford and Mary Louise Clifford, *Nineteenth-Century Lights: Historic Images of American Lighthouses* (Alexandria: Cypress Communications, 2182), 168.

182 **Notwithstanding the**: William B. Shubrick to W. P. Fessenden, October 5, 1864, in *RLHB*, 1864 (Washington: U.S. Government Printing Office, 1864), 166.

183 **"The operations"**: Cipra, *Lighthouses*, 16.

183 **"The war is over"**: James M. McPherson, *Battle Cry of Freedom: The Civil War Era* (New York: Oxford University Press, 1988), 849-50.

184 **"In the rotunda"**: "Sherman," *Philadelphia Inquirer* (April 26, 1865); and Duffus, *The Lost Light*, 140.

184 **"Some broken"**: Duffus, *The Lost Light*, 142.

184 **Meigs also . . . to the state**: Ibid., 142–44.

184 **Although hopes . . . New York**: Ibid., 147–49.

185 **The flood . . . French manufacturers**: Levitt, *A Short*, 213.

185 **"as soon as"**: Duffus, *The Lost Light*, 153.

185 **rebuilt or repaired**: Shubrick to McCullough (October 16, 1866), in *RLHB*, September 30, 1866, 227.

CHAPTER 9: FROM BOARD TO SERVICE

187 **"The character"**: Joseph Henry to W. A. Richardson (October 14, 1873), in *ARLHB*, December 1, 1873 (Washington, D. C.: U.S. Government Printing Office, 1873), 587–88.

187 **One of the most . . . demand continued**: *RLHB*, June 30, 1855 (Washington: Beverley Tucker, 1855), 251; Holland, *America's Lighthouses*, 23; and Lance E. Davis, Robert E. Gallman, and Karin Gleiter, *In Pursuit of Leviathan: Technology, Institutions, Productivity, and Profits in American Whaling, 1816–1906* (Chicago: University of Chicago Press, 1997), 376–77, 379.

188 **distributing colza seeds**: *RLHB*, June 30, 1863 (Washington: U.S. Government Printing Office, 1863), 162.

188 **"too volatile"**: Ibid, 162–63.

188 **Indeed, a small**: "Lard Oil," *New England Farmer, & Horticultural Register* (December 28, 1842), 204; and Henry L. Ellsworth, *Improvements in Agriculture, Arts, &c of the United States* (New York: Greeley & McElrath, 1843), 50.

189 **Joseph Henry's experiments:** *ARLHB*, 1875 (Washington: U.S. Government Printing Office, 1875), 87–88; and Henry C. Cameron, "Reminiscences," in *Smithsonian Miscellaneous Collections*, vol. 21 (Washington: Smithsonian Institution, 1881), 309.

189 **by 1867 virtually:** *ARLHB*, 1867 (Washington: U.S. Government Printing Office, 1868), 194.

189 **in light of an accident:** *ARLHB*, 1875 (Washington: U.S. Government Printing Office, 1875), 99.

189 **by 1885:** *ARLHB*, June 30, 1885 (Washington: U.S. Government Printing Office, 1885), 16.

189 **The main type . . . industrial settings:** Jane Brox, *Brilliant: The Evolution of Artificial Light* (New York: Houghton Mifflin Harcourt, 2010), 102–9.

190 **When the Frenchman . . . feeble performance:** Carole L. Perrault, "Liberty Enlightening the World, Part I," *The Keeper's Log* (Spring 1986), 2–15; and Carole L. Perrault, "Liberty Enlightening the World, Part II," *The Keeper's Log* (Summer 1986), 6–17.

191 **"more like a glow":** Lois Wingerson, "America Cleans Up Liberty," *New Scientist* (December 25, 1986–January 1, 1987), 32.

191 **"The light in":** National Park Service, *Liberty Enlightening the World: The Statue of Liberty National Monument, Historic Structure Report* (New York: National Park Service, 2011), 76.

191 **The lamp . . . the locals:** Putnam, *Lighthouses*, 62; and Hans Christian Adamson, *Keepers of the Lights* (New York: Greenburg, 1955), 129–30.

192 **In this lamp . . . many other lighthouses:** Putnam, *Lighthouses*, 186; and *ARCL*, June 30, 1915, 3–4.

194 **"The mercury":** Thomas Tag, "The Clock Without Hands," *The Keeper's Log* (Spring 2008), 30–31.

194 **built a few:** James Woodward, "Lightening Lamps," 31–35.

196 **The board also . . . its replacement:** Holland, *America's Lighthouses*, 109–11; and Sara E. Wermiel, *Lighthouses* (New York: W. W. Norton, 2006), 225.

197 **opted for caisson lighthouses:** Background or caisson lighthouses comes from Francis Ross Holland, Jr., *Lighthouses* (New York: Barnes & Noble, 1997), 71–72; Putnam, "Beacons," 25–27; Ray Jones, *The Lighthouse Encyclopedia: The Definitive Reference* (Guilford: The Globe Pequot Press, 2004), 70.

199 **Sharps Island Lighthouse:** The background for the Sharps Island

Lighthouse comes from *ARLHB,* June 30, 1894 (Washington: U.S. Government Printing Office, 1894), 253–55; Pat Vojtech, *Lighting the Bay: Tales of Chesapeake Lighthouses* (Centreville, MD: Tidewater Publishers, 1996), 35; "Ice Damage in the Chesapeake" *Baltimore Sun* (February 14, 1881); and *ARLHB, June 30, 1881* (Washington: U.S. Government Printing Office, 1881), 39.

201 **It wasn't only ice:** Background for this section on the Thimble Shoal Lighthouse comes from "A Lighthouse is Burned," *Baltimore American* (December 28, 1909); *ARLHB, June 30, 1910* (Washington: Government Printing Office, 1910), 17; and Judy Bloodgood Bander, "The Thimbles Bug," *Lighthouse Digest* (April 2002), 20–21.

202 **A little after . . . thousands homeless:** U.S. Geological Survey, "San Francisco Earthquake of 1906," *Encyclopedia of Earth*, retrieved from http://www.eoearth.org/view/article/164914, accessed on May 31, 2015.

203 **"A heavy blow":** Gregory W. Coan, "Point Arena Light Station and the 1906 Earthquake," *The Keeper's Log*, 13–14. See also, Point Arena Lighthouse Logbook, April 18, 1906, RG26, E80, Lighthouse Station Logs, NAB.

203 **Given the . . . at hand:** Wayne C. Wheeler, "The History of Fog Signals, Part 1," *The Keeper's Log* (Summer 1990), 20–23; Wayne C. Wheeler, "The History of Fog Signals, Part 2," *The Keeper's Log* (Fall 1990), 8–13; and Holland, *America's Lighthouses*, 202–6.

203 **Since such . . . absolute necessity:** Holland, *America's Lighthouses*, 202.

203 **2,734 Hours:** *LSB* (August 1912), 31–32.

204 **"a screech like":** "Siren Is Breaking Up Happy Homes," *New York Herald* (June 19, 1905).

205 **"jaded attendants":** Dewey Livingston, "The Keepers of the Light: Point Reyes," *The Keeper's Log* (Winter 1991), 18.

205 **"be made happier":** *ARLHB,* 1875 (Washington: U.S. Government Printing Office, 1875), 10.

205 **Thus seeking to. . . more than five hundred:** *ARLHB, June 30, 1876* (Washington: U.S. Government Printing Office, 1877), 5; Holland, *America's Lighthouses*, 50; and Johnson, *The Modern Light-House Service*, 104.

206 **"aid in maintaining":** *ARLHB,* June 30, 1885 (Washington: U.S. Government Printing Office, 1885), 12.

207 **"efficient party . . . the oil":** "Keeping the Light," *Gazette of the Union,*

Golden Rule & Odd-Fellows' Family Companion (December 8, 1849), 369.

208 **"In regard to"**: *ARLHB,* December 1, 1873 (Washington: U.S. Government Printing Office, 1873), 591.

208 **"Mr. Lawrence was"**: Elinor De Wire, *Guardians of the Lights: Stories of U.S. Lighthouse Keepers* (Sarasota: Pineapple Press, 1995), 48.

208 **during President Lincoln's**: George R. Putnam, *Sentinel of the Coasts: The Log of a Lighthouse Engineer* (New York: W. W. Norton, 1937), 303-5.

208 **"new plan for"**: "Clippings," *Deseret News* (January 2, 1861).

208 **"A tall building"**: Ambrose Bierce, *The Unabridged Devil's Dictionary,* edited by David E. Schultz & S. T. Joshi (Athens: University of Georgia Press, 2000), 151.

208 **"You are superseded"**: Putnam, *Sentinel,* 127.

208 **The board did. . . of security**: Holland, *America's Lighthouses,* 39-41; Johnson, *The Modern,* 102-3; and "Congressional Patronage is the Greatest Obstacle to Every Reform," *The Civil Service Chronicle* (August 1894), 155.

210 **purchase of Alaska**: The background for this section on Alaska's lighthouses comes from Adamson, *Keepers,* 255-56; Wayne Wheeler, "Northern Lights: Lighthouse Development in the Alaskan Territory," *The Keeper's Log* (Spring 1990), 2-13; Shannon Lowry and Jeff Schultz, *Northern Lights: Tales of Alaska's Lighthouses and Their Keepers* (Harrisburg: Stackpole Books, 192), 5-16; and F. Ross Holland, *Lighthouses,* 97-99.

210 **"There are no"**: *Lieutenant Zagoskin's Travels in Russian America, 1842-1844,* edited by Henry N. Michael (Toronto: University of Toronto Press, 1967), 66.

211 **With so many . . . coast in 1898**: Steven C. Levi, *The Clara Nevada: Gold, Greed, Murder and Alaska's Inside Passage* (Charleston: History Press, 2011), 17-32; "SS Clara Nevada," *San Francisco Call* (February 15, 1898); Lowry and Schultz, *Northern Lights,* 43-44; and Gibbs, *Lighthouses of the Pacific,* 37-38.

212 **"The *Nevada* affair"**: "Klondike Steamer Lost," *The New York Times* (February 15, 1898).

212 **spurred demands**: *ARLHB,* June 30, 1899 (Washington: U.S. Government Printing Office, 1899), 41.

213 **"Tombstone Twins"**: Walter C. Dudley and Min Lee, *Tsunami* (Honolulu University of Hawaii Press, 1998), 1.

213 **Two other major . . . interests in Asia:** Samuel Eliot Morison, *The Oxford History of the American People* (New York: Oxford University Press, 1965), 800–805; and Julia Flynn Siler, *Lost Kingdom: Hawaii's Last Queen, the Sugar Kings, and America's First Imperial Adventure* (New York: Atlantic Monthly Press, 2012), 208–12, 220–22, 280–87.

213 **The board didn't. . . Puerto Rico:** Wayne C. Wheeler, "The Lighthouses of Puerto Rico, Part I," *The Keeper's Log* (Spring 1991), 23–27; Wayne C. Wheeler, "The Lighthouses of Puerto Rico, Part II," *The Keeper's Log* (Summer 1991), 12–17; and Holland, *Lighthouses*, 90–91.

214 **"generally of":** *ARLHB*, 1906 (Washington: U.S. Government Printing Office, 1906), 221–22.

214 **The board immediately initiated. . . used in the United States:** Love Dean, *The Lighthouses of Hawaii* (Honolulu: University of Hawaii Press, 1991); 38–44; "Pacific Mail Liner Manchuria Strikes a Reef," *The American Marine Engineer* (September 1906), 11; and Levitt, *A Short*, 222–24.

216 **The more than 2,500:** Putnam, *Lighthouses*, 52; H. R. Doc. 14 (1850), 3; and Putnam, "Beacons," 1.

216 **At the same . . . been illuminated:** *ARLHB*, June 30, 1908 (Washington: U.S. Government Printing Office, 1908), 9; George Putnam, "Beacons," 1; and U.S. Department of Commerce, *The United States Lighthouse Service*, 12.

218 **Despite this . . . and projects:** *ARLHB*, 1909 (Washington: U.S. Government Printing Office, 1910), 49; and *The Papers of Joseph Henry*, edited by Marc Rothenberg, vol. 11 (Washington, D. C.: Smithsonian Institution Press, 2004), xli.

218 **In his 1909:** William Howard Taft, *Message of the President of the United States, Communicated to the Two Houses of Congress at the Beginning of the Second Session of the SixtyFirst Congress* (Washington: U.S. Government Printing Office, 1909), 35–36.

218 **Congress did so:** "An act to authorize additional aids to navigation in the Light-House establishment, and to provide for a Bureau of Light-Houses in the Department of Commerce and Labor, and for other purposes," in *The Statutes at Large of the United States of America from March 1910, to March, 1911*, vol. 35 (Washington: U.S. Government Printing Office, 1911), 534–39.

219 **"rolled in an":** Putnam, *Sentinel*, 11.

219 **"bitter wastes":** Ibid, 32.

220   "made no other": Ibid, 120.

220   "The lighthouse": Putnam, *Lighthouses*, v.

220   Putnam strove . . . bad weather: Putnam, *Sentinel*, 199–205; and Jones, *Lighthouse Encyclopedia*, 120–21.

220   "Only the radio": Putnam, *Sentinel*, 200

221   Evidence of: Ibid, 199–205, 213.

221   by the 1930s: Holland, *America's Lighthouses*, 24.

221   But it was not. . . maintain keepers: Michael J. Rhein, *Anatomy of the Lighthouse* (New York: Barnes & Noble Books, 2000), 163–66; Putnam, *Lighthouses and Lightships*, 189; and Tag, "From Braziers and Bougies to Xenon, Part II," *The Keeper's Log* (Winter 2003), 26–27.

222   hundreds of lighthouses: *ARCL*, June 30, 1922 (Washington: U.S. Government Printing Office, 1922), 5.

223   "Although the": "Our Lighthouse Service," *LSB* (November 2, 1925), 101.

223   With each passing year: Putnam, *Sentinel*, 234.

223   When Putnam became . . . out the door: Putnam, *Sentinel*, 227–28; and Adamson, *Keepers*, 16, 30.

224   The pension law: United States Department of Labor, *Labor Legislation of 1918* (Washington: U.S. Government Printing Office, 1919), 21–22.

224   "I am heartily": Putnam, *Sentinel*, 282.

224   After attending . . . certain disaster: D'Entremont, *The Lighthouses of Massachusetts*, 402; and Holland, *America's Lighthouses*, 79.

225   "due to vicious": George Weiss, *The Lighthouse Service: It's History, Activities and Organization* (Baltimore: Johns Hopkins Press, 1926), 77.

225   Keepers began complaining . . . out of work: *ARCL*, June 30, 1917 (Washington: U.S. Government Printing Office, 1917), 27; *ARCL*, June 30, 1919 (Washington: U.S. Government Printing Office, 1919), 14; *Message of the President of the United States Transmitting the Budget for the Service of the Fiscal Year Ending June 30, 1932* (Washington: U.S. Government Printing Office, 1930), 219; and Wayne C. Wheeler, "The Keeper's Pay," *The Keeper's Log* (Fall 2003), 26–30.

225   thousand dollars per year: *Historical Statistics of the United States: Earliest Times to the Present, Millennial Edition*, vol. 2, part B, edited by Susan B. Carter, et. al. (Cambridge: Cambridge University Press, 2000), 2–273.

226   "Lighthouse Bureau": Adamson, *Keepers*, 31.

226   It was not uncommon: Leffingwell, *Lighthouses*, 87.

226　**"Well," the superintendent said:** Ralph C. Shanks, Jr., and Janetta Thompson Shanks, *Lighthouses and Lifeboats on the Redwood Coast* (San Anselmo: Constano Books, 1978), 80.

227　**"The secret":** "Ashore After 38 Years in Lighthouse Service," *LSB* (May 2, 1921), 177–78.

227　**In May and June . . . fiery explosion:** "Explosion at Makapuu Point Lighthouse, Hawaii," *LSB* (June 1, 1925), 80.

227　**"charred black":** Dean, *Lighthouses of Hawaii*, 45.

227　**"Stand by":** "Alexander D. Toomey," *LSB* (May 1, 1925), 76.

228　**"bright lookout":** Ellen J. Henry, *The Lighthouse Service and the Great War* (Ponce Inlet, FL: Ponce de Leon Inlet Lighthouse Preservation Society, 2013), 7.

228　**Soon after:** Weiss, *The Lighthouse Service*, 25–27.

228　**"Submarine Silhouette Book":** "Submarine Silhouette Book No. 1," The United States Navy Department Library website, http://www.history .navy.mil/library/online/sub_silhouette.htm, accessed on July 14, 2014.

228　**"Food Will":** George H. Nash, *The Life of Herbert Hoover: Master of Emergencies, 1917–1918* (New York: W. W. Norton, 1996), x.

228　**encouraged keepers:** "Cultivation of Lighthouse Reservations," *LSB* (May 1917), 269.

228　**"good quality":** "Potatoes Grown in Sand," *LSB* (September 1, 1917), 281.

229　**instead of cultivating . . . his lead:** Leffingwell, *Lighthouses*, 86; and Elinor De Wire, *The Lightkeepers' Menagerie: Stories of Animals at Lighthouses* (Sarasota: Pineapple Press, 2007), 226.

229　**Lightships too . . . German sumbarine:** Holland, *America's Lighthouses*, 66; "Sinks Lightship off Cape Hatteras," *New York Times* (August 7, 1918); and Walter C. Capron, *The U.S. Coast Guard* (New York: Franklin Watts, Inc., 1965), 122.

229　**During his tenure:** Putnam, *Sentinels*, 328.

229　**According to Lloyd's:** Adamson, *Keepers*, 376.

230　**"He was one":** "Putnam of the Lights," *New York Times* (June 9, 1935).

230　**Harold D. King:** "Mr. King Appointed Commissioner of Lighthouses," *LSB* (August 1, 1935), 213.

CHAPTER 10: KEEPERS AND THEIR LIVES

232　**The primary responsibility:** The background for this section on keeping the light and fog signal comes from USLB, *Instructions and Directions* *to Guide Light-House Keepers and Others Belonging to the Light-House Establishment Issued January 1, 1870* (Washington: U.S. Government Printing Office, 1870); USLB, *Instructions to Light-Keepers, July 1881* (Washington: U.S. Government Printing Office, 1881); USLB, *Instructions to Light-Keepers and Masters of Light-House Vessels, 1902* (Washington: U.S. Government Printing Office, 1902); and Holland, *America's Lighthouses*, 45.

232   **This kept . . . explosive situation:** James Woodward, "Myths, Misnomers, and Mistakes: Straightening Some of the Twisted Ideas About Lighthouses," *The Keeper's Log* (Fall 2006), 38.

234   **"O what is":** Robert Thayer Sterling, *Lighthouses of the Maine Coast and the Men Who Keep Them* (Brattleboro, VT: Stephen Daye Press, 1935), 33–34.

235   **Just seventeen . . . medical doctor:** George W. Easterbrook, "The Lightkeeper's Night of Peril," part 1, *Washington Historian* (April 1900), 124–27; and George W. Easterbrook, "The Lightkeeper's Night of Peril," part 2, *Washington Historian* (July 1900), 175–78. All the quotes from Easterbrook come from the second of these two sources.

237   **nearly 25,000:** Leffingwell, *Lighthouses*, 109

238   **"switchies":** De Wire, *Guardians*, 14.

238   **"Principal keeper":** Putnam, *Sentinels*, 254.

239   **"[My] wife died":** LighthouseFriends.com, "Burnt Island, ME," website http://www.lighthousefriends.com/light.asp?ID=503, accessed on July 4, 2014.

240   *Captain January*: Laura E. Richards, *Captain January* (Boston: Dana Estes and Lauriat, 1890).

242   **"And, while they":** Celia Thaxter, "The Watch of Boon Island," *Atlantic Monthly* (March 1872), 272.

242   **With the rise:** Mia Fineman, "Kodak and the Rise of Amateur Photography," on the Metropolitan Museum of Art website, http://www.metmuseum.org/toah/hd/kodk/hd_kodk.htm, accessed on June 30, 2014.

243   **"arms" . . . "Show Me Dirt":** Richard Cheek, "Beacons for Business: The Commercial Use of Lighthouse Design," in *From Guiding Lights to Beacons for Business: The Many Lives of Maine's Lighthouses*, edited by Richard Cheek (Thomaston: Tilbury House, 2012), 192.

245   **"to make the":** Henry David Thoreau, *Cape Cod* (Boston: Ticknor and Fields, 1866), 155.

245   **I thought it":** Ibid., 157–58.

245 **"You will find"**: Robert Louis Stevenson, "The Old Pacific Capital," *Library Magazine of American and Foreign Thought*, vol. 6 (New York: American Book Exchange, 1880), 181.

245 **"It's the first"**: Jim Merkel, "Devil's Island Light Station—A 'Landmark' in Western Lake Superior," *Lighthouse Digest* (January 1999), 14–15. See also "The President Visits a Lighthouse," *LSB* (September 1, 1928), 255.

245 **The number of people . . . the tour**: "Visitors at Split Rock Light Station," *LSB* (February 1938), 38; James A. Gibbs, *Oregon's Seacoast Lighthouses* (Medford: Webb Research Group, 2000), 33; Berger, *Lighthouses*, 58; and Putnam, *Lighthouses and Lightships*, 82.

247 **"was of a"**: Frank Perry, *The History of Pigeon Point Lighthouse* (Santa Cruz: Otter B. Books, 2001), 54.

248 **At least . . . heads-up**: De Wire, *Guardians*, 50–52.

248 **"There were times"**: Philmore B. Wass, *Lighthouse in My Life: The Story of a Maine Lightkeeper's Family* (Camden: Down East Books, 1987), 39.

249 **One of the most endearing**: Background for this story, and all quotes come from Cheryl Shelton-Roberts and Bruce Roberts, *Lighthouse Families* (Birmingham, AL: Crane-Hill Publishing, 1997), 49–50.

250 **"love of the"**: Dewey Livingston, "The Keepers of the Light: Point Reyes," *The Keeper's Log* (Winter 1991), 17.

250 **"fomenting trouble . . . slovenly appearance"**: "Punishments," *LSB* (March 1912), 11.

250 **"It is the duty"**: *ARLHB*, June 30, 1894 (Washington: U.S. Government Printing Office, 1894), 254.

250 **"The light first"**: Thomas Wilson, "The Hermits of the Deep," *Los Angeles Herald* (July 12, 1908).

252 **A somewhat amusing . . . their newborn**: Putnam, *Sentinel*, 242–43; and Adamson, *Keepers*, 327–28.

253 **Abbie Burgess**: "Twenty-Two Years on Matinicus Rock," *Record of the Year* (February 1876), 181–83; and Gustav Kobbe, "Heroism in the Lighthouse Service: A Description of Life on Matinicus Rock," *Century Magazine* (June,1897), 219–30.

254 **"I took"**: Burgess, "Twenty-Two Years on Matinicus Rock," 182.

254 **"I can depend"**: D'Entremont, *The Lighthouses of Maine*, 238.

254 **"her only . . . the rock"**: Burgess, "Twenty-Two Years on Matinicus Rock," 182.

254 **"Though at times"**: Ibid.

255 **According to the lighthouse**: J. Candace Clifford and Mary Louise Clif-

ford, *Maine Lighthouses: Documentation of Their Past* (Alexandria, VA: Cypress Communications, 2005), 162; and Mary Louise Clifford and J. Candace Clifford, *Women Who Kept the Lights: An Illustrated History of Female Lighthouse Keepers* (Alexandria, VA: Cypress Communications, 2000), 2, 201–24.

255 **The first woman . . . to John:** Clifford and Clifford, *Women*, 5–11; D'Entremont, *The Lighthouses of Massachusetts*, 245–47; "Resolve on the Petition of Hannah Thomas," in *The Acts and Resolves, Public and Private, of the Province of The Massachusetts Bay*, vol. 20 (Boston: Wright & Potter, 1918), 267; and Benjamin Lincoln to Alexander Hamilton, March 19, 1790, in *The Papers of Alexander Hamilton*, vol. 6, edited by Harold C. Syrett and Jacob E. Cooke (New York: Columbia University Press, 1962), 307–8.

256 **"It must . . . and respectable":** Stephen Pleasonton to Thomas Corwin, 7 June 1851, in *Report of the Officers,* 270.

257 **"Life to me":** Elizabeth Whitney Williams, *A Child of the Sea; And Life Among the Mormons* (n.p.: privately printed, 1905), 214–15.

257 **When Van Riper . . . twenty-nine years:** Williams, *A Child*, 215; and Clifford and Clifford, *Women*, 139–43.

257 **Katherine Walker:** Background for Walker comes from "At Seventy She Keeps the Light of New York's Inner Harbor," *Literary Digest* (July 13, 1918), 57–58; Clifford and Clifford, *Women*, 167–75; Timothy Harrison, "Kate Would be Proud," *Lighthouse Digest* (March, 2011), 40–45; and Cliff Gallant, "Mind the Light, Katie," *The Keeper's Log* (Summer 1997), 16–18.

258 **"The day we":** "At Seventy She Keeps," 57.

258 **"Mind the light":** Mary Louise Clifford and J. Candace Clifford, *Mind the Light, Katie: The History of Thirty-Three Female Lighthouse Keepers* (Alexandria, VA: Cypress Communications, 2006), 94.

258 **"I am happy as":** B. J. O'Donnell, "Hunting Happiness in the Joy Capitol of the World!" *Day Book* (October 30, 1916).

259 **"I am in fear":** Eileen O'Connor, "The Woman Warder of City's Inner Harbor," *New York Sun* (May 26, 1918).

259 **"It has surprised":** "Mrs. Walker dies; lighthouse keeper," *New York Times* (December 7, 1931).

259 **"the only manifestly":** "At Seventy She Keeps," 57. This quote and the following ones pertaining to the rescue of the dog, Scotty, all come from this article.

260 "A great city's": Gallant, "Mind the Light, Katie," 18.

260 Laura Hecox: Frank Perry, *Lighthouse Point: Illuminating Santa Cruz* (Santa Cruz, CA: Otter B. Books, 2002), 55–75; and "Long Vigil at Lamp That Guides Seamen," *Los Angeles Times* (October 25, 1908).

261 "pleasant little": Perry, *Lighthouse Point*, 57.

261 he honored Hecox: A. G. Wetherby, "Some Notes on American Land Shells," *Journal of the Cincinnati Society of Natural History* (April 1880), 38–39.

262 "Why, the sea": Leffingwell, *Lighthouses*, 108.

263 Though it was . . . her job: Clifford and Clifford, *Women*, 67–70.

263 Emily Maitland Fish's story: Background for this comes from Clifford Gallant, "Emily Fish: The Socialite Keeper," *The Keeper's Log* (Spring 1985), 8–13; and Jean Serpell Stumbo, *Emily Fish: Socialite Lighthouse Keeper of Point Pinos Lighthouse, Pacific Grove, California* (Pacific Grove: Pacific Grove Museum of Natural History Association, 1997).

264 "was one of": "The Life She Loves Best," *Kansas City Star* (September 8, 1900).

265 "Socialite Keeper": Gallant, "Emily Fish: The Socialite Keeper."

266 "an elegant": *History of the Celebration of the Fiftieth Anniversary of the Taking Possession of California and Raising of the American Flag at Monterey, Cal.* (Oakland: Carruth & Carruth Printers, 1896), 41.

266 Interestingly enough . . . exemplary actions: "Heroines of the Lighthouse Service. There Are Twenty-Seven Stationed at the Beacons throughout the United States" *Lexington Herald* (January 7, 1912); JoAnn Chartier, "Juliet Fish Nichols: The Angel of Angel Island," *Lighthouse Digest* (March 2005), 44–45.

266 In addition to the 140: Clifford and Clifford, *Women*, 209.

268 "The present evidence": Holland, *America's Lighthouses*, 41.

268 lighthouse historian and genealogist: Sandra MacLean Clunes, "African American Lighthouse Keepers of the Chesapeake Bay," *Chesapeake Lights* (Winter 2004), 1–6.

268 For many . . . 184 years: Adamson, *Keepers*, 318; Charles K. Hyde, *The Northern Lights: Lighthouses of the Upper Great Lakes* (Detroit: Wayne State University Press, 1995), 52–53; and De Wire, *Guardians*, 41.

268 Lighthouse families . . . deteriorating health: Snow, *The Lighthouses*, 9–11; and Clifford and Clifford, *Women*, 53–55.

269 "Sometimes I": Kobbe, "Heroism," 225.

270 Robert Israel: Katherine B. Menz, *Historic Furnishings Report, Point*

Loma Lighthouse (Harpers Ferry, VA: National Park Service, December 1978), 5–6, 12–13.

271 **"three sickly"**: Kirk Munroe, "From Light to Light: A Cruise of the America, Supply-Ship," *Scribner's Magazine* (October 1896), 469.

271 **"God's Rock Garden"**: Mary Ellen Chase, *The Story of Lighthouses*, 93–94. See also, Adamson, *Keepers*, 75.

272 **"Mule Patty"**: White, *The Farallon*, 61.

272 **"soon recovered"**: Munroe, "From Light to Light, 470.

273 **One dog . . . lighthouse keepers' lives**: Snow, *The Lighthouses*, 159–61; and Stanley Coren, *Why Does My Dog Act That Way: A Complete Guide to Your Dog's Personality* (New York: Free Press, 2006), 247–48.

273 **At least one dog**: Snow, *The Lighthouses*, 39–41; and from De Wire, *The Lighthouse Menagerie*, 21–24.

274 **"My husband speaks"**: Snow, *The Lighthouses*, 40.

275 **Sometimes it . . . relief keeper**: James A. Gibbs, *Sentinels of the North Pacific: The Story of Pacific Coast Lighthouses and Lightships* (Portland: Binfords & Mort, 1955), 212–13.

276 **"After the first"**: Adamson, *Keepers*, 232–33.

276 **In August 1897**: "Race for Life," *Boston Globe* (August 13, 1897); "Madman in a Lighthouse," *New York Times* (August 15, 1897); and Jeremy D'Entremont, *The Lighthouses of Rhode Island* (Beverly, MA: Commonwealth Editions, 2006), 50–51.

277 **"O, I'll murder"**: "Race for Life," *Boston Globe*.

277 **"He was almost"**: Ibid.

277 **"smashed crockery"**: Ibid.

278 **no more dramatic example**: The background for the battle at the Ship Shoal Lighthouse comes from "The Crime of Jim Wood," *Daily Picayune* (April 4, 1882); "A Desperado of the Sea," *Daily Picayune* (March 9, 1882); and "A Thrilling Experience," *New York Times* (January 25, 1886).

281 **involved education**: Holland, *America's Lighthouses*, 47–48; "School Facilities," *LSB* (May 1915), 178; Chase, *The Story of Lighthouses*, 142; and De Wire, *Guardians*, 169–72.

282 **"growing up"**: Alexander P. MacDonald, "The Children of the Lighthouses," *Outlook* (January 18, 1908), 150.

282 **"It was a"**: Wass, *Lighthouse*, 232.

282 **On Christmas Day**: The background for this section on Royal's illness and the journey to try to save him comes from White, *Farallon*, 64–66;

Shanks and Shanks, *Lighthouses*, 53–54; Casey, *The Devil's*, 86–88; and Farallon Island Lighthouse Logbook, December 25–29, 1898, RG26, E80, Lighthouse Station Logs, NAB.

283 **"He was in"**: "She Proved That There is No Love Like a Mother's Love," *San Francisco Examiner* (December 31, 1898).

284 **"A man had"**: Robert DeGast, *The Lighthouses of the Chesapeake* (Baltimore: Johns Hopkins University Press, 1973), 9.

284 **One of . . . an end**: Bruce Roberts and Ray Jones, *Pacific Northwest Lighthouses: Oregon, Washington, Alaska, and British Columbia* (Old Saybrook, CT: Globe Pequot Press, 1997), 30; and Gibbs, *Lighthouses*, 149.

285 **"Oh! The loneliness"**: Stella M. Champney, "Four Days of Terror," *Detroit News* (May 17, 1931).

285 **"When I left"**: "The Mother Tragedy of the Lonesome Lighthouse," *Morning Tulsa Daily World* (September 10, 1922).

285 **"had grown morose"**: "Lighthouse Mother Kills Self and Son," *New York Times* (June 10, 1922).

285 **"Out at sea"**: Annie Bell Hobbes, "Another Lighthouse Story," *The Nursery: A Monthly Magazine for Youngest Readers*, vol. 19 (Boston: John L. Shorey, 1876), 67–68.

286 **"Nothing ever"**: "Fifty Years' Work: Woman Lighthouse Keeper's Record of Half a Century," *New York Daily Tribune* (June 20, 1903).

286 **"The trouble"**: Kobbe, *Life in a Lighthouse*, 373.

286 **"When I was living"**: Lewis Samuel Feuer, *Einstein and the Generations of Science* (New Brunswick: Transaction Publishers, 1974), 88.

286 **"who fitted"**: Thoreau, *Cape Cod*, 158.

286 **William Hunt Harris**: Dean, *Lighthouses of the Florida Keys*, 149; and Gideon Dowse Harris, *Harris Genealogy* (Columbus, Miss.: privately printed, 1914), 79.

287 **"I don't know"**: "Lighthouse No Longer Place of Monotony," *Berkeley Daily Gazette* (March 29, 1929).

287 **"At best"**: "Hoover Appeals to Listeners to Donate Sets for Lighthouses," *New York Times* (March 21, 1926).

288 **"At other times"**: "Light Keepers Find a Boon in Radio," *New York Times* (June 23, 1929).

288 **Wincapaw decided**: Backgground for Flying Santa comes from Brian Tague, "The Origins and History of the Flying Santa," on the Friends of Flying Santa website, http://www.flyingsanta.com/HistoryOrigins.html, accessed on July 21, 2014; Snow, *Famous*, 1–14;

"Flier Carries Cheer to 70 Lonely Lighthouses; Safely Drops Gifts for Crews Who Aided Him," *New York Times* (December 26, 1933); and Max Karant, "Santa Now Uses an Airplane," *Popular Aviation* (March 1937), 23–24, 56.

290   **"I have been"**: Snow, *Famous*, 1.

291   **"I love the"**: "A Fragile Woman of 80 Years is Uncle Sam's Oldest and Most Reliable Lighthouse Keeper," *Chicago Tribune* (October 2, 1904).

291   **"I'm happy here"**: Champney, "Four Days of Terror."

291   **"You ever see"**: *DeGast, The Lighthouses*, 55.

291   **"When we were"**: Jeremy D'Entremont, "Women of the Lights: In Their Own Words," *Lighthouse Digest* (June 2007).

292   **"I dunno"**: "Christmas Cheer in a Lighthouse," *Stamford Advocate* (December 17, 1908).

CHAPTER 11: LIGHTHOUSE HEROES

294   **Idawalley Zoradia Lewis**: The background for this section on Ida Lewis comes from George D. Brewerton, *Ida Lewis: The Heroine of Lime Rock* (Newport, RI: A. J. Ward, 1869); Lenore Skomal, *The Keeper of Lime Rock* (Philadelphia: Running Press, 2002); and D'Entremont, *The Lighthouses of Rhode Island*, 187–91.

294   **"It was her father"**: Skomal, *The Keeper*, 36.

296   **"so far gone"**: Zoradia Lewis, affidavit, Archives, RG26, Correspondence Concerning Lifesaving Medals, 1874–1920, Entry 235, Box 10, NAB.

297   **"Oh Holy Vargin"**: Brewerton, *Ida Lewis*, 19.

297   **"Ida, oh my"**: Ibid., 25.

297   **"blowing a living"**: Zoradia Lewis, affidavit.

298   **"barely able"**: Brewerton, *Ida Lewis*, 27.

298   **"When I saw"**: Skomal, *The Keeper*, 17.

299   **"Guardian angel"**: "Ida Lewis: The Grace Darling of America," *New-York Tribune* (April 12, 1869).

299   **This last comparison . . . twenty-six**: Skomal, *The Keeper*, 19–21; William J. Hardy, *Lighthouses: Their History and Romance* (New York: Fleming H. Revell, 1895), 48–52; and Jessica Mitford, *Grace Darling had an English Heart: The Story of Grace Darling, Heroine and Victorian Superstar* (New York: E. P. Dutton, 1998), 13–15, 33–53, 75–79.

301   **"was a most"**: "Ida Lewis, The Newport Heroine," *Harper's Weekly* (July 31, 1869), 484.

301 **"Her size"**: Skomal, *The Keeper*, 23.

301 **The coverage . . . in marriage**: Brewerton, *Ida Lewis*, 29–47; Skomal, *The Keeper*, 21–26, Margaret C. Adler, "To the Rescue: Picturing Ida Lewis," *Winterthur Portfolio* (Spring 2014), 85.

302 **Elizabeth Cady Stanton and Susan B. Anthony**: Adler, "To the Rescue: Picturing Ida Lewis," 99.

302 **"I have come"**: Skomal, *The Keeper*, 57.

302 **"I am happy"**: *The Papers of Ulysses S. Grant, vol. 19, July 1, 1868–October 31, 1869*, edited by John Y. Simon (Carbondale: Southern Illinois University Press, 1995), 229, n6.

302 **"If there were"**: Skomal, *The Keeper*, 23–24.

303 **Late on the afternoon . . . for treatment**: Affidavits of Frederick O. Tucker, Giuseppe Gianetti, Harriet Lewis, Mrs. M. E. Connell, Charles Abbott, Cassius W. Hallock, in Archives, RG26, Correspondence Concerning Lifesaving Medals, 1874–1920, Entry 235, Box 10, NAB; F. E. Chadwick to George Brown (June 24, 1881), in Archives, RG26, Correspondence Concerning Lifesaving Medals, 1874–1920, Entry 235, Box 10, NAB; and Skomal, *The Keeper*, 92–95.

303 **"endanger their own"**: "An Act to provide for the establishment of life-saving stations and houses of refuge upon the sea and lake coasts of the United States, and to promote the efficiency of the life-saving service," in *United States Congress, Acts and Resolution of the United States of America Passed at the First Session of the Forty-Third Congress, December 1, 1873–June 23, 1874* (Washington: U.S. Government Printing Office, 1874), 152.

303 **"Dear good brave"**: Skomal, *The Keeper*, 96.

304 **"The Grace Darling of"**: "The Passing of Ida Lewis, the Heroine of Newport," *New York Times* (October 29, 1911).

304 **More than fourteen hundred . . . Lewis saved**: D'Entremont, *The Lighthouses of Rhode Island*, 196–97; and Skomal, *The Keeper*, 127–37.

305 **Hanna's story begins**: The background for the wreck of the *Australia* and the rescue comes from the following documents: Marcus Hanna to J. M. Richardson (February 6, 1885); Affidavit of Nathaniel Staples, February 28, 1885; Affidavit of Hiram Staples, March 7, 1885; Affidavit of Irving Pierce, March 10, 1885; Affidavit of Henry E. Dyer, March 9, 1885. All these are in Marcus Hanna file, RG 26, Entry 235, Correspondence Concerning Lifesaving Medals, 1874–1920, Box 9, NAB. All the quotes are from the February 6 letter from Hanna to Richardson.

306 **Forty-three . . . transferred to Cape Elizabeth Lighthouse**: D'Entremont, *The Lighthouses of Maine*, 76, 206, 223–24.

307 **During the Civil War . . . Medal of Honor:** Walter F. Beyer and Oscar F. Keydel, Deeds of Valor: *How American Heroes Won the Medal of Honor*, vol. (Detroit: Perrien Keydel Company, 1901), 208–9.

310 **On April 29:** "Gold Medals Awarded," *Boston Herald* (April 30, 1885).

310 **more than 1,234:** Adamson, *Keepers*, 21–22.

310 **"The sky seemed":** Herbert Molloy Mason, Jr., *Death From the Sea: The Galveston Hurricane of 1900* (New York: Dial Press, 1972), 78–79.

310 **A killer of massive:** The background for this section on the Galveston Hurricane and the Bolivar Point Lighthouse comes from William H. Thiesen, "Saving Lives during America's Deadliest Disaster," *Naval History* (December 2012), 46–52; Erik Larson, *Isaac's Storm: A Man, A Time, and the Deadliest Hurricane in History* (New York: Vintage Books, 1999), 102–8; 111–14; 141–43; 163–66; 264–65; Mason, *Death*, 85–86; 162–63; "Gen. Scurry Is in Charge," *Dallas Morning News* (September 13, 1900); "52,000 Candles Are Set in the Window of Galveston," *Galveston Daily News* (July 25, 1915); and J. R. Selfridge to Light-House Board, September 15, 1900, RG26, E24, Letters Received From District Engineers and Inspectors (1853–1900), box 287, NAB.

313 **Fifteen years later:** Bolivar Point Lighthouse Logbook, August 15–18, 1915, RG26, E80, Lighthouse Station Logs, NAB.

314 **"The big tower":** "Bolivar Weathered Another Big Storm," *Galveston Daily News* (August 30, 1915).

314 **The water receded . . . the lighthouse:** "Bolivar Point Lighthouse, Texas," *The Keeper's Log* (Fall 1995), 26–27.

314 **In the case of the:** The background for this section on the *Bird of Paradise* comes from Lester J. Maitland, *Knights of the Air* (Garden City, NY: Doubleday, Doran & Company, 1929), 305–9, 318–27; William J. Horvat, *Above the Pacific* (Fallbrook, CA: Aero Publishers, 1966), 63–70; and Ross R. Aiken, *Kilaeua Point Lighthouse: The Landfall Beacon on the Orient Run* (Kilauea: Kilauea Point Natural History Association, 1988), 70–81.

316 **"saw a light":** Maitland, *Knights*, 326.

317 **"These aviators":** "Kilauea Point Light First Landfall Made by Army Aviators in Hawaiian Flight," *LSB* (August 1, 1927).

317 **"the Kilauea":** Dean, *The Lighthouses of Hawaii*, 146.

CHAPTER 12: MARVELS OF ENGINEERING AND CONSTRUCTION

319 **named after:** Snow, *Famous*, 53.

319 **In 1838 . . . deaf ears:** Nathaniel Spooner, *Gleanings From the Records of*

the Boston Marine Society, Through its First Century (Boston: Published by the Society, 1879), 131.

319 "is more required . . . a 'Stevenson' ": U.S. H.R. Doc. 183, 11.

319 the British engineer John Smeaton: Bella Bathurst, The Lighthouse Stevensons: The Extraordinary Story of the Building of the Scottish Lighthouses by the Ancestors of Robert Louis Stevenson (New York: HarperCollins, 1999), 58–60; and Majdalany, The Eddystone, 116–18, 154.

320 "broad at . . . being uprooted": Bathurst, The Lighthouse, 58–60.

320 The resulting edifice . . . wave-swept location: Ibid.

320 One such . . . his masterpieces: Ibid., 63–96.

321 William Henry Swift: The background for this section on Swift and his selection of the site, the proposed plan for the lighthouse, and its construction comes from "Report of the Colonel of the Corps of Topographical Engineers" (November 14, 1850), in Message from the President of the United States, to the Two Houses of Congress at the Commencement of the Second Session of the Thirty-First Congress, part 2 (Washington: Printed for the House, 1850), 432–43, 452–55; Edward Rowe Snow, The Story of Minot's Light (Boston: Yankee Publishing, 1940), 23–31; and George W. Cullum, Biographical Sketch of Captain William H. Swift, of the Topographical Engineers (New York: A. G. Sherwood & Co., 1880), 3–10.

323 "Here was the": Thoreau, Cape Cod, 243.

323 "A tremendous . . . my trust": Snow, The Story, 39–42.

323 Even the kitten . . . frazzled life: Ibid., 37–38.

324 "At intervals": "Minot's Rock Lighthouse," Appletons Mechanics' Magazine and Engineers Journal (February 1, 1851), 98.

325 "Time, the great": United States Lighthouse Board, Compilation of Public Documents and Extracts From Reports and Papers Relating to . . . 1789 to 1871 (1871), 549.

325 "The lighthouse won't": Snow, Famous, 59.

325 Exactly when . . . recovered later: Snow, The Story, 50–57; "The Gale and the Flood," Boston Atlas (April 18, 1851).

326 There were . . . inferior quality: John W. Bennett, "The Minot's Rock Lighthouse," Boston Herald (May 21, 1851); and "Minot Rock Lighthouse," Appleton's Mechanics' Magazine & Engineers' Journal (July 1, 1851), 398–402.

327 Totten went with: J. G. Barnard, "Eulogy on the Late Joseph G. Totten, Brevet Major General," in Annual Report of the Board of Regents of the Smithsonian Institution Showing the Operations, Expenditures, and

Condition of the Institution for the Year 1865 (Washington: U.S. Government Printing Office, 1866), 166.

327 **"whether it be"**: Snow, *The Story*, 64. For general background on the construction of the second Minot's lighthouse see ibid., 61–84; and Barton S. Alexander, "Minot's Ledge Lighthouse," in *Transactions, American Society of Civil Engineers* (April 1879), 83–94.

327 **"There had to be"**: John G. Barnard, "Lighthouse Construction," *Johnson's Universal Cyclopaedia: A Scientific and Popular Treasury of Useful Knowledge*, vol. 4 (New York: A. J. Johnson & Co., 1886), 825. (Emphasis in original.)

328 **"We would watch"**: Charles A. Lawrence, "The Building of Minot's Ledge Lighthouse," *New England Magazine* (October 1896), 138.

328 **In 1856 . . . when necessary**: Alexander, "Minot's Ledge Lighthouse," 86–87; Snow, *The Story*, 73; and Snow, *Famous*, 62.

328 **"If tough"**: Lawrence, "The Building of Minot's Ledge Lighthouse," 136.

328 **despair evaporated**: Snow, *The Story*, 65–66.

329 **The tower's granite . . . used throughout**: Alexander, "Minot's," 91–92; and D'Entremont, *The Lighthouses of Massachusetts*, 275.

330 **"A light-house"**: "Laying the Corner Stone of the Minot's Ledge Light-House," *Freemason's Monthly Magazine* (November 1, 1858), 1–2.

331 **"Let us remember"**: Ibid, 7.

332 **"ranks, by the"**: John G. Barnard, "Lighthouse Engineering as Displayed at the Centennial Exhibition," *Transactions, American Society of Civil Engineers* (March 1879), 59.

332 **"rises out"**: Henry Wadsworth Longfellow, *Life of Henry Wadsworth Longfellow*, edited by Samuel Longfellow, vol. 3 (Boston: Houghton, Mifflin and Company, 1891), 184.

332 **Long after the . . . on their minds**: *ARLHB*, June 30, 1893 (Washington: U.S. Government Printing Office, 1893), 233–34; Snow, *The Story of Minot's Light*, 98; and D'Entremont, *Lighthouses of Massachusetts*, 279–80.

333 **A continent . . . the Columbia**: G. L. Gillespie, "Report Upon the Construction of Tillamook Rock Light Station, Sea Coast of Oregon," appendix in *ARLHB*, June 30, 1881, 99; and Portland Board of Trade, *Report of the President and Secretary for the Year Ending August 1, 1879* (Portland, OR: Board of Trade, 1879), 1–20.

334 **Tillamook Rock**: For background for this section on the design and

building of Tillamook Rock Lighthouse comes from Gillespie, "Report Upon," 99–134; and James A. Gibbs, *Tillamook Light* (Portland: Binford & Mort, 1979), 37–57.

334 **with ridicule:** "Tillamook Rock," *Oregonian* (November 20, 1879).

336 **"a large rounded":** Gillespie, "Report," 103.

336 **To handle this . . . West Coast:** Dennis M. Powers, *Sentinel of the Seas: Life and Death at the Most Dangerous Lighthouse Ever Built* (New York: Citadel Press, 2007), 13–16; "Wolf Rock," Trinity House website, http://www.trinityhouse.co.uk/lighthouses/lighthouse_list/wolf_rock.html, accessed on May 25, 2015; and David Stevenson, *Life of Robert Stevenson* (London: Adam and Charles Black, 1878), 172.

337 **Appointing Ballantyne . . . by example:** Powers, *Sentinel of the Seas*, 13–16.

337 **"idle talk":** Gillespie, "Report," 103.

339 **"rather disagreeable":** Ibid., 126.

341 **For two more . . . in satisfactory shape:** "In Awful Peril," *Oregonian* (January 20, 1880).

342 **On January 3:** *Lewis & Dryden's Marine History of the Pacific Northwest*, edited by E. W. Wright (Portland: Lewis & Dryden Printing Company, 1895), 289; and Gibbs, *Tillamook*, 54–57.

343 **"Hard aport":** "Marine Disaster," *Philadelphia Inquirer* (January 10, 1881).

344 **"From that hour":** Adamson, *Keepers*, 237.

344 **The storm that struck:** Background for this storm and its impact on the lighthouse comes from "Tremendous Seas Sweep Tillamook Rock," *LSB* (November 1, 1934); and Sam Churchill, "The Day 'Terrible Tilly's' Light Nearly Died in a Sea of Terror," *Northwest Magazine* (December 3, 1972), 6–10.

345 **"As an example":** Putnam, *Sentinel*, 236.

345 **St. George Reef Lighthouse:** Background for this section on the building of the lighthouse comes from A. H. Payson, "Report Upon the Construction of Saint George's Reef Light-Station, Sea-Coast of California," in *ARLHB*, June 30, 1884 (Washington: U.S. Government Printing Office, 1884), 113–26; Alexander Ballantyne to W. H. Heuer, January 1, 1892, in *ARLHB*, June 30, 1891 (Washington: U.S. Government Printing Office, 1891), 271–78; Powers, *Sentinel*, 3–48; 71–171; and Wayne C. Wheeler, "St. George Reef Lighthouse: A Nineteenth-Century Engineering Feat," *The Keeper's Log* (Fall 2003), 2–13.

345 **"Dragon Rocks":** John Vancouver, *A Voyage of Discovery to the North Pacific Ocean, and Round the World*, vol. 1 (London: G. G. and J. Robinson, 1798), 202.

346 **During a gale . . . the danger:** Powers, *Sentinel*, 5, 29; "The Brother Jonathan Wreck," *San Francisco Bulletin* (August 3, 1865).

346 **again in 1881:** *ARLHB*, June 30, 1881, 8.

349 **"made of two":** Payson, "Report," 120.

349 **"At my cry":** Powers, *Sentinel*, 72.

349 **But safety . . . major damage:** Ibid., 73.

351 **"In four years":** Alexander Ballantyne to W. H. Heuer, 273.

353 **"The men's":** Ibid., 275.

354 **The entire endeavor . . . and all:** Charles Graves, "Statue of Liberty," *Encyclopedia Americana*, vol. 17 (New York: Encyclopedia Americana Corporation, 1919), 350; and Powers, *Sentinel*, 168–69.

CHAPTER 13: OF BIRDS AND EGGS

355 **It was a noise . . . strewn about the lighthouse:** M. Eldridge, "History of Hog Island Light Station, Virginia" (April 1951), clipping file for Hog Island, RG 26, NAB.

356 **still do not know:** Sidney A. Gauthreaux, Jr., and Carroll G. Belser, "Effects of Artificial Light on Migrating Birds," in *Ecological Consequences of Artificial Night Lighting*, edited by Catherine Rich and Travis Longcore (Washington: Island Press, 2006), 71–74.

357 **"The lighthouse":** Celia Thaxter, *Among the Isle of Shoals* (Boston: James R. Osgood and Company, 1873), 110–11.

357 **"As soon as":** J. A. Allen, "Destruction of Birds by Light-Houses," *Bulletin of the Nuttall Ornithological Club* (July 1880), 134–35.

357 **December 1920:** "Damage Cape Ann Light Station," *LSB* (February 1, 1921), 165–66.

358 **A few days . . . in years:** Sterling, *Lighthouses*, 55–56.

359 **"a great bird":** William Dutcher, "Bird Notes From Long Island, N.Y." *The Auk* (April 1888), 182. See also William Dutcher, "Notes on Some Rare Birds in the Collection of the Long Island Historical Society," *The Auk* (July 1893), 276.

359 **"The largest":** Wells Woodbridge Cooke, *Distribution and Migration of North American Warblers* (Washington: U.S. Government Printing Office, 1904), 17–18.

360 **keepers contributed to:** "Banding of Birds," *LSB* (December 1, 1922), 256.

360 **In a particularly:** Eric Jay Dolin and Bob Dumaine, *The Duck Stamp Story: Art, Conservation, History* (Iola, WI: Krause Publications, 2000), 16.

360 **On a stroll:** T. Gilbert Pearson, *The Bird Study Book* (New York: Doubleday, 1919), 146–47.

361 **In 1900:** William Dutcher, "Results of Special Protection to Gulls and Terns Obtained Through the Thayer Fund," *The Auk* (January 1901), 76–77.

361 **The results ... previous years:** William Dutcher, "Report of the Committee on the Protection of North American Birds for the Year 1900," *The Auk* (January 1901), 92.

361 **The success:** "State Reports," *Bird Lore* (February 1, 1905), 113.

362 **"spirit of protection":** Notes and News, *The Auk* (April 1900), 199.

362 **Two years later:** USLB, *Instructions to Light-House Keepers*, 1902, 12–13.

362 **When the ... Audubon Society's employ:** B. S. Bowdish, "Ornithological Miscellany from Audubon Wardens," *The Auk* (April 1909), 116–28; Larkin G. Mead, "The Minute-Men of the Coast," *Harper's Weekly* (January 11, 1908), 25; and Ted Panayotoff, "Lighthouse Keepers Saved Lives of Birds, as Well as Humans," *Lighthouse Digest* (July 2008), 14–16.

362 **most dramatic story:** Background for this story is from White, *The Farallon*, 42–55, 108–9; Doughty, "San Francisco's," 554–72; Casey, *The Devil's*, 81–85; and "The Farallones," *San Francisco Bulletin* (June 15, 1880).

363 **"who was":** Amos Clift to Horace Clift (November 30, 1859), San Francisco History Center of the San Francisco Public Library.

363 **"If I could":** Ibid.

363 **"drawn lines":** "Disputed Claims to the Farallones," *Daily Alta California* (November 23, 1859).

363 **"armed to":** White, *The Farallon*, 43.

363 **"egg co.":** Amos Clift to Horace Clift (June 14, 1860), San Francisco History Center of the San Francisco Public Library.

364 **"the undue":** White, *The Farallon*, 43.

364 **"at their peril":** Ibid., 53.

364 **"in spite":** "The Farallones Egg War—Coroner's Inquest of the Body of Perkins," *Daily Alta California* (June 7, 1863).

364 **"God damn":** Ibid.

364   **Both sides claimed:** "The Farallones War—Arrests for Murder," ibid. (June 6, 1863).

364   **Batchelder was:** "Farallons Egg War," ibid., (December 10, 1864).

365   **All of . . . eviction notice:** *ARLHB, June 30, 1880* (Washington: U.S. Government Printing Office, 1880), 63–64; *ARLHB*, June 30, 1881, 70–71.

365   **"We steamed":** Charles Warren Stoddard, *In the Footprints of the Padres* (San Francisco: A. M. Robertson, 1912), 157–58.

366   **"engaging in":** "Report of the A.O.U. Committee on Protection of North American Birds," *The Auk* (January 1898), 109–10.

CHAPTER 14: A CRUEL WIND

367   **One of the earliest:** George Dutton to John Y. Mason, October 14, 1846, *New York Municipal Gazette* (March 15, 1847), 736; and Dean, *Lighthouses of the Florida Keys*, 54.

367   **The hurricane that roared:** Putman, "Beacons," 29; *ARLHB*, June 30, 1907 (Washington: U.S. Government Printing Office, 1907), 95–99; and Timothy Harrison, "The Hero of Horn Island Lighthouse, Pascagoula, Mississippi," *Lighthouse Digest* (July/August, 2011), 70–71.

368   **Edwin S. Babcock . . . half mile away:** The background for the ordeal of Plum Beach Lighthouse and its keepers during the hurricane comes from Lawrence H. Bradner, *The Plum Beach Light: The Birth, Life, and Death of a Lighthouse* (n.p.: privately published by author, 1989), 95–140.

369   **Great Hurricane of 1938:** The background for the hurricane comes from Everett S. Allen, *A Wind to Shake the World: The Story of the 1938 Hurricane* (New York: Little, Brown and Company, 1976); R. A. Scotti, *Sudden Sea: The Great Hurricane of 1938* (New York: Little, Brown and Company, 2003), 23, 37–50, 81, 93–94, 216–17; Cherie Burns, *The Great Hurricane: 1938* (New York: Atlantic Monthly Press, 2005), 74–78; and National Weather Service, The Great Hurricane of 1938, at http://www .weather.gov/box/1938hurricane, accessed on August 23, 2014.

370   **"If the lighthouse":** Bradner, *The Plum*, 123.

371   **"like an eggshell":** Ibid., 124.

371   **"If it had":** Ibid.

372   **Walter Eberle:** D'Entremont, *The Lighthouses of Rhode Island*, 49–54; and "Detailed Reports Indicate Violence of September Hurricane," *LSB* (December 1938), 145–46.

373   **"The light is":** D'Entremont, *The Lighthouses of Rhode Island*, 54.

373   **Prudence Island Lighthouse:** Background for this section, and all of the quotes, comes from Edward Rowe Snow, *A Pilgrim Returns to Cape Cod* (Boston: Yankee Publishing Company, 1946), 364–66.

375   **Dumpling Rock Lighthouse:** The background for this section on Dumpling Rock, and all the quotes, comes from Seamond Ponsart Roberts, with Jeremy D'Entremont, *Everyday Heroes: The True Story of a Lighthouse Family* (Portsmouth, NH: Coastlore Media, 2013), 10–13.

377   **Sidney Z. Gross:** Background for this section, and all of the quotes, comes from "Detailed Reports Indicate," 146.

379   **Its keeper, Arthur Small:** The background for this section on Palmer Island Lighthouse and its bout with the hurricane comes from Allen, *A Wind*, 320–26; "Secretary of Commerce Addresses Conference of Lighthouse Superintendents," *LSB* (October 1938), 133–34; and D'Entremont, *The Lighthouses of Massachusetts*, 21–25.

379   **"It is a popular":** Snow, *The Lighthouses*, 305–6.

380   **"Whenever they say:"** Allen, *A Wind*, 321.

381   **"I was hurt":** Ibid, 322.

382   **"No keeper":** Ibid.

383   **"one of the most":** Ibid, 323.

383   **All told:** "September Hurricane Causes Loss of Life and Extensive Property Damage," *LSB* (October 1938), 135–36.

383   **By the time . . . American history:** Allen, *A Wind*, 348–49; and Scotti, *Sudden Sea*, 23, 216–17, 226.

CHAPTER 15: THE NEW KEEPERS

385   **"devoted, efficient":** "Public Resolution No. 16," U.S. Sen. Doc. 130 (1939), 652.

385   **The celebration . . . through consolidation:** Robert Erwin Johnson, *Guardians of the Sea: History of the United States Coast Guard, 1915 to the Present* (Annapolis: Naval Institute Press, 1987), 162–65; U.S. Coast Guard, *The Coast Guard at War—Aids to Navigation* (Washington: Public Information Division, U.S. Coast Guard, July 1, 1949), 4; and Franklin D. Roosevelt: "Message to Congress on Plan II to Implement the Reorganization Act," May 9, 1939, at *The American Presidency Project*, http://www.presidency.ucsb.edu/ws/?pid=15760, accessed on August 30, 2014.

385   **While some . . . petty officers:** Johnson, *Guardians*, 163; and Holland, *America's Lighthouses*, 38.

385 **Many keepers . . . operate smoothly:** Adamson, *Keepers*, 31; Johnson, *Guardians*, 164; and De Wire, *Lighthouses of the South*, 96.

386 **a million dollars:** Johnson, *Guardians*, 164.

386 **Many lighthouses . . . against invasion:** U.S. Coast Guard, *The Coast Guard at War*, 5–10; and J. McCaffery, *Point Pinos, Pacific Grove, California Lighthouse* (Point Pinos: Printed by author, 2001), 81.

386 **Scotch Cap Lighthouse:** The background for this section comes from the Scotch Cap Radio Station Logbook, April 1–8, 1946, RG26, E80, Lighthouse Station Logs, NAB (all quotes, except one, come from this); Adamson, *Keepers*, 249–54; Michael J. Mooney, "Tragedy at Scotch Cap," *Sea Frontiers* (March/April 1975), 84–90; "Memorandum Kept by Chief Radio Electrician Horan B. Sandford, U. S. Coast Guard," transcript at the Office of the Historian, U.S. Coast Guard; and Dudley and Lee, *Tsunami!*, 1–5, 41.

388 **"The light!":** Adamson, *Keepers*, 252.

389 **One of the . . . out to sea:** Wermiel, *Lighthouses*, 323; Bruce Roberts, Cheryl Shelton-Roberts, and Ray Jones, *American Lighthouses: A Comprehensive Guide to Exploring our National Coastal Treasures* (Lanham, MD: Rowman and Littlefield, 2012), 155; and LighthouseFriends.com, "Charleston (Sullivan's Island), SC," at http://www.lighthousefriends .com/light.asp?ID=334, accessed on September 2, 2014.

390 **Beyond building . . . critical jobs:** National Park Service, U.S. Coast Guard, and Department of Defense, *Historic Lighthouse Preservation Handbook* (Washington: U.S. Government Printing Office, 1997), part 2, 2.

391 **in 1968:** Ibid.

391 **Automation, during . . . four years:** DeGast, *The Lighthouses*, 7; and Skip Rozin, "Who mourns the vanishing wickies?" *Audubon* (May 1972), 31–32.

391 **One that is . . . little maintenance:** Jones, *The Lighthouse*, 136; and e-mail communication with Jeremy D'Entremont, May 31, 2015.

393 **"This place . . . stinks!":** De Wire, *Guardians*, 262.

393 **"When I had the":** Robert G. Müller, *Long Island's Lighthouses: Past and Present* (Patchogue: Long Island Chapter of the U.S. Lighthouse Society, 2004), 157–58.

393 **By 1989 . . . fog signal:** Jeremy D'Entremont, "Coney Island Light Station, New York," *The Keeper's Log* (Fall 2009), 2-6; and Robert D. McFadden, "Frank P. Schubert, Lighthouse Keeper Since 1939, Dies at 88," *The New York Times* (December 13, 2003).

395 **"was nuts"**: Myrna Oliver, "Obituary: Frank Schubert, 88, Last Civilian Lighthouse Keeper in the United States," *Los Angeles Times* (December 19, 2003).

395 **"because of public relations"**: "The Last Lighthouse Keeper," *All Things Considered*, National Public Radio, http://www.npr.org/templates/story/story.php?storyId=1137620, accessed on September 2, 2014

396 **"My head's"**: Charlie LeDuff, "So, It's a Lighthouse. Now Leave Me Alone," *New York Times* (April 18, 2002).

396 **"The Coast Guard mourns"**: Oliver, "Obituary: Frank Schubert, 88."

397 **For example, in 1925 . . . Museum and Lighthouse**: James Boylan and Betsy Wade, *Stonington's Old Lighthouse and Its Keepers* (Stonington: Stonington Historical Society, 2013), 98–102; Holland, *America's Lighthouses*, 164; and Elinor De Wire, "Fairport Harbor Lighthouse: The Freedom Light," *The Keeper's Log* (Winter 2009), 11.

398 **The Chesapeake . . . prime attractions**: Vojtech, *Lighting*, 151.

398 **East Brother Lighthouse**: Background for this section comes from Frank Perry, *East Brother: History of an Island Light Station*, a book published by the East Brother Light Station, Inc., 1984, accessed at http://www.ebls.org/book.html, on September 4, 2014.

401 **Fire Island Lighthouse**: Background for the Fire Island Lighthouse restoration comes from an interview by author with Robert LaRosa, president of the Fire Island Lighthouse Preservation Society, September 5, 2014; Fire Island Lighthouse Preservation Society website, http://fireislandlighthouse.com/index.html, accessed on September 6, 2014; Casey Rattner, "Long Island Volunteer Hall of Fame Archive Project, Inception to Induction, Fire Island Lighthouse Preservation Society" (April 14, 2011), at the following website, accessed on September 6, 2014, http://www.livolunteerhalloffame.org/uploads/Fire_Island_Lighthouse_Preservation_Society.pdf; Dennis Hanson, "The Tide Is Turning for Old Beacons Adrift at Land's End," *Smithsonian* (August 1, 1987), 99–108; and Paul Vitello, "Thomas Roberts, Who Led Fight to Save Fire Island Lighthouse, Dies at 75," *New York Times* (June 15, 2013).

403 **Rose Island Lighthouse Foundation**: Background for this section comes from Rose Island Lighthouse Foundation website, at http://www.roseislandlighthouse.org/index.html, accessed on September 5, 2014; and D'Entremont, *The Lighthouses of Rhode Island*, 176–79.

404 **Maine Lights Program**: Island Institute, "Maine Lights Program: Over-

view and Conclusions – January, 2000," at http://www.islandinstitute
.org/documents/mainelights.pdf, accessed on September 7, 2014.

405 **"You solved a"**: James M. Loy, "Maine Lighthouse Transfer Ceremony,
Rockland, Maine, June 20, 1998,"at http://www.uscg.mil/history//CCG/
Loy/docs/MLHS062098.pdf, accessed on September 7, 2014.

406 **As of 2015**: Personal communication with Patrick J. Sclafani, Regional
Public Affairs Officer, New England Region, U.S. General Services
Administration, January 29 and June 2, 2015.

407 **"It's said you can't"**: Clay Risen, "Preserving the Lighthouse, Not Just
the Light," *New York Times* (September 5, 2014).

407 **"like nothing else"**: Virginia Sole-Smith, "Who Owns America's Lighthouses?" *Coastal Living* (August 2012), 87–88.

408 **"an enormously . . . we're going"**: Interview with Dave Waller, September 10, 2014.

409 **"always been"**: Jacqueline Tempera, "Beacon Thrill: What It's Like to
Live in a Lighthouse," *Boston Globe* (August 3, 2104).

409 **"there is nothing"**: Interview with Nick Korstad, September 10, 2014.

410 **"Nonprofit groups "**: Sole-Smith, "Who Owns," 88.

410 **"It burns me up"**: Alexander Abnos, "Coast Guard Auctions of Lighthouses," *USA Today* (April 2, 2008).

410 **"One part"**: Amy Gamerman, "The Lure of the Lighthouse," *Wall
Street Journal* (August 15, 2013).

410 **"Doomsday List"**: Tim Harrison, "The Doomsday List—America's
Most Endangered Lighthouses," *Lighthouse Digest*, at http://www.light
housedigest.com/news/doomsdaystory.cfm, accessed on September 17,
2014; and telephone interview with Tim Harrison, September 16, 2014.

411 **finally toppled**: Holland, *America's Lighthouses*, 76–77.

412 **The most challenging . . . this century**: Mike Booher and Lin Ezell,
Out of Harm's Way: Moving America's Lighthouse (Annapolis: Eastwind
Publishing, 2001), 10-94; "Cape Hatteras Light Station," National Park
Service Web page accessed on May 16, 2015, at http://www.nps.gov/caha
/planyourvisit/chls.htm; Orrin H. Pilkey, David M. Bush, and William J.
Neal, "Lessons from Lighthouses: Shifting Sands, Coastal Management
Strategies, and the Cape Hatteras Lighthouse Controversy," in *The Earth
Around Us: Maintaining a Livable Planet*, edited by Jill S. Schneiderman
(New York: W. H. Freeman, 2000), 198–200; and telephone interview with
Tyler Finkle, Project Manager at International Chimney Corporation, July
24, 2015.

415   **"the head"**: "A Perfumed Ghost," *The Savannah Tribune* (February 16, 1889).

415   **In 1880**: Telephone interview with Mimi Rogers, curator, Coastal Georgia Historical Society, September 16, 2014; and S. E. Schlosser, *Spooky Georgia: Tales of Hauntings, Strange Happenings, and Other Local Lore* (Guilford, CT: Globe Pequot Press, 2012), 62.

Epilogue

419   **Marblehead Lighthouse stands**: D'Entremont, *The Lighthouses of Massachusetts*, 351–57.

419   **"good harbor"**: Richard Whiting Searle, "Marblehead Great Neck," *Essex Historical Institute Collections* (July 1937), 228.

420   **"gallant Marblehead men"**: "One of the Veterans," *Salem Register* (October 26, 1857).

SELECT BIBLIOGRAPHY

. . . .

THIS BIBLIOGRAPHY CONTAINS BUT A SMALL FRACTION OF THE sources cited in *Brilliant Beacons*, and it includes only books, not articles or government reports. It is intended as a starting point for the general reader who wants to learn more about the history of American lighthouses. For additional information about specific topics and particular lighthouses covered in the text, please refer to the notes.

Adams, William Henry Davenport. *Lighthouses and Lightships: A Descriptive and Historical Account of Their Mode of Construction and Organization*. London: T. Nelson and Sons, 1870.

Adamson, Hans Christian. *Keepers of the Lights*. New York: Greenburg, 1955.

Allen, Everett S. *A Wind to Shake The World: The Story of the 1938 Hurricane*. New York: Little, Brown and Company, 1976.

Arago, François. "Fresnel," in *Biographies of Distinguished Scientific Men*. London: Longman, Brown, Green, Longmans, & Roberts, 1857.

Baker, T. Lindsay. *Lighthouses of Texas*. College Station: Texas A&M University, 2001.

Bathurst, Bella. *The Lighthouse Stevensons: The Extraordinary Story of the Building of the Scottish Lighthouses by the Ancestors of Robert Louis Stevenson*. New York: HarperCollins, 1999.

Berger, Todd R. *Lighthouses of the Great Lakes*. St. Paul: Voyageur Press, 2002.

Bostick, Douglas W. *The Morris Island Lighthouse: Charleston's Maritime Beacon*. Charleston, SC: History Press, 2008.

Carr, Dawson. *The Cape Hatteras Lighthouse: Sentinel of the Shoals*. Chapel Hill: University of North Carolina Press, 2000.

Chase, Mary Ellen. *The Story of Lighthouses*. New York: W. W. Norton, 1965.

Cheek, Richard, ed. *From Guiding Lights to Beacons for Business: The Many Lives of Maine's Lighthouses*. Thomaston, ME: Tilbury House, 2012.

David L. Cipra, *Lighthouses, Lightships, and the Gulf of Mexico*. Alexandria, VA: Cypress Communications, 1997.

Clifford, J. Candace, and Mary Louise Clifford. *Nineteenth-Century Lights: Historic Images of American Lighthouses*. Alexandria: Cypress Communications, 2000.

———. *Women Who Kept the Lights: An Illustrated History of Female Lighthouse Keepers*. Alexandria: Cypress Communications, 2000.

———. *Maine Lighthouses: Documentation of Their Past*. Alexandria: Cypress Communications, 2005.

Dean, Love. *The Lighthouses of Hawaii*. Honolulu: University of Hawaii Press, 1991.

———. *Lighthouses of the Florida Keys*. Sarasota: Pineapple Press, 1998.

D'Entremont, Jeremy. *The Lighthouses of Connecticut*. Beverly, MA: Commonwealth Editions, 2005.

———. *The Lighthouses of Rhode Island*. Beverly, MA: Commonwealth Editions, 2006.

———. *The Lighthouses of Massachusetts*. Beverly, MA: Commonwealth Editions, 2007.

———. *The Lighthouses of Maine*. Beverly, MA: Commonwealth Editions, 2009.

———. *The Lighthouse Handbook of New England*. Kennebunkport, ME: Cider Mill Press, 2012.

De Wire, Elinor. *Guardians of the Lights: Stories of U.S. Lighthouse Keepers*. Sarasota: Pineapple Press, 1995.

———. *Lighthouses of the South*. St. Paul: Voyageur Press, 2004.

———. *The Lightkeepers' Menagerie: Stories of Animals at Lighthouses*. Sarasota: Pineapple Press, 2007.

Duffus, Kevin P. *The Lost Light: The Mystery of the Missing Cape Hatteras Fresnel Lens*. Raleigh, NC: Looking Glass Productions, 2003.

Gibbs, James A. *Sentinels of the North Pacific: The Story of Pacific Coast Lighthouses and Lightships*. Portland, OR: Binford & Mort, 1955.

———. *Lighthouses of the Pacific*. Atglen, PA: Schiffer Publications, 1986.

———. *Tillamook Light*. Portland: Binford & Mort, 1979.

———. *Oregon's Seacoast Lighthouses*. Medford: Webb Research Group, 2000.

Gleason, Sarah C. *Kindly Lights: A History of the Lighthouses of Southern New England*. Boston: Beacon Press, 1991.

Heap, David P. *Ancient and Modern Light-Houses*. Boston: Ticknor and Company, 1889.

Holland, Francis Ross, Jr. *America's Lighthouses: Their Illustrated History Since 1716*. Brattleboro, VT: Stephen Greene Press, 1972.

———. *Lighthouses*. New York: Barnes & Noble, 1997.

Hurley, Neil E. *Florida's Lighthouses in the Civil War*. Oakland Park, FL: Middle River Press, 2007.

Hyde, Charles K. *The Northern Lights: Lighthouses of the Upper Great Lakes*. Detroit: Wayne State University Press, 1995.

Johnson, Arnold Burges. *The Modern Light-House Service*. Washington: Government Printing Office, 1890.

Jones, Ray. *The Lighthouse Encyclopedia: The Definitive Reference*. Guilford, CT: Globe Pequot Press, 2004.

Levitt, Theresa. *A Short, Bright Flash: Augustin Fresnel and the Birth of the Modern Lighthouse*. New York: W. W. Norton and Company, 2013.

Leffingwell, Randy. *Lighthouses of the Pacific Coast*. St. Paul: Voyageur Press, 2000.

Lowry, Shannon, and Jeff Schultz. *Northern Lights: Tales of Alaska's Lighthouses and Their Keepers*. Harrisburg, PA: Stackpole Books, 1992.

Noble, Dennis L. *Lighthouses & Keepers: The U.S. Lighthouse Service and its Legacy*. Annapolis: Naval Institute Press, 1997.

Osmers, Henry. *On Eagle's Beak: A History of the Montauk Point Lighthouse*. Denver: Outskirts Press, 2008.

Porter, Jane Molloy. *Friendly Edifices: Piscataqua Lighthouses and Other Aids to Navigation, 1771–1939*. Portsmouth, NH: Portsmouth Marine Society, 2006.

Powers, Dennis M. *Sentinel of the Seas: Life and Death at the Most Dangerous Lighthouse Ever Built*. New York: Citadel Press, 2007.

Putnam, George Rockwell. *Lighthouses and Lightships of the United States*. Boston: Houghton Mifflin Company, 1917.

———. *Sentinel of the Coasts: The Log of a Lighthouse Engineer*. New York: W. W. Norton, 1937.

Rhein, Michael J. *Anatomy of the Lighthouse*. New York: Barnes & Noble, 2000.

Shanks, Ralph C., Jr., and Janetta Thompson Shanks, *Lighthouses and Lifeboats on the Redwood Coast*. San Anselmo, CA: Constano Books, 1978.

Shelton-Roberts, Cheryl, and Bruce Roberts. *Lighthouse Families*. Birmingham, AL: Crane-Hill Publishing, 1997.

Skomal, Lenore. *The Keeper of Lime Rock*. Philadelphia: Running Press, 2002.

Smith, Fitz-Henry, Jr. *The Story of Boston Light, With Some Accounts of the Beacons in Boston Harbor*. Boston: privately printed, 1911.

Snow, Edward Rowe. *The Story of Minot's Light*. Boston: Yankee Publishing, 1940.

———. *Famous Lighthouses of America*. New York: Dodd, Mead & Company, 1955.

———. *The Lighthouses of New England*, updated by Jeremy D'Entremont. Beverly, MA: Commonwealth Editions, 2002.

Snowman, Sally R., and James G. Thompson, *Boston Light: A Historical Perspective*. North Andover, MA: Flagship Press, 1999.

Stevenson, Alan. *A Rudimentary Treatise on the History, Construction, and Illumination of Lighthouses*. London: John Weale, 1850.

Stevenson, D. Alan. *The World's Lighthouses Before 1820*. London: Oxford University Press, 1959.

Vojtech, Pat. *Lighting the Bay: Tales of Chesapeake Lighthouses*. Centreville, MD: Tidewater Publishers, 1996.

Weiss, George. *The Lighthouse Service: Its History, Activities and Organization*. Baltimore: Johns Hopkins Press, 1926.

Wermiel, Sara E. *Lighthouses*. New York: W. W. Norton, 2006.

White, Peter. *The Farallon Islands: Sentinels of the Golden Gate*. San Francisco: Scottwall Associates, 1995.

ILLUSTRATION CREDITS

. . . .

Page xi: N. P. Willis, *American Scenery*, vol. 2 (London: George Virtue, 1840)

Page 1: Courtesy Library of Congress

Page 3: *A New Geographical Dictionary*, 2 vols. (London: J. Coote, 1759–60)

Page 5: William Henry Davenport Adams, *Lighthouses and Lightships: A Descriptive and Historical Account of Their Mode of Construction and Organization* (London: T. Nelson and Sons, 1870)

Page 8: Courtesy Library of Congress

Page 10: © Eric Jay Dolin

Page 11: Courtesy Library of Congress

Page 12: Courtesy Library of Congress

Page 14: Courtesy U.S. Coast Guard Historian's Office

Page 20: Courtesy New London County Historical Society, New London, Connecticut

Page 27: © Jeremy D'Entremont

Page 30: © Jeremy D'Entremont

Page 32: Courtesy National Archives

Page 38: Courtesy Library of Congress

Page 44: Courtesy Library of Congress

Page 46: "DESCRIPTION of the LIGHT-HOUSE at SANDY-HOOK," *New-York Magazine; or, Literary Repository* (August 1, 1790)

Page 47: Courtesy Library of Congress

Page 49: Courtesy National Archives

Page 51: Courtesy Library of Congress

Page 59: Courtesy Library of Congress

Page 65: United States Coast Guard, *Aids-to-Navigation Manual* (1945)

Page 68: Courtesy Library of Congress

Page 69: William Henry Davenport Adams, *Lighthouses and Lightships: A Descriptive and Historical Account of Their Mode of Construction and Organization* (London: T. Nelson and Sons, 1870)

Page 71: Courtesy Library of Congress

Page 72: Courtesy U.S. Coast Guard Historian's Office

Page 78: "Along the South Shore," *Harper's New Monthly Magazine* (June 1878)

Page 80: Courtesy Library of Congress

Page 81: Courtesy Library of Congress

Page 89: © HistoryMiami, 1985-223-3

Page 92: Leonor Fresnel, *Oeurves Complètes D'Augustin Fresnel*, vol. I (Paris: Imprimerie Impèrials, 1866)

Page 93: William Henry Davenport Adams, *Lighthouses and Lightships: A Descriptive and Historical Account of Their Mode of Construction and Organization* (London: T. Nelson and Sons, 1870)

Page 94: William Henry Davenport Adams, *Lighthouses and Lightships: A Descriptive and Historical Account of Their Mode of Construction and Organization* (London: T. Nelson and Sons, 1870)

Page 97: Leonor Fresnel, *Oeurves Complètes D'Augustin Fresnel*, vol. I (Paris: Imprimerie Impèrials, 1870)

Page 98 (top): William Henry Davenport Adams, *Lighthouses and Lightships: A Descriptive and Historical Account of Their Mode of Construction and Organization* (London: T. Nelson and Sons, 1870)

Page 98 (bottom): © Thomas Tag

Page 99: Edmund Atkinson and Arnold W. Reinold, *Natural Philosophy for General Readers and Young People* (London: Longmans, Green, and Co., 1905)

Page 100: Leonor Fresnel, *Oeurves Complètes D'Augustin Fresnel*, vol. III (Paris: Imprimerie Impèrials, 1870)

Page 103: Courtesy Smithsonian American Art Museum / Art Resource, NY

Page 116: Courtesy National Archives

Page 120: Courtesy National Archives

Page 122: Courtesy U.S. Coast Guard Historian's Office

Page 130: Courtesy Library of Congress

Page 132: Courtesy National Archives

Page 136: Courtesy Library of Congress

Page 138: William Henry Davenport Adams, *Lighthouses and Lightships: A Descriptive and Historical Account of Their Mode of Construction and Organization* (London: T. Nelson and Sons, 1870)

Page 139: Courtesy U.S. Coast Guard Historian's Office

Page 141: William Henry Davenport Adams, *Lighthouses and Lightships: A Descriptive and Historical Account of Their Mode of Construction and Organization* (London: T. Nelson and Sons, 1870)

Page 142: Courtesy Evanston History Center, in Evanston, Illinois

Page 143: Courtesy U.S. Coast Guard Historian's Office

Page 147: Courtesy Annie Schmidt

Page 149: Charles S. Greene, "Los Farallones de los Frayles," *Overland Monthly* (September 1892)

Page 151: Courtesy U.S. Coast Guard Historian's Office

Page 154: Courtesy U.S. Coast Guard Historian's Office

Page 155: Courtesy of National Archives

Page 157: Courtesy Library of Congress

Page 158: Courtesy Library of Congress

Page 168: Courtesy National Archives

Page 175: Courtesy Tybee Island Historical Society

Page 179: Courtesy U.S. Naval Historical Center

Page 183: Courtesy National Archives

Page 186: Private collection

Page 190: Courtesy Library of Congress

Page 192: Courtesy Library of Congress

Page 193: Courtesy U.S. Coast Guard Historian's Office

Page 194: Courtesy Library of Congress

Page 196: © Jeremy D'Entremont

Page 197: Courtesy U.S. Coast Guard Historian's Office

Page 198: Courtesy National Archives

Page 199: Courtesy National Archives

Page 201: © Craig Bruce

Page 202: Courtesy Library of Congress. © Carol M. Highsmith

Page 204: Courtesy National Archives

Page 205: Courtesy Milwaukee County Historical Society and North Point Lighthouse
Museum

Page 207: Courtesy Library of Congress. © Martin Stupich

Page 209: Courtesy U.S. Coast Guard Historian's Office

Page 212: Courtesy U.S. Coast Guard Historian's Office

Page 214: Courtesy U.S. Coast Guard Historian's Office

Page 216: Courtesy U.S. Coast Guard Historian's Office

Page 217 (top): Courtesy National Archives

Page 217 (bottom): Courtesy Library of Congress. © Robert Brewster

Page 219: Courtesy Library of Congress

Page 231: Charles S. Greene, "Los Farallones de los Frayles," *Overland Monthly* (September
1892)

Page 233: Courtesy National Park Service, Cape Hatteras National Seashore

Page 235: Courtesy James W. Claflin Collection

Page 237: Courtesy Library of Congress

Page 239: Courtesy Library of Congress

Page 243 (top): Courtesy Alan Gottlieb, Oldpostcards.com

Page 243 (bottom): Courtesy Maine Lighthouse Museum

Page 244: Courtesy Eric Jay Dolin

Page 246: Courtesy Historic New England. Original photograph by Baldwin Coolidge

Page 247: © Bruce Roberts

Page 251: Courtesy U.S. Coast Guard Historian's Office

Page 252: Courtesy Tim Harrison

Page 253: Courtesy U.S. Coast Guard Historian's Office

Page 255: Courtesy U.S. Coast Guard Historian's Office

Page 258: Courtesy U.S. Coast Guard Historian's Office

Page 262: Courtesy Library of Congress

Page 264: John Drake Sloat, *History of the Celebration of the Fiftieth Anniversary of the Taking Possession of California* (Oakland: Carruth & Carruth Printers, 1896)

Page 265: Courtesy National Archives

Page 270: © Eric Jay Dolin

Page 271: Courtesy U.S. Coast Guard Historian's Office

Page 273: Courtesy Library of Congress

Page 274 (top): Courtesy U.S. Coast Guard Historian's Office

Page 274 (bottom): © Eric Jay Dolin

Page 278: Courtesy National Archives

Page 289: © Dolly Snow Bicknell

Page 290: Courtesy Jeremy D'Entremont and the Collection of Dolly Snow Bicknell

Page 293: Courtesy Library of Congress

Page 295: "Ida Lewis: The Newport Heroine," *Harper's Weekly* (July 31, 1869)

Page 298: U.S. Coast Guard Art Program

Page 299: "Ida Lewis: The Newport Heroine," *Harper's Weekly* (July 31, 1869)

Page 307: Courtesy U.S. Coast Guard Historian's Office

Page 312: Courtesy U.S. Coast Guard Historian's Office

Page 316: Courtesy Smithsonian National Air and Space Museum (NASM 00168237)

Page 318: Courtesy National Archives

Page 322: Courtesy U.S. Coast Guard Historian's Office

Page 326: Courtesy Library of Congress

Page 330: Courtesy U.S. Coast Guard Historian's Office

Page 332: Private Collection Photo / © Christie's Images / Bridgeman Images

Page 333: Courtesy U.S. Coast Guard Historian's Office

Page 336: David P. Heap, *Ancient and Modern Light-Houses* (Boston: Ticknor and Company, 1889)

Page 338: David P. Heap, *Ancient and Modern Light-Houses* (Boston: Ticknor and Company, 1889)

Page 342: Courtesy Library of Congress

Page 343: Courtesy Library of Congress

Page 350: Courtesy Library of Congress

Page 352: Courtesy National Archives

Page 354: Courtesy U.S. Coast Guard Historian's Office

Page 355: William Henry Davenport Adams, *Lighthouses and Lightships: A Descriptive and Historical Account of Their Mode of Construction and Organization* (London: T. Nelson and Sons, 1870)

Page 358: Courtesy National Park Service: Statue of Liberty National Monument

Page 367: Courtesy National Oceanic and Atmospheric Administration

Page 372: © Jeremy D'Entremont

Page 374 (top): Courtesy Beavertail Lighthouse Museum Association

Page 374 (bottom): Courtesy U.S. Coast Guard Historian's Office

Page 375: Courtesy U.S. Coast Guard Historian's Office

Page 378: Courtesy Collection of The New Haven Railroad Historical & Technical Association, Inc.

Page 380: Courtesy U.S. Coast Guard Historian's Office

Page 381: © Jeremy D'Entremont

Page 382: Courtesy U.S. Coast Guard Historian's Office

Page 384: Courtesy The Chesapeake Bay Maritime Museum, St. Michaels, Maryland

Page 387: Courtesy Library of Congress

Page 388: Courtesy U.S. Coast Guard Historian's Office

Page 390: Courtesy Library of Congress

Page 392: © Jeremy D'Entremont

Page 394 (top): Courtesy U.S. Coast Guard Historian's Office

Page 394 (bottom): Courtesy Library of Congress

Page 398: © Eric Jay Dolin

Page 399: Courtesy The Chesapeake Bay Maritime Museum, St. Michaels, Maryland

Page 400: © Bruce Roberts

Page 402: © George Bacon

Page 403: Courtesy Library of Congress. Photograph by Carol M. Highsmith

Page 405: © Eric Jay Dolin

Page 408: Courtesy U.S. Coast Guard Historian's Office

Page 409: © Nick Korstad

Page 411: Courtesy City of Fernandina Beach, Florida

Page 412: Courtesy National Archives

Page 413: Courtesy National Park Service, Cape Hatteras National Seashore

Page 417: © Brian Tague

Page 420: Courtesy U.S. Coast Guard Historian's Office

Page 421: © Eric Jay Dolin

Insert

1. Courtesy The Collection of the Redwood Library and Athenaeum, Newport, Rhode Island, gift of Roger King
2. © The Metropolitan Museum of Art / Art Resource, NY
3. © The Huntington Art Collections
4. From the Collection of Studebaker National Museum, South Bend, Indiana
5. © Jim Patterson
6. © Art Noble
7. © Jeff Stephens, At Lands End Photography, LLC
8. © Michael Blanchette
9. © Tom Gill
10. © Nick Korstad
11. © Jamie Wyeth
12. Courtesy Library of Congress. © Carol M. Highsmith
13. Courtesy National Park Service, Cape Hatteras National Seashore
14. Courtesy Library of Congress. © Carol M. Highsmith
15. Courtesy Library of Congress. © Carol M. Highsmith
16. © Edward Nunez
17. © Michael DiRenzo
18. © Todd Reed of Todd and Brad Reed Photography
19. © Lily Dolin

INDEX

· · · · · · · · · · · · · ·

Page numbers in *italics* refer to illustrations.

ABOUT THE AUTHOR

ERIC JAY DOLIN is the author of *Leviathan: The History of Whaling in America*, which was chosen as one of the best nonfiction books of 2007 by the *Los Angeles Times* and the *Boston Globe*, and also won the 2007 John Lyman Award for U.S. Maritime History; and *Fur, Fortune, and Empire: The Epic History of the Fur Trade in America*, which was chosen by the *Seattle Times* as one of the best nonfiction books of 2010, and also won the James P. Hanlan Book Award, given by the New England Historical Association. He is also the author of *When America First Met China: An Exotic History of Tea, Drugs, and Money in the Age of Sail*, which was chosen by *Kirkus Reviews* as one of the 100 best nonfiction books of 2012. A graduate of Brown, Yale, and MIT, where he received his Ph.D. in environmental policy, Dolin lives in Marblehead, Massachusetts, with his family. For more information on his background, books, and awards, please visit his website ericjaydolin.com. You can also follow Dolin's posts on Facebook on his author page, at Eric Jay Dolin.